Race

Race

A Study in Social Dynamics

Oliver Cromwell Cox

Monthly Review Press
New York

Library of Congress Cataloging-in-Publication Data

Cox, Oliver Cromwell, 1901–1974.
   [*Caste, class & race*. Chapters 16–25]
   Race : a study in social dynamics / Oliver Cromwell Cox ;
introduction by Adolph Reed, Jr.
     p.   cm.
   Previously published as the final section (chapters 16–25) of the
author's *Caste, class & race*. 1948.
   Includes bibliographical references and index.
   ISBN 1-58367-006-8 (pbk.). — ISBN 0-85345-941-X (cloth)
   1. Race. 2. Social classes. 3. Race relations. I. Title.
HT1521.C69   1999
305.8—dc21   98-48876
                                                       CIP

Monthly Review Press
122 West 27th Street
New York NY 10001

Manufactured in Canada
10 9 8 7 6 5 4 3 2 1

Contents

Introduction to Oliver C. Cox

Adolph Reed, Jr.

Oliver Cromwell Cox's *Caste, Class, and Race* was first published in 1948 by Doubleday, which, in line with the anti-leftist imperatives of the time, almost immediately let the book go out of print. Fortunately, it was reissued in 1959 by Monthly Review Press, which has enabled subsequent generations to read Cox's extraordinary text. Indeed, I discovered Cox through Monthly Review's Modern Reader paperback edition in 1970; coincidentally, that was also the year of the only occasion on which I heard him speak, at the annual meeting of the Association of Social and Behavioral Scientists, the black social scientists' group.

Cox is a curious figure in black American and left intellectual life. He is difficult to fit into a genealogy of black intellectuals or activists. Unlike some of his contemporaries, such as Ralph Bunche, Abram Harris, or E. Franklin Frazier, Cox was not particularly prominent within the racial advocacy or political activist groups of the day, though he did comment on contemporary affairs in venues such as the *Journal of Negro Education.* Cox neither produced a school of intellectual followers nor does he seem to have passed on his professional DNA through the founding of an interpretive tendency or the production of a visible cohort of students who would trace their intellectual lineage through him. Moreover, although he earned a doctorate in sociology from the University of Chicago, his work differed in focus and intellectual disposition from that of other black scholars associated with the Chicago School, including Frazier, Charles S. Johnson, and even St. Clair Drake, who shared with Cox an orientation that was at least compatible with and probably sympathetic to Marxism.

Cox stands out, however, as a scholar whose work consistently and rigorously proceeded from the conviction that making sense of the meaning of race and the character of race relations in American life requires an understanding of the dynamics of capitalism as a social system and its specific history in this country. *Caste, Class, and Race* was Cox's most elaborate attempt to follow through on that conviction. This new, abbreviated Monthly Review Press edition reprints *Race*, the third section of *Caste, Class, and Race*, which comprised nearly half of the original volume. This should make the central thrust of Cox's critique more accessible, if only because *Caste, Class, and Race*'s length—nearly six hundred pages of text—made the book seem overly daunting to many potential readers. Moreover, Cox's meticulous, if suspiciously formalistic, discussion of the Indian caste system that was the topic of the more-than-one-hundred-page Part One of the original book is easily dispensable for contemporary readers. Cox's consideration of the Indian caste order was preliminary to the argument that he laid out in *Race* against a scholarly tendency in the study of American race relations that had gained momentum during the interwar years, a tendency that invoked the metaphor of caste to describe racial stratification in the United States.

Cox took pains to chart the differences between the Indian caste system and the dynamics of racial stratification in this country, and he argued that the dissimilarities of the two systems were so great that the caste notion could not clarify American race relations. However, his main brief against the "caste school of race relations" was that it abstracted racial stratification in the United States from its origins and foundation in the evolution of American capitalism. In so doing, he argued, the caste school treated racial hierarchy as if it were a timeless, natural form of social organization. The caste approach to the study of American race relations has not been in vogue for several decades; other equally misleading metaphors have long since supplanted it.

Cox's critique of the caste school was linked to his broader view of the inadequacy and wrong-headedness of attitudinal or other idealist approaches to the discussion of racial inequality. He emphatically rejected primordialist notions of racial antipathy or ethnocentrism as explanations of racial stratification. He insisted that racism and race prejudice emerged from the class dynamics of capitalism and its colonial and imperial programs. This was the basis of his critical assessment of other prominent tendencies in the liberal scholarly treatments of American race relations, including the work of Robert Park and Ruth Benedict, as well as Gunnar Myrdal's singularly influential volume, *An American Dilemma*.

Cox believed that the theories of Robert Park, one of the founders of the Chicago School of Sociology and Booker T. Washington's former ghostwriter, in effect naturalized notions of fundamental difference in two ways. First, said Cox, Park alleged that "the beginnings of modern race prejudice may be traced back to the immemorial periods of human associations." Second, Park maintained that the racial subordination that prevailed in the South stemmed from custom and "mores," a static, ahistorical notion of core beliefs and norms around which populations supposedly cohere organically. Similarly, while acknowledging that Ruth Benedict, the anthropologist of race relations and a former student of Franz Boas, improved on Park in recognizing racism's historically specific, modern origins, Cox objected to Benedict's construing of racism as an example of a universal tendency to ethnocentrism. The consequence, he argued, was that Benedict "conceives of race prejudice as essentially a belief and gives almost no attention to the materialistic source of the rationalization." In his critique of Myrdal, the Swedish economist and sociologist commissioned by the Carnegie Foundation to produce a systematic study of American race relations, Cox was most critical of the tendency to locate American racial dynamics within abstract, transhistorical dispositions or attitudes. Myrdal's *An American Dilemma*, Cox charged, was built around an evasion, the attempt to avoid a class analysis of American race relations. Thus Myrdal resorted to explaining American racism through airy, reified formulations, such as assertion of tensions and ambivalence around an idealized American Creed or a struggle for the "national soul." Because the Myrdal study has had such lasting influence on American racial discourse, quoting Cox's summary judgment of the document is useful both for clarifying his critique and for giving a flavor of his intellectual style.

> *An American Dilemma*, the most exhaustive survey of race relations ever undertaken in the United States, is for the most part a useful source of data. In detail it presents many ingenious analyses of the materials. But it develops no hypothesis or consistent theory of race relations; and, to the extent that it employs the caste belief in interpretations, it is misleading. Clearly, the use of "the American Creed" as the "value premise" for his study severely limits and narrows Dr. Myrdal's perspective. Even though we should grant some right of the author to limit the discussion of his subject to its moral aspects, he still

develops it without insight. He never brings into focus the two great systems of
morality currently striving in our civilization for ascendancy, but merely assumes
a teleological abstraction of social justice toward which all good men will
ultimately gravitate. Moreover, since we can hardly accuse him of being naïve,
and since he clearly goes out of his way to avoid the obvious implications of
labor exploitation in the South, we cannot help concluding that the work in many
respects may have the effect of a powerful piece of propaganda in favor of the
status quo. If the "race problem" in the United States is preeminently a moral
question, it must naturally be resolved by moral means, and this conclusion is
precisely the social illusion which the ruling political class has constantly sought
to produce.

Cox advanced a perspective on race, racial difference and racial stratification that we would today describe as a social constructionist view.
Bypassing biological or physical anthropological definitions, he proposed
that "race may be thought of as simply any group of people that is generally
believed to be, and generally accepted as, a race in any given area of ethnic
competition." (He defined an ethnic group as "a people living competitively
in a relationship of superordination or subordination with some other people
or peoples within one state, country or economic area.") He acknowledged that
such races are not real in the sense of having a meaning and content apart
from the specific patterns of social relations in which they are enmeshed;
he opted for a "social definition of the term race." Cox did not address in
any depth the empirical or biological status of race as a category for sorting
human populations. Indeed, he made no attempt to refute racist pseudos-
cience, contending that "the laboratory classification of races, which began
among anthropologists about a hundred years ago, has no necessary relationship with the problem of race relations as sociological phenomena.
Race relations developed independently of anthropological tests and measurements." Nevertheless, the thrust of his argument was a clear refutation
of such scientific racialism.

For Cox, race was most fundamentally an artifact of capitalist labor
dynamics, a relation that originated in slavery. "Sometimes, probably
because of its very obviousness," he observed, "it is not realized that the
slave trade was simply a way of recruiting labor for the purpose of
exploiting the great natural resources of America." This perspective led to
one of Cox's most interesting and provocative insights, that "racial exploitation is merely one aspect of the problem of the proletarianization of labor,

regardless of the color of the laborer. Hence racial antagonism is essentially political-class conflict." We should not make too much of the adverbs "simply" and "merely." Seeing race as a category that emerges from capitalist labor relations does not necessarily deny or minimize the importance of racial oppression and injustice or the need to fight against racism directly.

Contrary to the claims of critics such as David Roediger, Cox did not dismiss racism among working-class whites. He argued that "the observed overt competitive antagonism is produced and carefully maintained by the exploiters of both the poor whites and the Negroes." He recognized that elite whites defined the matrix within which non-elite whites crafted their political agency, and he emphasized the ruling-class foundations of racism as part of his critique of the liberal scholars of race relations who theorized race relations without regard to capitalist political economy and class dynamics. Cox's perspective goes right to the heart of how we should try to understand race by encouraging us to move beyond categories for defining and sorting supposedly discrete human populations, beyond concepts of racial hierarchies, and beyond racist ideologies—all components of a singular, indivisible unholy trinity—and instead recognize that race is the product of social relations within history and political economy. More than a half-century after its initial publication, Cox's interpretation is a refreshing alternative to the idealist frames that have persisted in shaping American racial discourse and politics. The lucidity and groundedness of his interpretation stand out strikingly, for example, in relation to ontological arguments the equivalent of devil theories that either trace racism back to the Ice Ages or attribute racism to ideas of the Enlightenment; his viewpoint contrasts just as sharply with arresting but uninformative and strategically useless metaphors, such as the characterization of racism as a "national disease" or the chestnut that racism "takes on a life of its own" or other such mystifications. Racism is not an affliction; it is a pattern of social relations. Nor is it a thing that can act on its own; it exists only as it is reproduced in specific social arrangements in specific societies under historically specific conditions of law, state, and class power.

Cox was not a political strategist; he did not approach political analysis with the instrumentalist specificity of an organizer or cadre. Nor did he ever affiliate with or move in the orbit of any political organization. He did not propound a clearly defined path for pursuit of the radical social and economic change that he viewed as necessary. Like many intellectuals of his era the vision of revolution embraced by W.E.B. Du Bois in his 1928 novel, *The Dark Princess,* comes most readily to mind. Cox gravitated toward a view of radical political change that by and large lacked a complex vision of popular agency. He considered the working-class political party, the labor party, to be the vehicle for effecting transformation to socialism, but he opposed parliamentary gradualism as hopeless. Similarly, he recognized the union as the basic organizational form of the working class. Although he acknowledged business unionism's accomplishments, he condemned it as divisive and inimical to class struggle. However, he did not engage in issues bearing either on political processes and participation within the movement or strategies for building solidarity and broadening the political base within the working class, except insofar as he endorsed in very general terms the principle that the political class organization should represent not just the unionized, but all workers, on the model of the nineteenth-century Knights of Labor.

I suspect that the limitation of his strategic vision was reinforced by the combination of his teleological faith in capitalism's inevitable replacement by socialism and an apocalyptic notion of revolution as the mechanism of millennial change. If the script is already written and a quantum leap is the sole necessary and sufficient condition for its realization, then there is little need to puzzle over how to get there from here. The only warrant is to preach the gospel and wait for enlightened adherents. This view suggests the convergence of Fabian and revolutionary notions of transformation, and as a practical matter it emphasizes the place of intellectuals as propagators of the gospel. It also devalues, or at least ignores the significance of, democratic, participatory processes for creating and shaping the sort of class-conscious movement that Cox calls "political-class struggle"on which the goal of social transformation must depend. This mindset may also reflect Cox's failure to break with the familiar petit bourgeois romance of revolution as *jacquerie*, and it quite likely blunted his critique of the idea of black race leadership.

In the early post–Second World War period the notion of the race leader as the source of effective black political agency retained conceptual force in conventional American racial discourse. Myrdal and other scholars and commentators assumed the category to be central for understanding black political action. However, the model of singular race spokesmanship, embodied most prominently by Booker T. Washington and Marcus Garvey, was being supplanted by a more plural, organizationally–based racial advocacy. Perhaps it was the disjunction between the new political forms and the residual rhetoric of leadership that led Cox to be so sharply, and perceptively, critical of the "persistent lament" that black Americans lacked a "great leader, whose function must be to bring about solidarity among Negroes." He argued that no such entity could ever emerge, characterizing it as a fantasy. The black race leaders, he argued,

> must be specialists in the art of antagonistic cooperation. Their success rests finally in their ability to maintain peace and friendship with whites; yet they must seem aggressive and uncompromising in their struggle for the rights of Negroes. They dare not identify all whites as the enemy, for then they will themselves be driven together into a hostile camp. This tentative nature of Negro solidarity presents a particularly baffling problem for the Negro leader. He must be a friend of the enemy. He must be a champion of the cause of Negroes, yet not so aggressive as to incur the consummate ill will of whites. He knows that he cannot be a leader of his people if he is completely rejected by whites; hence no small part of his function is engaged in understanding the subtleties of reaction to the manipulation of the whites of his community. No contemporary Negro leader of major significance, then, can be totally void of at least a modicum of the spirit of "Uncle Tom"; ingratiation, compromise, and appeasement must be his specialties.

Cox's critique of black leadership stemmed partly from his own political teleology; in his view black Americans' "destiny" was "integration and fusion with the larger American society." "To develop a powerful leader," he argued, "Negroes must retract themselves, as it were, from their immediate business of achieving assimilation, and look to him for some promised land or some telling counterblow upon their detractors." Not only was this course hopeless because of the limits and contradictions of the actual practice of race leadership that he described, but Cox felt also that it played into the hands of the opponents of black aspiration.

Cox's analysis of black leadership was incisive and insightful, though not in tune with the style of race-conscious politics that originated in the Black Power era of the late 1960s and early 1970s and is hegemonic today. Yet his critique did not cut quite to the core of the problem with the notion of a race leader: that its ideal of an individual or individuals "whose function must be to bring about solidarity among Negroes" presumes the existence of or potential for a unitary racial consciousness. This in turn underscores a connection between the leaders and the led that circumvents or suppresses questions of genuine political differentiation, accountability, and popular participation. For Cox and other of his radical contemporaries, such as the elder Du Bois and Ralph Bunche in the 1930s and early 1940s, this inattentiveness to democratic concerns among black Americans was in tension with the larger egalitarian commitments of their politics. The imagery of "the masses" obscured and perfumed that tension, justifying a view of the rank-and-file population as fundamentally monolithic and passive by associating it with the rhetoric of apocalyptic revolution, according to which this population contains within it an emergent collective political subject, indeed the crucial political subject. The promise of paramount political agency in the millennial future could thus substitute for attention to popular agency and democratic participation in the present. Besides, to Cox and other black radicals operating before the victories of the civil rights movement, assuming an unproblematic racial political consensus simply expressed common sense insofar as that consensus was held to cohere around opposition to the Jim Crow regime and practices of racial exclusion and subordination. Cox, in particular, saw those objectives as exhaustive of the basis of a distinctively black politics. However, the rhetoric of "the masses" was nonetheless an evasion of the thorny problem of crafting a popular politics in the here-and-now.

This imagery of the masses has been normalized in black political discourse over the last three decades, but its associations with ideological radicalism have dissipated. In this environment, and with erosion of the objective basis for the presumption of coherent racial aspiration on which the notion was grounded, its limitations become clearer than they could have been to Cox and his contemporaries. Despite its superficial evocations of potential agency in motion, "the masses" is the conceptual negation of a discourse of political mobilization. Some of Cox's formulations will seem mechanistic especially to sensibilities honed in a time when capitalist power relations somehow seem more diffuse (despite their unprecedented global hegemony), when prevailing social theoretical discourses seem more nuanced and less scientistic, and when current political criticism focuses on categories of political identity other than those that emerge directly from the capitalist-labor relationship. Cox also displays a visceral, conventionally petit bourgeois moralism in his perception that "social instability" and "disreputable communal life" prevailed among poor black Americans. His views in this area may have been reinforced by the Chicago School's focus on social disorganization and pathology. In this way Cox stands out neither from his contemporaries nor from ostensibly leftist intellectuals today who imagine a degraded black "underclass" mired in pathology, "moral crisis," and "nihilism." ("The masses" and "the underclass" are, after all, two sides of the same coin: both representing monolithic, passive populations, though with different normative valuations.) However, I urge readers not to fixate on those occasional flaws, which in any case will probably often appear to be more egregious than they are, and to approach the text with an openness to the challenge that Oliver Cromwell Cox has bequeathed us: to think systematically about race as a category of social classification and hierarchy that emerged from and is a constitutive element of—not distinct from or alternative to—capitalist labor relations. This is the crucial entailment of the insight that race is a social construct and a prerequisite to the development of a genuinely transformative politics in the United States.

The Life and Career of Oliver C. Cox

Herbert M. Hunter

The Early Years

Oliver Cromwell Cox was born on August 24, 1901, in Port-of-Spain, Trinidad, the son of Virginia Blake and William Raphael Cox.[1] His family was economically stable and was less impoverished than the majority of Trinidadians. His father, a "wavy-haired," light-skinned man, was able to achieve middle-class status for his relatively large family by working as the captain of a revenue schooner, a government ship that sailed around the island enforcing the sea laws,[2] and then as a customs and excise officer, collecting duties and checking for contraband and pilferage for the British colonial authorities. William Cox was a demanding father and encouraged all nine of his children (six sons and three daughters) to be thrifty, hard working, and disciplined.[3]

The experience of growing up in the West Indies under the British colonial system in the first two decades of the twentieth century provided Oliver Cox with a cultural heritage that was to be unique among black American sociologists of his generation. In Trinidad, Cox was far removed from the racial discrimination and hostility that characterized race relations in the United States, and in addition had experienced living in a country where whites were a minority and considered outsiders. Poverty, illiteracy, and exploitation were common, but unlike in the United States, where blacks were a minority in a white majority society and culture, living primarily in racially segregated communities maintained by force, Cox was a member of the majority group. Without explicit legal restrictions or a rigidly defined color bar separating the races, there were opportunities for Trinidadians who had the appropriate skin color, wealth, education, and/or family status—it was the interplay among these factors that set the pattern of power and privilege.[4] While it is difficult to know the extent to which an individual's background influences his or her later development, it can be argued that Oliver Cox was able to develop an independent path in his life and work in part at least because he was freer intellectually to see the problems of black America in a manner not typical of U.S. social scientists, who tended to be preoccupied with the racial victimization of blacks by race prejudice, discrimination, and segregation.

Cox's Education and Intellectual Development in the United States

Cox's father had an unremitting determination to further his children's education, and insisted that they (especially the males) go to the United States to prove themselves. All three sons received financial support for the initial passage, but it was only the eldest—his father's favorite—who received assistance while attending school. Once the eighteen-year-old Oliver Cox arrived in the United States, he was on his own. The following year he began to prepare for college by attending the Central Y.M.C.A. High School in Chicago, from which he graduated in 1923. He then spent two years at the Lewis Institute, majoring in history and economics, and received his associate degree in 1927. In the fall of that year he entered Northwestern University to study law, and received his Bachelor of Science in Law degree in 1929. He expected to become a successful lawyer and return to Trinidad, but his plans were destroyed when he was stricken with poliomyelitis. With full recovery in doubt—he walked with crutches for the rest of his life—he was forced to rethink his plans. He felt that he would not be mobile enough to be a lawyer, and that he would neither be able to marry nor make Trinidad his permanent home.

He was nevertheless determined to survive despite his disability, and in 1930, after a year and a half spent recovering, he entered the department of economics at the University of Chicago, believing that academic work "would not require too much footwork."[5] It was during this period that Cox developed an analytic approach that later placed him at odds with the ahistorical and empiricist approach of many of his sociological contemporaries.

Cox later shifted to sociology. He explained this as being in part because of the inability of the Chicago economists to explain adequately the Great Depression of the 1930s. According to Cox, "I felt that if economics did not explain what I wanted to know; if economics did not explain the coming of the depression; if economics did not help me to understand that great economic change, then I felt I did not need it. Thus, I changed over to sociology."[6]

Cox enrolled in courses in preparation for the doctorate. His first introductory course covered the work of Park and Burgess, whose *Introduction to the Study of Sociology* had become the established primer for introductory courses across the country. He also attended courses given by such prominent Chicago sociologists as William F. Ogburn, Herbert Blumer, Faris, and others, and was exposed to the historical approach to social problems and institutions adopted by Louis Wirth.

Cox wrote his dissertation, entitled "Factors Affecting the Marital Status of Negroes in the United States," under Ogburn. In it he concentrated "on those aspects which are amenable to quantitative techniques" by demonstrating the effect of demographic variables—such as sex ratios, urbanization, population increase, age, employment status, school attendance, and farm tenancy—on marital status.[7]

Unlike virtually all of his fellow black students who had been trained in the department of sociology at Chicago, Cox was attracted to the quantitative methods emphasized by Ogburn and Samuel Stouffer, rather than the more qualitative case-study method and ecological approach. On August 26, 1938, two days after his thirty-seventh birthday, Cox received his doctorate in sociology. His childhood socialization to the values of hard work, discipline, and thrift appear to have been his guides, as, with great persistence and little financial help, he achieved the education that he had come to the United States to pursue.

Teaching in a Black College

Like many of his black contemporaries, Cox was now well prepared for a career as an academic. With graduate degrees in economics and sociology from a leading university, he was in a position to teach both disciplines, which should have considerably widened his employment opportunities. Despite this, he was unable to secure a position in any of the larger white institutions, with their greater resources, and instead—as was customary for even the brightest young black scholars well into the 1950s—was forced to seek employment in a black college, where the teaching load was heavy, the salary low, and there were few graduate students or resources for carrying out research.[8] In fact, Cox was destined to spend his career in both intellectual and geographical isolation, not only working within a framework that removed him from the mainstream of academic sociology but working in institutions where few of his colleagues could match his academic credentials and scholarly accomplishments and that were in geographical isolation, far from the intellectual centers of activity. Despite these problems, however, he was able to surmount the intellectual limitations imposed on racially segregated southern black colleges. He attended professional meetings around the country, and traveled during the summer months and during sabbatical years. He maintained contact with the scholarly world through reading and by contributing to the most important journals in his field.

Cox's first major teaching position was at Wiley College, a small Methodist school in Marshall, Texas.[9] There he taught economics and was director of the Bureau of Social Research, a position he shared with his friend and colleague V. E. Daniels from 1939 to 1944. While at Wiley, Cox began his critique of the "caste school of race relations," a theory that was rapidly gaining popularity among social scientists. The conceptualization was first initiated by the social anthropologist W. Lloyd Warner, in his article "American Caste and Class," which appeared in the *American Journal of Sociology* in 1936. Here Warner brought together the concepts of caste and class to explain the social organization of the U.S. South in terms of a biracial system of social stratification. He argued, accordingly, that while caste and class were two concepts often thought to be antithetical, they could nevertheless operate within a single community. Thus whereas class describes a situation where intergroup movement, including marriage, is possible, caste describes a situation where both social mobility and intermarriage between blacks and whites are restricted through extralegal codes of behavior and patterns of deference between the races. According to Warner, in the U.S. South, caste and class structures could coexist and accommodate themselves to internal conflict and hostility because both the dominant white group and the subordinate black group participated in maintaining the caste system.

Cox's critique of Warner and his associates and students first appeared in 1942 in the journal *Social Forces,* in a piece entitled "The Modern Caste School of Race Relations." Although not recognized as such at the time, it was this article that established Cox as one of the first U.S. sociologists to present an alternative to the accepted proposition that black-white relations in the United States constituted a caste system similar to that found in Hindu society. Cox found this analogy completely unacceptable because it ignored the historical differences between the two societies and discounted the political and economic imperatives undergirding race relations in the United States. His article was only the first salvo in what was to become a comprehensive critique of the conceptual framework of the entire field of race relations and social stratification—a critique that emerged in a number of articles and culminated, in 1948, in the magnum opus *Caste, Class, and Race.*

The working conditions at Wiley were unsatisfactory to a scholar of Cox's ability. In 1944, because of the low salary and the absence of any prospect for advancement, he decided to accept an offer from Tuskegee Institute, the most celebrated black vocational school in the South, founded by Booker T. Washington, and located in the heart of the Alabama Black Belt.

While at Tuskegee Cox primarily taught economics and sociology. He taught a graduate course on race and culture that, according to the school's bulletin, focused on "racial theories of culture as a factor determining race relations in different situations," a concern Cox also addressed in his writings. He also taught a course on the socioeconomic problems of the rural South, which was directed particularly at the predominantly rural and southern Tuskegee student, as well as basic economics and courses on labor problems, consumer economics, and the U.S. economy—all subjects in keeping with his training at Chicago. But since Tuskegee was primarily a vocational institution, Cox had few students who were interested in graduate study in sociology, or even in sociological theory; they preferred to concentrate on the practical applications of sociological research that they could use after graduation.[10]

Cox's reputation as a sociologist continued to grow while he was at Tuskegee, and it was at this point that his radical critique of the prevailing notions of caste, class, and race relations began to gain him the label of

"Marxist." But although those of his writings on race relations published between 1944 and 1948 were powerful critiques of mainstream theories, they were probably read by a relatively small number of people: Many appeared in *The Journal of Negro Education,* which was read by few social scientists. With the publication of *Caste, Class, and Race* in 1948, however, Cox's label of Marxist sociologist was well established, as the many reviewers ideologically opposed to his ideas dismissed his work as "Marxist dogma" and "Communist propaganda," pernicious labels that were to shadow him throughout the rest of his career and deny him the scholarly recognition he deserved.

Given that this was a time when Marxism and Communism were both anathema to post–Second World War America, it was not surprising that Cox's approach clashed with a "conservative religious-oriented black school which spent a great deal of its time trying to present a positive image to powerful white capitalist philanthropists who kept the school financially alive."[11] Other evidence suggests, however, that Cox's growing reputation as an intellectual and ideological radical had little effect on his position at Tuskegee. He had many friends, and there was great respect for his ideas—which in any case often seemed more radical than he was. He was personally austere and conservative in his ways, and did not espouse a particular political philosophy publicly. In fact, since many black civil rights organizations were considered—by white politicians—to be "Communist-inspired," even F. D. Patterson, president of Tuskegee College, could be considered something of a radical for serving as an adviser to the militant Southern Negro Congress.[12] Cox's own intellectual radicalism certainly went far beyond the civil rights activities of many of his Tuskegee colleagues, but the alleged conservatism at Tuskegee in the late 1940s was not so pervasive that Cox's ideas could not be tolerated.

If Cox was condemned at all, it was for his attack on the school's founder and idol, Booker T. Washington, for being a "quisling," a term Cox used to describe those individuals who aligned themselves with the white ruling class.[13] The "old-timers" at the school, who firmly supported Washington's philosophy of vocational education and self-help and who were proud of their founder's success in the white world, were furious at Cox's attack.

Cox did not relent, however, and in a paper entitled "The Leadership of Booker T. Washington," which was read before the annual meeting of the

Association of Social Science Teachers—a primarily black group—in Jefferson City, Missouri, in 1949, Cox reiterated that Washington was a class collaborator and that his leadership was "spurious":

> He was not a leader of the masses in the Garvian sense; his function was rather that of controlling the masses. He deflated and abandoned their [the Negroes'] common cause. He demanded less for the Negro people than that which the ruling class had already conceded. And because he was in reality sent with a mission to subdue the spirit of protest in the masses instead of his arising among them as a champion of their cause he was frequently insulting and harsh towards them.[14]

Cox continued to develop this theme in several articles written in the early 1950s.

When Cox finally left Tuskegee in the spring of 1949, however, it was not because of these tensions but because of the inadequate support he thought the school was giving to the social sciences. He wanted to teach in a university that would support his research.

Cox was now forty-eight years old, and his academic record was so impressive that he should have been able to obtain a position wherever he chose. He had published more than twenty articles in the major professional journals in his field, including the *American Journal of Sociology,* the *American Sociological Review,* and *Social Forces,* and belonged to a number of professional organizations, including the Society for Social Research, the Southern Sociological Society, the American Sociological Society, and the National Educational Association. *Caste, Class, and Race,* although never accepted into the mainstream of sociological thought, did earn him recognition outside the sociological fraternity. In 1948, the book's publisher, Doubleday and Company, awarded Cox the George Washington Carver Award. In addition, he was in the process of preparing a second major volume, to be titled *The Foundations of Capitalism,* a study of the historical origins, growth, and development of the capitalist world system.

But there were still few opportunities for a man like Cox in predominantly white colleges and universities, and in July 1949 he therefore accepted a position as associate professor at Lincoln University. There Cox continued to develop his reputation as a demanding teacher who took his scholarship seriously and expected the same from his students—or those who were brave enough to enroll in his courses.

Institutional constraints gave Cox a teaching load of twelve to fifteen hours a week, which left little time for research and writing. Yet the administration understood Cox's research needs and also knew that his success as a scholar would bring prestige to the university. Thus, although he funded much of his own research and travel expenses, the university supported him by granting him sabbaticals with half pay, and providing funds for travel to conferences and for typing manuscripts. Nevertheless, while many of his sociological peers, both black and white, served on study commissions and received foundation support for their research, Cox received no such institutional amenities.[15]

Despite the limited resources at his command, the scholarly record Cox established at Lincoln University was remarkable. During his twenty-one years there, he published articles in professional journals and completed his trilogy on capitalism—*The Foundations of Capitalism* (1959), *Capitalism and American Leadership* (1962), and *Capitalism as a System* (1964). Together, these volumes reexamined the historical origins and development of the world capitalist system and provided the basis for an explanation of the political economy of race relations. Cox argued that a significant feature of European capitalist societies, beginning with early Venetian capitalism of the thirteenth century, was the commercial relations they fostered with "backward" areas in the world system. Racial antagonisms found throughout the world were not the cause but the effect of capitalist domination of the less-developed countries. The basis of his argument was that for a capitalist nation to dominate in the world capitalist system it had to maintain uneven patterns of development. Cox was introducing a world-system perspective that predated by at least a decade the work of Immanuel Wallerstein and his followers.[16]

In March 1970, at the age of seventy, Cox decided to retire. He left very quietly, declining festivities and testimonials.[17] He debated moving back to Trinidad, but, as he wrote to his sister, "Too many problems seem to come to mind—not money, but other problems," a probable reference to his physical condition.[18] At the invitation of Alvin W. Rose, chairman of the department of sociology at Wayne State University in Detroit, Michigan, Cox accepted the post of Distinguished Visiting Professor of Sociology. He would only have to teach one seminar a semester and assist doctoral students with their dissertation research in the area of race relations. Rose thought Cox would benefit from having a larger audience, advanced graduate students, and a large faculty with whom to discuss his ideas:

> I think he was lonely and very glad that I had invited him. . . . It was a push, more than a pull, in the sense that Lincoln was barren intellectually for his purposes. There wasn't a community of sociologists there at Lincoln and I wanted the students, both black and white, to have a chance to see a good sociologist in seminars and to have him on campus.[19]

As it turned out, however, Wayne State proved to be a disappointment to Cox. He in fact had limited contact with his colleagues, and most of the graduate students were either not interested in his courses or unprepared to meet his rigorous standards. His classes were therefore small, and few students stayed for more than one semester.

In addition, the climate of the times had changed dramatically. No longer was Marxism necessarily something to be avoided—indeed, it was often forcefully defended. Ironically, this created something of a problem for Cox. In some of his classes he came into conflict with black Marxists who adhered to a rigid analysis of capitalism and who went so far as to accuse him of being "an apologist for the system."[20] But Cox refused to engage in polemics or speak from a "soap box," and he constantly asserted that he was not a Marxist. He insisted on examining both the positive and negative aspects of Marx's thought, as well as of capitalism in general. As one student, Bruce Williams, reports:

> I specifically remember in his course on the sociology of capitalism Cox was attempting to establish the positive contributions of capitalism, i.e., that capitalism had brought the world into a unified, interdependent system—ending isolation; that it replaced mysticism with science and rational thinking. . . . The black Marxists in the class (three) cursed him out, stormed out and dropped the class, accusing him of being a traitor to the revolution. . . . Those who stayed received one of the best analyses of the system available.[21]

While Cox did not influence a large group of students, he did influence individuals at all the places he taught. As Williams put it, "The brilliance of the man would eventually be demonstrated if one had the patience to wait and listen closely. Thus the key to being a student in his class was to be patient and keep your ears open. You could only do this if you gave him his due as a genius and a scholar."[22]

At Wayne State, Cox continued to write and to generate controversy. He published several articles in the early 1970s, as well as his last major book,

Race Relations: Elements and Social Dynamics (1976). Much of this work was in response to the re-emergence of the black nationalist movement in the late 1960s, and to the resurgence of ethnic consciousness among whites that followed, and was significantly encouraged by the writings of Michael Novak, Andrew Greeley, and others. A strong proponent of assimilation, especially among blacks, Cox was opposed to ethnic solidarity movements of any type, and was critical of those sociological perspectives that were linked with such movements. In one article, published in the British journal *Race* (to which he was a contributing editor for many years), Cox challenged what he believed to be an imprecise use of the term "pluralism." As he noted, the term had been given at least three inconsistent meanings in the social science literature: It had been used as (1) a political concept, in order to discuss the concentration and dispersal of power in society; (2) a legal concept, in order to identify the aims of minority groups in protecting their civil rights and heritage through judicial means; and (3) an economic concept, in order to analyze the larger societal process of colonialism, where capitalism came to dominate and disrupt indigenous native cultures. This debate on ethnic pluralism was not unconnected to Cox's earlier opposition to, and debates with, the caste theorists. For Cox, a concept of ethnic pluralism that lends support to the revitalization of black urban ghettos, or to separate political, economic, and cultural development for blacks, was not dissimilar to the earlier attempts to explain race relations within the framework of a caste system—both concepts paradoxically implied that blacks should remain estranged from the larger U.S. social system.

Cox triggered further controversy in an article entitled "Jewish Self-interest in 'Black Pluralism'" (1974), published shortly before his death. Here he noted that anti-Semitism was an ancient social attitude, related to the rise of Jewish identity, and that it would therefore arise wherever Jews asserted this identity. He believed that Jewish support for the notion of pluralism, used to enhance Jewish self-respect and survival, was similar to certain elements of black nationalism, but that neither blacks nor Jews had anything to gain from the strategy. Black self-interest, therefore, should lead to support for integration and assimilation. Cox's observation, in a footnote to the article, that Andrew Greeley, one of the foremost proponents of ethnic pluralism, "is a converted Irish ethnic contributing to publications of the American Jewish Committee,"[23] brought forth a chorus of scathing and critical rebuttals, from Greeley and other readers of Cox's paper. Cox was accused of not offering empirical evidence for many of his assertions and of addressing important issues with generalities and stereotypes about an unfounded Jewish conspiracy to promote ethnicity. Greeley wrote the following: "I can only use the word flabbergasted to describe my reaction to Oliver Cox's article in your spring issue. Such a piece might have been acceptable in Nazi Germany in the middle 1930s, but it surely is not acceptable in a responsible social science publication in the middle 1970s. It is a tendentious, wandering, vicious diatribe and you should be ashamed of yourself for publishing it."[24] Cox died on September 4, 1974, before he was able to reply to his critics.

A Neglected Scholar

Oliver Cox's writing was never incorporated into the mainstream of sociological thinking, even after the publication of *Caste, Class and Race* in 1948. To be sure, the economic and political milieu in the United States at the end of World War II was far from propitious for the kind of Marxist-inspired analysis that Cox was engaged in. The prosperity generated by the New Deal and the war appeared to have laid to rest any fears about the viability of capitalism. A consumer-oriented society was launched with the $100 billion that Americans had saved during the war.[25] When Stalin announced in 1946 that there would be no long-term relations between the "young, dynamic world of socialism and the dying, corrupt world of capitalism," the stage was set for a wave of virulent anti-Communism that would last a decade. The House Committee on Un-American Activities (HUAC), which had gone into eclipse during the war, was reinvigorated and granted the status of a standing committee of the Congress. Its members saw a vast conspiracy across the nation.[26] Few academicians who expressed disapproval of U.S. society could escape the hysteria:

> Pressures on colleges and universities tended to be implicit when federal, explicit when locally instigated; although explicit enough was HUAC's letter of June, 1949, to eighty-one colleges and high schools, demanding lists of textbooks in use in the fields of literature, economics, government, history, political science, social science and geography.[27]

Serious constraints were placed on academic freedom "as communists and socialists were thought to be lurking in all the dark corners of academe."[28] Even the accusation of being associated with the Communist party or harboring radical ideas could mean being passed over for promotion—or the loss of a job and "blacklisting" from future employment.

Thus there were few people—either social scientists or ordinary citizens—who were prepared to embrace the concept of class struggle or endorse a probing critique of capitalist society. Nor were the times conducive to the publication of a sociological treatise that asserted—as did *Caste, Class, and Race*—that "from the standpoint of degrees of development in democracy in the three great nations of the world—the United States, England, and Russia—the United States is probably most backward and Russia farthest advanced,"[29] or argued that racial prejudice was used by the ruling class to prevent the unification of black and white workers.

Though never called before HUAC, Cox was not immune from the pressures of the times. At least one prominent sociologist, Howard Becker, refused to write an introduction to the book because of its putative "Marxist" orientation, and one publisher turned it down because the ideas were reminiscent of "Communism." In a letter to Cox, Becker wrote:

> After much soul-searching and a very painstaking second perusal of your transcript, I am compelled to say that it will be absolutely impossible for me to write an introduction to your book which would not do more harm than good. Your Marxism is so undiluted, especially in the part on class and in the conclusion, that I should have to dissociate myself completely from these proportions.

He added: "I don't know who your publisher is, but I should be greatly surprised—assuming that his office reader is prudent—if he accepted the book without modification."[30] Indeed, one editor provided the following assessment:

> Dear Professor Cox:
> It's no use, I can't stomach the communist line.
>
> Sincerely Yours,
> Wm. B. Selgby[31]

When Cox consulted Paul M. Sweezy, editor of *Monthly Review,* an independent socialist magazine, about publishing some of his work, Sweezy wrote: "Needless to say, we are very well aware of the fact that many people can't write what they want to these days, and we are perfectly willing to publish articles anonymously where protection is needed."[32]

The reviews of the book in scholarly journals, magazines, and newspapers were mixed. Some reviewers believed that it was a significant contribution and placed Cox among the ranks of such leading scholars as Ruth Benedict, Gunnar Myrdal, Aldous Huxley, and Ashley Montagu.[33] Few failed, however, to label Cox a "Marxist sociologist." For instance, Elmer P. Martin has reported that out of one hundred reviews on Cox's books, between 75 and 80 percent referred to Cox as a Marxist. There were some reviewers who expressed a reluctance to make a statement about Cox's work because, as one put it, "it is so deeply steeped in Marxism that it may do interracial relations more harm than good." Others believed that although Cox's writings were Marxist, his approach "differed from the exponents of Marxism" in not taking an orthodox approach to race relations.[34] And even those reviewers who praised Cox's erudition and the "freshness" of his approach expressed a concern that he was advocating political action within the Marxist framework, rather than producing a scientific study of human society.[35]

Those few who responded directly to Cox's arguments were also concerned with his inattention to the rules of science (as they were defined at the time). While the question of the relation between values and scientific sociology had come to the fore in the 1940s, as sociologists became involved in applied research,[36] most still believed that an "objective" or "value-free" sociology was possible. Thus while Cox's Marxism was the issue for some, for others the criticism was expressed in more "scientific" terms. Cox's entire theoretical orientation was considered unscientific, deterministic, polemical, and incapable of addressing the complex problems of a modern industrial society. Alvin Rose has commented on the atmosphere of the time:

> I think that exacerbated the problem for him. Marxism in those days was a dirty word. Sociologists generally believed that Marx was naive. The assumption that there are really only two important social classes was seen as a gross oversimplification. They did not blame Marx. Marx wrote in another time. But they thought that it was naive for people in this day to be spouting that out as contemporary sociology. The class system was seen as being much more complex.[37]

A similar view was expressed by many of the sociologists who, like Cox,

had been trained in sociology and anthropology at the University of
Chicago. For example, Robert Park, a leading mentor of many Chicago
sociologists, was at the forefront in the quest to make sociology "scientific,"
and he impressed upon his students a view of the scientific role of the
sociologist.[38] Furthermore, Park believed that "one's personal status depended on one's ability to gain access to unusual research sites and establish
rapport with key respondents," which he saw as the opposite of adhering
to a particular ideological framework.[39] Thus going into the field, collecting
data, and having group discussions of research results were all part of a
work style that was believed to be conducive to developing and producing
a community of sociologists that would be maintained after their graduate
education.

Cox's black peers gave him no more recognition than his white ones.
They too had largely been trained at Chicago and while their minority status
compelled them to be critical of racial segregation and discrimination, they
were less critical of research in this area than was Cox. As Charles Smith
and Lewis Killian have written in their analysis of social protest in the
writings of the black sociologists of this generation, these scholars did not
attack white American civilization and its values to the extent that we would
expect today from those associated with black cultural and/or revolutionary
nationalism.[40] Cox, in contrast, was openly suggesting that fundamental
political and economic problems had to be resolved in order for race
relations in the United States to change. One result of the neglect of Cox's
work is that there are few discussions of his ideas in the works of the black
sociologists of the 1940s and 1950s, and he received few invitations to
lecture from those black institutions that had attained some visibility and
prestige in the social sciences.

Cox avoided what he perceived to be white intellectual paternalism,
which locked many black sociologists into the prevailing view of the race
problem. Aware of the professional rewards to be accrued by those closely
associated with the institutional establishment in sociology, he was nevertheless uncompromisingly critical of those whites he believed were perpetuating a conservative view of race relations behind the facade of value
neutrality and scientific objectivity. For Cox, the race problem in the United
States could not be solved with moralistic arguments proving that society

was wrong, or by pursuing a detached "science" that did not raise structural issues and place intellectual problems in the context of the wider society.

Cox's Work Reconsidered

Caste, Class, and Race was allowed to go out of print as soon as the first edition was exhausted in 1949.[41] It was ten years before it was reissued, a task undertaken by Monthly Review Press, a small enterprise publishing only a few books a year. Regardless of the rationale underlying Doubleday's decision—whether it was the result of succumbing to Cold War hysteria or because of lack of sales (an indication of a wider neglect)—the fact remains that Cox's ideas continued to be ignored. Moreover, Cox was omitted from John H. Bracy, August Meier, and Elliot Rudwick's *The Black Sociologists*, one of the first anthologies to present selections from the writings of black sociologists. In their introduction, the editors defend their omission by claiming that "Cox, an independent thinker, stood apart from the dominant tradition in the sociology of American race relations, and exerted little influence on later scholars."[42]

What little recognition Cox has received has come from a group of younger black social scientists, themselves often outside the mainstream of the discipline. The Association of Social and Behavioral Scientists, composed largely of black scholars, awarded Cox its first W. E. B. Du Bois Award in 1968 for his contribution in the field of race relations. A few years later, as black sociologists saw the need to rediscover the contribution of older scholars, Cox was (ironically) the first to receive the Du Bois-Johnson-Frazier Award (in 1971), sponsored by the Caucus of Black Sociologists.

Cox's association with Marxism has both facilitated and hindered his subsequent recognition by young sociologists. On the one hand, as Marxism has emerged as a valid alternative perspective within U.S. sociology in general, both Marxist and non-Marxist writers interested in the role of class conflict and power in race relations have begun to reexamine Cox's work. On the other hand, as mainstream sociology continues to consider Marxism a "limited" way of interpreting class, Cox continues to be branded a Marxist and dismissed. On both counts, the critique has in part been the result of a narrow reading of Cox's work, with *Caste, Class, and Race* the only work considered (and not all of it at that), while the writings on capitalism are ignored.

Cox: A Marxist Intellectual or an Intellectual Radical?

This is, then, a good place to consider what Cox's theoretical orientation really was. Cox's approach to Marx, and to Marxist theory in general, often seems inconsistent, and Marxists and non-Marxists alike have engaged in much argument over the precise nature of his theoretical orientation.[43] Cox relied unabashedly on Marx for much of his critique of capitalist society and recognized the outstanding contributions of Marx's theory to the study of society in general. On the other hand, he firmly objected to being affiliated with what he called the "religious Marxists" because of their rigid adherence to a dogmatic brand of Marxism. Moreover, he criticized some of Marx's essential theoretical precepts, and disavowed Marx himself whenever that name was associated with unscientific thinking. Thus he criticized Marx's theory of class, which he argued failed to offer a precise enough definition of classes themselves; and, as noted below, when he analyzed the historical origins, growth, and development of capitalism as a world system, he repudiated Marx's labor theory of value, arguing that surplus value was derived not simply from the exploitation of labor in the sphere of the factory (within the nation-state), but also in trade among nations in the larger world economy.

It might seem, then, that Cox was a "plain" Marxist, as C. Wright Mills used the term. He argued that one could work openly and flexibly with Marx's ideas without embracing all that Marx said.[44] Yet Cox's acceptance of Marx and Marxist theory was a cautious one, an acceptance predicated on two essential factors: First, Cox did not embrace Marxist theory out of direct theoretical and political conviction, but rather as the end result of a process of independent investigation and theoretical elimination. Second, Cox was primarily concerned with Marx's method, and rejected outright any ideological commitment that might be associated with an adherence to Marxism. Thus in the preface to *Caste, Class, and Race,* he declared that his attachment to Marxist theory rested on its greater explanatory power when compared to other theories: "If, therefore, parts of this study seem Marxian, it is not because we have taken the ideas of the justly famous writer as gospel, but because we have not discovered any other that could explain the facts so consistently." He drew a distinction between Marx and the "religious Marxists," disclaiming any association with the latter:

> At best, Marxian hypotheses are "servants, not masters." Indeed, it has been said that Karl Marx himself was not a Marxian because in his studies he strived to understand modern society, while religious Marxists, in their exegetical discussions, center their attention not upon the ongoing social system but rather upon an explanation and criticism of Marx—a sort of rumination of his conclusions, incidental errors and all.[45]

In other words, independent thinkers should be free to draw on any body of knowledge as long as it proved scientifically sound—one need not be a Marxist in order to benefit from Marx's approach.

Cox leaned on two principal aspects of Marx's methodology. First, like Marx, his approach was historical, and his research into the actual conditions of human social life was anti-idealist, fundamentally materialist, and historically specific. Thus, to give but one example, he challenged the widely accepted notion that racism had existed throughout history, instead arguing that it emerged with the advent of capitalism and colonialism.

Cox followed Marx in another significant respect. He, like Marx, placed a great deal of emphasis on the significance of labor and on the centrality of class divisions in the development of racism. Thus, after discussing the spread of European capitalism, he demonstrated the role of African slaves and black tenant farmers in the system of capitalist production relations. On the basis of economic interests, he argued, the "white ruling class" developed a corresponding ideology in order to justify and rationalize existing relations of production. The resulting "political-class struggle" is inextricably connected to racial antagonism and constitutes its central dynamic core.

Thus in methodological approach, conceptual language, and mode of analysis, Cox seems to us today to be very much a Marxist. Indeed, any reader of *Caste, Class, and Race,* Marxist or non-Marxist, can hardly come to any other conclusion. Yet in his trilogy on capitalism, Cox is not content to accept Marx's theory of capitalism at face value. He finds it necessary to rediscover and rethink the origin of capitalism from its early beginnings in Venice. One of the most controversial points he makes in *The Foundations of Capitalism,* for example, is that capitalism originated in Venice as a result of chance circumstances that led the city-state to rise to prominence. He then argues that an unbroken process of growth links the "infant" capitalism of Venice to the "mature" capitalism of the United States. Venice prospered and gained influence throughout Europe and the East through the development of foreign trade—a pattern that was followed by other Italian city-states, by the Hanseatic League, and by Holland. Cox thus argues two related points: that capitalism has always expanded and developed on the basis of foreign trade; and that capitalist societies have been from their inception part of a world system and thus by nature open and dynamic, not closed. This argument directly challenged both Marx and those of his followers who argued that capitalism grew out of the declining feudal order, and developed in the closed system of English industrial capitalism.[46] Cox further argues that even the amendments to Marx's theory made by Lenin, Rosa Luxemburg, and Maurice Dobb, while placing more emphasis on the imperialistic strivings of the capitalist nations, do not correct the fundamental errors in Marx's theoretical conception of capitalism:[47]

> Having accepted the fundamental Marxian postulates on the nature of capitalist society, Marxists cannot go back to Venetian, Hanseatic, Dutch or even early English imperialism for the essential concepts of the components of that phenomenon. It thus becomes a crucially limiting position which entails procrustean operations in the handling of the facts of modern social change as they relentlessly impose themselves upon us. The rigid ideas concerning the role of industrial workers in modern revolutionary movements, and the earlier Marxian predictions giving precedence to the more advanced capitalist nations in the succession of socialist revolutions, are all derivatives of the theory.[48]

But it is one thing to point out Marx's shortcomings—many Marxists, after all, do that, placing Marx in the context of the time in which he lived and developed his theory. It is quite another to claim that Marxism, as practiced by Marx's followers, is simply the "ideological" consequence of political practice—and this is what Cox argues in *Capitalism as a System*:

> But Marx and his immediate colleague, Frederick Engels, were also major leaders of anti-capitalist action groups; and, in that capacity, they assumed the normal charismatic aura of outstanding leadership. The completely rational analysis of society formulated by these thinkers can scarcely be expected of their followers. To be sure, this is also true—in reverse fashion, so to speak—of the capitalist leadership and its dedicated scholars: a diabolical image tends spontaneously to be evoked whenever any Marxian concept is brought into their

purview. They do not allow critical thinking free play. Moreover, because the preponderance of power rests in the existing elite, we should expect and find more flagrant and effectual manifestations of intolerance on their side.[49]

According to Cox, Marx's theory is not based on a scientific analysis, as one ought to expect, but appears as a theoretical justification that is used to cloak his "proletarian ideology." To quote Cox once again:

> He [Marx] contrived with remarkable success to become the ideological leader of this [proletarian] class; and then devoted the rest of his intellectual life mainly to a study of the economics and sociology of capitalism in order to provide a theoretical foundation for his proletarian ideology. It goes without saying that if Marx's preoccupation had originally been the *scientific* study of capitalism as a form of social organization, with only a derived interest in the contemporary class struggle, his entire theoretical work would have been differently informed.[50]

Two related points should be noted about this passage. First, assuming that Marx did indeed seek a theoretical foundation for his proletarian ideology, there is no reason to conclude that such a pursuit would of necessity be *unscientific*. After all, Marx's theorizing and political praxis went hand in hand. Second, Cox suggests that had Marx remained detached from the ongoing class struggle, he would have developed a different (a Coxian?) view of capitalism. Here Cox reveals his own view of science while simultaneously failing to grasp an essential aspect of Marx's theory: the notion of social praxis.[51]

Perhaps Cox is best described as a critical theorist, one who draws on a number of "classical" thinkers (including Weber, Sombart, Marx, Durkheim, to name only a few) to pursue a line of inquiry using a historical materialist and comparative approach. But it is important to point out that Cox was not eclectic in his approach, even though he was influenced by a number of thinkers with opposing views (e.g., Durkheim and Marx). Rather, Cox always began with a historically specific society viewed as a system—be it the Venetian city-state, the Hanseatic League, Hindu caste society, or U.S. capitalism:

> After addressing themselves in this fashion to the economic aspects of race relations, these scholars usually move on to emphasize certain startling psychological or political incidents, implying that these are at least as significant for an analysis of the society. Such approaches may seem to satisfy the requirements of a detached eclecticism, but they can hardly arrive at a conception of race

relations as societally determined, that is, if we think of society as a definable pattern of social relations. The economics of all societies are socially defined, but social factors do not limit the operation of the economic order in the same way in all societies.[52]

Cox's respect for, and dependence on, the classical sociological thinkers puts him in the company of C. Wright Mills, another contemporary sociologist who was often disparagingly labeled a radical. Both men shared a respect for the classical tradition in sociology and saw themselves as a part of it. Both men respected Marx and used his insights, and both were repeatedly accused of dogged adherence to simple economic and political formulas and interpretations. With Cox, in particular, a concern for societal and controversial issues was interpreted as Marxist; a creative application of certain aspects of Marx's theory and method was seen as confirming their dogmatism; and, finally, a respect for Marx's colossal intellectual production was reason for excommunication from the sociological community. Cox was then a radical intellectual in the classical tradition of both C. Wright Mills and Thorstein Veblen. He thought of himself as an independent thinker, a scholar, and a social scientist. As an intellectual craftsman, he pursued a line of inquiry reminiscent of an earlier period of classical thinkers. Like them, he preferred to tackle the most controversial issues of the day. Unlike many of his contemporaries, he refused to sidestep or blindly malign Marx (even though he disagreed with some essential aspects of Marx's theory) in order to demonstrate his orthodoxy in the sociological fraternity and thus gain success and fame in official circles. He was a rebel and an iconoclast at a time when it was fashionable to vociferously pronounce one's anti-Marxism and adherence to an official canon. He paid dearly for his unwillingness to conform. His works were relegated to relative obscurity in the sociological profession and he was never offered an academic post commensurate with his achievements. He refused to compromise his integrity as a scholar, even when he was roundly criticized for his Marxist borrowings. He openly declared his intellectual debt to Marx, but freely renounced those aspects of Marx's theory that he found dogmatic or incompatible with the historical dynamics of capitalism as a world system and the transition from capitalism to socialism. He may have seen himself as an "independent" radical thinker, but in today's class-and-race-divided world, Oliver C. Cox can justifiably be considered a distinguished and creative fellow-traveler among Marxists, albeit an independent one.

Notes

1. Some of the material included in this introduction has appeared in a previously published article and has been revised for this book; see Herbert M. Hunter, "Oliver C. Cox: A Biographical Sketch of His Life and Work," *Phylon* 44, no. 4 (December 1983): 249–61.

2. Elmer P. Martin, "The Sociology of Oliver C. Cox: A Systematic Inquiry" (Master's Thesis, Atlanta University, 1971), p. 12.

3. Virginia Blake Cox gave birth to six children, four sons and two daughters. Through a second marriage, to Louisa Cox, two additional sons and a sister were added to the Cox family. Several of Oliver Cox's brothers and sisters died at a relatively early age.

4. Interview with Stella Awon-Cox.

5. Interview with Oliver C. Cox by Elmer P. Martin, November 19,1970.

6. Interview with Oliver C. Cox by Elmer P. Martin.

7. Oliver C. Cox, "Factors Affecting the Marital Status of Negroes in the United States," (Ph.D. diss., The University of Chicago, 1938).

8. An excellent analysis of the experiences of black social scientists teaching in black colleges may be found in Butler Jones, "Tradition of Sociology Teaching in Black Colleges: The Unheralded Professionals," in *Black Sociologists: Historical and Contemporary Perspectives,* ed. James E. Blackwell and Morris Janowitz (Chicago, 1974), pp. 121–63.

9. In Hunter, "Oliver C. Cox: A Biographical Sketch of His Life and Work," Wiley College is identified as a Baptist school. It has since been brought to our attention that the religious denomination of Wiley College is Methodist. We are indebted to Darnell D. Thomas of Texarkana, Texas, for this correction.

10. Telephone interview with Charles G. Gomillion, Washington, D.C., May 23, 1978.

11. Martin, "The Sociology of Oliver C. Cox," p. 17.

12. In fact, one author has referred to the Southern Negro Congress as a "communist front organization"; see William A. Nolan, *Communism Versus the Negro* (Chicago, 1951), p. 578.

13. See footnote in Oliver C. Cox, *Caste, Class, and Race* (New York, 1970), p. 578.

14. See Oliver C. Cox, "The Leadership of Booker T. Washington," *Social Forces* 30, no. 1 (October 1951): 95. See also "The New Crisis in Leadership Among Negroes,"*Journal of Negro Education 19* (Fall 1950): 459–65; "Leadership Among Negroes in the United States," in *Studies in Leadership,* ed. Alvin Gouldner (New York, 1950), pp. 228–71; "The Programs of Negro Civil Rights Organizations,"*Journal of Negro Education* 20 (Summer 1951): 354–66.

15. Cox did seek support for his research from the Carnegie and Ford Foundations during his career, but in both cases his proposals were rejected.

16. Cf. Immanuel Wallerstein, *The Modern World System* (New York, 1974), and Barbara Hockey Kaplan, ed. *Social Change in the Capitalist World Economy* (Beverly Hills, Calif., 1978).

17. Interview with Lorenzo Greene, Lincoln University, Jefferson City, Missouri, February 17, 1978.

18. Letter from Oliver C. Cox to Stella Awon-Cox, June 8, 1970.

19. Interview with Alvin W. Rose, University of Miami, Coral Gables, Florida, May 16, 1980.

20. Correspondence with Bruce Williams, Vanderbilt University, Nashville, Tennessee, March 16, 1980.

21. Ibid.

22. Ibid.

23. Oliver C. Cox, "Jewish Self-interest in Black Pluralism," *The Sociological Quarterly* 15 (Spring 1974): 183–189.

24. "Comments on Cox," *The Sociological Quarterly* 16, no. 1. (Winter 1975): 131–134.

25. Geoffrey Perrett, *A Dream of Greatness: The American People, 1945–1963* (New York, 1979), p. 72.

26. Cabell Phillips, *The 1940s: Decade of Triumph and Trouble* (New York, 1975), p. 364.

27. David Caute, *The Great Fear: The Anti-Communist Purge under Truman and Eisenhower* (New York, 1978), p. 404.

28. Ibid.

29. Cox, *Caste, Class, and Race*, p. 223.

30. Letter from Howard Becker to Oliver C. Cox, August 23, 1946; quoted in Martin, "The Sociology of Oliver C. Cox," p. 85.

31. Letter from William B. Selgby, editor, Public Affairs Press to Oliver C. Cox, August 26, 1960; quoted in Martin, "The Sociology of Oliver C. Cox," p. 22.

32. Letter from Paul M. Sweezy to Oliver C. Cox, July 20,1949; quoted in Martin, "The Sociology of Oliver C. Cox," p. 80.

33. Letter from Benjamin J. Davis, Jr., to Oliver C. Cox, September 9, 1948; quoted in Martin, "The Sociology of Oliver C. Cox," p. 2.

34. Quoted in ibid., p. 83.

35. Ibid.

36. See Roscoe C. Hinkle, Jr., and Gisela J. Hinkle, *The Development of Modern Sociology* (New York, 1954), p. 47.

37. Interview with Alvin W. Rose.

38. See Winifred Raushenbush, *Robert E. Park: Biography of a Sociologist* (Durham, N.C., 1979), p. 197.

39. James T. Carey, *Sociology and Public Affairs: The Chicago School* (Beverly Hills, Calif., 1975), p. 155.

40. Charles U. Smith and Lewis Killian, "Black Sociologists and Social Protest," in *Black Sociologists*, p. 199.

41. This section draws on an earlier paper by Sameer Y. Abraham, "Oliver C. Cox's (Neglected) Contributions Toward a Theory of Race Relations," presented at the annual meeting of the North Central Sociological Association, Dayton, Ohio, May 1–3, 1980.

42. John H. Bracy, Jr., August Meier, and Elliot Rudwick, *The Black Sociologist: The First Half Century* (Belmont, Calif., 1971), p. 12.

43. This section draws on an earlier paper by Sameer Y. Abraham, "Oliver C. Cox: An Independent Contribution to Marxist Theory," presented at the Fourth Annual Conference on the Current State of Marxist Theory, University of Louisville, November 15–17, 1979. Also see Herbert M. Hunter, "Oliver C. Cox: Marxist or Intellectual Radical?" *Journal of the History of Sociology* 5, no. 1 (Spring 1983): 1–27.

44. C. Wright Mills was accused by many of being a Marxist, although many thought him un-Marxist or even anti-Marxist. In 1957, he said he had never been a Marxist; in 1962 he wrote as a "plain Marxist" in criticizing "vulgar" and "sophisticated" Marxists for trying to rationalize and repair Marx's outmoded model rather than using Marx's method to construct a new and credible picture of a changed reality. See *The Marxist* (New York, 1962), pp. 96–104.

45. Cox, *Caste, Class, and Race*, p. xi.

46. Marx's view of the subject can be located in Eric J. Hobsbawm, *Karl Marx: Pre-Capitalist Economic Formations* (New York, 1964), and Maurice Dobb, "Marx and Pre-Capitalist Economic Formations," *Science and Society* 30 (Summer 1966): 1–11.

47. Cox specifically refers to the following Marxists here: Vladimir Lenin, *Imperialism: The Highest Stage of Capitalism* (Peking, 1967); Maurice Dobb, *Political Economy of*

Capitalism (London, 1937); and Rosa Luxemburg, *The Accumulation of Capital* (New Haven, 1951).

It appears odd that so thorough a scholar as Cox would deliberately neglect key works in this area, namely, Nikolai Bukharin, *Imperialism and World Economy* (New York, 1929); idem, *Imperialism and the Accumulation of Capital* (New York, 1973); and Paul Baran, *The Political Economy of Growth* (New York, 1962). This seeming neglect points to Cox's superficial reading of the Marxist literature.

48. Cox, *Capitalism as a System* (New York, 1964), p. 218.

49. Ibid., p. 210.

50. Ibid., p. 212.

51. For a discussion of social praxis, the reader is referred to Karl Korsch, *Three Essays on Marxism* (New York, 1972), and Shlomo Avineri, *The Social and Political Thought of Karl Marx* (New York, 1968).

52. Oliver C. Cox, *Race Relations,* p. 6.

Introduction

The term "ethnic" may be employed generically to refer to social relations among distinct peoples. Accordingly, an ethnic may be defined as a people living competitively in relationship of superordination or subordination with respect to some other people or peoples within one state, country, or economic area. Two or more ethnics constitute an ethnic system or regime; and, naturally, one ethnic must always imply another. In other words, we may think of one ethnic as always forming part of a system.

Ethnic systems may be classified:

1. According to the culture of the ethnics:
    a. Degrees of cultural advancement (simple or complex).
    b. Type variation, e.g., Occidental or Oriental.
    c. Pattern, e.g., variation in language, religion, nationality, or other ways of living.
2. According to physical distinguishability:
    a. Race, e.g., black, brown, red, white, etc.
    b. Mixed bloods.

Thus, difference among ethnics may center about variations in culture, such as those claimed by British, Afrikander, and Jews of South Africa; or it may rest upon distinguishability, such as that of whites, East Indians, Bantu, and Cape Colored of the same area. When the ethnics are of the same race—that is to say, when there is no significant physical characteristics accepted by the ethnics as marks of distinction—their process of adjustment is usually designated nationality or "minority-group" problems. When, on the other hand, the ethnics recognize each other physically and use their physical distinction as a basis for the rationale of their interrelationships, their process of adjustment is usually termed race relations or race problems.

Cultural or national ethnics and racial ethnics are alike in that they are both power groups. They stand culturally or racially as potential or actual antagonists. The degree of the interethnic conflict can be explained only by the social history of the given relationship; and neither race nor culture seems in itself to be an index of the stability of the antagonism. The status relationship of both cultural and racial ethnics may persist with great rigidity for long periods of time or it may be short-lived. The opposition between the English and the Irish and between the Jews and Catholics in Spain are instances of rather long-time cultural antagonisms. The Mohammedans and the Hindus in India present a situation in which the formerly subordinated Hindus are apparently about to take the place of their old Mohammedan masters, but the centuries-old hostility persists. Both culture and race prejudices are dynamic group attitudes varying in intensity according to the specific historical situation of the peoples involved.[1]

Ethnic, political class, social class, estate, and caste may be compared. Castes, estates, and social classes belong to or comprise status systems of socially superior and inferior persons. These systems are peaceful, and degrees of superiority are taken for granted according to the normal expectations of the system. Lower-status persons are not preoccupied with ways and means of demoting their superiors. When these systems are functioning at their best, social acts recognizing degrees of superiority in the status hierarchy are yielded with the same kind of alacrity as that which college boys lavish upon their athletic heroes.

On the other hand, political-class and ethnic relations do not constitute ordered systems but rather antagonistic regimes. Political classes tend to break up the orderly working of a status system and struggle toward or against revolutionizing it. The aggressive political class aims at social disorder for the purpose of instituting a new order.[2] Ethnics are peoples

[1]It appears that the principle of racial and nationality assimilation laid down by Lloyd Warner and Leo Srole is too simple. As they see it: ". . . the greater the difference between the host and the immigrant cultures, the greater will be the subordination, the greater the strength of ethnic social systems, and the longer the period necessary for assimilation of the ethnic groups. . . . The greater the racial difference . . . the greater the subordination of the immigrant group . . . and the longer the period necessary for assimilation." The process of assimilation is further delayed if the immigrant is divergent in both cultural and physical traits. There is probably some truth in this birds-of-a-feather hypothesis, yet it seems that it may be too truistic and crude for significant analysis of internationality and racial assimilation. See *The Social Systems of American Ethnic Groups*, pp. 285–86.

[2]Abraham Lincoln was pertinent when in 1848 he said in Congress: "It is a quality of revolutions not to go by old lines and old laws; but to break up both, and make new ones." J. G. Nicolay and John Hay, *Abraham Lincoln, Complete Works*, Vol. I, p. 105.

living in some state of antagonism, and their ambitions tend to vary with the situation. Some ethnics are intransigent; others seek or oppose assimilation; still others struggle for positions as ruling peoples. In political-class action not only status groups but also ethnics may be split to take sides on the basis of their economic rather than their ethnic interests or status position. On the contrary, ethnic antagonism may so suffuse other interests that political-class differences are constantly held in abeyance.[3]

We shall discuss further the problems of national ethnics in a following chapter, and we shall use the popular expression "race relations" to refer to the problems of adjustment between racial ethnics.

The Concept—Race Relations

It is evident that the term "race relations" may include all situations of contact between peoples of different races, and for all time. One objection to the use of this term is that there is no universally accepted definition of race. The biologist and the physical anthropologist may indeed have considerable difficulty with this, but for the sociologist a race may be thought of as simply any group of people that is generally believed to be, and generally accepted as, a race in any given area of ethnic competition. Here is detail enough, since the sociologist is interested in social interaction. Thus, if a man looks white, although, say in America, he is everywhere called a Negro, he is, then, a Negro American. If, on the other hand, a man of identical physical appearance is recognized everywhere in Cuba as a white man, then he is a white Cuban. The sociologist is interested in what meanings and definitions a society gives to certain social phenomena and situations. It would probably be as revealing of interracial attitudes to deliberate upon the variations in the skeletal remains of some people as it

[3]Edgar H. Brookes describes the situation in South Africa which illustrates this: "Economically the Poor White, the Coloured man and the detribalized, urban Native are in the same category. Yet no political party in South Africa, with the exception of the Communists, has made any serious or sustained attempt to draw them all together in opposition to capitalism. It is most significant that the Poor White proletariat of the towns does not in general vote for Communist or even for Labour candidates; but for some Party—whether the main National Party or not—which claims to be 'nationalist.' they are not class-conscious. They prefer to join with their fellow-white men, even if capitalists, than with their non-white fellow-workers. . . . As was long the case in the Southern States of America, as indeed still is the case there, the Poor White has sacrificed his economic to his sentimental interests, and the immediate economic protection offered him on colour lines." *The Colour Problems of South Africa*, p. 29.

would be to question an on-going society's definition of a race because, anthropometrically speaking, the assumed race is not a *real* race. What we are interested in is the social definition of the term "race." To call that which a group has been pleased to designated race by some other name does not affect the nature of the social problem to be investigated.[4]

We may think of race relations, therefore, as that behavior which develops among peoples who are aware of each other's actual or imputed physical differences. Moreover, by race relations we do not mean all social contacts between persons of different "races," but only those contacts the social characteristics of which are determined by a consciousness of "racial" difference. If, for example, two persons of different racial strains were to meet and deal with each other on their own devices—that is to say, without preoccupation with a social definition of each other's race—then it might be said that race here is of no sociological significance. But if their behavior tended to be fashioned by ethnic attitudes toward each other's actual or purported physical differences, then the situation may be called a social contact between ethnics, and it may be also referred to as race relations. However, these ethnic attitudes are based upon other and more fundamental social phenomena.

[4]Cf. William Oscar Brown, "Race Prejudice," Ph.D. thesis, University of Chicago, 1930, pp. 4–5. It should be made patently clear that the laboratory classification of races, which began among anthropologists about a hundred years ago, has no necessary relationship with the problem of race relations as sociological phenomena. Race relations developed independently of anthropological tests and measurements.

1.

Race Relations—Its Meaning, Beginning, and Progress

A Definition

In a discussion of "the origin" of race relations it should be well to determine at the outset exactly what we are looking for. We shall proceed, therefore, by first eliminating certain concepts that are commonly confused with that of race relations. These are: ethnocentrism, intolerance, and "racism."

Ethnocentrism, as the sociologists conceive of it, is a social attitude which expresses a community of feeling in any group—the "we" feeling as over against the "others." This attitude seems to be a function of group solidarity, which is not necessarily a racial phenomenon. Neither is social intolerance (which we shall consider in more detail in a subsequent chapter) racial antagonism, for social intolerance is social displeasure or resentment against that group which refuses to conform to the established practices and beliefs of the society. Finally, the term "racism" as it has been recently employed in the literature seems to refer to a philosophy of racial antipathy. Studies on the origin of racism involve the study of the development of an ideology, an approach which usually results in the substitution of the history of a system of rationalization for that of a material social fact.[1] Indeed, it is likely to be an accumulation of an erratic pattern of verbalizations cut free from any ongoing social system.

What then is the phenomenon, the beginnings of which we seek to determine? It is the phenomenon of the capitalist exploitation of peoples and its complementary social attitude. Again, one should miss the point entirely if one were to think of racial antagonism as having its genesis in

[1] See Hannah Arendt, "Race-Thinking Before Racism," *The Review of Politics,* Vol. 6, January 1944, pp. 36–73; and Fredrick G. Detweiler, "The Rise of Modern Race Antagonisms," *The American Journal of Sociology,* Vol. 37, March 1932, pp. 738–47.

some "social instinct" of antipathy between peoples. Such an approach ordinarily leads to no end of confusion.[2]

The Beginning of Racial Antagonism

Probably a realization of no single fact is of such crucial significance for an understanding of racial antagonism as that the phenomenon had its rise only in modern times.[3] In a previous chapter on "the origin of caste" we have attempted to show that race conflict did not exist among the early Aryans in India, and we do not find it in other ancient civilizations.* Our hypothesis is that racial exploitation and race prejudice developed among Europeans with the rise of capitalism and nationalism, and that because of the world-wide ramifications of capitalism, all racial antagonisms can be traced to the policies and attitudes of the leading capitalist people, the white people of Europe and North America.

By way of demonstrating this hypothesis we shall review briefly some well-known historical situations. In tracing the rise of the Anglo-Saxons to their position as the master race of the world[4] we shall omit consideration

[2]Consider, for instance, the following definitive statement by Professor Robert E. Park: "This [prejudice against the Japanese] is due to the existence in the human mind of a mechanism by which we inevitably and automatically classify every individual human being we meet. When a race bears an external mark by which every individual member of it can infallibly be identified, that race is by that fact set apart and segregated. Japanese, Chinese, and Negroes cannot move among us with the same freedom as members of other races because they bear marks which identify them as members of their race. This fact isolates them. . . . Isolation is at once a cause and an effect of race prejudice. It is a vicious circle—isolation, prejudice; prejudice, isolation." In Jesse F. Steiner, *The Japanese Invasion,* p. xvi.

Since, however, we may assume that all races "bear marks which identify them as members of their race," it must follow, according to Park, that a certain human capacity for classification makes it impossible for races to come together without racial antagonism and prejudice. We shall attempt to show that this instinct hypothesis is too simple.

[3]Cf. Ina Corine Brown, *National Survey of the Higher Education of Negroes,* U.S. Office of Education, Misc. No. 6, Vol. I, pp. 4–8.

*Publisher's note: This is a reference to the original version of this book. Consult Oliver Cromwell Cox, *Caste, Class and Race* (New York: Monthly Review Press, 1959), pp 82–120.

[4]Professor G. A. Borgese makes an observation pertinent to this remark: "The English-speaking mind is not fully alive to the gravity of this issue. Unlike their German cousins and foes, the Anglo-Saxon stocks did not strive to *become* the master race or Herrenvolk holding sway over the world and mankind. . . . Yet, unlike their German cousins and rivals, they have succeeded in *being* a Herrenvolk, a race of masters." "Europe Wants Freedom from Shame," *Life,* March 12, 1945, pp. 41-42. (Italics Borgese's.)

"The Germans needed all of Hitler's ranting and daily doses from the Goebbels propaganda machine to persuade them that they were better than other people. Englishmen

of the great Eastern civilizations from which Greece took a significant cultural heritage. There seems to be no basis for imputing racial antagonism to the Egyptians, Babylonians, or Persians. At any rate, the Greeks were the first European people to enter the stream of eastern Mediterranean civilization, and the possibility of racial exploitation did not really occur until the Macedonian conquest. Our point here is, however, that we do not find race prejudice even in the great Hellenistic empire which extended deeper into the territories of colored people than any other European empire up to the end of the fifteenth century.

The Hellenic Greeks had a cultural, not a racial, standard of belonging, so that their basic division of the peoples of the world were Greeks and barbarians— the barbarians having been all those persons who did not possess the Greek culture, especially its language. This is not surprising, for the culture of peoples is always a matter of great moment to them. But the people of the Greek city-states, who founded colonies among the barbarians on the shores of the Black Sea and of the Mediterranean, welcomed those barbarians to the extent that they were able to participate in Greek culture, and intermarried freely with them. The Greeks knew that they had a superior culture to those of the barbarians, but they included Europeans, Africans, and Asiatics in the concept Hellas as these peoples acquired a working knowledge of the Greek culture.

The experience of the later Hellenistic empire of Alexander tended to be the direct contrary of modern racial antagonism. The narrow patriotism of the city-states was given up for a new cosmopolitanism. Every effort was made to assimilate the barbarians to Greek culture, and in the process a new Greco-Oriental culture with a Greco-Oriental ruling class came into being. Alexander himself took a Persian princess for his wife and encouraged his men to

simply take it for granted and rarely waste a syllable discussing it." See John Scott, *Europe in Revolution*, p. 216.

[5]In describing the composition of Alexander's army invading India, E. R. Bevan says: ". . . mingled with Europeans were men of many nations. Here were troops of horsemen, representing the chivalry of Iran, which had followed Alexander from Bactria and beyond, Pashtus and men of the Hindu Kush with their highland-bred horses, Central-Asiatics who ride and shoot at the same time; and among the camp-followers one could find groups representing the older civilizations of the world, Phoenicians inheriting an immemorial tradition of shipcraft and trade, bronzed Egyptians able to confront the Indians with an antiquity still longer than their own."*The Cambridge History of India*, Vol. I, p. 351.

intermarry with the native population.[5] In this empire there was an estate, not a racial, distinction between the rulers and the un-Hellenized natives.

Moreover, the inclination of Alexander to disregard even cultural differences in his policy toward the peoples of his empire seemed to have stimulated one of the most remarkable philosophies of all time: that of the fundamental equality of all human beings. In Athens, in about 300 B.C., Zeno developed a system of thought called stoicism which held in part that "all men should be fellow citizens; and there should be one life and order, as of a flock pasturing together, which feeds together by a common law." This doctrine was not a reaction to race prejudice but rather to certain invidious cultural distinctions among the peoples of the time; and the idea has come down to us by way of the Roman law, the preaching of St. Paul, and the writings of the philosophers of the Enlightenment. It has been given a democratic emphasis in the American Declaration of Independence and in amendments to the Constitution of the United States.

The next great organization of peoples about the Mediterranean Sea—and in so far as European civilization is concerned this may be thought of as constituting the whole world—was the Roman Empire. In this civilization also we do not find racial antagonism, for the norm of superiority in the Roman system remained a cultural-class attribute. The basic distinction was Roman citizenship, and gradually this was extended to all freeborn persons in the municipalities of the empire. Slaves came from every province, and there was no racial distinction among them. Sometimes the slaves, especially the Greeks, were the teachers of their masters; indeed, very much of the cultural enlightenment of the Romans came through slaves from the East. Because slavery was not a racial stigma, educated freedmen, who were granted citizenship upon emancipation, might rise to high positions in government or industry. There were no interracial laws governing the relationship of the great mass of obscure common people of different origin. Moreover, the aristocracy of the empire, the senators and *equites,* was constituted largely from responsible provincials in the imperial administration.

One should not mistake the social relationship among the various social estates of the Greek and Roman world for race relations. The Spartiates, *Perioikoi,* and Helots of Laconia, for instance, were not races but social estates; neither did the *Metics*,[6] the alien residents of Periclean Athens, constitute a race. In early republican Rome intermarriage was forbidden between the privileged patrician class and the plebeian mass, but this was a social-estate partition rather than a racial accommodation.

If we have not discovered interracial antagonism in ancient Greece and Rome, the chances of discovering it in the system which succeeded the fall of the Roman Empire are even more remote. With the rise of the politico-religious system of Christianity, Western culture may be thought of as having entered its long period of gestation. Its first signs of parturition were the Crusades. But during all this time and even after the Renaissance the nature of the movement and of the social contact of peoples in this area precluded the possibility of the development of race prejudice.

The general pattern of barbarian invasions was that of a succession of peoples of increasing cultural inferiority moving into areas of higher culture. Thus, the German nations which invaded the Roman Empire had a smaller capacity for maintaining a complex culture than the Romans had when they conquered the Greeks; and probably the Celtic people of Britain had still fewer resources to continue their Roman cultural heritage. In the movement of barbarian peoples from the East and North toward the general area of the Mediterranean no nationalistic sentiments stood in the way to limit their amalgamation with the native populations.

One aspect of this era of barbarian invasion, the movement of Asiatics into Europe, is of especial significance. The Asiatics were better warriors than rulers. We may say rather conclusively that the white man's rise to superiority over the colored peoples of the other continents is based pivotally on his superiority as a fighter. This is, however, a rather recent achievement. In the Middle Ages the Asiatics outfought him. The Huns, Saracens, Moors, Seljuk Turks, Ottoman Turks, Tartars—all went deep into Europe, subjugated and sometimes enslaved white peoples who today are highly race-prejudiced. At any rate, we shall not find racial antagonism among these invaders. The most powerful of them were Moslems, and both

---

[6]The Metics may probably be better thought of as presenting a multinationality situation. On this point Gustave Glotz, referring to the Metics of various national origins, concludes: ". . . there was formed in Greece in the fifth and sixth centuries a kind of international nation which was preparing, chiefly in economic interests but also in the domain of ideas and in the very framework of society, for the cosmopolitanism of the Hellenistic period." *Ancient Greece at Work*, p. 191.

the economic base and religious sanctions of Mohammedanism are opposed to race prejudice. Under Mohammedanism—at least in so far as it has not been recently corrupted by capitalist ideals—the criterion of belonging is a cultural one; furthermore, Islam is a proselytizing culture.

In Europe itself the policies of the Roman Catholic Church presented a bar to the development of racial antagonism. The Church, which gradually attained more or less religious, economic, and ideological dominance, had a folk and personal—not a territorial or racial—norm of belonging. The fundamental division of human beings was Christian and non-Christian. Among the non-Christians the heathen, the infidel, and the heretic were recognized by differential negative attitudes; however, as a means of entering the Christian community, conversion or recantation was freely allowed and even sought after. There was in medieval Europe—indeed in the Christian world—an effective basis for the brotherhood of peoples. Although a man's economic, contractual relationship in his community determined his livelihood, to be excommunicated by the Church almost had the effect of putting him beyond the purview of society itself. In the Middle Ages, then, we find no racial antagonism in Europe; in fact, Europeans were, at this time, more isolated and ignorant about foreign peoples and world geography than the Romans and Greeks were.

But gradually, under a commercial and religious impulse, Europe began to awaken and to journey toward strange lands. The First Crusade may be taken as the starting point which finally led to world dominance by Europeans. When after their travels in the last quarter of the thirteenth century the Polos returned from the court of the great Kublai Khan in China to tell Europeans a story of fabulous wealth and luxury, the astonished people could hardly believe what they heard. Yet Marco Polo's memoirs were a great stimulant to traders. It was not until the discovery of America and the circumnavigation of the globe, however, that the movement assumed a decidedly irreversible trend. The period between the First Crusade and the discovery of America continued to be characterized by the religious view of world order; but it set a pattern of dealing with non-Christian peoples which was to be continued, minus only its religious characteristics, to this day. To the extent that the religious controls remained effective, racial antagonism did not develop; what really developed was a Jew-heathen-infidel antagonistic complex which was to color European thought for some centuries.

Up to the eleventh century Christian Europe was hemmed in from the North, East, and South by heathens and infidels; the Mediterranean was almost encircled by the Arabian Mohammedans, a people whose culture was superior to that of the northern Europeans. In the eleventh century, however, under the organizing influence of the popes, the holy warriors of Christendom began to carry conquering crusades into the territory of the heathen Slavic and infidel Asiatic peoples. As a general rule the Church made the lands and even the peoples of the non-Christian world the property of the Crusaders, and the trader ordinarily followed the cross.

In fact, it was this need for trade with the East, especially by the Italian, Spanish, and Portuguese merchants, and its obstruction by the Mohammedans whose country lay across their path in the Near East, which induced the Portuguese, in the fifteenth century, to feel their way down the African coast in the hope of sailing around this continent to the East Indies. Here began the great drama that was, in a few hundred years, to turn over the destiny of the world to the decisions of businessmen. But our concern at this point is to indicate that racial antagonism had not yet developed among the Europeans.

In the first place, the geography of the world was still a mystery, and some of the most fantastic tales about its peoples were believed. Stories of the splendor, luxury, and wisdom of the peoples of the East held all Europe in constant wonderment. No one would have been surprised if some traveler had returned from the heart of Africa to break the news that he had found a black monarch ruling over a kingdom surpassing in grandeur and power any that had then existed in Europe. In short, the white man had no conception of himself as a being capable of developing *the* superior culture of the world— the concept "white man" had not yet its significant social definition—the Anglo-Saxon, the modern master race, was then not even in the picture.

But when the Portuguese began to inch their way down the African coast they knew that the Moors and heathens whom they encountered were inferior to them both as fighters and as culture builders.[7] This, however, led

---

[7]It should be noted that the Portuguese felt they were superior because they were Christians, not because they were white. In an address to his men just before they attacked an unsuspecting west-coast community, the captain of a caravel declared: ". . . although they are more in number than we by a third yet they are but Moors, and we are Christians one of whom ought to suffice for two of them. For God is He in whose power lieth victory, and He knoweth our good wills in His holy service." Azurara, *The Discovery and Conquest of Guinea*, p. 138.

to no conclusions about racial superiority. Henry the Navigator, himself, sought in those parts a Christian prince, Prester John, with whom he planned to form an alliance "against the enemies of the faith." All through the latter half of the fifteenth century the Portuguese sailors and explorers kept up this search for the kingdom of the lost black prince.

Of more significance still is the fact that there was as yet no belief in any cultural incapacity of these colored people. Their conversion to Christianity was sought with enthusiasm, and this transformation was supposed to make the Africans the human equals of all other Christians. The Portuguese historian Gomes Eannes de Azurara, writing in the middle of the fifteenth century, gives us some idea of the religious motives for Prince Henry's exploits among the peoples on the West African coast. One reason for the Navigator's slave raids:

> . . . was his great desire to make increase, in the faith of our lord Jesus Christ and to bring to him all souls that should be saved,—understanding that all the mystery of the Incarnation, Death, and Passion of our Lord Jesus Christ was for this sole end—namely, the salvation of lost souls, whom the said Lord Infant [Henry] by his travail and spending would fain bring into the true faith. For he perceived that no better offering could be made unto the Lord than this. For if God promised to return one hundred goods for one, we may justly believe that for such great benefits, that is to say, for so many souls as were saved by the efforts of this Lord, he will have so many hundreds of guerdons in the Kingdom of God, by which his spirit may be glorified after this life in the celestial realm. For I that wrote this history saw so many men and women of those parts turned to the holy faith, that even if the Infant had been a heathen, their prayers would have been enough to have obtained his salvation. And not only did I see the first captives, but their children and grandchildren as true Christians as if the Divine grace breathed in them and imparted to them a clear knowledge of itself.[8]

This matter of cultural conversion is crucial for our understanding of the development of racial antagonism. For the full profitable exploitation of a people, the dominant group must devise ways and means of limiting that people's cultural assimilation. So long as the Portuguese and Spaniards continued to accept the religious definition of human equality, so long also the development of race prejudice was inhibited. Although it is true that the forays on the African coast were exceedingly ruthless, the Portuguese did

---

[8]Op. cit., p. 29. See also C. Raymond Beazley, *Prince Henry the Navigator.*

not rationalize the fact with a racial argument. To kill or to take into slavery the heathen or infidel was to serve the highest purpose of God. As Azurara pointed out: ". . . though their bodies were now brought into subjection, that was a small matter in comparison to their souls, which would now possess true freedom for evermore."[8a] In granting to Prince Henry a "plenary indulgence," Pope Eugenius IV gave "to each and all those who shall be engaged in the said war [slave raids], complete forgiveness of all their sins."[8b]

The Portuguese people themselves had developed no racial hatred for the captives. Azurara relates how the townspeople at Lagos wept in sympathy for the suffering of the Moors as families were broken to be distributed among different masters. And, it seems, the captives were quite readily assimilated into the population.

> . . . from this time forth [after their partition] they began to acquire some knowledge of our country, in which they found great abundance; and our men began to treat them with great favour. For as our people did not find them hardened in the belief [i.e., Islam] of the Moors, and saw how they came unto the law of Christ with a good will, they made no difference between them and their free [Portuguese] servants, born in our own country. But those whom they took [captured] while still young, they caused to be instructed in mechanical arts. And those whom they saw fitted for managing property, they set free and married to women who were natives of the land [of Portugal], making with them a division of their property as if it had been bestowed on those who married them by the will of their own fathers. . . . Yea, and some widows of good family who bought some of these female slaves, either adopted them or left them a portion of their estate by will, so that in the future they married right well, treating them as entirely free. Suffice it that I never saw one of these slaves put in irons like other captives, and scarcely any one who did not turn Christian and was not gently treated.
>
> And I have been asked by their lords to the baptisms and marriages of such; at which they, whose slaves they were before, made no less solemnity than if they had been their children or relations.[9]

The Portuguese had no clear sense of racial antagonism, because its economic and rationalistic basis had not yet developed among them. Indeed the Portuguese and Spaniards never became fully freed of the

[8a] Op. cit., p. 51.
[8b] Ibid., p. 53.
[9] Op. cit., p. 84.

crusading spirit, which constantly held in check their attainment of a clear appreciation of the values of competitive labor exploitation.[10] The Church received its share of African servants; as yet, however, it had no idea of the economic uses of segregation and "cultural parallelism"—of the techniques for perpetuating the servile status of the black workers. It had developed no rationalizations of inborn human inferiority in support of a basic need for labor exploitation. On the contrary, its obsession with the spiritual values of conversion left the Negroes free to be integrated into the general population. It is reported that before the returning captains of one commission of caravels "did anything else [in the distribution of captured Moors] they took as an offering the best of those Moors to the Church of that place; and another little Moor, who afterwards became a friar of St. Francis, they sent to St. Vincent do Cabo, where he lived ever after as a Catholic Christian, without having understanding or perception of any other law than that true and holy law in which all the Christians hope for salvation."[11]

The next era in the history of race relations commenced with the discovery of America. If we see that race prejudice is an attitudinal instrument of modern human, economic exploitation, the question as to whether race prejudice was found among the primitive peoples of the world will not arise. It would be, for instance, a ridiculous inversion of thought to expect the native peoples of America to have had race prejudice for the white invaders.[12] But modern society—Western civilization—began to take

---

[10]Speaking of the activities of the Portuguese at Goa, India, soon after 1498, L. S. S. O'Malley says: "The Portuguese territories were intended to be outposts of their empire and their religion. . . . Colonization was effected not so much by immigration as by marriage with Indian women. There was no color bar, and the children of mixed marriages were under no stigma of inferiority. . . . Proselytization began soon after the capture of Goa. . . . At the same time the spread of Christianity was assisted by an appeal to material interests. Converts were to be provided with posts in the customs, exempted from impressment in the navy, and supported by the distribution of rice." *Modern India and the West*, pp. 44–45.

[11]Azurara, op. cit., p. 80.

[12]Although Columbus participated in the enslavement of the Indians of the West Indies, which finally led to their extermination, his first impression of them is well known: "They are a loving uncovitous people, so docile in all things that I do assure your Highness I believe in all the world there is not a better people or a better country; they love their neighbours as themselves, and they have the sweetest and gentlest way of speaking in the world and always with a smile." Again, "As they showed us such friendship and as I recognized they were people who would yield themselves better to the Christian faith and be converted more through love than by force, I gave them some coloured buttons and some glass beads . . . and [they] became so attached to us that it was a marvel to behold." See Francis A. MacNutt, *Bartholomew De Las Casas*, pp. 18, 19.

on its characteristic attributes when Columbus turned the eyes and interests of the world away from the Mediterranean toward the Atlantic. The mysticism of the East soon lost its grip on human thought, and the bourgeois world got under way. The socioeconomic matrix of racial antagonism involved the commercialization of human labor in the West Indies, the East Indies, and in America, the intense competition among businessmen of different western European cities for the capitalist exploitation of the resources of this area, the development of nationalism and the consolidation of European nations, and the decline of the influence of the Roman Catholic Church with its mystical inhibitions to the free exploitation of economic resources. Racial antagonism attained full maturity during the latter half of the nineteenth century, when the sun no longer set on British soil and the great nationalistic powers of Europe began to justify their economic designs upon weaker European peoples with subtle theories of racial superiority and masterhood.

It should be observed that this view is not generally agreed upon. A popular belief among writers on modern race relations is that the phenomenon has always been known among most, if not all, peoples. This approach apparently tends to give theories of race relations a "scientific" aspect, but it contributes little to an understanding of the problem.

For instance, Jacques Barzun may be misleading in his saying that "if anyone deserves burning in effigy for starting the powerful race-dogma of Nordic superiority" it is Tacitus. This is supposed to be so because Tacitus, in his admiration of the primitive "Germans," made assertions "embodying the germ of present-day Nordicism."[13] Yet it seems evident that neither Tacitus, St. Paul, Noah, nor the Rig-Vedic Aryans are responsible for the racial practices and ideologies developed among modern Europeans. Moreover, the use of the metaphor "germ" is likely to convey the idea that this excursus of Tacitus, his "noble-savage" description of the virtues of the tribal Germans, was continually built upon by them over the centuries, until at last it blossomed into nazism.

We might just as well rely upon that notable charge of Cicero to Atticus in the first century B.C., "Do not obtain your slaves from Britain because they are so stupid and so utterly incapable of being taught that they are not

[13]*Race, A Study of Modern Superstition,* pp. 11, 28.

fit to form a part of the household of Athens," as a basis for the explanation of modern race prejudice against the British—the only difficulty being that there has never been any such prejudice.

When white scholars began their almost desperate search of the ancient archives for good reasons to explain the wonderful cultural accomplishments among the whites, European economic and military world dominance was already an actuality. Most of the discoveries which explain the racial superiority of the tall, long-headed blond may be called Hamite rationalizations; they are drawn from bits of isolated verbalizations or deductions from cultural situations which cannot be identified with those of modern race relations. Probably the most widely accepted of these has been the biblical story of the descendants of Ham as a people cursed forever to do the menial work of others.

When English, French, and German scholars discovered the Aryans in the Sanskrit literature of the Hindus, the Hindus themselves were unaware of the Aryans' racial potentialities. The concept "Arya" meant practically nothing to them. It remained for the nationalistic Germans to recognize that the term "Aryan" designated Germans particularly and that, because of this, the right of Germans to exploit all other peoples of the world, not excluding the Hindus, was confirmed.

In the study of race relations it is of major importance to realize that their significant manifestations could not possibly have been known among the ancients. If we had to put our finger upon the year which marked the beginning of modern race relations we should select 1493–94. This is the time when total disregard for the human rights and physical power of the non-Christian peoples of the world, the colored peoples, was officially assumed by the first two great colonizing European nations. Pope Alexander VI's bull of demarcation issued under Spanish pressure on May 3, 1493, and its revision by the Treaty of Tordesillas (June 7, 1494), arrived at through diplomatic negotiations between Spain and Portugal, put all the heathen peoples and their resources—that is to say, especially the colored peoples of the world—at the disposal of Spain and Portugal.[14]

[14]As early as 1455 Pope Nicholas V had granted the Portuguese exclusive right to their discoveries on the African coast, but the commercial purpose here was still very much involved with the crusading spirit.

Sometimes, probably because of its very obviousness, it is not realized that the slave trade was simply a way of recruiting labor for the purpose of exploiting the great natural resources of America.[15] This trade did not develop because Indians and Negroes were red and black, or because their cranial capacity averaged a certain number of cubic centimeters; but simply because they were the best workers to be found for the heavy labor in the mines and plantations across the Atlantic.[16] If white workers were available in sufficient numbers they would have been substituted. As a matter of fact, part of the early demand for labor in the West Indies and on the mainland was filled by white servants, who were sometimes defined in exactly the same terms as those used to characterize the Africans. Although the recruitment of involuntary labor finally settled down to the African coasts, the earlier kidnapers did a brisk business in some of the most enlightened European cities. Moreover, in the process of exploiting the natural resources of the West Indies, the Spanish conquistadors literally consumed the native Indian population.

This, then, is the beginning of modern race relations. It was not an abstract, natural, immemorial feeling of mutual antipathy between groups, but rather a practical exploitative relationship with its socio-attitudinal facilitation—at that time only nascent race prejudice. Although this peculiar kind of exploitation was then in its incipiency, it had already achieved its significant characteristics.[17] As it developed and took definite capitalistic

[15] In a discussion of the arguments over slavery during the Constitutional Convention, Charles A. Beard observes: "South Carolina was particularly determined, and gave northern representatives to understand that if they wished to secure their commercial privileges, they must make concessions to the slave trade. And they were met half way. Ellsworth said: 'As slaves multiply so fast in Virginia and Maryland that it is cheaper to raise than import them, whilst in the sickly rice swamps foreign supplies are necessary, if we go no farther than is urged, we shall be unjust towards South Carolina and Georgia. Let us not intermeddle. As population increases, poor laborers will be so plenty as to render slaves useless.'" *An Economic Interpretation of the Constitution,* p. 177. Quote from Max Farrand, *Records,* Vol. II, p. 371.

[16] In a discussion of the labor situation among the early Spanish colonists in America, Professor Bailey W. Diffie observes: "One Negro was reckoned as worth two, four, or even more Indians at work production." *Latin American Civilization,* p. 206.

[17] Francis Augustus MacNutt describes the relationship in Hispaniola: "Columbus laid tribute upon the entire population of the island which required that each Indian above fourteen years of age who lived in the mining provinces was to pay a little bell filled with gold every three months; the natives of all other provinces were to pay one *arroba* of cotton. These amounts were so excessive that in 1496 it was found necessary to change the nature of the payments, and, instead of the gold and cotton required from the villages, labour was substituted, the Indians being required to lay out and work the plantations of the colonists in their vicinity." *Bartholomew De Las Casas,* p. 25.

form, we could follow the white man around the world and see him repeat the process among practically every people of color. Earl Grey was directly in point when he described, in 1880, the motives and purpose of the British in one racial situation:

> Throughout this part of the British Dominions the colored people are generally looked upon by the whites as an inferior race, whose interest ought to be systematically disregarded when they come into competition with their own, and who ought to be governed mainly with a view of the advantage of the superior race. And for this advantage two things are considered to be especially necessary: first, that facilities should be afforded to the white colonists for obtaining possession of land heretofore occupied by the native tribes; and secondly, that the Kaffir population should be made to furnish as large and as cheap a supply of labor as possible.[18]

But the fact of crucial significance is that racial exploitation is merely one aspect of the problem of the proletarianization of labor, regardless of the color of the laborer. Hence racial antagonism is essentially political-class conflict. The capitalist exploiter, being opportunistic and practical, will utilize any convenience to keep his labor and other resources freely exploitable. He will devise and employ race prejudice when that becomes convenient.[19] As a matter of fact, the white proletariat of early capitalism had to endure burdens of exploitation quite similar to those which many colored peoples must bear today.

However, the capitalist spirit, the profit-making motive, among the sixteenth-century Spaniards and Portuguese, was constantly inhibited by the philosophy and purpose of the Roman Catholic Church. A social theory supporting the capitalist drive for the impersonal exploitation of the workers never completely emerged. Conversion to Christianity and slavery among the Indians stood at cross-purposes; therefore, the vital problem presented to the exploiters of labor was that of circumventing the assimilative effects of

---

[18]Quoted by E. D. Morel, *The Black Man's Burden*, p. 30.

[19]In our description of the uses of race prejudice in this essay we are likely to give the impression that race prejudice was always "manufactured" in full awareness by individuals or groups of entrepreneurs. This, however, is not quite the case. Race prejudice, from its inception, became part of the social heritage, and as such both exploiters and exploited for the most part are born heirs to it. It is possible that most of those who propagate and defend race prejudice are not conscious of its fundamental motivation. To paraphrase Adam Smith: they who teach and finance race prejudice are by no means such fools as the majority of those who believe and practice it.

conversion to Christianity. In the West Indies the celebrated priest, Las Casas, was touched by the destructive consequences of the ruthless enslavement of the Indians, and he opposed it on religious grounds. But work had to be done, and if not voluntarily, then some ideology had to be found to justify involuntary servitude. "The Indians were represented as lazy, filthy pagans, of bestial morals, no better than dogs, and fit only for slavery, in which state alone there might be some hope of instructing and converting them to Christianity."[20]

The capitalist exploitation of the colored workers, it should be observed, consigns them to employments and treatment that is humanly degrading. In order to justify this treatment the exploiters must argue that the workers are innately degraded and degenerate, consequently they naturally merit their condition. It may be mentioned incidentally that the ruling-class conception of degradation will tend to be that of all persons in the society, even that of the exploited person himself; and the work done by degraded persons will tend to degrade superior persons who attempt to do it.

In 1550, finally, the great capitalist interests produced a champion, Gaines de Sepulveda, brilliant theologian and debater, to confront Las Casas in open debate at Valladolid on the right of Spaniards to wage wars of conquest against the Indians. Sepulveda held that it was lawful to make war against (enslave) the Indians:

1. Because of the gravity of their sins. . . .
2. Because of the rudeness of their heathen and barbarous natures, which oblige them to serve those of more elevated natures, such as the Spaniards possess.
3. For the spread of the faith; for their subjection renders its preaching easier and more persuasive [and so on].[21]

It is not surprising that Sepulveda won the debate. His approach was consistent with the exploitative rationalizations of the time. He contrived a reasonably logical justification for the irrepressibly exploitative situation. This clearly was in answer to an urgent necessity for such an authoritative explanation; the whole world, so to speak, was calling for it. As a charac-

---

[20]Francis Augustus MacNutt, op. cit., p. 83.

It should be kept clearly in view that this colonial movement was not a transference of the feudal manorial economy to America. It was the beginning of an entirely different economic enterprise—the dawn of colonial capitalism, the moving out of "white" capital into the lands of colored peoples who had to be exploited unsentimentally and with any degree of ruthlessness in the interest of profits.

[21]MacNutt, op. cit., p. 288.

teristic, it should be observed that no explanation at all need have been made to the exploited people themselves. The group sentiment and feeling of the exploited peoples were disregarded entirely.

Sepulveda, then, may be thought of as among the first great racists;[22] his argument was, in effect, that the Indians were inferior to the Spaniards, therefore they should be exploited. Yet the powerful religious interest among the Spaniards limited the establishment of a clear philosophy of racial exploitation. Some years earlier an attempt was made to show "that the Indians were incapable of conversion," but this was finally squelched by a threat to bring the advocate before the tribunal of the Inquisition.[23] It remained for later thinkers, mainly from northern European countries, to produce the evidence that "native peoples" have an inferior, animal-like capacity for culture.[24]

In the years to follow there will be unnumbered sermons preached and "scientific" books written to prove the incapacity for cultural conversion of exploitable peoples, and always with the implied or expressed presumption that this incapacity should stand as a bar to movements for the cultural assimilation of such peoples. (The ultimate purpose of all theories of white superiority is not a demonstration that whites are in fact superior to all other human beings but rather to insist that whites must be supreme. It involves primarily a power rather than a social-status relationship.) Assimilation diminishes the exploitative possibilities. This social situation is not

[22]Among the Spanish writers of the time (about 1533 onward) who were in rather complete accord with the drastic methods of human exploitation in the New World was Gonzolo Fernandez de Oviedo, whose prolific works have been collected in the commentary, *Historia General y Natural de las Indias,* 4 vols. It was Oviedo's opinion, even after visiting America on a royal commission, that the Indians were not far removed from the state of wild animals, and that coercive measures were necessary if they were to be Christianized and taught the uses of systematic labor.

[23]MacNutt, op. cit., pp. 94–95.

[24]Beasts of burden do not have rights which human beings are bound to respect; they may be exploited at will. The latter convenience is a desideratum in the capitalist exploitation of labor, regardless of the color of the laborer. However, the fact of difference in color and culture makes available to the exploiters of colored workers a valuable means of securing their dehumanization in the eyes of a certain public, that is to say, the public of the exploiting class. When a philosophy for the dehumanizing of the exploited people has been developed with sufficient cogency, the ruling class is ready to make its grand statement, sometimes implicitly, and to act in accordance with it: the colored people have no rights which the master race is bound to respect. The exploiting class has an economic investment in this conviction and it will defend it with the same vigor as it would an attack upon private property in land and capital.

especially a derivative of human idiosyncrasy or wickedness, but rather it is a function of a peculiar type of economic order which, to repeat, has been developed in the West among Europeans. The exploitation of native peoples, imperialism, is not a sin, not essentially a problem of morals or of vice; it is a problem of production and of competition for markets.[25] Here, then, are race relations; they are definitely not caste relations. They are labor-capital-profits relationships; therefore, race relations are proletarian bourgeois relations and hence political-class relations.

The commercial activities of the merchant adventurers from the northern European cities were much less involved with the universal interests of the Church. The Anglo-Saxon and Germanic merchants came later to the great area of capitalist opportunities, and their profit-making purpose was much more clearly defined. Here, too, the bitter economic competition between different groups of raiders and traders cradled the nationalism which was to become a characteristic political trait of modern peoples. Out of this early economic war of shifting national fortunes England soon emerged as the "great slave trader of the world" and at the head of the most powerful economic empire.

It may be well to emphasize that the white people who went out from Europe to "civilize" and exploit the resources of the colored peoples were mainly capitalists, urban dwellers, business people from the beginning. Their way of life was basically antagonistic to the feudal and prefeudal agricultural systems which they encountered everywhere; therefore, the colored people had to be suppressed if the urgent purpose of the white

[25]Of course one should not be particularly disturbed about the fact that, although one never had the necessity or even the thought of exploiting colored people, yet an almost irresistible bitterness seems to well up as one finds himself in certain social situations with colored people. It is this very reaction which derogatory racial propaganda sets out to achieve and, knowing that even human nature itself is a social product, it would be surprising if the people did not hate whichever group the ruling class convinced them should be hated. Moreover, we naturally tend to dislike people who are degraded or brutalized. A degraded person is a contemptible person who should be despised and kept at a distance—the Christian Gospels notwithstanding.

Such ambivalent conclusions as the following by Dr. Louis Wirth may be misleading: "Ethnic, linguistic, and religious differences will continue to divide people, and the prejudices that go with them cannot suddenly be wiped out by fiat. But whereas personal prejudices and antipathies can probably be expected to yield only to the tedious process of education and assimilation, collective programs and policies can be altered considerably in advance of the time when they have unanimous group consent. Law and public policy can go far toward minimizing the adverse effect even of personal prejudices." In Ralph Linton, ed., *The Science of Man in the World Crisis,* p. 368.

opportunists was not to go unanswered.[26] In this connection Max Weber asserts:

> A man does not "by nature" wish to earn more and more money, but simply to live as he is accustomed to live and to earn as much as is necessary for that purpose. Wherever modern capitalism has begun its work of increasing the productivity of human labor by increasing its intensity, it has encountered an immensely stubborn resistance of this leading trait of pre-capitalistic labor. And today it encounters it the more, the more backward (from a capitalistic point of view) the laboring forces are with which it has to deal.[27]

The system of chartered companies, adopted by the colonizing European countries, ordinarily put the welfare and destiny of whole peoples directly into the hands of profit makers. What E. D. Morel says of the British South African Company for the exploitation of Southern Rhodesia is characteristic of the system:

> In such a fashion were the powers of government and administration, involving the establishment of a police force, the making of laws, the raising of revenue,

[26]Leonard Woolf makes a pertinent observation on this point: "The manufacturers and traders who were the harbingers of imperialism in the hills and plains of Asia and the forests of Africa went there with certain definite economic objects: they wanted to sell cotton or calico, to obtain tin or iron or rubber or tea or coffee. But to do this under the complicated economic system of Western Civilization, it was necessary that the whole economic system of the Asiatic and African should be adjusted to and assimilated with that of Europe. . . . In the process the lives of the subject peoples have been revolutionized and the bases of their own civilization often destroyed. . . . Nothing like this and upon this scale has ever happened in the world before." *Imperialism and Civilization*, pp. 48–49.

See also James Mill, *The History of British India*, Vol. I, pp. 22–23, for an interesting account of a taboo against the employment of "gentlemen" by the early seventeenth-century "adventurers" in their East India trade; also Henry Stevens, *The Dawn of British Trade to the East Indies, as Recorded in the Court Minutes of the East India Company 1599–1603*, p. 28.

[27]*Protestant Ethic and the Spirit of Capitalism*, p. 60. Concerning England itself, Paul Mantoux writes about this process of the proletarianization of labor: "Once the problem of capital and plant had been solved, that of labour arose. How was it to be recruited and governed? Men used to working at home were generally not inclined to go to the factory. In the early days factory labour consisted of the most ill-assorted elements. . . . All these unskilled men, unused to collective work had to be taught, trained, and above all disciplined, by the manufacturer. He had, so to speak, to be turned into a human machine, as regular in its working, as accurate in its movements, and as exactly combined for a single purpose as the mechanism of wood and metal to which they became accessory. Hard-and-fast rules replaced the freedom of the small workshop. Work started, meals were eaten and work stopped at fixed hours, notified by the ringing of a bell. . . . Everyone had to work steadily . . . under the vigilant eye of a foreman, who secured obedience by means of fines or dismissals, and sometimes by more brutal forms of coercion." *The Industrial Revolution in the Eighteenth Century*, p. 384. See also J. L. and Barbara Hammond, *The Town Labourer, 1760–1832*, Chap. II.

the administration of justice, the construction of public works, the grant of mining and forestry concessions, and so on, in an African country three times the size of England, eventually conferred upon a corporation, whose interest in that country was to make money out of it.[28]

Probably it is unnecessary for us to restate the history of the planter class in the West and its problems of exploitation, or the drama of white colonization in other parts of the world. Yet it may be in place to indicate further the relationship of race antagonism to the broader bourgeois-proletariat conflict. As we mentioned previously, the relationship of producers to white workers has been frequently such as to demonstrate the common status of workers as a factor of production, regardless of color. In some of the early experiments with labor in the West Indies both white and black workers were used in the field and their treatment and value were ordinarily determined by their relative economic productivity.[29] But it is the early mercantilist labor theory and practice which show naïvely the fundamental exploitative drive; and we may illustrate this from the situation in England, the leading capitalist nation.

Mercantilism may be thought of as that system of economic philosophy, trading practice, and direction of production which has for its purpose the securing of advantages to a nation in international economic competition. It is the state capitalism which the postfeudal capitalists developed.[30] Nationalism is the emotional matrix of this state, economic competition. Although mercantilism reached some sort of high point in overt expression in the late eighteenth century, its essential ideology continues in what has been sometimes called neomercantilism. Roughly speaking, the early mercantilist defined the "wealth of the nation" in terms of the monetary payments

---

[28]Op. cit., p. 36.

[29]See Frank Wesley Pitman, *Development of the British West Indies, 1700–1763*, p. 45; Eric Williams, *Capitalism and Slavery*, pp. 3–29; and Lowell Joseph Ragatz, *The Fall of the Planter Class, passim.*

[30]Gustav Schmoller gives a significant definition: ". . . in its innermost kernel [mercantilism] is nothing but state making—not state making in a narrow sense, but state making and national-economy making at the same time; state making in the modern sense, which creates out of the political community an economic community, and so gives it a heightened meaning. The essence of the system lies not in some doctrine of money, or the balance of trade; but in something far greater:—namely, in the total transformation of society and its organization, as well as of the state and its institutions, in replacing of a local [town] and territorial economic policy by that of the national state." *The Mercantile System*, pp. 50–51. Cf. Carl Bucher, *Industrial Evolution*, p. 136.

which other nations were compelled to pay in order to offset their unfavorable balance of trade; today more emphasis is put upon the success of the
heavy industries of a nation. The worker's place in the system has been
primarily related to production, and he has been regarded as an item of
cost—that is to say, as both a necessary and important factor of production
and as an impediment to the entrepreneur in his basic urge to undersell his
competitors. The worker, then, was indispensable, but he should be paid
only so much as would be sufficient to keep him alive and able to labor—a
subsistence wage. Thus, as Eli F. Heckscher concludes: "With practically
insignificant exceptions, all official wage-fixing . . . prescribed maximum
wages. Out of every ten interferences with the relationship between employers
and employed, at least nine were in the interest of the employers."[31] And, says
Rees, "The desideratum was a population as large as possible, as fully
occupied as possible, and living as near as possible to the margin of
subsistence."[32]

But low wages were supposed to have other values besides those of
limiting cost of production. They tended to keep the worker in a constant
state of necessity, which disposed him to labor. In this respect the mercantilists'
characterization of the English workers is very much like that continually
addressed to colored workers and native peoples. A man will not work seven
days a week if he could live by the earnings of one; therefore, if the employer
is to have a sufficient supply of labor, a day's wage should be no more than
that which the worker must spend in that day. Edgar S. Furniss calls this "the
doctrine of the utility of poverty." According to Arthur Young, writing in 1770,
"[Great earnings] have a strong effect on all who remain the least inclined
to idleness or other ill courses, by causing them to work but four or five
days to maintain themselves the seven; this is a fact so well known in every
manufacturing town that it would be idle to think of proving it by
argument."[33] There were riches, then, in the poverty and necessitous state

[31]*Mercantilism,* Vol. II, p. 167.

[32]J. F. Rees, "Mercantilism and the Colonies," *Cambridge History of the British Empire,*
Vol. I, p. 563. To the same effect Heckscher observes: "By forcing down wages . . . the export
of such products as contained relatively more human labor could be increased; and such a
policy could at the same time restrict the import of the same group of products. . . . The
corollary was that efforts had to be made to maintain as abundant supply of labour as possible
at as low a price as possible." Op. cit., Vol. II, p. 153.

[33]Quoted by Edgar S. Furniss, *The Position of Labor in a System of Nationalism,* pp. 119–20.

of the masses: "in a free nation where slaves are not allowed of, the surest wealth consists in a multitude of laborious poor."[34]

If, however, low wages did not produce the desired results, it was felt that the law should compel idle workers to find employment. As one writer suggested in a series of questions:

> Whether if human industry be the source of wealth, it doth not follow that idleness should of all things be discouraged in a wise state? Whether temporary servitude would not be the best cure for idleness and beggary? Whether the public hath not the right to employ those who cannot or will not find employment for themselves? Whether sturdy beggars may not be seized and made slaves to the public for a certain term of years?[35]

To be sure, no producer will express himself so bluntly in England today, but this attitude and practice of forced labor is still common among Europeans in their dealings with native peoples. Vagrancy laws are still posted in courthouses and city halls in the Southern states of the United States. The technique of "keeping books" and making commodity advances to workers also tends to secure the planter's labor supply.

Moreover, the mercantilist feared the prospects of the laborer's getting out of his place. It was felt that some class of people should be depended upon to do the common work, and that the status of this class as common workers should remain permanent. It was some tendency in the working class to be independent which called forth reactions akin to racial antagonism. Says William Temple in 1770: "Our manufacturing populace have adopted a notion that as Englishmen they enjoy a birth right privilege of being more free and independent than any country in Europe. . . . The less the manufacturing poor have of it, the better for themselves and for the estate. The laboring people should never think of themselves independent of their superiors for, if a proper subordination is not kept up, riot and confusion will take the place of sobriety and good order."[36]

[34]B. Mandeville, *Britannia Lenguens,* p. 153, quoted by Eli F. Heckscher, op. cit., Vol. II, p. 164.

[35]George Berkeley (1750), quoted by Edgar S. Furniss, op. cit., p. 80. Furniss also cites an anonymous author on the duties of the laboring classes: "Such journeymen, day laborers, or others, who shall refuse to work the usual hours, for the price hereby stipulated, shall immediately, by the peace officer of the parish, be carried before a neighboring Justice of the Peace, and be by him committed to Bridewell, there to be kept to hard labor till they shall think proper to obey the laws of their country." Ibid., p. 84.

[36]Ibid., p. 56.

This is, let us interpose, precisely the idea of "the Negroes' place" in the United States.

Undoubtedly the most persistent menace to the peace and good order of the classes was the rise of popular education. For, as Mandeville said in 1723: "To make the society happy and people easy under the meanest circumstances, it is requisite that great numbers of them should be ignorant as well as poor."[37] Therefore, it became the immediate business of the ruling class to obstruct or at least to direct the education of the common people. If the workers had to be educated, they should receive vocational and industrial education; they should be turned back to their natural duty and not away from it, since "few that have once learnt to write and read, but either their parents or themselves are apt to think that they are fit for some preferment, and in order to it, despise all laboring employments."[38] And Thomas Ruggles made the typical statement: "There must be in society hewers of wood and drawers of water. If all are good penmen, where are those who will contentedly live through a life of toil?"[39] Thus, the training advocated for the workhouse children, the children of the poor, was intended to keep them within the occupational level of their parents; and intellectual pursuits were ruled out.[40] Professor Furniss describes the position of the eighteenth-century white workers in England as a class, which

[37]See Heckscher, op. cit., Vol. II, p. 167. And in 1763 an anonymous author of *Considerations of the Fatal Effects to a Trading Nation of the Excess of Public Charity* declared: "The charity school is another universal nursery of idleness; nor is it easy to conceive or invent anything more destructive to the interest and very foundation principles of a nation entirely dependent on its trade and manufactures than the giving an education to the children of the lowest class of her people that will make them contemn those drudgeries for which they were born." Quoted by Furniss, op. cit., p. 148.

[38]J. Prollexfen, *A Discourse of Trade, Coyn, and Paper Credit,* quoted by Heckscher, op. cit., pp. 166–67.

[39]*History of the Poor.* Although Ruggles was making a plea for the just treatment of the common people, he did not go beyond the following demand: "By this expression [the claims of the poor on society] no abstract ideas of a claim to equality, either in legislation or property, have been canvassed; but simply that claim to a fair retribution for their strength and ability to labor, which is their only birthright." Ibid., 1797 ed., p. ix.

[40]It is to this characteristic of capitalist society Harold Laski refers when he says: "There is a vested interest in the perpetuation of ignorance which is endemic in our civilization. We cannot get rid of ignorance save as we are willing to attack that vested interest; and the signs are clear that it will bitterly defend itself if we move to the attack." *Reflections on the Revolution of Our Time,* p. 3. See also J. A. Hobson, *Democracy and a Changing Civilization,* pp. 105–6.

is virtually a description of the position of colored people in certain modern racial situations:

> The proponents of the workhouse in both of its forms evidently conceived of the laboring population as a class united to the social body by bonds of duty and drawing from their connection with the nation certain rights. The fact that the laboring population was viewed as a *class* and dealt with as a class shows that individualistic concepts of society did not embrace them. As a class they were to be patronized by the government; as a class, coerced, disciplined, punished, when patronage failed to awaken the expected response. Much was said of their duties and their station in life, little or nothing of their opportunities for advancement in the social scale; few were the proposals to throw them upon their own resources as individuals, many those which advocated comprehensive government action to control their conduct as a group.[41]

The white common people, after continual struggle along the way to democracy, have gained more or less right to be educated freely. But colored people, in South Africa and the Southern United States typically, are still suffering from the crude pressures of exploitation. The argument still holds that the Negro should be taught "labor, not learning." The desperate resistance to the giving of Negroes an equal opportunity for education is well known. It is necessary, so to speak, that their educable potentialities remain as nearly as possible undiscovered.

Sometimes, in studies of education in the South, the backward state of the system is attributed to the economic poverty of the region. This, however, does not seem to be the primary reason. The South does not want its poor white people and its Negroes particularly to be educated away from "those drudgeries for which they were born." If, for instance, some jinnee were to appear before the assembled governors, senators, and bankers of the South and present them a little hill of gold bricks to be used for educational purposes, they would probably begin to discuss among them-

[41]Op. cit., p. 87. The Hammonds quote the president of the Royal Society, Giddy (1767–1839), as developing the following logic: "[Giving education to the laboring classes] would teach them to despise their lot in life, instead of making them good servants in agriculture, and other laborious employments to which their rank in society had destined them; instead of teaching them subordination, it would render them factious and refractory . . . it would enable them to read seditious pamphlets, vicious books, and publications against Christianity; it would render them insolent to their superiors; and in a few years the result would be that the legislature would find it necessary to direct the strong arm of power toward them, and to furnish the executive magistrate with much more vigorous laws than were now in force." Op. cit., p. 57.

selves what effect it might have on the stability of the social system; but if the jinnee interrupts with the condition that every time a gold brick is taken for the education of a white child another should also be taken for that of a Negro child, then we should expect the council to say without hesitation, "Gather up your bricks as fast as you can and betake yourself to Hades." Today it is almost as easy to get Federal funds for education in the South, but little general enthusiasm and certain possibilities of Negroes participating equally result in rejection of the aid.

It is, moreover, on this principle of vocational and industrial education— "teaching black workers to work"—that Booker T. Washington felt sure of himself. He knew that on this ground the ruling class had to listen to him; and, indeed, it accepted him as leader of the Negroes and watched carefully the program of the school which he established. However exalted his motives might have been, yet he enunciated one of the deepest intents of the exploiters of labor—of black labor especially—when in giving utterance to an essentially mercantilist labor philosophy he declared: "We shall prosper in proportion as we learn to dignify and glorify common labor and put brains and skill into the common occupations of life. . . . No race can prosper till it learns that there is as much dignity in tilling a field as in writing a poem." And, turning to the white exploiting class, he said confidently: "You are in debt to the black man for furnishing you with labor that is almost a stranger to strikes, lock-outs, and labor wars; labor that is law-abiding, peaceful, teachable . . . labor that has never been tempted to follow the red flag of anarchy, but always the safe flag of his country and the spotless banner of the Cross."[42]

[42]*Selected Speeches of Booker T. Washington,* E. D. Washington, ed., pp. 33, 82.
      In Washington's own words: ". . . The bulk of opinion in the South had little faith in the efficacy of the 'higher' or any other kind of education for the Negro. . . . While the education which we proposed to give at the Tuskegee Institute was spontaneously welcomed by the white South, it was this training of the hands that furnished the first basis for anything like united and sympathetic interest and action between the two races.
      "Many white people of the South saw in the movement to teach young Negroes the necessity and honour of work with the hands a means of leading them gradually and sensibly into their new life of freedom. . . . They perceived, too, that the Negroes [the slaves] who were master carpenters and contractors under the guidance of their owners could greatly further the development of the South if their children were not too suddenly removed from the atmosphere and occupation of their fathers. . . . The individual and community interest

Thus the white ruling class tended to agree with Washington when he advocated dignity in common labor—the doing of manual occupations efficiently and dignifiedly; that is to say, in essence, the doing of menial occupations contentedly. This very class would have brought him to his knees had he advocated *superior education* on the grounds of its enhanced productivity and inevitably inherent dignity. A superior education tends to make the individual superior, because it puts him in a position to accept occupations that the society has defined as superior; whereas there is no assurance that the ordinary, efficient worker would be able to arrogate to himself an artificial dignity that the social system itself does not generally recognize. One reason why there is in fact little dignity in manual labor is that the laborer himself is ordinarily not dignified.[43] To dignify a person is to refine and educate him far beyond the training necessary for the successful performance of a manual skill; and when this is done in a capitalist society, manual labor usually loses such a person.

This, of course, is not a criticism of Washington; it may be indeed a commendation of his intuition in sensing the basis of race relations. It makes no reference to his widely recognized contribution to the advancement of Negroes among skilled workers. Yet, so long as Washington accepted the

of the white people was directly appealed to by industrial education. . . . Almost every white man in the South was directly interested in agricultural, mechanical, or other manual labor; in cooking and serving of food, laundering and dairying, poultry raising, and everything related to housekeeping in general. . . .

"Therefore there came to be a growing appreciation of the fact that industrial education of the black people had a practical and vital bearing on the life of every white family in the South. There was little opportunity for such appreciation of the results of mere literary education." *Working with the Hands,* pp. 13–14.

[43] As a matter of fact, the white planters were accustomed to see their skilled black workers as slaves. On this point Richard B. Morris observes: "Failing to maintain an adequate number of white artisans, the Southern colonies then trained Negro slaves for the skilled trades. The files of the *South Carolina Gazette* revealed that Negroes were trained and practicing virtually all the crafts needed for maintaining the plantation economy. In addition to those engaged in husbandry, the well-organized plantation employed carpenters, coopers, stone-masons, a miller, a black-smith, shoemakers, spinners, and weavers. The wealthier planters often carried on industrial enterprises on a considerable scale, necessitating the employment of a sizable number of skilled workmen. . . . Some white artificers were generally needed to start such enterprises, but they were in the main carried on almost exclusively by negro slaves who were often hired out by their masters to others in need of skilled help." *Government and Labor in Early America,* p. 31.

Vocational education as a technique of exploitation was practiced with fervor and zeal among the sixteenth-century Latin-American colonists. See Bailey W. Diffie, *Latin American Civilization,* p. 359, *passim.*

morality of capitalism, he had to conceive of the labor power of colored people in this fashion. "Washington was in some respects a greater leader of white opinion than he was of Negro opinion,"[44] and "white opinion" was inevitably against the best interest of Negroes, as it still is to this day. There are many sincere Southern white people who believe that the success of the Negroes depends upon their adopting the industrial philosophy of the English eighteenth-century workhouses.

Although both race relations and the struggle of the white proletariat with the bourgeoisie are parts of a single social phenomenon, race relations involve a significant variation. In the case of race relations the tendency of the bourgeoisie is to proletarianize a whole people—that is to say, the whole people is looked upon as a class—whereas white proletarianization involves only a section of the white people. The concept "bourgeois" and "white people" sometimes seems to mean the same thing for, with respect to the colored peoples of the world, it is almost always through a white bourgeoisie that capitalism has been introduced. The early capitalist settlers among the colored peoples were disposed to look upon the latter and their natural resources as factors of production to be manipulated impersonally with "white capital" in the interest of profits. It is this need to impersonalize whole peoples which introduces into the class struggle the complicating factors known as race problems. If the colored people themselves are able to develop a significant bourgeoisie, as among the Japanese and East Indians, race relations are further complicated by the rise of conscious nationalism. As we shall attempt to show in a later chapter, situations of race relations may be distinguished according to the exploitative convenience of the white bourgeoisie.

The Progress of Racial Antagonism

This, then, is the nature of racial antagonism; developing in Europe, it has been carried to all parts of the world. In almost fateful terms Kipling's celebrated poem written in 1899 describes a desperate conflict, "the white man's burden," a like obligation, incidentally, never assumed by any other race in all the history of the world:

[44]Guy B. Johnson, "Negro Racial Movements and Leadership in the United States," *American Journal of Sociology,* July 1937, Vol. 43, p. 63.

Take up the White Man's burden—
Send forth the best ye breed—
Go bind your sons to exile
To serve your captives' need;
To wait in heavy harness,
On fluttered folk and wild—
Your new-caught, sullen peoples,
Half-devil and half-child.[44a]

The Europeans have overthrown more or less completely the social system among every colored people with whom they have come into contact. The dynamism and efficiency of capitalistic culture concluded this. The stability of color and inertness of culture, together with effective control over firearms, subsequently made it possible for whites to achieve a more or less separate and dominant position even in the homeland of colored peoples. "The white man's conception of himself as the aristocrat of the earth came gradually through the discovery, as surprising to himself as to anyone else, that he had weapons and organization which made opposition to his ambition futile."[45]

It should be made clear that we do not mean to say that the white race is the only one *capable* of race prejudice. It is probable that without capitalism, a cultural chance occurrence among whites, the world might never have experienced race prejudice. Indeed, we should expect that under another form of economic organization, say socialism, the relationship between whites and peoples of color would be significantly modified.[46]

The depreciation of the white man's color as a social gift goes hand in hand with the westernization of the conquered peoples of color. The

[44a]*Rudyard Kipling's Verse, 1885–1926,* p. 320.

[45]Josef W. Hall (Upton Close), *The Revolt of Asia,* p. 4. In this early period there was a more or less conscious development of the exploitative system. In later years, however, the infants that were born into the developed society had, of course, to take it as they found it. The social system determined their behavior *naturally;* that is to say, the racial exploitation and racial antagonisms seemed natural and the *conscious* element frequently did not exist.

In other words, the racial fate of the individual was determined before he was born.

[46]See a popular discussion relative to this by Hewlett Johnson, *The Soviet Power,* Book V; Bernhard J. Stern, "Soviet Policy on National Minorities," *American Sociological Review,* June 1944, pp. 229–35, and particularly Joseph Stalin, *Marxism and the National Question.*

Hindus, for example, are the same color today as they were in 1750, but now the white man no longer appears to them to be the cultural magician of other days. His secret of domination has been exposed, and the Hindus are now able to distinguish between his white skin and that secret. Therefore, he is now left with only his nationalism and superior might, for should he pull a cultural rabbit out of his hat, some Hindu would promptly pull another, which might even overmatch the first. Krishnalal Shridharani puts it thus: "[The Saxon] has been accustomed to regarding himself as a supreme being for centuries. Now he faces a world which refuses to recognize him as such. With all his civilized values, he will have to go on the role of military tyrant."[47] There is no assumption, then, that race prejudice is a biological heritage of the white race.

But we should not lose sight of the fact that whites have pre-empted this attitude.[48] Since the belief in white superiority—that is to say, white nationalism—began to move over the world, no people of color has been able to develop race prejudice independent of whites. It may be, however, that the Japanese have now reached that stage of industrial development, nationalistic ambition, and military power sufficient to question their assignment to inferior racial rank; no other colored race

[47]*Warning to the West*, p. 274.

[48]Pearl S. Buck likes to repeat the fact that "we differ in one important regard from the peoples of Asia. Race has never been a cause for any division among those people. But race prejudice divides us deeply." "The Spirit Behind the Weapon," *Survey Graphic*, Vol. XXXI, No. 11, November 1942, p. 540.

In a broad historical description of this process Leonard Woolf says: "In no other period of world's history has there been such a vast revolution as the conquest of Asia and Africa by Europe. . . . Until very nearly the end of the nineteenth century, Europeans themselves regarded it with complacent pride as one of the chief blessings and glories of Western Civilization. The white race of Europe, they held, was physically, mentally, and morally superior to all other races; and God, with infinite wisdom and goodness, had created it and developed it so that it might be ready, during the reign of Queen Victoria in England, to take over and manage the affairs of all other people on earth and teach them to be, in so far as that was possible for natives and heathens, good Europeans and good Christians. Indeed, until the very end of the century, the natives and heathens themselves seemed to acquiesce in this view of the designs of providence and the blessings of being ruled by Europeans. It is true that in almost every case originally a considerable number of Africans and Asiatics had to be killed before the survivors were prepared to accept the domination or, as it was called, protection of the European State; but once the domination was established there were few revolts against European rule which could not be met with a punitive expedition." Op. cit., pp. 15–16.

has ever dared to do this.[49] Indeed, since 1905 the Japanese have known how it felt to overcome the white man and make him like it.

Furthermore, the Japanese are culturally ripe for a belief of their own in yellow superiority. But the problem now confronting them is not similar to that which lay before the Europeans when they began to take on the burden of exploiting the colored peoples of the world. The white opportunists had then come upon no race able to fathom their cultural superiority and power. Today, however, the Japanese are not only blocked at every point by powerfully entrenched whites but also relatively limited in their possible area of dominance.

A still more crucial question is whether this world is large enough to accommodate more than one superior race. Barring the apparent illogic of the superlative, we should bear in mind that color prejudice is more than ethnocentrism; race prejudice must be actually backed up by a show of racial excellence, secured finally by military might.[50] No race can develop

[49]And we should expect that all peoples of color will be gratified and inspired by this kind of accomplishment. It tends to restore their self-respect as nothing else can. "When the white man began his series of retreats before the yellow hordes," Shridharani writes, "it was soothing balm to the ancient wounds of Asia. More than any Japanese words the Japanese deeds made propaganda. The white man, the most hated creature in Asia, was put to flight at Hong Kong, in Malaya, in Burma, and above all at Singapore." Op. cit., p 196.

Dr. Sun Yat-sen finds inspiration for all the colored peoples in Asia in the exploits of Japan. "Japan," he says, "is a good model for us, if we wish for prosperity of China. . . . Formerly it was thought that of all the people in the world only the whites were intelligent and gifted"; but today Japan has shown all this to be false and hope has returned to the peoples of Asia. *Le Triple Demisme,* French trans. by Pascal M. d'Elia, pp. 20–21.

One fairly widely read East Indian, P. S. Joshi, puts it in this way: "The whiteism steps an insane dance in all the continents of the world. There are in Asia only a handful of whites. . . . Still they have, by reason of their political might, introduced the colour bar in India, China, the Philippines, and other countries. Had not Japan been triumphant over Russia, had not white prestige suffered a severe blow, the same colour bar would have spread . . . throughout the continent of Asia." *The Tyranny of Colour,* p. 4.

[50]Raymond Kennedy emphasizes the point that in the belief of racial superiority the confidence in superior might is elemental. Thus he writes: "The European peoples were enabled, some four hundred years ago, to extend conquest over the entire 'native' world. The 'natives,' who were just as good, man for man, as the Europeans, lacked the superior material equipment of the latter, and were either slaughtered or subjugated. The possessors of guns came to believe that they were also possessors of superior racial endowments, and attributed their success not to material advantages, but to innate mental and physical superiority. They were white and the beaten peoples mostly black, brown, yellow, and red; consequently inferiority must be linked with color and race." *The Ageless Indies,* pp. 185–86. To the same effect see Leonard Woolf, op. cit., p. 12.

Lin Yutang puts the idea in his own way: "How did nineteenth century imperialism begin,

color prejudice merely by wishing to do so. It would be ridiculous for the
Chinese to say that they are prejudiced against whites when Europeans
segregate the Chinese even in China.[51]

Of course one should not mistake reactionary racial attitudes for prime
movers. One has only to imagine a situation developing in Asia in which
whites come to recognize themselves as inferior to, say, Japanese—in
which whites come to look upon Japanese as a master race in the same sense
in which Europeans have been looked upon—to realize what a tremendous
revolution in nationalistic feeling and power relationship must transpire. It
would involve an exchange in the exploitative position of the races, which
could not be fully established until the yellow and brown people actually
subdued the Europeans in their homes and there, in Europe, directed the
economy in the interest of great capitalists living in the East. Josef W. Hall
(Upton Close) states graphically the nature of white superiority in the East:

> The white man walked as a god, above the law . . . secure in exploitation. In
> his "sacred cities" there were parks, into which no native was allowed to come.
> His clubs excluded the native, however high born or well educated. His person
> was sacrosanct. . . . He could pass through contending armies—carrying any
> information he might wish. He could shelter any native political criminal and
> assist in any plot and remain inviolate. He could exert himself at will to tear down
> native custom, religion and industry, and still be protected according to treaty
> stipulations.[52]

Then, too, it is even more difficult to conceive of a race becoming
superior in the East without being so also in the West.

and how did the white man go about conquering the world, and what made him think he was
superior to other peoples? Because the white man had guns and the Asiatics had none. The
matter was as simple as that." And he brings the argument up to date: "China will never
. . . be accorded true equality until she is like Japan, twenty years from now, when she can
build her own tanks and guns and battleships. When that time comes, there will be no need
to argue about equality, such being the standards of the modern age." *Between Tears and
Laughter,* pp. 21, 4.

[51]In reporting on social conditions in China, Theodore H. White says: "No one can
understand China today . . . who does not understand the hatred and bitterness of the
intelligent Chinese for the foreign businessman who treated him like a coolie in his own land.
In some cities this foreigner closed the public parks to Chinese; on some boats Chinese were
not allowed to ride first-class." See "Life Looks at China," *Life,* May 1, 1944, p. 100. See
also Nathaniel Peffer, *The White Man's Dilemma,* Chap. IX.

[52]Op. cit., pp. 109–10.

Still another primary consideration serves to indicate the insuperable difficulties in the way of any other race aspiring either to duplicate the racial record of Europeans or to dominate them. Today communication is so far advanced that no people of color, however ingenious, could hope to put a cultural distance between them and whites comparable to that which the Europeans of the commercial and industrial revolution attained in practical isolation over the colored peoples of the world. And such a relationship is crucial for the development of that complex belief in biological superiority and consequent color prejudice which Europeans have been able to attain. Therefore, we must conclude that race prejudice[53] is not only a cultural trait developed among Europeans, but also that no other race could reasonably hope to duplicate the phenomenon. Like the discovery of the world, it seems evident that this racial achievement could occur only once.

The color prejudice of whites has other potentialities; it functions as a regulator of minor racial prejudices. Whenever there are two or more races in the same racial situation with whites, the whites will implicitly or explicitly influence the relationship between these subordinate races. In other words, the whole racial atmosphere tends to be determined by the superior race. This is a consideration of highest significance in understanding race relations. In the more or less tacit admission of white superiority and in competition among subordinate races for white favor, the situation is set for channelization.

The race against whom the whites are least prejudiced tends to become second in rank, while the race that they despise most will ordinarily be at the bottom. Thus more or less directly the superior race controls the pattern of all dependent race prejudices.[54] However, the whites are not entirely free

[53]It should be borne in mind that race prejudice is not simply dislike for the physical appearance or the attitudes of one person by another; it rests basically upon a calculated and concerted determination of a white ruling class to keep some people or peoples of color and their resources exploitable. If we think of race prejudice as merely an expression of dislike by whites for some people of color, our conception of the attitude will be voided of its substance.

[54]The noted Southern writer, David L. Cohn, gives an illustration of this process. "The Anglo-Saxon," he writes, "bitterly hates, and prevents wherever possible, the marriage of his kind with black or yellow peoples. There are separate schools for Chinese in Mississippi, because by statute they are not permitted to attend white schools. . . . There are many Chinese in the [Mississippi] Delta. They are successful merchants. Some of them live with their Chinese wives; others have Negro mistresses and families of half-breed children. To the

in the exercise of their prejudice. The actual cultural advancement or national power of the subordinate races may not be without some reciprocal effect in the final adjustment of the races. Referring to the South African situation, P. S. Joshi declares: "The whites estimate all non-whites as inferior to themselves. The natives are the 'untouchables' of their country. The Asiatics rank lower than whites, and claim to be higher than the coloured or natives. This caste-phobia is a derivation of the colour bar."[55]

Europeans have mixed their blood with that of practically every colored people in the world. In no situation, however, where whites have interbred with colored races have they accepted the mixed-bloods without discrimination.[56] The tendency has been to accept the mixed-bloods according to their lightness of color, and this notwithstanding interracial laws socially proscribing all persons of colored blood. The anti-color codes merely limit acceptability.

Caste prejudice is an aspect of culture prejudice, while race prejudice—as distinguished from culture prejudice—is color-and-physique prejudice. The latter is prejudice marked by visibility, physical distinguishability; it is not, however, caused by physical differences. We may repeat that precise anthropometrical definitions of race are not of crucial significance.[57] Racial attitudes are based upon simple obvious criteria, and

casual eye these children are often indistinguishable from full-blooded Chinese. The fear arose in the white community that if Chinese children were permitted to attend the public schools, these Chinese-Negro half-breeds would go along. The result was that separate schools for the Chinese, at the expense of the community, were provided for by law. Theoretically, these schools are of the same quality as the white schools. Actually, it is impossible to make them of the same quality without prohibitive expense. Chinese children, therefore, do not enjoy the same facilities for education that are open to white children.

"The leaders of the Chinese, knowing the real reason for the exclusion of their children from the public schools, hope, one day, to have the barriers removed. To this end, they are insisting that their men shall refrain from having Negro mistresses, and no half-breed children. When they feel that they can prove to the satisfaction of the white community that the children whom they present for admittance to the white schools are racially pure Chinese, they may attempt to have the statute repealed." *God Shakes Creation,* pp. 219–20.

Should the Chinese make the necessary response, we should expect them to show an even greater hatred for Negroes than that of the whites, but the view of this racial situation would be very much distorted if one attempts to understand Chinese-Negro relationship independently of the controlling white prejudice.

See also Krishnalal Shridharani, "Minorities and the Autonomy of India," *Group Relations and Group Antagonisms,* R. M. MacIver, ed., pp. 200–6.

[55]Op. cit., p. 28.

[56]The writer is not unmindful of the situation in some parts of Brazil.

the findings of anthropometry, whether genuine or spurious, may simply provide a basis for their rationalization. Color prejudice, as a psychological phenomenon, is a complex emotion manifested by a positive attitude of distance and a reaction; specifically it is an insistent attitude of white superiority and dominance and an accommodating reaction of persons of color. It is a cultural trait of Western society which took form during the era of explorations.

To achieve a simple understanding of the concept, it may be well for us to observe the problem from the point of view of the initiating factor; that is to say, the white factor in the relationship. As stated above, in the contact of color groups, whites have set the stage for the pattern which the racial adjustment will assume. It varies according to their needs and aspirations, while the colored groups attempt to meet the aggressor on whatever seem to them the most favorable grounds. Therefore, an understanding of modern race relations will be achieved only if we look at the situation from the point of view of the desires and methods of Europeans in their dealings with peoples of color. The caste hypothesis of race relations will hardly help us to understand why the white ruling classes in the West Indies contend with most exacting logic that the contact of East Indians and Negroes there is socially advantageous, while in Kenya they reason with equal verve that the contact of Indians and Negroes is socially insalubrious.[58] It would hardly give us a hint to the reason for the Portuguese's remarkable freedom from

[57]We may illustrate this point. After delivering an invective against the assumed racial superiority of the whites in India, Krishnalal Shridharani declares: "An overwhelming majority of the Indian people belongs to the so-called white race, according to all anthropological and ethnological data. The tropical sun may have imparted pigmentation to the skin of the Indo-Aryan . . . but the ethnologist knows that the Indo-Aryan is of Caucasian origin." *Warning to the West,* p. 191. The ethnologist may be equally convinced about the race of white American Negroes, but just as the British in India pays him no attention, so also white Americans turn to him a deaf ear. Says Robert Briffault, in his incisive review of the ways of the white sahibs in India, "The Hindus were treated, as they have been ever since, as 'niggers.'" *The Decline and Fall of the British Empire,* p. 78.

[58]See *Report of the Committee on Emigration from India to the Crown Colonies and Protectorates,* London, 1910.

Warren S. Thompson comments upon the situation in Africa: "When all is said that can truly be said about the nefarious practices of the Indians in their dealings with the Negroes in East Africa, it seems more than probable that the chief objection to their economic relations with the natives is to be found in the fact that they render the white man's exploitation of the Negroes more difficult and less profitable than it would otherwise be. Naturally this is resented, and it certainly sounds better to object to the nefarious exploitation of the Negro by the Indian than to say that the Indian is not wanted because he makes white people work

race prejudice in Brazil as compared with their scrupulousness about color in Hawaii. We should have no clue at all concerning the irreconcilable ways of the Dutch—their anti-color attitudes in South Africa as against their comparative liberality in Java.

What the white dominant group will do depends upon the nature of the color situation—the exploitative situation. The Australians are too white-conscious to permit "olive-skinned" Italian immigration;[59] and recently white Americans who risked very much to introduce Africans into the United States and who mixed their blood rather freely with them have become too white-conscious to allow southern Europeans and Levantines to immigrate to the United States. In the following chapter we shall discuss some typical racial situations.

harder to maintain their profits, and renders their lives less pleasant than they would be if they did not have to compete with him. This is too frank an avowal of their own exploitative purposes." *Danger Spots in World Population,* p. 169. See also India, Central Bureau of Information, *India in 1930–31,* pp. 49ff., and Maurice S. Evans, *Black and White in South East Africa,* p. 291.

In 1919 the Kenya Economic Commission reported: "Physically the Indian is not a wholesome influence because of his repugnance to sanitation and hygiene. In this respect the African is more civilized than the Indian, being naturally cleanly in his ways. . . . The moral depravity of the Indian is equally damaging to the African. . . . The presence of the Indian in this country is quite obviously inimical to the moral and physical welfare and the economic advancement of the native." Quoted by Raymond Leslie Buell, *The Native Problem in Africa,* Vol. I, p. 291.

[59]Warren S. Thompson, op. cit., pp. 223ff.

2.
Situations of Race Relations

Let us now examine some *modern* situations of free relationship between whites and persons of color; situations, to repeat, in which the aggressive whites have sought most conveniently and efficiently to exploit the human and natural resources of the colored peoples.

1. Situations in which the colored person is a stranger in a white society, such as a Hindu in the United States or a Negro in many parts of Canada and in Argentina—we shall call this the stranger situation.

2. Situations of original white contact where the culture of the colored group is very simple, such as the conquistadors and Indians in the West Indies, and the Dutch and Hottentots in South Africa—the original-contact situation.

3. Situations of colored enslavement in which a small aristocracy of whites exploits large quantities of natural resources, mainly agricultural, with forced colored labor, raised or purchased like capital in a slave market, such as that in the pre–Civil War South and in Jamaica before 1834—the slavery situation.

4. Situations in which a small minority of whites in a colored society is bent upon maintaining a ruling-class status, such as the British in the West Indies or the Dutch in the East Indies—the ruling-class situation.

5. Situations in which there are large proportions of both colored and white persons seeking to live in the same area, with whites insisting that the society is a "white man's country," as in the United States and South Africa—the bipartite situation.

6. Situations in which colored-and-white amalgamation is far advanced and in which a white ruling class is not established, as in Brazil—the amalgamative situation.

7. *Situations in which a minority of whites has been subdued by a dominantly colored population, as that which occurred in Haiti during the turn of the eighteenth century, or the expulsion of whites from Japan in 1638—the nationalistic situation.*

A little more detail should help to elucidate these situations.[1]

The Stranger Situation

In cases where colored persons in the total population are so few that they can neither be expected to compete with whites nor serve any considerable purpose as a labor force there is usually little racial antagonism against them—until, perhaps, they attempt to enter the higher rungs of society where participants are fewer and competition keener. In certain parts of Canada, for example, Negroes have relatively wide social opportunities, and Negro-white intermarriage goes on with a freedom that is wholly unknown in the United States.[2] Although in the United States Hindus suffer far greater legal disabilities than Negroes, no Hindu will willingly exchange his status for that of a Negro. He falls within a general Asiatic ban which is a sort of official prophylaxis against his coming into the country in numbers large enough to make him a significant competitor; but socially he is a stranger.

There have been cases of West Indian Hindus in the United States who had long since given up the turban and the sari; as they came to understand the nature of Negro-white relationship, however, they returned to the Oriental dress and marked well their distance from American colored people. As Hindus, they are conceded certain privileges and opportunities which are denied Negroes even of much lighter complexion. But not so in Natal. In the United States the Hindu is still a romantic figure; in South Africa he is a "damn coolie."

[1]There may be other situations of race contacts, but it does not seem advisable to attempt a permutation of those cited. To do this may not only result in situations which do not exist in fact but also in some that are totally fanciful. In a following chapter we shall discuss the racial situation on the Pacific Coast, which presents a different pattern.

[2]It should be pointed out that Canadians are by no means unmindful of the destiny of whites in their relationship with peoples of color. In British Columbia no Chinese, or Japanese, or East Indian can vote; these are discriminated against; and whether the person of color is or is not a British subject is of no moment. [Voting rights were gained in 1947.]

Yet fewness in number is not necessarily the prime factor in the situation. If the individual goes into a community where a negative attitude has been indirectly nurtured, he will not then really be a stranger. He will be singled out for differential treatment on the basis of prepared racial sentiments. An individual Negro is not a stranger in all-white communities of the South. Furthermore, developed attitudes may be transferred to new communities.

> If a man with African ancestry known as a Porto Rican goes to a certain barber shop in Honolulu—one that seeks to attract tourist patronage—he can get his hair cut. But if a man with African blood is identified as a Negro of mainland origin, he, when he seeks the service of this shop is told that he has come to the wrong place.[3]

Probably the extreme of this situation was that of the American Indian in Europe during the age of discovery. The relatively few American Indians who either went or were carried to European countries were known to be "savages," but everywhere the reaction toward them was that of mass curiosity and wonderment. They encountered no socially established ethnic definition; sometimes they were entertained and honored by royalty and sometimes they were pitied for their cultural backwardness. In so far as their exploitation was concerned, however, they were frequently made to review the military might of certain nations so that on their return home they might recount their experience to overawe their tribal fellows. On the brighter side of their living abroad Carolyn T. Foreman writes:

> The Indians proved a source of great interest to scientists; the portraits of many of them were painted by famous artists in Europe; kings and queens received them as fellow sovereigns, showering them with gifts of money, jewels, and clothing while entertaining them in royal style; philosophers, poets, and historians wrote of them; gala performances were staged at the theatres and operas of European cities for their entertainment.[3a]

During the world wars Negro American soldiers in Europe were largely racial strangers. In every country the cordiality of the people was in remarkable contrast to the normal racial antagonism of their white American comrades. It has been reported that the restrictions and difficulties set up in the way of intermarriage by the United States Army have left hundreds of World War II Negro babies in England with anomalous status, a striking

[3]Romanzo Adams, *Interracial Marriage in Hawaii*, p. 24.
[3a]*Indians Abroad. 1493–1938*, p. xix.

example of a positive racial attitude impinging upon a social situation of diffused racial norms.

The Original-Contact Situation

The original-contact situation is not so much a type as a stage in the process of developing a more or less stable pattern of race relations. It may precede others which we are considering. When the native colored groups have a very simple culture, they are almost completely at the disposal and mercy of the whites. They are subordinated and awed by the latter's sophistication and calculations. In some cases the preliterates are looked upon practically as game to be exploited and dispossessed at will. Civilized ethics are abandoned, and the law of the frontier is justice.

"Forced trading" soon creates an economic vacuum in their old way of life. Native women are ordinarily considered booty, hence miscegenation is common but intermarriage rare. Indeed, there is ordinarily such great disparity between the cultures that the common understanding necessary for intermarriage is seldom attained. From a cultural point of view the natives are thought of as little children or savages.

If there is great exploitative zeal among the whites and the native population is comparatively small, it may be exterminated, as was the case of the Indians in the West Indies and the Tasmanians of Australasia;[4] or, in case there is sufficient hinterland, it may be pushed back, as were the Indians of the United States and the Negroes of East Africa.[5] Here they may

[4]For instances of native extermination on contact with whites, see James Bryce, *The Relations of the Advanced and Backward Races of Mankind,* 2d ed., pp. 10–11. Sometimes the physical durability and resistance of the people are so great that they may survive even the cruelest atrocities and pressures. A classic example of this is the survival of the peoples of the Belgian Congo under Leopold II.

[5]The authority and decision with which native peoples may be dispatched are illustrated by the method used in Kenya and described by Warren Thompson: "In Kenya there are highland areas in which the white man can live in reasonable comfort even though they are under the equator. This was called by the British a 'white man's country' and it was desired to reserve it for future white settlement. In order to so reserve considerable parts of it, it was necessary to clear out some of the native tribes, and this was done with what looks to the outsider like complete indifference to their right and with much unnecessary suffering. It so happened that one of the peoples whose lands were coveted was a particularly friendly group of Negroes which had been of great assistance to the British in actually bringing the country under their control. They thus merited special consideration at the hands of their masters, but instead of receiving it, they were compelled to leave their native lands for much poorer lands in a less favorable situation. Moreover, the migration was not well planned and resulted in great hardship both in direct suffering on the road and through the loss of a very

be able to endure the pains of acculturation more easily. In time, however, they may become more or less adapted to Western culture, in the process of which race problems develop and multiply.

The Slavery Situation

The slavery situation is probably the purest form of established race relations. Without disguise it defines the slaves, the colored people, as chattel, and exploits them in production virtually on the same economic principle as that employed in the exploitation of beasts of burden. It is in this situation that the capitalist, exploitative basis of race relations with its powerful drive toward dehumanizing the worker is most clearly observed. The master may consciously decide to use up his slaves because their replacement is cheaper than their conservation.

Modern slavery necessarily demands that the social system define the colored bondmen as irredeemably subsocial; it is upon this basis only that the ideological superstructure of the exploitative interest of the master class may be contrived. The pith of this ideology is not so much that the colored people are inferior as that they must remain inferior. Slaves can have no social organization of their own, no rights independent of their master's personal wishes; they can have neither status, function, nor social and geographical mobility like a caste; they cannot be permitted to contradict or dispute any question with the master. They are immediately and perpetually manipulable as instruments of production and must remain completely below the level of conscious organization and direction of community life.

Modern slavery may be thought of as developing out of a need for the rapid proletarianization of workers. In this situation white common laborers, already highly proletarianized, are scarce or non-existent, and therefore the colored people, as slaves, ordinarily constitute "the masses." The experienced white worker is ordinarily employed in such administrative

considerable part of their cattle, on which they depended for a living. . . .

"When this land became available, the British found that they needed laborers to develop it. For a 'white man's land' in east Africa does not mean land in which the white man expects to do his own work as a settler in Canada or Australia would, but a climate in which he can live in moderate comfort and ease, provided he can get cheap labor to do the actual field work. It being necessary to have labor now that the land was available, it was decided that the natives should work for the white man whether they cared to do so or not. It would be for their good to be kept busy and would prevent their getting into mischief and having so much time to 'plot against the whites.'" Op. cit., pp. 165–66.

positions as overseers, drivers, or gang foremen. Labor unions of any kind are generally unknown. The master class, having more or less complete freedom to employ its labor force at any function, is able to use its slaves in competition with any plethoric, white, manual workers until the latter, in desperation, are driven to some extremity of existence as poor whites.

The situation is usually dangerous, unstable, and apprehensive. Teachers, preachers, free-colored people, humanitarians, all tend to become threats to the peace and order of the community. A system of etiquette, which has to be sensitive enough to detect any tendency in the slave toward insubordination, is developed. Moreover, since slave uprisings are constant social expectations, this etiquette conveniently contrives to involve and implicate the poor whites, so that, even though the latter are economically disadvantaged in competition with slave labor, they tend to become, nevertheless, morally obligated and bound up in a common fate with the white master class. Then, too, since the system never gets into the "mores" of the people, considerable reliance is put upon physical coercion and exemplary cruelty in its maintenance.

Here the colored people do not have social status in the sense that whites do. The slave derives his social status not particularly from any attribute of his own, but from the social status and power of his master. In other words, a slave who has ingratiated himself with a powerful master is likely to be treated with circumspection even by whites of the community. An ill-treatment of such a slave may be construed as disrespect for the master. On the whole, however, slaves are not respected as persons; among the slaves themselves there is no self-respect independent of the master. Indeed, the slave can have no personality capable of responsible, self-assertive behavior. His individuality remains submerged beneath the overwhelming authority of the master.

The sexual and familial life of the slaves are determined by the master. Slaves may be bred and raised like animal stock, with one or a few males functioning as sires to a community of breeding females. Children, of course, are the property of the master. In some slavery situations, mainly among Latin peoples, masters have been known to marry slave women. This relationship, however, has been usually forbidden by law; concubinage has been somewhat more common.

Ordinarily the sexual relations between master and slave have been promiscuous and, in the South at any rate, even this never gained social sanction. In fact, the primary social definition of the slave as a sub-social, working animal leads to the corollary definition of sex relations between white men and slave women as sodomy; the white man "defiles his body by lying with a Negro." Quite frequently, however, the powerful sexual urge confronted by the easy sexual opportunities of the bond-women overrides the social fiction and many mulatto children are born. The latter, in turn, tend to become socially restless and consequently more or less serious threats to the system.

In this situation sex relations between slave men and white women are very rare. Marriage, of course, could not be sanctioned; the social disadvantages to the white woman of even a clandestine relationship are so great that she tends to be effectively inhibited. A pregnancy of this kind is a social calamity of the first order. To bear a child for a "beast of the field," a slave, is to "dishonor God" and abuse one's self most shamefully. Such a white woman always expects to be scorned and ridiculed as a sexual pervert by the community; her colored child presents her with an insoluble social problem. Public authorities must find a way either to relieve her of it or to institutionalize her with it.

Since the colored man, the slave, tends to be a social nonentity, slave women who have become concubines of white men gain in social status. Such women tend to rise in the estimation of other slaves and may even be envied by interested white women. The relationship, however, is always more or less surreptitious. It is probably most convenient among great plantation owners who practically dominate the community.

There are tremendous natural urges and social compulsives in the slavery situation determining the behavior pattern of the slaves. The purposeful, independent slave is ordinarily "sold down the river"; the runaway or insurrectionist, "the lover of freedom," is ordinarily "broken on the wheel" or "quartered." The obsequious, ingratiating, and resigned slave ordinarily reaches the best adjustment in the system. The Bush Negroes of the Guianas, the Maroons of Jamaica, and the runaways in the North are examples of slaves breaking away to freedom; yet slaves as a whole tend to achieve some workable degree of accommodation.

The finally accommodated slave, a rather exceptional individual in modern slavery, conceives of himself as inconsequential and worthless except as he is able to satisfy his master by his work; he also tends to define the members of his group as having no other reason for existence. This supine devotion of the accommodated slave and the tremendous power of the master over his life fate may occasionally affect the master so deeply that in sympathy the relationship becomes personalized and much of the cruel necessities of exploitation may be tempered with condescension.

Matthew G. Lewis, an absentee Jamaican planter, presents, in his *Journal of a West Indian Proprietor,* a classic illustration of accommodated slaves:

> Whether the pleasure of the Negroes was sincere may be doubted; but certainly it was the loudest that I ever witnessed: they all talked together, sang, danced, shouted, and, in the violence of their gesticulations, tumbled over each other, and rolled upon the ground. . . .
>
> The shouts, the gaiety, the wild laughter, their strange and sudden bursts of singing and dancing, and several old women, wrapped up in large cloaks, their heads bound round with different-colored handkerchiefs, leaning on a staff, and standing motionless in the middle of the hubbub, with their eyes fixed upon the portico which I occupied, formed an exact counterpart of the festivity of the witches in Macbeth. Nothing could be more odd or more novel than the whole scene; and yet there was something in it by which I could not help being affected. Perhaps it was the consciousness that all these human beings were my slaves. . . .
>
> Soon after reaching the lodging house at Savannah la Mar, a remarkably clean-looking Negro lad presented himself with some water and a towel—I concluded he belonged to the inn—and, on my returning the towel, as he found that I took no notice of him, he at length ventured to introduce himself by saying, "Massa not know me; me your slave!"—and really the sound made me feel a pang at the heart. The lad appeared all gaiety and good humor, and his whole countenance expressed anxiety to recommend himself to my notice, but the word "slave" seemed to imply that, although he did feel pleasure then in serving me, if he had detested me, *he must have served me still.* [Italics added.]

The Ruling-Class Situation

Where whites are mainly sojourning rulers, their numbers are usually relatively small. Ordinarily "home" is in Europe or America, and they seldom set their roots in the area. Here there is little hope of developing a significant white population. The white man's principal need is not a home but a satisfied and exploitable people to develop the resources of the country. This ruling class adopts a policy of "co-operation"; and, other things being equal, favors are distributed to the mixed-bloods on the basis of their apparent degrees of admixture. In other words, a premium is put upon degrees of whiteness among the people of color. Degrees of color tend to become a determinant of status in a continuous social-class gradient, with whites at its upper reaches. Thus, assuming cultural parity among the group, the lighter the complexion, the greater the economic and social opportunities. In this situation, then, there are significant color distinctions among the colored people themselves. Usually a color scheme is established, with generally recognized names for the different shades; and color problems of a more or less momentous nature come into being.

The system tends to generate among even those of light complexion a painfully morbid bitterness against fate, a diffused attitude of hatred and despair, the basis of which appears to be without social definition.[6] The colored people as a whole tend to become perennially preoccupied with the problem of degrees of pigmentation and lament the luck of their dusky progenitors. Brothers of different color may become estranged, and dark parents may keep themselves out of the way of their lighter children. Indeed, children may implicitly disavow their darker parents, while lighter persons who have been awarded in social status for their lightness may become rigid and even fierce at any attempt of darker persons to recognize them publicly and familiarly.[7] This constricting sense of color shame tends

[6]Many students of race relations have resorted to a biological interpretation of this attitude and with rather sterile results. The conclusion of Olive Schreiner is at hand: "'I could bite my own arm,' a coloured girl once said in our presence, 'when I see how black it is. My father was a white man!' The half-caste alone of all created things is at war within his own individuality. The white man loves the white man incarnate in him, and the black man loves the black." *Thoughts on South Africa,* quoted with approval by Everett V. Stonequist, *The Marginal Man,* p. 21.

[7]At the basis of this attitude there is a powerful implicit play of racial sentiment. The prejudice of the mixed-blood is derived from the dominant prejudice of the whites; and it waxes or wanes directly as the situation gives the white man an opportunity to hold the mixed-blood responsible for the blackness of his aspiring associate. The mixed-blood, in his association with whites, strives to identify his racial sentiments with those of the whites; in fact, one criterion of complete achievement of whiteness by the native is the complete identification of his racial sentiments with those of the European. Now, the black man who attempts a familiarity with the mixed-blood in the presence of whites or other mixed-bloods of comparative whiteness puts the mixed-blood in a difficult situation. In the eyes of the whites he is caught red-handed in a debasing revelation; he thus stands accused until he can clear himself. If he can make it obvious to the whites that he has put a supercilious distance between himself and the darker person, very little or no explanation may be necessary. But

to be heightened when the relationship is under the surveillance of white people. Lighter persons seek to group themselves and to clique darker aspirants into oblivion. In fact, true friendship between lighter and darker young people is scarcely possible, for even schoolboys evaluate the color of their pals.

In business and official positions, darker colors are particularly penalized. These may go farthest in those occupations which call for unusual talent. In this situation, therefore, colored people cannot be asked to recognize all white persons as superior to themselves; yet the color obsession has its existence in that very fact. Coveted goals are made to appear available to all men alike, and the occasional attainment of high position by a darker colored person is all the more tantalizing. The color question is seldom, if ever, discussed in the press or on the platform, but it has extensive currency in esoteric discussion. Among the colored people there may be pride in lightness of color; pride of race, however, is a meaningless imponderability.

Ordinarily the basis of the system is only vaguely recognized. In an ideal situation the position of the white ruling class is impregnable. Its members are envied, admired, and imitated religiously, but they are never questioned. The rest of the population is too absorbed with the immediate business of achieving increments of whiteness or their equivalent to give much attention to the inciting social force in the system. The system tends to be self-regulating. The colored people as a whole do not look upon whites as a people particularly prone to race prejudice, but rather each aspiring color stratum grapples with the problem of holding its own and of whittling away the distance attitudes from the stratum above. Therefore, to any given color group, the persons who are most exasperatingly color-prejudiced are not necessarily white people, but rather the cold-shouldering, snubbing, lighter-color group immediately above.

The ambitious individual who has been rebuffed is particularly disconsolate, for he must usually bear his ill fortune alone. He cannot appeal to color

if the darker person be a relative, say his mother, he is likely to suffer the deepest kind of emotional disturbance. He may hate her for her untimely appearance, which, she ought to have known, could have only a degrading effect upon him, and proceed to estrange himself from her for the occasion. He may decide to recognize her and thus reveal the true extent of his pollution, with its consequent penalty of demotion in social status; or he may take some middle ground in the hope that he will be able subsequently to talk himself out of guilt.

groups below him, since to do so might induce familiarity; neither could he allow the latter groups to observe his misfortune, for they might take the situation as an opportunity for gloating. He cannot disclose the whole truth even among his own group without revealing that he had planned to steal a march on them. He is left finally to reconstruct his self-respect and to devise new methods of approach. To many the struggle is exceedingly exhausting, for ground gained is seldom secure. The goal is apparently attained when the mixed-blood has become so light in complexion that he is generally accepted as a *native white.*

The white ruling class seldom contests the claim of such a person. It merely assigns him a different and more insidious social task, that of the social climber. This is usually sufficient to maintain the desired distance, for the social life of the white upper class is ordinarily carefully organized on a "private-club" basis, and it is a past master of the blackball. The native whites are the real bulwark of the status quo. To the colored people of darker shades they are serious, sensitive, and meticulous in their demands that the full etiquette of class distinction be observed; on the other hand, the European whites, free from any suspicion, are able to relax in the easy assurance that deference comes to them *naturally.*

In this situation there is never a lynching; interracial conflicts are practically unknown and, though they are in the majority, colored men are never stigmatized with a propensity, say, to rape white women. Furthermore, the poor-white problem never develops. Colored men may marry white women with impunity, and laws are never openly biased in favor of whites. When the colored population consists of many colored races, the situation becomes particularly favorable for amalgamation. The small white ruling class, already limited in its power to segregate, now finds it practically impossible to identify any one group for racial discrimination. "Equality among all peoples" tends to become the social philosophy. Instances of this are found in the island of Trinidad, and in Hawaii especially.[8]

---

[8]The assimilation policy of the French in West Africa falls into this category. Here a cultured black elite serves as the control group. Jealous of its privileges and sensitive to its importance, this elite has no sense of solidarity with the uneducated black masses. See Raymond Buell, op. cit., Vol. II, pp. 81–86.

For a discussion of this situation of race relations, see Everett V. Stonequist, "Comparison of Race Relations in Hawaii and Jamaica," *The West Indian Review,* September 1935.

The Bipartite Situation

Where whites are in numbers large enough to fill all preferred occupations or where there is possible competition with a large colored population along the whole cultural hierarchy, definite racial attitudes are developed. Here the tendency is to dichotomize the society into color groups, for any system of increasing acceptability according to degrees of lightness of color will quickly threaten white dominance. We do not have, in this case, merely a white ruling class, but a white population; therefore, anything short of dichotomy will leave masses of white persons subordinated to numbers of enterprising colored persons, a situation extremely favorable for rapid amalgamation and consequent depreciation of color per se as a social value.

Then, too, the social definition of the dominant place of husbands in the family tends to put a white wife of a man of color in a situation embarrassing to the whites. She is the embodiment of their pretensions; hence their sympathies must follow her in her yielding and subordination to the "inferior" colored man. In a most realistic way this tends to abrogate the theoretical claims of all whites to dominance. And for this reason, in the United States, for instance, even Negro women are not fundamentally displeased over the marriage of Negro men and white women.

In the ruling-class situation there are colored "ladies" in the upper social classes; but in this, the bipartite situation, the whites ordinarily define all colored females as "Negresses" or "nigger women." This is necessary because, should it appear that colored womanhood possesses some remarkable degree of refinement and elegance, it would be inconsistent to characterize all white men who marry colored women as depraved. There must be some tacit, if not expressed, suggestion that all colored women are prostitutes, polluted, and carnal, so that only the most disreputable white men may reach moral depths sufficiently low to marry them.

Accordingly, among many whites, it has become second nature to say that "only low-class white men have anything to do with colored women." This attitude—legal restrictions aside—has made most colored women in the South particularly opposed to the idea of marrying white men. Indeed, other things being equal, even Negro men who look white are no ideal of colored women. They abhor the suggestion that they are concubines.

But this technique of racial defamation is not so effective in the case of Negro men. Ordinarily a man's character is not nearly so delicate as that of a woman. Once it has been established that all Negro women are wenches, the white man who marries one automatically identifies himself as degenerate. In the case of the Negro-man–white-woman marriage, however, the principal attack is shifted not to all white women but to those particular white women who marry Negroes.

These are supposed to be women with ungovernable sexual passions who may find satisfaction only in the assumed animal appetites of Negro men. It follows that a "white lady" with refined sensibilities will never marry a Negro man, and of course the white policy makers must inevitably insist that all white women should be white ladies. But this defense does not cause Negro men to recoil from the relationship as Negro women tend to do. The accusation of animal virility is not necessarily a derogatory one; furthermore, the man brings his white spouse among Negroes, where the white stereotypes are largely impotent. It is to Negro society that he looks for approbation, and the character of his wife tends to be measured by his own social stature.

Therefore, those white persons who conceive of themselves as being charged with the maintenance of continued white dominance will contrive segregation barriers and rationalizations to secure a bipartite racial system. Here the term "social equality" is taboo, racial laws are always partial, and cultural merit among people of color is given minimal recognition.

In this situation, lightness of color within the colored group is not nearly so highly prized as in the preceding illustration. In fact, it appears that a certain shade of brownness[9] (at least in men), rather than increasing whiteness, may become an ideal among the colored people. Here the lighter person is hardly rewarded with wider opportunities, and the possession of a darker complexion is hardly so unfortunate an attribute.

Moreover, the tendency of whites is to be less discriminating about color values within the colored group, a fact which naturally tends to make degrees of color a social factor of less moment to colored people themselves. The social distance between shades of color is narrowed. Some colored people, especially those who are definitely dark, may even welcome the definition of the whites: "If you are not white, you are black."

---

[9]See Charles S. Johnson, *Growing Up in the Black Belt,* and Charles Henry Parrish, *The Significance of Color in the Negro Community* (i.e., in Louisville, Kentucky), Ph.D. thesis, University of Chicago, 1944.

However, the vulgarism that all Negroes or all Hindus look alike may be particularly poignant to an accomplished light-complexioned person. None the less colored persons who try in a way that would be acceptable in the preceding situation to capitalize their light color are, in this situation, marked men within their race.

Thus, we may conclude that, the greater the insistence of the dominant whites upon a bipartite system of social segregation of the races, the less the social advantage of lightness of color within the colored group. Because marriage is ordinarily more important in the life of women than in that of men, and because the tendency of colored men to marry lighter is scarcely abated in this situation, we should expect the foregoing principle to be truer for colored men than for colored women. Incidentally, it may be mentioned also that, the greater the insistence upon, and accomplishment of, a bipartite racial system, the greater the relative cultural advantage of being white.

When there are more than one significant colored group in the population, it becomes the interest of the whites to prevent their coalescence. In the United States, for example, laws are enacted prohibiting intermarriage between Negroes and Indians or Negroes and Malays, and so on, while in South Africa the Negro-East Indian mixed-blood is particularly detested.[10]

---

[10]Arthur F. Raper cites an interesting case in Bolivar County, Mississippi: "The small Chinese element in Bolivar and other delta counties is racially significant, because it occupies a position midway between the Negroes and the whites, thereby giving rise to unique situations. One of the best grocery stores in Rosedale is owned and operated by a Chinese. They are permitted limited social privileges with the whites in proportion as they do not mingle socially with the Negroes.

"Recently in Greenville, thirty miles south, a Chinese boy who married a white girl was forced to leave. This marriage would probably have been permitted to pass, except for the fact that the boy's brother had previously married a Negro. Since that time the white people have held several anti-Chinese meetings, to which Negroes were invited. The Negroes, however, did not attend, and subsequently a white committee waited upon them to ascertain their attitude toward the Chinese. The immediate purpose of the movement was to establish a boycott against Chinese business, in which the co-operation of the Negroes was essential." *The Tragedy of Lynching*, p. 106.

The 1926 Native Policy Bill of General Hertzog separates the natives from every other racial group, whites, colored, or Indian. The "bill grants the franchise to the *existing* colored population." But "persons born of mixed unions in future shall be regarded as natives," inheriting all the latter's social disadvantages. And Hertzog said in his Smithfield speech supporting the bill: "The result of this policy has been that an alliance of [the colored people] and the native population has been stopped. Luckily they [the Cape Colored] felt that their interests were more closely allied to those of the Europeans than that of the Native. It is their wish just as much as it is ours that they should stand by themselves with regard to the franchise." Quoted by Raymond Leslie Buell, op. cit., Vol. I, p. 142.

Dominance can always be more easily maintained by keeping these people apart; and the dissemination of ingenious pure-blood myths facilitates this purpose. Whereas in our third situation the white-colored mixed-bloods are generally welcomed as a racial liaison group, in the present one they are usually branded inferior mongrels.

In the ruling-class situation the white ruling class encourages cultural refinement among the colored people. So long as the colored person eschews antagonistic political ideas, he is complimented, at least ostensibly, for striving to acquire all the amenities of the upper class. To speak well, to dress fashionably, to live in an attractively appointed home, to assume a dignified bearing, to develop family pride is to merit the favor of the ruling class. Here, then, colored people may brush off their lower-class fellows with impunity. The cultural rapprochement of the ruling-class whites and the upper-class colored people facilitates the use of the latter as a cultural cushion and an instrument of exploitation of the masses.

In the situation under discussion, however, the whites carefully suppress such attitudes; here colored persons may acquire marks of cultural distinction only by sufferance. Moreover, the cultural degradation of the colored people as a whole is believed to be an asset to the whites, and they strive to achieve it.[11] In the South, for example, the Negro who speaks good English to a typical Southern white man insults him; such a person is characterized a "cocky nigger" and merits reduction. The colored person is most acceptable in the clothes of the manual worker, and he who perchance acquires material goods of some worth must be careful not to make it appear that his conception of himself as a citizen has advanced commensurably, for this would be the surest indication that he is getting out of place. The cry that Negroes are inferior is an illusion; what is real is the fierce insistence by the white ruling class that Negroes do nothing which might lead either

Of course it would be as undesirable for the native tribes to come together. Says Edgar H. Brookes, "We may . . . rule out the association of the Bantu with other Africans in a great movement of pan Africanism. Such a movement would be regarded by most nationalist thinkers as highly dangerous to White supremacy." *The Colour Problems of South Africa*, p. 30; see also p. 34.

[11]With reference to an earlier age of race relations in the United States, de Tocqueville makes a similar observation. Since the whites, he says, "will not raise the Negroes to their own level, they sink them as nearly as possible to the brutes." *Democracy in America*, Vol. II, pp. 246–47.

themselves or other people to believe that they are equal or superior to whites.

In this situation, even severe states of social pathology among the colored people may serve the implicit purpose of the whites. Since cultural *rapprochement* is fatal to this purpose, the whites in South Africa, for example, advocate cultural parallelism; while those in the Southern United States practice cultural repression among the colored people. Actually, the latter policy is also intended to achieve cultural parallelism.[12] In the United States a relatively illiterate, criminal, diseased, base, poor, and prostituted colored people serves by comparison as proof to the world that Negroes do not deserve the social opportunities available to whites. This state of degradation tends to characterize the cultural life of the Negroes and to make it distinct from that of whites. It is, of course, in the interest of the ruling-class whites to keep it thus distinct. They seek, through myriad and powerful devices, to make the colored person, as a human being, ashamed of his very existence; indeed, the accomplishment of racial shame is a psychological goal of the Southern oligarchs. In the South Negroes have been lynched for "trying to act like white men."[13] As Myrdal observes: "The South did not want—and to a great extent, still does not want—the Negro to be successful as a freedman. White southerners are prepared to abstain from many liberties and to sacrifice many advantages for the purpose of withholding them from the Negroes."[14]

For this reason emphasis is never put upon improvement of the colored people; in fact, the idea of "improvement" or "progress" is looked upon with apprehension by whites. Hence jails are always more tolerable than schools and Old Testament preachers more acceptable

[12]Observe, for instance, the intent of the Honorable Chauncey Sparks, governor of Alabama, in his declaration: "There is no need for racial jealousies, no need for racial conflicts, but there is a great field for racial pride. This pride cannot be maintained unless each race is developed along its own lines." Founder's Day address delivered at Tuskegee Institute, April 4, 1943. This, obviously, is a plea to Negroes that they should co-operate with their exploiters in isolating themselves. Naturally, if Negroes in the South can be made to believe that they have "lines" of development distinct from those of whites, segregation may be more easily imposed upon them.

[13]See Arthur F. Raper, op. cit., p. 36.

[14]Gunnar Myrdal, *An American Dilemma*, Vol. I, p. 223.

thansocial-serviceworkers.[15] However, the ruling-class whites never intend that the disease and crime perpetuated among the colored people should overflow among them. The spread of disease is limited by segregation, and for crime by colored people against whites the criminal is punished mercilessly. Excessive criminality and social disorder within the colored group tend to keep its members occupied with self-criticism, recrimination, individual expressions of hatred for the colored group as a whole, and with desperate social devices contrived by individuals or families in their attempts to develop, more or less isolatedly, decent living conditions. Among the masses it has been said, "Their cares are brutish because they are treated as brutes."

A social fact of major significance in this situation is the insistence upon a suppression of civic pride among colored people. Although in the ruling-class situation the colored people are ruled by whites, the masses are never deprived of the sense of having a country. Here the colored people know that they have a permanent home and, if pressed, they will readily become conscious of the fact that the whites are foreigners. Therefore, these people can develop a genuine patriotism; and, in spite of their exploitation, their lives are more frequently planned; they are securely anchored in the social system. It is not uncommon to hear an East Indian or a West Indian, with head erect and confident, say of himself: "I am a British subject!" Out of these attitudes defensive nationalism among the colored people tends to have a comparatively easy growth.

But civic pride is denied colored people in the bipartite situation, and this fact is in no small measure responsible for their social instability. It keeps them spiritually on the move; it denies them the right to call their country home; it limits patriotism severely, thus making a genuine love of one's country virtually impossible. Implicitly or explicitly the white ruling

[15]Without recognizing the inciting force in the situation Dr. Gunnar Myrdal says: "The low plane of living . . . and all the resulting bodily, intellectual, and moral disabilities and distortions of the average Negro make it natural for the ordinary white man not only to see that the Negro is inferior but also to believe honestly that the Negro's inferiority is inborn. This belief means . . . that all attempts to improve the Negro by education, health reforms, or merely by giving him his rights as a worker and a citizen must seem to be less promising of success than they otherwise would be. The Negro is judged to be fundamentally incorrigible and he is, therefore, kept in a slum existence which, in its turn, leaves the imprint upon his body and soul which makes it natural for the white man to believe in his inferiority." Ibid., p. 101.

class has insisted upon Negro dependence, upon gearing the existence of Negroes to its interest, and as a consequence Negroes tend to be irresponsible and uninspired for civic pride and initiative. Restrictions upon co-operative efforts of colored people in communal life tend to determine their pattern of community organization. Here their effort becomes tentative, they establish impermanently, and their impaired sense of ownership in their country tends to be reflected in their comparatively disreputable communal life. In America especially, fanatical gambling and the emergence of wealthy messiahs register somewhat the mental atmosphere of the colored community.[16]

Few, if any, colored persons in the Southern United States, for example, are able to assume the full bearing of Americans, with all its privileges and responsibilities; and their inelegant material appointments are ordinarily symptomatic of the absence of this vital social drive. This condition, of course, is a desirable end of the white ruling class; indeed, its purpose is epitomized in its boast: "This is a white man's country." Spiritual and physical instability among the colored people perpetuate their dependence and render them the more easily exploitable. It is in this sense that George W. Cable says caustically: ". . . The master-caste [in the South] tolerates, with unsurpassed supineness and unconsciousness, a more indolent, indifferent, slovenly, unclean, untrustworthy, ill-mannered, noisy, disrespectful, disputatious, and yet servile domestic and public menial servant than is tolerated by any other enlightened people."[17]

Civic pride among the colored people, then, if permitted at all, must be limited to some tentative racial pride, which in turn must be carefully voided of nationalism, the very pith of such an attitude.

Although both the United States and South Africa are "white men's countries," they differ somewhat in the potentialities of their racial dichotomy. In the United States the great majority of the population is white; in South Africa it is black. There is comparatively little fear in the United

---

[16]In this connection Alexis de Tocqueville makes a point that still has a modicum of validity: "The Negro, who is plunged in this abyss of evils, scarcely feels his own calamitous situation. Violence made him a slave, and the habit of servitude gives him the thoughts and desires of a slave; he admires his tyrants more than he hates them, and finds his joy and his pride in the servile imitation of those who oppress him: his understanding is degraded to the level of his soul." Op. cit., Vol. II, p. 183.

[17]*The Negro Question*, p. 23; see also pp. 67–68.

States that Negroes will use force in asserting themselves. Hence segregation and discrimination practices may be adopted with a high degree of finality. In South Africa, however, the whites are concerned about the mixed-bloods. In a sense, the latter occupy a position similar to that of the *gens de couleur* in pre-revolutionary San Domingo; and the whites are not unmindful of the possibility that they may assume a similar role in a racial crisis. They are, therefore, allowed only so much social privilege as will keep them apart from the natives, yet not enough to close the social breach between them and the whites.

The planned racial dichotomization of South Africa is revealing. Here the policy-making whites have sought to utilize even more basic means of keeping the races socially isolated. Their policy is to prevent the acculturation of the natives, a plan which is obviously expected to accomplish both the territorial and cultural segregation of the natives and thus ensure their continued exploitation. The policy is conducted under the anthropological euphemism "that the natives should be allowed to develop along their own lines." W. O. Brown's generalization that "dominant races have a vested interest in the perpetuity of the cultures of weaker races"[18] fits this situation. "Many English speaking colonists," Maurice S. Evans observes, "seem to have a repugnance to hearing the natives using the English language, and go so far as to decline to carry on a conversation in it; and so Kitchen-Kaffir is invariably the medium used in the towns and is the rule even in the country districts."[19] But this cultural antagonism is readily translatable into economic terms:

[18]"Culture Contact and Race Conflict," *Race and Culture Contacts*, E. B. Reuter, ed., pp. 43–44. See also Jawaharlal Nehru, op. cit., p. 276.

[19]Maurice S. Evans, op. cit., p. 51. In commenting upon the use of "Bazaar Malay" by the Dutch as an interracial language in Indonesia, G. H. Bousquet asserts: "The real truth is that the Dutch desired and still desire to establish their superiority on the basis of native ignorance. The use of Dutch diminishes the gap between inferior and superior—and this must be avoided at all cost." *A French View of the Netherlands Indies*, trans. by Philip E. Lilenthal, p. 88.

How the ruling-class whites may profit by the continuance of certain parts of the native culture is illustrated by an incident which took place when the Prince of Wales visited India in 1921. A number of leaflets were issued in the vernacular by the Government of the Central Provinces explaining that, "according to Hindu Scriptures, the King's Son was a part of God, therefore all Hindu boys should fulfil their religion by assembling to cheer the Prince of Wales." See Reginald Reynolds, *The White Sahibs in India*, p. 277.

In South East Africa, the white man draws a distinction between what he considers the work of a white man and Kaffir work, and is very jealous of any infringement of what he thinks are his labor rights; all clerical work, practically all handicrafts, all skilled work in connection with machinery, all supervision are regarded as the prerogative of the European. If a firm employed native clerks, they would probably be boycotted; if a native was seen doing the skilled work in connection with the erection of a building, the press would teem with indignant letters. To plough, to dig, to hoe, to fetch and carry, to cook—all laborious and menial toil is the duty of the black man.[20]

Even more than in the Southern states it is thought that parallel development is possible. The native must be educated so that he will be able to govern himself according to the principles of his African institutions,[21] the object being a planned cultural isolation. Thus Edgar H. Brookes declares that "we are driven to define the Nationalist programme for the future of the Natives . . . as the building up side by side with the [White] South African nation of a parallel nation. . . . The Bantu nation will embrace all the Natives of the Union of South Africa, and it will be kept clear by sharp lines of distinction both from Europeans in South Africa and also from Natives outside the Union borders."[22] It must be obvious, of course, that no such thing as the development of an independent nation is really intended, for it is well known that long before this the Bantu would have tested their strength against the whites.[23]

The Amalgamative Situation

Where there is no white ruling class answerable to a foreign white power, and where amalgamation between the white and black population is far advanced, it becomes practically impossible to make lightness of complexion a definite mark of status. The color scheme is confused, and attempts

[20]Maurice S. Evans, op. cit., pp. 154–55.

[21]It should be observed that no native custom which contravenes the exploitative purpose of the white man will be allowed to stand.

[22]Op. cit., p. 31.

[23]Brookes puts it in this way: "Here then would be a subject race, which was at the same time proletariat, asked in a shrinking world to keep clear of both pan-Africanism and Bolshevism, and be contented with a permanently inferior position in its own land. It would have become by education and experience group-conscious. It would have constantly dinned into its ears theories of nationalism and before its eyes examples of nationalism in practice. It would organize in self-defense. And it would not be otherwise than that that organization should be of an anti-white character." Ibid., p. 32. See also Lord Olivier, *The Anatomy of African Misery*, pp. 68–84.

to arrange it involve delicate and socially distasteful issues. Even though a preponderance of dark-colored people are in the lower economic strata, the population is necessarily marbled with color. Therefore, the group cannot attain a white "universe of discourse" and consensus sufficiently strong to achieve clear-cut white dominance. In the interest of social peace, therefore, an official policy of non-interference with color relationships must be followed. Intermarriage becomes a matter of personal tastes, and there arises no organized sentiment for or against it. Individual cultural achievements tend to be estimated on their merits; and unless some powerful foreign white economic clique, such as American tourists and businessmen in Brazil, initiates opposite racial tendencies, such a population is well on its way to complete amalgamation.

It is interesting to inquire into the reasons for these highly amalgamated populations. Europeans of Mediterranean stock settled Latin America and they have mixed quite readily with the colored peoples. The Anglo-Saxons have also mixed their blood in the north. But there are no intermarriage prohibition laws in Latin America. We have suggested that in race relations the desires of the whites are controlling and that these will manifest themselves differently in different situations. These desires are affected, however, by still other social determinants. Among these the intensity of nationalistic and imperialistic social attitudes of the European nation from which the whites came seems most significant.[24]

Directed nationalism gives the individual his group conception of himself; his personal ego tends to be raised to the level of his national pretensions. Therefore, the greater the nationalism, the more inflated will be the individual's conception of himself, and the greater his unwillingness to intermarry with other peoples. Nationalism emphasizes to the individual the vital necessity of retaining and enhancing group identity. It propagates the feeling that the individual is an altogether superior being even among persons of his own color though of another nation. It stimulates "group conceit." While the sex urge may overcome nationalistic sentiments, the

[24]Parker T. Moon associates these concepts: "Nationalism means that people considering themselves similar in language, 'race,' culture, or historical traditions should constitute a separate sovereign state; imperialism, on the contrary, means domination of non-European native races by totally dissimilar European nations. Antithetical as these two principles may seem, the latter is derived from the former through economic-nationalism or neo-mercantilism." *Imperialism and World Politics,* p. 33.

latter may be strong enough to retard intermarriage significantly. Among the Japanese (a people of color) intense nationalism and exploitative zeal have evidently limited the possibility of their amalgamating with their conquered peoples. It should be stated also that nationalism had its beginnings and achieved its highest perfection among white peoples, Europeans. "Nationalism is unthinkable before the emergence of the modern state in the period from the sixteenth to the eighteenth century." Like the racial antagonism which it inspires, then, "nationalism is not a natural phenomenon, not a product of 'eternal' or 'natural' laws; it is a product of the growth of social and intellectual factors at a certain stage of history."[25]

Intense nationalism such as that developed among the northern industrial European states tends to transform the subjects of a nation into a sect with national prayers and national hymns. These appeals strive to be mandatory upon the Deity, aggressive, and symbolic of national destiny in a context of assumed aspirations of other peoples and nations. The religious loyalties of the Middle Ages were "transmuted into the political loyalties" of the rising state. "European nationalism," says Leonard Woolf, "became a religion with the state as the object of worship. The idea of an empire became closely connected with the idea of patriotism in the minds of nationalists."[26] This state religion, nationalism, may be as effective in limiting intermarriage between, say, Englishmen and some people of color as Mohammedanism is in restricting the marriage of Moslems with, say, Christians.

Groups, even within single states, who are bent upon racial aggression always carry the flag and sing the national hymn. Moreover, it should be observed as a fact of prime significance that bourgeois nationalism is anti-democratic and consequently anti-proletarian. In saying that nationalism is the emotional basis of race prejudice we are not presenting the question one step removed from solution. Nationalism is an integral

[25]Hans Kohn, *The Idea of Nationalism,* pp. 4, 6. See also *Nationalism, A Report by a Study Group of Members of the Royal Institute of International Affairs,* Chap. III.

[26]Op. cit., p. 44. "The violent racialism to be found in Europe today," says Julian Huxley, "is a symptom of Europe's exaggerated nationalism: it is an attempt to justify nationalism on a non-nationalist basis, to find a basis in science for ideas and policies which are generated internally by a particular economic and political system." *Race in Europe,* Oxford Pamphlets on World Affairs, No. 5, p. 31.

part of the non-material cultural imperatives of capitalism, and it has developed as a function of the rise of capitalism.[27] It provides the collective attitude for capitalist aggression and exploitation of other peoples. Says Carlton J. H. Hayes:

> . . . prior to the advent of modern nationalism obvious physical differences were generally viewed as interesting results of climate or curious freaks of nature, and the popular prejudice was not so great as to prevent the New World from a very considerable fusion of white emigrants, especially those from tradition- ally Catholic countries of Portugal, Spain, and France with red Indians, and even with blacks. . . . It was only in the nineteenth century—the century of rising, raging nationalism—which universally magnified racial prejudices and racial intolerances.[28]

Of course love for one's country, the desire to be among one's own people, is not nationalism. This is the more passive emotion, which may be called patriotism. Says Sombart: "Patriotism . . . is that indefinable power exercised upon the soul by the sound of the mother tongue, by the harmony of the [folk] song, by many peculiar customs and usages, by the whole history and poetry of the home land."[29]

But nationalism is more than the emotional set of a people in inter- national competitive struggle; it is particularly an exploitative, socio- psychological instrument of actual or potential ruling classes; and it seeks its principal support and effective expression in an organized capi- talist state. The more nationalistic a people, the more secure the state, which is always at the service of the ruling class especially. Therefore, the propagation and intensification of nationalism becomes the indispensable duty of the ruling class; and when, as a ruling people, whites find themselves among a people of color, their nationalism tends to be exclusive. Should counternationalism arise, there will be conflict on the spot.

In the past offensive nationalism has been most thoroughly developed among the British, who have been fairly consistent in maintaining their identity among peoples of color. The British and Americans take their nationalism for granted. On the other hand, one has simply to glance at the

---

[27]See Carlton J. H. Hayes, *Essays on Nationalism,* Chap. II.

[28]Ibid., pp. 235–36.

[29]*Socialism and the Social Movement in the Nineteenth Century.*

teachings of modern Germany and Italy to perceive the relationship between nationalism and ethnic relations.[30]

Besides the foregoing explanation we may observe the difference in colonizing policy of the Latin and Anglo-Saxon peoples. Spain and Portugal, in their early contact with colored peoples, were influenced by the medieval idea of Christianizing the heathen and of commercial exploitation of native resources. In pursuance of this end, therefore, amalgamation with the colored peoples was advocated as a salutary colonial policy; the white population grew imperceptibly upon this basic social attitude. Where, however, as in North America, the whites came later as settlers with the avowed purpose of taking over and of making the country their home, amalgamation has not been accepted as a policy. Thus, in addition to nationalism, the purpose of the whites, whether exploitation or settlement, tends to determine the type of race relationship which will develop.

[30]"In no way conceived as an anti-Black movement, South African nationalism has become so, as a result of the psychological impossibility of including the Bantu in a program appealing inevitably so largely to sentiment and emotion." Edgar H. Brookes, op. cit., pp. 26–27.

Recently both Dr. Robert E. Park and Dr. Donald Pierson attempted to explain the ethnic situation in Brazil. Both, however, seem unconvincing. "Brazil," says Park, "is a vast country and has been colonized . . . by a wide variety of peoples. . . . With the exception of the Italians, these different peoples have settled in more or less closed communities in widely separated parts of a vast territory. Dependent upon water transportation rather than upon rail to maintain economic and political unity, Brazil has been haunted by the fear that the country would some day fall apart. Under these circumstances, it has seemed that the security and solidarity of the nation depended upon its ability to assimilate and ultimately to amalgamate its different immigrant populations. From this point of view, the Negro has not constituted a problem." *Negroes in Brazil,* by Donald Pierson, pp. xix–xx.

From this statement we do not know whether Park means that Brazil adopted a formal policy of white integration and national solidarity; and certainly it does not follow that Negroes must necessarily have been included in any assimilation policy among Brazilian whites.

Pierson's explanation is truistic. "It may be," he hypothesizes, "that the Portuguese, like the Moors and other Mohammedans, were . . . a 'color blind' people; that is, awareness of color and other racial differences were not so pronounced with them as with us." Ibid., p. 327. Probably this does not say much more than that the Portuguese are not a color-conscious people because they were not color-conscious. Furthermore, the statement has a biological ring. Reference to retinal capacity or any other such implication of innate conditioning ordinarily leads through sociological blind alleys. It will not help us very much in an explanation of the relationship of the Portuguese and the natives in, say, Angola, East Africa.

Moreover, the Protestant religion of the northern European whites, whose early colonization was mainly private enterprise,[31] and the Roman Catholic faith of the Latins, whose early colonization was under the aegis of a monarch, are important considerations in explaining the difference in these racial situations.[32] Among the Latins there was a strong tradition in favor of a continuation of the old religious criterion of equality, while among the Anglo-Saxons an objective, capitalistic orientation facilitated the maneuvering of the colored people into positions which seemed most suitable to their continued segregation. In this discussion it has been taken as understood that neither Spain nor Portugal ever attained the industrial development of northern Europe.

The Nationalistic Situation

In reaction to white dominance, a large colored population may possibly become restless and revolt against the system. Usually, for a short period of time, whiteness becomes exceedingly depreciated, while persons of color assume the prestige of former white rulers. There is such a budding reaction in India today; the Indian Mutiny of 1857 almost succeeded in turning the color scheme. "In Haiti, discrimination runs against the white man rather than against the Negro. A public career for a person of purely Caucasian origin would be rarely, if ever, possible."[33]

Such a country, however, cannot be isolated from the rest of the world; hence, in spite of possible local desires, its world policies must be couched in terms of world opinion, and with this goes an ever-present insistence upon white supremacy.[34] Thus all the local variants of race relations are

[31]For a brief discussion of this, see Edward Potts Cheyney, *European Background of American History,* pp. 123–46.

[32]In describing the place of religion in the colonization of Latin America, Professor Bailey W. Diffie concludes: "It is doubtful whether there is an example of an institution in any country, in, any epoch, whose responsibility for the type of civilization was as great as that of the colonial Catholic Church."Op. cit., p. 269.

[33]Chester Lloyd Jones, *Caribbean Backgrounds and Prospects,* p. 28.

[34]Jacques Barzun expresses this idea: "Equally important, though generally overlooked, is the fact that articulate minorities in other countries than Germany are fully as much engaged in thinking and talking about race. The only difference is that no other government has yet gone so far as the Nazi regime in adopting race as a popular slogan. . . . But read attentively the press and political literature, not only of England, France, Italy, and the United States, but also Mexico, Turkey, Rumania, and Scandinavia: you will not read very far before you are told or left to infer that whites are unquestionably superior to the colored races; that Asiatic

more or less conditioned by this international belief. The idea of white superiority hangs over the world like a great mist, and former attempts to lift it have resulted only in its condensation over the intractable area. In this Great Britain has set the ultimate pattern of intrigue, subtlety, and force in dealings with peoples of color; she is the great modern stabilizer of world white dominance. As Briffault puts it: "There is indeed no parallel in history, ancient or modern, to the dominance which, in the nineteenth century, England came to wield over the world."[35] And the source of this domination is undoubtedly England's imperialistic achievements among colored peoples.

A Special Case?

We have presented here some typical patterns of race relations; some of their features, however, may vary from case to case. Cuba and the Dominican Republic are countries with highly mixed populations; they should be like Brazil in racial adjustment, but they are smaller and too dependent upon the United States and Great Britain. Thus they are more like those countries where there is a small white ruling class. Haiti and Liberia ought to be free from "color consciousness"; if they were, however, they would be further atrophied in isolation. For instance, in establishing personal contacts with the English and Americans especially, Haiti understands that it is expedient to send forward her lighter colored persons. Our whole analysis, of course, rests upon the basic idea of a white-colored relationship. Indeed we now have a conceptual basis for a world study of race relations. By following Europeans in their contacts with peoples of color a world map of types of race prejudice and discrimination may be made.

But it may not be easy to retire the belief that race prejudice and racial domination are inherent social attitudes among all races. A friendly critic expostulated with the writer on the score that he has not accounted for the prejudices obtaining between non-white races. That he has not shown, for

Peril is a race-peril; that the Japanese of late seem to have become very yellow indeed . . . that the great American problem is to keep the Anglo-Saxon race pure from the contamination of Negro (or southern European, or Jewish) 'blood.' The quarrel about race and blood is often carried even closer home, as when we are informed that among the whites the tall blond Nordics are a superior breed, destined to rule the world, and that brown-eyed, round-headed Latins, whether in Europe or in South America, are a degenerate, revolutionary lot." *Race, A Study of Modern Superstition*, pp. 6–7.

[35]*Decline and Fall of the British Empire*, p. 9.

instance, what kind of race prejudice exists between Chinese and Japanese or between Japanese and Filipinos in Hawaii, and that Hawaii itself should not have been included in the typical ruling-class situation described above.

The racial situation in Hawaii seems so complex and even unique that it may be well to inquire whether, indeed, it should be excluded from our generalization. In the first place, the history of early contact between whites and Hawaiians has not been exceptional. The effects of early white contact were the liquidation of Hawaiian culture, the decimation of the population, and the control of economic life in the country by whites. The Beards summarize it in this way: "Though [the Hawaiians] were converted to Christianity and taught to read and write, economic competition, whisky, and disease cut them down like grain before a sickle. And in the process the whites got control of nearly all the land in the kingdom, overcoming the cupidity and resistance of the dusky proprietors by the lure of money and pressures of various kinds."[36]

The Hawaiians were humanely subdued, but the purpose of the white man was as determined as ever; and in the end, Queen Liliuokalani, in the hands of the sugar planters, was as pathetic and helpless a figure as the great Inca, Atahualpa of Peru, before Friar Valverde and Pizarro. Only the conquistadors had a less understanding world with which to rationalize and, consequently, could work upon the "primitives" with greater expedition and acclaim. At any rate, there was no trace of race prejudice among the Hawaiians on first contact with whites.

Hawaii is not a white man's country; white men constitute a small ruling class. And typical of this situation, there are no Anglo-Saxon laborers or field workers. What the Beards say about conditions even before the fall of royalty in Hawaii is essentially true today. "In spite of the royal government maintained in the 'palace' at Honolulu, approximately five thousand whites, mainly Americans, were the real masters of eighty thousand natives, Chinese, and Japanese. In short, the fate of the Hawaiian Islands was already sealed. They were to become an imperial province inhabited by Orientals and directed by white capitalists."[37]

[36]Charles A. and Mary R. Beard, *The Rise of American Civilization*, p. 357.

[37]Op. cit., p. 358. For a discussion of later population figures, see *The American Empire*, William H. Haas, ed., pp. 228–35; and William C. Smith, "Minority Groups in Hawaii," *The Annals*, Vol. 223, September 1942, pp. 38–39.

We should expect in Hawaii that, the more individuals of mixed-blood approach the physical appearance of whites, the more, other things being equal, they would be favored by the ruling class. And such is in fact the case. Here the mixed-bloods form a liaison group, and a man's light color has economic value. Says Romanzo Adams, "White employers and executives, who tend to favor the lighter complexioned part-Hawaiians for the positions of greater dignity and income, would say that they are more capable."[38] It must follow, then, that lightness of color would be an asset in the marriage bargain and that the birth of a light-complexioned child would be a blessing.[39] In explanation Adams says: "At first the light complexion was associated with superiority of status, then it became a sign of superiority, and now tends to be regarded as superior in itself."[40]

Furthermore, we should not expect the whites to raise a racial issue publicly in Hawaii, and consequently not to have it so raised at all. But this, of course, does not preclude their playing one race against the other in their own interest. When during the last quarter of the nineteenth century the Chinese began to leave the plantations to seek opportunities about the cities, the white planters conducted a bitter campaign against them; but it was relatively weak because it lacked anti-racial content. On the West Coast it would have had different results. The few thousand whites in Hawaii had to appeal to other colored races, and an anti-racial campaign would surely have rebounded. "Had a white man coined a color slogan to fling at the Chinese, it would have hit the Hawaiians, whose friendly co-operation was necessary, with even greater offense."[41]

Sometime later the sugar and pineapple growers leveled the same kind of attack against the Japanese. Now they said that the Chinese made good laborers but that the Japanese were "cocky, quarrelsome, independent, and altogether too numerous."[42] The Japanese, of course, were brought in to take the place of the formerly unmanageable Chinese. One thing, however,

---

[38]Op. cit., p. 106.

[39]Ibid., pp. 104, 106, 107.

[40]Ibid., p. 107. Cf. William C. Smith, "The Hybrid in Hawaii as a Marginal Man," *The American Journal of Sociology*, XXXIX, pp. 462ff.

[41]Romanzo Adams, op. cit., pp. 59, 61.

[42]See Louis R. Sullivan, "The Labor Crisis in Hawaii," *Asia*, Vol. XXIII, No. 7, July 1923, pp. 511ff.

they did not dare to call the Japanese yellow, a fact which deprived them of their keenest weapon of exploitation.

In Hawaii there is considerable intraracial organization, especially among first-generation immigrants; but this fact is not crucial in the situation. Naturally, if there are unassimilated colored races in the population, they will not be struggling against their color for position in the culture. The first-generation East Indians in Trinidad, for example, are plantation workers; they live like Hindus. They must first be ensnared by the capitalist compulsives of European culture before their striving for advancement comes face to face with the purpose of the white ruling class. The new immigrants continue to live more or less in the cultural haven of their fellow immigrants.[43]

William C. Smith indicates clearly the spirit of the racial situation in Hawaii:

> It is a matter of tradition and principle that there is or should be no prejudice. That is a doctrine to which the leading spokesmen for the Territory subscribe, and practically all members of the community feel bound to maintain it. . . . Beneath this apparently calm surface, however, are found inequality, discrimination, prejudice, cynicism, and bitterness. The plantation system . . . has manipulated the importation of laborers . . . so that a small group of white Americans are in control not only of the sugar industry but of all aspects of life in the Territory.
>
> Much is said about the educational opportunities in the islands, and the young people are urged to use them in order to become good Americans. They are told about the "room at the top" that is open to all on an equal basis. The children go through the schools and even through the university looking forward to the days when they will play important roles in the further unfolding of the great American epic. . . . Many, however, are awakened quite rudely from their dreams when,

[43]Jitsuichi Masuoka has studied race preference among Japanese in Hawaii, the most solidly organized and least assimilated racial group in the islands. Briefly, he finds that the first- and second-generation Japanese together prefer to have, as playmates of their children: first Japanese, second the ruling-class whites, then Chinese, and lastly—the tenth and eleventh racial choice—the Filipinos and Puerto Ricans. They show a decided preference for white-Hawaiian mixed-bloods over the Asiatic-Hawaiian. Barring the influence of certain cultural sympathies developed in the Orient, such as those toward the Koreans, the Japanese follow in their preference the racial status pattern dominated by the ruling-class whites in Hawaii. Masuoka explains variations from this pattern in terms of reaction. "Not infrequently," he says, "[members of the second-generation Japanese] resent the superior status of the whites, their tendency to maintain an obvious air of superiority, and their disposition to patronize other races." "Race Preference in Hawaii," *The American Journal of Sociology,* Vol. XLI, March 1936, pp. 635–41.

with diplomas in hand, they seek employment. Then they find barriers, some of them very subtle, to be sure, while their Caucasian classmates . . . move unopposed into the preferred positions.[44]

In Hawaii, then, a man's color is a matter of no little concern to him. Officially all persons, white or colored, are equal; but in practice the color of the Anglo-Saxon is economically most valuable and, to be sure, socially most satisfying. Among the mixed-bloods, superiority ranks from this norm. In this situation, to study color prejudice from the point of view of the subordinated races would be to see the tail as wagging the dog.

Personality Factors

Two recognizable attitudes of superiority seem to develop in the ruling-class and bipartite situations. In the ruling-class situation colored people are not hopelessly depressed; for them the ceiling of opportunity is high, but attainable. Although the color ranks are practically checkmated by color cliques, color is never explicitly accepted by the group as a whole as a consideration limiting success. There are ordinarily sufficient instances of brilliant victories over color barriers to warrant sanguine illusions that they do not exist. Exemplifying cases of colored persons holding positions of enviable dignity are always available. As a consequence, colored people assume the bearing of freemen; indeed, not infrequently, success is accompanied by a show of exaggerated importance. The successful are impatient with the "degenerate masses," and they tend to remain aloof from any idea which seeks to identify them with the problems of colored people as a whole. The Negro leader, Marcus Garvey, on returning to Jamaica from the United States, realized the latter fact more vividly than he had expected.

Not so, however, in the bipartite situation. Here people of color tend to be humbled, not only by the engrossing importance of their color but also by the fact that the color interest is inevitably common to them all. Here the colored person of lowest class has an intuitive way of quickly establishing rapport with the most advanced colored gentleman, for the basis of their sympathy is elemental. It tends to keep the social-class hierarchy among them quite obtuse.

It is interesting to observe the pattern of behavior which develops when colored persons from these two cultures meet on common ground. In the

[44]Op cit., p. 43.

United States, West Indian Negroes are likely to be first admired by American Negroes for their intractability to color restrictions and for their relative absence of a sense of inferiority in their dealings with white people as such. Later, however, the West Indian who has been accustomed to picking his friends and who puts emphasis upon family status is likely to arouse resentment among Americans. The West Indian frequently finds the American wanting in dignity and class refinement; Americans, on the other hand, are likely to find him conceited and boring. The pattern of relationship is by no means thus limited, but we shall not dilate upon it.

In the case of whites, attitudes of superiority are more likely to arise in the bipartite situation. Here white gentlemen and aristocrats, who despise all forms of menial work, are developed. The upper classes assume a condescending, paternal attitude to all lower-class persons, and their sense of power tends to be fully supported by the obsequiousness of the colored masses. In the ruling-class situation, on the other hand, the white man is generally compromising. He is living in a colored man's country and his attitude toward white people "from home" tends to be apologetic. The latter usually have great prestige among them, and the need for explaining their position usually puts whites in such a situation on the defensive. Usually they are working toward the end that they shall be able to merit retirement and a comfortable life "back home."

Probably the most significant difference between the ruling-class and the bipartite situations is to be found in their segregation practices. In the ruling-class situation there is ostensibly no segregation; in the bipartite situation, however, the races are segregated both in custom and in written law. There is what might be called white exclusiveness in the ruling-class situation; that is to say, the whites segregate themselves[45] in residential areas and in their social activities. Overtly the practice is made to rest on the presumption that every man has a right to choose his own associates and to live exclusively if he so desires. Yet the occasional acquisition of residential property by a colored family in a white community never results in a public disturbance; it never results even in a public discussion. Such notices as

---

[45]Self-imposed segregation need not be degrading. It is of the nature of privacy, and the whites resort to it primarily for the purpose of conserving and augmenting their powers of dominance and control.

FOR WHITES ONLY or *COLORED* and *WHITE* do not appear in this situation, while both colored people and whites ordinarily attend schools and churches without overt segregation.

In the bipartite situation, on the other hand, explicit segregation is at the foundation of all the racial discrimination and exploitative practices of the whites. In fact, segregation is here absolutely necessary to maintain white ruling-class dominance. The colored zones, belts, and camps are fundamental restrictions upon the colored people. They restrict the latter's freedom of physical movement, the *sine qua non* of a normal life under capitalism.

It would be an egregious error to think of imposed racial segregation as a mutually desirable spatial limitation between the races. What segregation really amounts to is a sort of perennial imprisonment of the colored people by the whites. Moreover, this imprisonment provides the proper milieu for the planned cultural retardation of the colored people. Here they may mill and fester in social degeneracy with relatively minimal opportunity for even the most ambitious of them to extricate themselves.

In this situation, also, the concrete evidence of what is known as white racial superiority is at hand. Gobinesque contrasts between whites and colored people can now be easily supported by even mensurative data. In the ruling-class situation there is the stark fact that the lighter the color of the individual the greater, other things being equal, his economic and cultural advantage. Ordinarily the colored people take this fatalistically; that is to say, they attribute it implicitly to some inherent misfortune of being born colored. But they will not understand an ideology built about the assumption of mental inferiority of colored people as a whole, for the evidence developed in this situation is ordinarily opposed to it.

In the bipartite situation, on the other hand, the cultural limitations achieved by segregation are so pervasive that color inferiority could be pointed out on almost any count. The ocular proof of this inferiority, of course, serves to justify the continued exploitation and discrimination of the colored people; it never serves to support a conclusion that, the greater the social handicap of a people, the greater the need for social assistance.

Crisis and Panic in Race Relations

Although in the foregoing discussion we have referred to the personality problems of individuals, it may be well to deal a little more specifically with this subject. In both the ruling-class and bipartite situations persons of color are likely to be confronted with a series of racial crises and panics due to discrimination. They may be called upon, even as children, to adjust and accommodate themselves to reactions ranging all the way from the simple snub to the baying of dogs and the lynchers' rope. This is part of the process by which the individual achieves a conception of himself as a colored person.

The slighting and snubbing which ordinarily crisscross the lower levels of intensity in race relations are sometimes identified with similar phenomena in social-class relationships. But they are not really identical. The social climber is better prepared to understand the pretensions to exclusiveness of upper-class persons; the poor man with resignation usually leaves the ways of the rich to God. At any rate, the social-class system is at relative peace with the techniques for maintaining social distance among status groups. Discrimination based upon color, on the other hand, may involve severe mental anguish and panic. The social norms do not allow a lower-class person the right to "rub elbows" with upper-class persons, but these norms do impel the colored person to rise in status individually as if the paradoxical restraints of color were non-existent. In other words, the system judges the colored person as if he were under no social handicaps of color; he is, therefore, frequently confounded and irked in the realization that his color is to him the decisive social fact of his life.

A rebuff due to one's color puts him in very much the situation of the very ugly person or one suffering from a loathsome disease who is made to feel suspected or exposed. The suffering which this is likely to engender may be aggravated by a consciousness of incurability and even blameworthiness, a self-reproaching which tends to leave the individual still more aware of his loneliness and unwantedness. The extreme situation of terror in racial antagonism is probably the manhunt of the lynching mob. Here the colored person becomes the baited beast frantically alone before the fully uncovered teeth of race prejudice.

There seem to be two principal situations in which the colored person may be distressed or tormented for his color: (a) among other persons of lighter color and (b) among whites. In the ruling-class situation discrimination is based upon smaller differences in shades of color, but it does not culminate in serious violence as in the bipartite situations. As a means of color control there is more overt teasing, laughing, and ridicule in the ruling-class situation than in the bipartite situation, but in both these situations the colored person who finds himself among whites—in school, at a hotel, or in semi-public social gatherings, such as dances and picnics—may be made to experience the same paroxysms of shifting emotions.

The dominant socio-psychological pressure of color prejudice seems to produce a collapsing effect upon the individual's self-respect—to render him ashamed of his existence. It is intended to reduce him to a condition of no social consequence, and to a lesser or greater extent he commonly accepts the definition. The achievement of a degree of enforced isolation by the various methods of overshadowing, excluding, and estranging the colored person regulates the color system and gives each individual a fairly accurate racial conception of himself.

In this section we have attempted only to characterize the situation in which the individual may be tortured by race prejudice. The conditions for specific cases may vary tremendously. Moreover, the range of possible incidents is probably unlimited. In the United States, for instance, the discriminatory attitude may produce results ranging all the way from a slight nettling of the colored person to a full-blown lynching for "trying to act like a white man."

The Eurasians

The ruling-class situation describes the relationship which characterizes the race problem of the Eurasians. The case of the Eurasians of India is particularly revealing, however, for they stand at the junction between caste and race relations. The Eurasians of India are a white-Indian mixed-blood people, and mainly a British-Indian mixture. Before the Portuguese, who came earlier than the British, fully understood the temper of the Hindus, they actually planned a mixed-blood intermediary. At Goa they encouraged the marriage of Portuguese men to Indian women. "No less than 450 of [Albuquerque's] men were thus married, and others who desired to follow their example were so numerous that [the navigator] had great difficulty in granting their requests."[46] These mixed-bloods, however, never assumed the role designed for them. Their status and identity dwindled with the failing fortunes of the Portuguese. Therefore, the significant group of Eurasians today are mainly of British descent.[47]

The problem of the Eurasians is different from that of any other mixed-blood group because the colored masses from which this class came belong to a caste system. Inadequate recognition of this fact has resulted in very much spurious thinking, not only about the status of the Eurasians themselves, but also about that of mixed-bloods in all other parts of the world.[48]

The Eurasians are naturally conditioned to seek assimilation with the British, but the caste system puts the British in a unique position of opposing strategy. Ordinarily this small white ruling class in India should have been constrained to yield many social privileges to the Eurasians, but the former has sensed its strategic position and is thus able to make almost unlimited demands upon these mixed-bloods without necessarily making any concessions to them.

As a characteristic of this situation, we observe Eurasian girls preferring to marry lighter men—even white men—while Eurasian men seek desperately the color status of native whites. As Kenneth E. Wallace, himself a Eurasian, says: "The light-hued Eurasian is often tempted to pose as a domiciled European."[49] The status of the Eurasians with respect to the caste system, be it remembered, is that of outcastes. The British are also outcastes, but they have a society of their own in India. The mixed-bloods are dependent upon this society not only because they were nurtured in it, but also because practically no other means of livelihood are open to them. No

[46]Edgar Thurston, *Castes and Tribes of Southern India,* Vol. II, pp. 233–34. See also Frederick Charles Danvers, *The Portuguese in India,* Vol. I, p. 217.

[47]"The descendants of the British in India have sorted out into three distinct groups. The first comprises those who were sent to England for their education and never returned to India, or who on retirement from service settled down in England. These have gradually been absorbed into the native population of England, and are no longer distinguished from the Britisher. The second continues in India as a distinct race. The third is being, or has been, absorbed into the Indian Christian population." Herbert A. Stark, *Hostages to India,* p. 36.

[48]The authors who have mistaken this situation are numerous indeed. The following may be taken as a type of reference: "The stigma which all countries attach to half-breeds is perhaps nowhere felt more keenly than in India, where the Eurasian is rejected both by the pure European whom he imitates and the natives of the country whom he affects to despise." *Bengal Census Report, 1881.* Quoted by William Crooke, *Things Indian,* p. 192. See also, to this effect, E. B. Reuter, *The Mulatto in the United States,* p. 19; Ogburn and Nimkoff, *Sociology,* p. 387; and Paul Fredrick Cressey, "The Anglo-Indians: A Disorganized Marginal Group," *Social Forces,* December 1935, Vol. 14, p. 267.

[49]*The Eurasian Problem,* p. 30.

wonder they are preoccupied with their color. "A peculiar snobbishness . . . might be noted, the fairer looking down on the darker, all despising the Indian and affecting the European. . . . It might also be observed that as a community they do not cohere, that they lack unity, pride of race, and initiative."[50] "Pride of race" is, of course, a sentiment which can hardly be achieved by these people. Their social pride can have no meaning in India unless they become a caste; on the other hand, bred to British culture, they have the alternative of pride in European civilization.

The Eurasians, then, unlike, say, the Jamaican mixed-bloods, are caught between caste prejudice and race prejudice. And indeed, although their cultural sophistication is generally above that of the darker colored masses, the repulsion of caste is probably more decisive than that of race. Thus the mixed-bloods in India cannot become the leaders of the Indian masses, for Brahmanism has already provided for non-intercourse with them. Their ostracism comes natural with the Hindus, since, unless the people are conquerors, their social system has no way of respecting persons outside of a caste. They cannot expect sympathy from the Hindu masses. Individually they may have social entree only by way of the lower strata of castes, and this at the dreadful expense of regressing toward an inferior cultural level. The British are conscious of the Indians' apathy toward the Eurasians; hence they can exploit them with impunity. Eurasians are inevitably dependent upon the British; they are Christian and Western in culture; their mothers were outcasted and their fathers insisted upon their westernization.

Here, then, is a mixed-blood group with a unique social problem. It is interesting to observe some verbal manifestations of the clash of social interests in this situation. The British call the Eurasians "half-castes." This term is inaccurate, but it serves well the former's derogatory purpose. The caste system has made no provision for half-castes. A person is either incaste or outcaste. Of course his caste status may be questionable, but then his living will ordinarily be precarious. The offspring of parents from two different castes are not half-castes; they are full members of some caste. What the whites in India really mean is that Eurasians are half-race or rather mixed-race. They are literally thinking of blood. On the other hand, the East

[50]Ibid., pp. 5–6.

Indians call the Eurasians "outcastes." In the sense that all people in the world who do not belong to the caste system are outcastes, the term is applicable. It is not so well used when it implies that Eurasians have either been expelled from some other caste or that they constitute part of the community of depressed castes. Finally, the mass of Eurasians look upon themselves as a true mixed-blood people who seek assimilation to the dominant culture. They exploit their lightness of color as a technique of achieving freedom of cultural participation[51] and call themselves Anglo-Indians or Eur-Asians.

The White Woman

We have mentioned the fact that in the ruling-class situation there are no coercive sanctions against men of color marrying white women; but in all color situations, with possible exception to caste members in India and nationalistic Japanese, there is a social urge among colored men to marry white women. This urge, of course, is not an "ungovernable sexual craving" for white flesh, as some rationalists would have us believe, for women of any color are totally sufficient for the satisfaction of any such simple desire. In fact, under such passion, white men have found colored women of every race fully adequate. Thus it must not be supposed that it is the white woman as a mere sexual object which is the preoccupation of colored men; it is rather her importance to him as a vehicle in his struggle for economic and cultural position. The particular advantage of a man's white skin is not that he has a supreme privilege of claiming a white woman in marriage; indeed, many do not choose to marry at all. His color, however, is a symbol of relatively unlimited cultural opportunity. So far as the sexual opportunity of marrying a white woman is concerned, some white men would gladly be colored; but so far as cultural opportunity is concerned, none would rather be colored.

The value of a white skin tends to depreciate directly with cultural advantage. When the Portuguese were forced to leave Goa, their proud light-skinned mixed-bloods stood face to face with the cold caste system.

[51]The Chinese Eurasians are evidently confronted with a similar situation. They are hedged between the powerful self-sufficient Chinese culture and the declining influence of the race-conscious Europeans. The irresponsibility of most of their white fathers is also against them. See Herbert Day Lamson, "The Eurasian in Shanghai," *The American Journal of Sociology,* Vol. XLI, 1936, pp. 642–48.

"Confronted with lack of patrons, lack of friends, lack of agricultural facilities, and lack of every resource, they sank rapidly in the social scale, and in the space of two centuries the majority of them have reverted to Indian stocks."[52]

In situations where Negroes may not marry white women the principal fear is not that if they did it would become more difficult for a white man to obtain a white wife, for the hostility is not diminished when Negroes come into the area with white women from abroad. The size of the white sex ratio is not ordinarily a factor. Neither are white Southerners, for example, particularly disturbed over the fact that in other countries there is considerable interracial marriage. We should miss the point entirely if we take as literally describing the situation the defense that white men must protect their sisters and daughters from the lust of black men. The status quo would be as effectively damaged if colored men went to Mars, married Martian white women, and brought them into the South as wives.

Therefore, it is not intermarriage, per se, which is determining, but rather the cultural advantage which restriction secures to the white group. Protecting the "honor and sanctity of white womanhood" constitutes a most convincing war cry and an excellent covering for the basic purpose that colored people must never be given the opportunity to become the cultural peers of whites. Incidentally, the greater the insistence upon the purity of white womanhood, the greater is the tendency of whites to conceive of colored women as undespoilable wenches. A Natal resident, Negro or Indian, may go to England and marry a white woman, but this would be practically out of the question in Natal. To return to South Africa with her would be to threaten white dominance in that area.

It is interesting to observe that the Bantu leader D. D. T. Jabavu, in listing some of the grievances of his people, never once intimated that they were handicapped by a limitation of the opportunity to marry white women. What seems important to him are such things as the extortionate poll tax on Bantu males only, the crowding of South African natives on restricted land areas, unfair wages and definite limitation of opportunity to rise occupationally, police brutality and the curfew, partiality of the laws and their unjust administration, grossly unequal provisions for education, and

[52]Herbert Alick Stark, op. cit., pp. 6–7.

denial of suffrage.[53] Yet, even so, there is a close association between cultural parity and intermarriage. As we have already intimated, amalgamation is the final solution of race problems. To grant cultural parity is to eliminate the basis of intermarriage restrictions; and to permit intermarriage is to make cultural discrimination on the basis of race impossible. Since the Negro man is ordinarily the cultural aggressor, he may proceed both to whittle away the cultural advantage of whites and to marry white women, so that the physical basis of color discrimination may be finally obscured. In this strategy the white man who aims to preserve his cultural advantage is particularly his foe. The role which the Negro woman will take depends upon the situation. Furthermore, there is no support either in fact or reason for the belief that it is only the dross of colored men who desire intermarriage with white women; on the contrary, we should expect this desire to be experienced particularly among the most ambitious and aspiring colored men.

Intermarriage between whites and people of color has never taken place principally among the dregs of society. That this is a current belief is evidence of the effectiveness of the propaganda of white exploiting classes, propaganda which goes to make up the substance of race prejudice. When it was convenient for white men to marry Hottentot, or East Indian, or Hawaiian, or any other women of color, they ordinarily obtained women from the upper class. And they themselves were not degenerate. Now that

[53]"It is the little things," says Jabavu, "that tell most in our social relationship with the whites. if I am stranded in the rural areas, I dare not go to a Boer farm speaking English and wearing boots and a collar without inviting expulsion and execration; but if I go barefooted and collarless and in rags I shall enjoy the warmest hospitality. . . . Once when I quietly boarded a train at Middledrift, I was unexpectedly hailed by a white lady: 'Heigh, where are you going to, you black devil?' . . . In seaside resorts, we blacks can bathe . . . only in an absurdly small section of the beach where the edge is least desirable, elbowed out by miles of excellent frontage available for the happy white race, there being no resting seats for us although we pay town rates.

"In public hospitals, where there are no Bantu nurses, our lot is not always a happy one, and I can confirm this from the experience of one of my children at the hands of an unsympathetic white nurse. . . . In the Civil Service we are confined to junior clerkships, even in our native areas. . . . Positions as interpreters in the Supreme Court and many lower courts are a preserve for whites who, at least, can never be as proficient as the Bantu in the vernacular languages. . . . In many cases salesmen in shops delight in keeping us waiting while they gossip with their European friends, and flare out in anger, hurling vituperative epithets, if you dare humbly to interrupt and ask to be served." "Bantu Grievances," in I. Shapera, *Western Civilization and the Natives of South Africa,* pp. 285–99. See also Raymond Leslie Buell, op. cit., pp. 58–70, 118ff.

men of color—African, East Indian, West Indian, Chinese—are occasionally marrying white women, it may be shown that on the whole these men are from the upper or middle classes of the population. Of course we are not here speaking of prostitution, which is pathological intraracially as well.

Our hypothesis, then, is that to conceive of the mere presence or absence of intermarriage—that is to say, the idea of "keeping blood pure"—as a postulate in studies of race relations will almost always lead to sterile results. In race relations, solicitude about purity of blood has been a means, not an end. "Pure blood" has value only when in preserving it a calculable social advantage can be maintained.

The social situation will be determined by racial expediency rather than by supposed basic attitudes of racial integrity. In fact, Europeans are particularly lacking in endogamous attitudes. So far as readiness to mix their blood with others is concerned, they are probably as willing as any people in the world. The black, caste-conscious Hindu of southern India would be far more reluctant to intermarry than any white people. In Hawaii, where there are many ethnics, it is not white people but the Japanese who intermarry with other groups least. "Why, of all the white peoples of the world," says Romanzo Adams, "have the race-conscious Americans and British played the leading role in amalgamation with the Hawaiians? . . . The civilian [white] men have been much less numerous since 1878 than the Chinese, and they have been better provided with women of their own race, but they have, nevertheless, intermarried with the Hawaiian and part-Hawaiian women more than the Chinese have."[54]

Western civilization and Christianity in particular have developed no definite sanction against race mixture. In fact, romantic love, the antitheses of endogamy, is a social trait of Western culture. Depending upon the social situation, however, endogamy among whites may or may not have practical value. In some situations it has proved a most effective instrument for maintaining white dominance over peoples of color. When this is the case, whole philosophies and schools of anthropology are developed to give it natural justification and explanation; they are constrained to define it as an instinct. As a theme, "the powerful biological urge to maintain the purity

---

[54]Op. cit., pp. 121–22. As a cause of the high white intermarriage rate, Adams thinks: "The most important thing is just the being away from home—away from his parents, relatives, and neighbors." But distance away from home should hardly be a factor, since these same whites in India or South Africa would hardly intermarry with colored people.

of the white race" has been most satisfying. What could be more natural, then, than to believe that intermarriage is the key to all problems of race relations? In racially dichotomized societies the status quo cannot be maintained without drastic sanctions against white-woman–colored-man marriage. In other words, the white woman is here in a critical position; defending her "purity" becomes a sacred duty. We may assume that the race problem is solved when the white woman becomes free to follow her sentiments in choosing either white man or colored man in marriage.

The Church and Race Relations

Elsewhere we have discussed the incompatibility of Christianity and caste and its freedom from anti-racial doctrines. The established Church, however, is far more flexible. All denominations of the Christian Church in whatever part of the world tend to follow the locally established pattern of race relations. Unlike applied Mohammedanism, for example, the Christian Church has no consistent ethical philosophy of race relations. Indeed, the Church has usually been the leader of the white purpose in the particular situation, and this is not entirely surprising. We do not expect the Church, as stabilizer of the morality of the social system, to counter the nationalism of the ruling class. Indeed, paradoxical as it may seem, race prejudice is in fact a decent and respectable attribute; it is a mark of refinement and a characteristic of aristocrats. Therefore, since the Church is ordinarily expected to be the author of social refinement, it has not only made terms with segregation and other discriminatory practices but also tends to perpetuate them in situations where even the popular social sanctions are relatively indifferent. One may expect, for example, to find frequent instances of Roman Catholics and Protestants segregating or excluding colored people from their schools and churches, not only in the South but also in the Northern United States where secular institutions may not segregate.

In color-class countries like Barbados, Jamaica, and Trinidad, the Church could be depended upon to perfect all the subtleties of color distinction. In short, the Church, being naturally conservative, sanctions and stabilizes the mundane interests of the ruling class.

Plan for Resolving a Racial Situation

We have already mentioned what seems to us to be the inevitable resolution of interracial conflict. Many conscientious students, however, believe that co-operation and good will between white and colored races will surely come if the whites are assured that the colored race has given up all designs upon race mixture. "For the fear of race-mixture," concludes R. F. Alfred Hoernle in reference to South Africa, "has poisoned in the past, and is still poisoning at present, all other relations between the two groups."[55] And this writer continues:

> The most we can aim at and hope is to reduce such relations to small proportions, by establishing the firmest possible will in both groups to maintain the rule that white shall marry white and black shall marry black, and that extramarital relations between white and black, with the resulting additions to the coloured population, are . . . to be avoided. It is a principle which has been established as one of the defining elements in group pride and group identity of the whites, and it is becoming similarly a defining element in the group pride and group identity of the Bantu. To ask whether it is right or wrong that both groups should build themselves upon this principle seems to me irrelevant and futile. . . .[56]

In these racially dichotomized societies the immediate problem tends to obscure long-run values, and they confuse symptoms with disease. The Bantu can give up neither the aim of amalgamation nor the desire for cultural equality without crystallizing his position of inferiority. The white man has made color a constituent element in economic competition; and to peoples of color, in immediate contact with whites, who cannot now or never become nationalistic, it is economically imperative that they accept this challenge and seek to liquidate the color impediment by amalgamation. The white man has set up the competitive norm; it seems, therefore, clearly preposterous to ask the colored people to remain unresponsive to it.

The Bantu, like other peoples of color, will certainly adopt the idea of progress with other traits of Western culture, and modern racial ideology goes with these. To follow a plan of racial segregation is to play completely into the hands of the white ruling class. Moreover, the apparent development of group pride among the Bantu can have but one meaning. It is a reaction; hence, the stronger it becomes, the greater the need for the expression of physical might among whites; in time we should expect this situation to be highly productive of Bantu nationalism.

[55]"Race Mixture and Native Policy in South Africa," in I. Shapera, op. cit., pp. 278–79.
[56]Ibid.

3.
Race Prejudice, Intolerance, and Nationalism

Race prejudice and intolerance are social attitudes that have not been clearly defined in discussions of intergroup antagonism. These attitudes have been confused particularly in descriptions and comparisons of Jews and Negroes as "minority groups," and the result has been an accumulation of many spurious conclusions. In this attempt to distinguish these attitudes we shall also consider in illustration the social situations of Negroes and Jews; then, by a somewhat different approach, we shall essay a definition of the social position of modern subordinate nationality groups and that of the Asiatics on the Pacific coast.

Intolerance

The common practice, in analyses of race relations, is to assume that race prejudice and intolerance are identical social facts. For instance, Dr. Ruth Benedict says:

> Traditional Anglo-Saxon intolerance is a local and temporal culture-trait like any other. . . . In this country it is obviously not an intolerance directed against a mixture of blood of biologically far-separated races, for upon occasion excitement mounts as high against the Irish Catholic in Boston, or the Italian in New England mill towns, as against the Oriental in California.[1]

We may illustrate this point further. According to Ellsworth Faris:

> The conflict between Jews everywhere and those among whom they live is a racial conflict. That the Jews belong to a separate biological race is doubtful and perhaps not true. Nevertheless the conflict is sociologically racial, for they are

---

[1] *Patterns of Culture*, p. 11. To the same effect Carlton Hayes asserts: "Intolerance toward Negroes in the United States is perhaps the acme of racial intolerance in modern nationalism . . . a nationalism which has been communicated from the West to the Far East may carry in its train to the Far East the racial intolerance as well as the international war which has characterized the West." *Essays on Nationalism*, pp. 237–38.

regarded as a separate race, are treated as a separate race, and hold themselves together as if they were a separate race.[2]

The conclusion here is explicit: there is no difference between anti-Semitism and race prejudice—and this is the question before us.

Anti-Semitism, to begin with, is clearly a form of social intolerance, which attitude may be defined as an unwillingness on the part of a dominant group to tolerate the beliefs or practices of a subordinate group because it considers these beliefs and practices to be either inimical to group solidarity or a threat to the continuity of the status quo. Race prejudice, on the other hand, is a social attitude propagated among the public by an exploiting class for the purpose of stigmatizing some group as inferior so that the exploitation of either the group itself or its resources or both may be justified. Persecution and exploitation are the behavior aspects of intolerance and race prejudice respectively. In other words, race prejudice is the socio-attitudinal facilitation of a particular type of labor exploitation, while social intolerance is a reactionary attitude supporting the action of a society in purging itself of contrary cultural groups.

Position of Jews and Negroes

We may think of intolerance as a suppressive attitude and of race prejudice as a limiting attitude. Anti-Semitism is an attitude directed against the Jews because they are Jews, while race prejudice is an attitude directed against Negroes because they want to be something other than Negroes. The Jew, to the intolerant, is an enemy within the society; but the Negro, to the race-prejudiced, is a friend in his place. As Joshua Trachtenberg points out, the Jew "is alien, not to this or that land, but to all Western society, alien in his habits, his pursuits, his interests, his character, his very blood. Wherever he lives he is a creature apart. He is the archdegenerate of the world, infecting its literature, its art, its music, its politics and economics with the subtle poison of his insidious influence, ripping out its moral foundation stone by stone until it will collapse in his hands."[3] Thus to the

---

[2]*The Nature of Human Nature*, p. 341. See also *Jews in a Gentile World*, Graeber and Britt, eds., p. 78, where J. O. Hertzler argues in support of Faris's conclusion that the Jews are a race "from the standpoint of sociology."

[3]*The Devil and the Jews*, p. 3. In the same vein Adolf Hitler attacked the Jew: "His blood-sucking tyranny becomes so great that riots against him occur. Now one begins to look more and more closely at the stranger and one discovers more and more new repellent features and characteristics in him, till the chasm becomes an unsurmountable one. In times of most

intolerant dominant group the Jew is not only an alien but also an aggressor against the society itself. "The Jew was the adversary without peer of Christendom, and *ipso facto* he was to be classed with all who sought destruction of the Church and of Christian society, whether they attacked from within or from without."[4]

This conception of the Jews as a guest-folk perverting and even damning the hospitality of their host has been turned to violent hostility against them.[5] Indeed, intolerance seems to contain an element of reciprocation, since the persecutor, irritated by the intractability or even the assumed destructive potentialities of the persecuted, tends also to feel tormented and persecuted. One anti-Semite has been quoted as saying: "While we pray for the Jews, they persecute and curse us!"[6] The Jews are thus conceived to be more than passively divisive; they are also charged with hating and betraying the society in which they live.

The Problem of Assimilation

Probably the clearest distinction between intolerance and race prejudice is that the intolerant group welcomes conversion and assimilation, while the race-prejudiced group is antagonized by attempts to assimilate. The Jews are a people who refuse to assimilate; that is to say, to give up their culture and lose their identity in the larger society. They conceive of the values of their culture as so significant or superior that they are willing to suffer considerable persecution rather than give them up. "[The Jews] have had a different faith, have refused intermarriage even when it was desired on the other side, have at times seemed to be impolite in refusing the Gentile's hospitality, and have regarded themselves as a special chosen people in a way which must often seem irritating to people who did not share the Jewish faith."[7] Thus, when

bitter distress the wrath against him finally breaks out, and the exploited and ruined masses take up self-defense in order to ward off the scourge of God. They have got to know him in the course of several centuries and they experience his mere existence as the same distress as the plague." *Mein Kampf,* p. 426.

[4]Joshua Trachtenberg, op. cit., p. 81.

[5]In an inverted expression of anti-Semitic aggression Hitler develops this passion for Jewish extermination: "[The Jew] pursues his course, the course of sneaking in among the nations and of gouging them internally, and he fights with his weapons, with lies and slanders, poison and destruction, intensifying the struggle to the point of bloodily exterminating his hated opponents." Op. cit., p. 960.

[6]Trachtenberg, op. cit., p. 182.

[7]Talcott Parsons in *Jews in a Gentile World,* p. 115.

the Jews are regarded as being stubborn, "as men who know the truth and deliberately reject it," violent emotions are ordinarily stirred up against them.

Probably most of the stability of the religio-cultural pertinacity of the Jews is due to the nature of their historical conflict with Christianity. After all, it is a Jew whom the Christians worship—a religious radical who causes the Jewish hierarchy so much embarrassment that they seem never to be able to accept him as their God. Jesus might have been able to organize His popular support for the forceful overthrow of the corrupt priesthood, the "serpents [who] devoured widows' houses," but the Romans would not have permitted such a show of physical power. The revolution was abortive, and the Jews encysted themselves with their traditional persecution ideology against all such future attacks.

Assuming the continuance of the present social order, the one condition of peace between Jews and Gentiles is that the Jews cease to be Jews. And they are apparently given extraordinary encouragement to do so. "If I were a Jew," Faris declares, "I should marry for love but I should try to marry a non-Jewish girl. There are excellent eugenic arguments for crossings of this sort and, if fate should work out this way, the gesture and example would count for much."[8] One has only to substitute the word "Negro" for "Jew" in the foregoing passage in order to appreciate the distinction between race prejudice and intolerance.

This fact of seeming to reward the object of intolerance for its conversion or contribution to social peace and harmony seems to be elemental in the phenomenon. Jesus had to ponder the implicit offer of the ruling elite—"All this power will I give thee, and the glory of them"—as a price of His selling out in the interest of the status quo. And, among many other instances, the purple of the Church was constantly held up before Erasmus of Rotterdam as a means of channeling his ideas. Indeed, some

---

[8]Ellsworth Faris, op. cit., p. 352. Probably no one will dream that it is possible for all Jews, say, in the United States to call a conference and thereupon decide to give up Judaism, after which anti-Semitism will have come to an end. The problem is infinitely more complicated. But this certainly is true: Almost any Jew, with comparatively little difficulty, may decide to marry a Gentile and bring up his children in the Christian tradition. As Edward A. Ross points out: "You may elude religious persecution by changing your creed, but you cannot dodge racial aggression by changing your race." "The Post-War Intellectual Climate," *The American Sociological Review,* Vol. 10, October 1945, p. 648.

of the best-paid, anti-socialist propagandists today are former "dangerous" radicals.[9] The intermarriage of Jews with Gentiles and of Negroes with whites are both infrequent occurrences, but the inhibiting social forces in each situation are essentially distinct.

Negroes and Jews as Allies

The question has been frequently raised as to the possibility of Negroes and Jews, as "minority groups," collaborating for the purpose of advancing their social position. Recently Dr. Werner Cahnman put it in this way: "Both Jews and Negroes are threatened by the same hatred and the same hostility. Upon the strength of this they could unite in action. But their reaction to the situation is different: the Jews are cautiously defending where the Negroes are militantly attacking."[10] Yet it is doubtful whether Jews and Negroes have a common basis for continuing action against the dominant group. In reality they are not "threatened by the same hostility," and there is some probability that there is as much reason for antagonism between them.[11]

In so far as Jews are bourgeois-minded businessmen and manufacturers, they are likely to be, at least implicitly, race-prejudiced. They will sooner understand the limiting racial policies of the ruling class than the ambition of Negroes for social equality. Because the Negroes are almost entirely a proletarian group, while the Jews tend to be professional and businessmen,[12]

[9]J. O. Hertzler, with some doubts about its ever occurring, reaches a similar conclusion. Says he: "To cease to be a cultural irritant the Jew must be completely assimilated . . . he must deliberately mould himself and his life on Gentile patterns. . . . He will have to be completely absorbed ethnically. That means he will have to marry non-Jews, generation after generation, until he has no grandparents who were considered as Jews and no children who by any chance might have any distinguishing 'Jewish' characteristics. . . . In general, he will have to disappear entirely as a Jew, be dissolved in the life and being of the larger world." In *Jews in a Gentile World,* p. 98.

[10]"An American Dilemma," *The Chicago Jewish Forum,* Vol. 3, No. 2, Winter, 1944–43, p. 94.

[11]For a discussion of Jewish and Negro relations in the United States, see Roi Ottley, *New World A-Coming,* pp. 122–36; Lunabelle Wedlock, *The Reactions of Negro Publications and Organizations to German Anti-Semitism;* Harold Orlansky, "A Note on Anti-Semitism among Negroes," *Politics,* Vol. 2, August 1943, pp. 250–52; and Kenneth B. Clark, "Candor about Negro-Jewish Relations," *Commentary: A Jewish Review,* Vol. I, February 1946, pp. 8–14.

[12]Gunnar Myrdal generalizes the situation this way: "Jews are the leading retail merchants in many Negro neighborhoods and are the leading employers of Negro servants in Northern cities. The natural dislike of the dominant person by the subordinate person in an unequal economic bargain thus seems to be the cause of any striking anti-Semitism that appears in certain Negro groups." Op. cit., p. 1143.

there is particular opportunity for the development of a disparity of interest between them. As Negroes become increasingly assimilated in the larger society, the likelihood is that they, too, will become intolerant.

There is a sense in which we may conceive of racial antagonism as contributing to the amelioration of anti-Semitism. The potentialities against which the present-day dominant whites struggle in their racial aggression are more dangerous than the possible disorganizing presence of the Jews. The threat to the entire social system is definitely increased if the black and the white proletariat are permitted to become unified and class-conscious—ruling-class Jews and all may be marked for liquidation. If the Jewish bourgeoisie can keep the fear of this threat before the minds of the dominant white Gentiles, it is likely that they will be able to establish a Jew-Gentile, bourgeois solidarity against the colored people and, of course, against the white proletariat also. This will tend to allay the intensity of anti-Semitism. To the extent, however, that the proletariat gains solidarity and power, to that extent also the Jewish bourgeoisie may come in for its full share of proletarian hatred, and probably more so from the most exploited group, the colored people.

Since the Jews are a traditionally persecuted group, they should not be expected to make a spectacle of their race prejudice. A South African Indian writer indicates the ground for antagonistic feeling between his race and the Jews:

> The Jews attempt to oust the Indians out of the commercial fields. . . . In general [they] may be termed inimical to the Indians. A certain writer has pointed out that the Jews never fight openly; they make a gentle rush. This has been true in South Africa. The Jews have never openly come out against the Indians. They have been playing a back-alley game.[13]

It would seem then that there is some real reason for the separate struggle of Negroes and Jews, for their social disabilities are rooted in different and apparently disparate social situations. And yet it may happen that the motives for both anti-Semitism and race prejudice call for heightened expression at the same time, a fact which may lead to the identification of a common enemy and thus drive the Jews and Negroes together in sympathy. When in 1934, for instance, the Nazi party declared that "the continuation of marriages with bearers of colored or Jewish blood is incompatible

---

[13]P. S. Joshi, op. cit., p. 37.

with the aims of the National Socialist party," the colored people and the Jews had to come together in opposition to a common danger.[14]

Naturalness of Race Prejudice and Intolerance

It is possible to conceive of any social fact as a natural phenomenon without implying that it is an inseparable function of social organization. Probably intolerance is as old as human society, but race prejudice has developed only recently in Western society, and this is a consideration of prime importance. An insufficient analysis of race prejudice and intolerance may lead one to conclude that "prejudice toward a racial or a religious group is a collective phenomenon with roots in the distant past."[15] The phenomena, however, do not have the same root.

If we assume that social solidarity is a desideratum in all societies, then leaders of the dominant intrasocietal group will always be intolerant of culturally divergent groups which threaten the stability of the social order. The presence of a different race need not be of itself a disorganizing factor, but a group which will not or cannot be assimilated ordinarily produces "social indigestion."[16] Moreover, there is probably no society so loosely organized as to permit subordinate groups to threaten its existence. As an insignificant Oriental cult, the followers of Jesus might have been tolerated or even disregarded. But when Jesus began to preach "to the multitude, and to his disciples, saying: 'Woe unto you, scribes and Pharisees, hypocrites! for ye are like unto whited sepulchres, which indeed appear beautiful outward, but are within full of dead men's bones, and of all uncleanness. . . . Ye generation of vipers, how can ye escape the damnation of hell?' " the time had come for the leaders of the Jews to be intolerant and to persecute Him and His followers. No society would bear such a threat to "law and order"—to the status quo.[17]

---

[14]In America, on the other hand, where the colored population is significant, the fascists may adopt a different strategy. In a crisis they will most likely set Negroes against Jews or vice versa, so that the major proletarian struggle may be subordinated to an augmented and intensified minor cultural conflict.

[15]Ellsworth Faris, op. cit., p. 348.

[16]Concerning the Jews, J. O. Hertzler observes: ". . . the Jewish culture is always a foreign culture—an undigested element—within the larger areal culture." In *Jews in a Gentile World*, p. 74.

[17]To this end, therefore, "assembled together the chief priests, and the scribes, and the elders of the people, unto the palace of the high priest . . . and consulted that they might take

So also it might have been possible for medieval religious leaders and modern nationalists to disregard the Jews as of no consequence; just as, for instance, the gypsies are ordinarily tolerated, if not encouraged. But Jews are seldom social non-entities; they enter effectively into the economic and political life of the community. Therefore, the anti-Semitic leader is never at a loss for spectacular instances of Jewish wealth, power, and prestige to vitalize his theme of Jewish cultural hostility.

There is apparently no reason to believe that with increasing democratic organization of society there will be a correlative decrease in social intolerance. The focus of intolerance may change—that is to say, Jews may be tolerated—but, since we may expect that even in an advanced democracy social values will be jealously defended, no group regarded as alien and disruptive of social harmony and solidarity could be assured a peaceful, tolerated existence. As Lord Acton observes: "The true democratic principle, that the people shall not be made to do what it does not like, is taken to mean that it shall never tolerate what it does not like."[18] Obviously, this does not mean to say that in a democracy Jews will be regarded as alien; it is not unlikely, however, that, say, anarchists might be. Moreover, anyone who challenges the status quo, whether he be a Socrates, Galileo, Hus, or Marx, must expect intolerance. Certain types of societies are able to tolerate a relatively large variety of beliefs and practices, but none will tolerate beliefs and practices which seem to threaten its existence.

To be sure, it is only necessary that the dominant group believes in the menace of the cultural tenets and practices of the other group; whether they are actually harmful or not is not the crucial circumstance. From the point of view of modern urban civilization, for instance, very much of the earlier persecution of Protestants by the Roman Catholic states of Europe was clearly ill advised; yet we still think that it was very fortunate that Catholic Europe did not allow itself to be swamped by Islam.

Jesus by subtlety and kill him." Indeed the final effects of counterpropaganda are pathetically illustrated as Jesus pleaded "to the multitudes: 'Are ye come out as against a thief with swords and staves for to take me? I sat daily with you teaching in the temple, and ye laid no hold on me." ' However, "they that laid hold on Jesus led him away to . . . the high priest, where the scribes and the elders were assembled." Intolerance does not argue or debate; it simply bares its teeth.

[18]*History of Freedom and Other Essays,* pp. 93–94.

It is this awareness, therefore, in a threat to the social order or the status quo, either by unassimilability or religio-political intractability, which constitutes the basis of intolerance and persecution.[19] The early Christians in Rome could not escape persecution, and when they finally dominated Western society they themselves gave to the world its classic lessons in persecution. We may think of intolerance, then, as the means by which the group through its ruling class seeks to protect or to enhance its social solidarity.

Race prejudice, on the other hand, developed gradually in Western society as capitalism and nationalism developed. It is a divisive attitude seeking to alienate dominant group sympathy from an "inferior" race, a whole people, for the purpose of facilitating its exploitation. In a previous chapter we have attempted to show that race prejudice is peculiar to the system of capitalist exploitation.[20]

The assertion that Jews have everywhere suffered very much injustice and persecution among other peoples may be a negative plea in a situation of rising anti-Semitic feeling, since the remedy for the devil is more, not less, persecution. Those who will not be converted and are supposed to have explicitly rejected the morality and social norms of the group may be thought of as willingly putting themselves beyond the purview of the social conscience. On the other hand, where race prejudice is mounting it may be idle or even aggravating to argue that the Negro seeks only social equality; that is to say, only the right to live as other men in the larger society. For it

[19]For a discussion of anti-Semitism from the point of view of ethnocentric or "unconscious nationalism" conflict, see Gustav Ichheiser, "The Jews and Antisemitism," *Sociometry,* Vol. IX, February 1946, pp. 92–108.

[20]It should be recognized, however, that with the rise of extreme racial antagonism in Europe an attempt has been made to reduce the Jews along with certain white nationalities to the status of exploitable racial groups. As Salo Baron observes: "Modern anti-Semitism led to another highly important consequence: for the first time it peremptorily refused assimilation of the Semitic Jews to the Aryan ruling majority. The view of former generations, that the difference between Jew and Gentile consisted chiefly in a difference of creed or culture, was abandoned. The new anti-Semites maintained that no matter how strong an effort was made by the individual, no matter how favorable the external circumstances, the attempt to assimilate was utterly futile." "Nationalism and Intolerance," *The Menorah Journal,* Vol. XVII, November 1929, p. 153. Having developed race prejudice, with its powerful conviction of immutable, human inferiority, a condition far more debasing than that of the "ostracized ideologists," it may become convenient to use the weapon of race prejudice in addition to that of intolerance against the persecuted group. And so, too, in order to make race prejudice more effective, it may be bolstered up by certain appeals to intolerance.

is against this very urge among Negroes to identify themselves with the dominant group that the hostility is aroused.

A Restatement

The dominant group is intolerant of those whom it can define as anti-social, while it holds race prejudice against those whom it can define as subsocial.[21] Persecution and capitalist exploitation are the respective behavior aspects of these two social attitudes. Thus we are ordinarily intolerant of Jews but prejudiced against Negroes. In other words, the dominant group or ruling class does not like the Jew at all, but it likes the Negro in his place. To put it in still another way, the condition of its liking the Jew is that he cease being a Jew and voluntarily become like the generality of society, while the condition of its liking the Negro is that he cease trying to become like the generality of society and remain contentedly a Negro.

From the point of view of the dominant group, the Jew is our irreconcilable enemy within the gates, the antithesis of our God, the disturber of our way of life and of our social aspirations; the Negro as our servant, on the other hand, is our indispensable friend. Therefore, it is conceivable that Negro Americans may become anti-Semitic; and Jews, in so far as they are businessmen, may learn to loathe forward and ambitious Negroes. Intolerance is probably as old as social organization, while race prejudice came into being only recently with the rise of a particular form of social organization. Intolerance demands recantation and conversion;[22] race prejudice loathes the idea of conversion.

When our social organization is threatened with internal disruption, as during the Black Death in Europe or the frantic attempt of the Germans to throw off the "shame of Versailles," we may become desperate and massacre the Jews.[23] They are the most stubbornly separative group that we can

[21]Professor J. F. Brown makes this observation: "Those whom we consider below us we may despise or pity, but we neither love nor hate them as we do our equals. . . . Negroes are discriminated against everywhere in the United States, but we do not have a wholesale anti-Negroism with the personalized virulence of anti-Semitism." In *Jews in a Gentile World,* p. 140.

[22]Conversion for the Jews, however, is not a simple matter. In Spain from the fourteenth century onward, the Jews who became converted, the *conversos,* continued in their economic prosperity and aroused thereby the suspicion and jealousy of the ruling class. The new Christians, having been converted under pressure, were always suspected of insincerity.

[23]See *Jews in a Gentile World,* pp. 94ff., for many classic instances of frenzied uprisings against Jews when the social order seemed to be threatened.

find. This negative attitude includes the phenomenon of scapegoating. But when we are under economic pressure, as during a depression, or made enraged by having to do our own menial labor while Negroes "idle," we pounce upon some of them, beat them into understanding, and command our police to pick them up as vagrants. A Jewish pogrom is not exactly similar to a Negro lynching. In a pogrom the fundamental motive is the extermination of the Jew; in a lynching, however, the motive is that of giving the Negro a lesson in good behavior.

We want to assimilate the Jews, but they, on the whole, refuse with probable justification to be assimilated; the Negroes want to be assimilated, but we refuse to let them assimilate.

Nationalism

Elsewhere in this study we have considered nationalism in its relation to racial antagonism; at this point we shall attempt to describe briefly the phenomenon as a factor determining the relationship among national ethnics. It is necessary first for us to differentiate the concepts "race" and "nation." A race, in so far as social interaction is concerned, may be thought of as any people who are distinguished, or consider themselves distinguished, in social relations with other peoples, by their physical characteristics. On the other hand, a nation or national ethnic may be thought of as a tribal group conscious of cultural unity; in addition we may think of modern nations as being nationalistic. The problems which develop when more than one of these nationalistic groups find themselves living under the same political state have been called national minority problems. We may repeat, these problems are of recent origin; before the rise of nationalism in Europe "nations" were landed estates. There was cultural difference without political unity and consciousness among peoples.

Probably the term "national minority" may best be thought of as meaning "subordinate nation"; thus we may speak of subordinate nationality problems.[24] This may be more cumbersome, yet more meaningful. As the

[24] A word should be said about the use of the term "minority group." Under this heading is ordinarily included any "group of people who, because of their physical or cultural characteristics, are singled out from the others in the society in which they live for differential and unequal treatment, and who therefore regard themselves as objects of collective discrimination." See Louis Wirth, "The Problem of Minority Groups," in *The Science of Man in the World Crisis,* Ralph Linton, ed., p. 347. This definition, which probably had to be as inclusive as it is because of the tremendous scope of the non-significantly modified concept "group,"

term "minority group" has been used, it may refer to a nationalistic group which exceeds in number of individuals the "majority" group. In fact, the idea of the position of the opposing group is not conveyed by the antonym "majority" but rather by such words as "dominant" or "superordinate."[25] The struggle among national groups, then, is a struggle for power.

But although the struggle between national ethnics is political, it is not exactly similar to political-class conflict. The principal concern of political classes is with the form of government; the revolutionists seek to reorganize the State in the interest of its class ideals—economic and political. More-over, an open class struggle is ordinarily an intrasocietal conflict, and it may take place among members of the same nationality, as, for instance, the French Revolution. On the other hand, the subordinate ethnic struggles for national independence or national recognition. Independence, of course, may mean the right to secede either for the purpose of establishing a separate state or of uniting with another state. In seeking to achieve greater political recognition the subordinate nationality may strive either for increased participation in the affairs of a state or for the attainment of a dominant position within it.

An exploited race tends to become a subordinate nationality when it has gained a degree of political unity and consequently makes appeals to national importance and rights as a basis for achieving political recognition. Most of the colonial native peoples are actual or potential subordinate nationalities. The Filipinos, East Indians, and Javanese are probably at the same stage of national development; the Trinidadians and Jamaicans are

promises and frequently accomplishes a confusing discussion. Indeed, it is practically unlimited, for under it we may discuss political-class problems, problems of religious sects, problems of particular economic interest groups, race, problems, nationality problems, and so on. Wirth even speaks of "where the minority occupies the position of a caste"! Ibid., p. 354.

Very much of the responsibility for the medley of incongruous ideas about race relations and nationality groups frequently encountered in Donald Young's *American Minority Peoples* is no doubt due to the false lead of the ill-defined concept "minority peoples." For a definitive attempt to derive some meaning of this amorphous concept, see "The Meaning of Minorities," by Francis J. Brown, in *Our Racial and National Minorities,* Francis J. Brown and Joseph S. Roucek, eds., Chap. I.

[25]The concept may lead to such word play as the following: "When the American speaks of problems of minorities, he is seldom conscious that he is actually speaking about himself and his own problems. Yet, both in size and in performance, the Caucasian rates a position as the world's number one minority problem. The Caucasian minority has a majority psychology." Buell G. Gallagher, *Color and Conscience,* p. 6.

only slightly nationalistic, while Haiti might be taken as the classic illustration of an exploited racial group which has achieved nationhood. Negro Americans will probably never become nationalistic; the numerical balance of the races will not allow the development of nationalistic antagonism on the part of the colored people. To say, as Robert E. Park does, that Negroes in the United States are a "national minority" may be misleading. Yet it is fairly certain that African Negroes in every continental colony will in time develop nationalism.

Subordinate nationalities are seldom, if ever, "assimilationist," for the nationalism itself which produces them is a separative social attitude; group integrity is the emotional core of nationalism. On the other hand, an exploited racial group may be assimilationist. Ordinarily, subordinate-nationality antagonisms are less divisive than racial antagonisms. In a bipartite racial situation, probably the most effective type of exploitative relationship, the white nationalities tend to act as a unit in dominating the colored people. This is especially true in South Africa.

In the United States we may consider the white Southerners and the Northerners as two nationalities of the same race, the Southerners being the subordinate group. The cultural difference in the South, with its peculiar economic pattern, gives it a sufficient basis for the development of nationalism. Although its attempts to form a separate and independent nation have been frustrated, its nationalistic fires still smolder. The Civil War, of course, was not an interracial strife; Negro slavery merely constituted a part of the essential circumstances about which the two nationalities struggled. We should have expected the white people of the North to take sides with the Southern whites, had the conflict been a nationalistic conflict between blacks and whites of the area.

The reason for this should probably not be sought in some "consciousness of kind" instinct, but rather in the political-class situation of the colored people. In our secular, exploitative system few, if any, economic conflicts between ruling political classes can be as dangerous as a conflict between one of these classes and a proletarian group. The white nationalities of South Africa, for instance, are implacably decided on their common purpose of exploiting the natives; this is their basic interest, and their internationality problems must not so divide them as to defeat it. It is a similar passion, which on little agitation wells up in the capitalist ruling classes, regardless of nationality, against organized proletarian movements. Adolf Hitler, with some considerable success, attempted to exploit it even in the very heat of his world-wide international conflict.

The Jews in the United States and probably in most parts of Europe do not constitute a subordinate nationality; neither do Roman Catholics. But in Palestine the Jews are a nationality group which cultivates Zionism, its nationalism, apparently with the intent of achieving national dominance in that country.[26] The positive behavior aspect of nationalism, it should be remembered, is international and imperialistic aggression.

Since nationalism developed recently mainly under the stimulation of international economic rivalry, we should seek the basis for the status relationship of different national ethnics in the pattern of conflict relationship among the nations involved. There seem to be two principal situations in which subordinate nationalities may be related to the dominant state: (a) that in which the entire national group is included within the dominant state, such as the many nationalities included within the Russian and the Austro-Hungarian states before 1917; and (b) that in which only a fraction of an independent nation is included within the dominant state, such as the Italians in France or the Germans in Poland. In these situations the pattern of internationality relationship will tend to be determined by the fortune of the nations in world politics and diplomacy.

To be sure, the immediate historical causes of the development of nationalism in a subordinate national group which is wholly included in a superordinate state will vary with the peculiarities of the international history and of the culture of the peoples involved. But we should expect such peoples to be intensely stirred by great wars and by the waves of idealism which ordinarily accompany them. After World War I many subordinate nationalities, mainly in the Baltic and Balkan areas, organized sovereign states.

[26]For a discussion of Jewish nationalism and the Zionist movement, see Louis E. Levinthal, "The Case for a Jewish Commonwealth in Palestine," *The Annals,* Vol. 240, July 1945, pp. 89–98. Says Levinthal: ". . . the Jewish people, as a people, has been homeless since A.D. 70. This national homelessness has prevented the free, normal, and creative development of Jewish cultural, spiritual, and religious values . . . a publicly recognized and legally secured national home will serve as a cultural, spiritual, and religious center, enriching Jewish life wherever Jews live." Ibid., p. 96.

Where the subordinate nationality is only a comparatively small fraction of a dominant nation, its behavior and fate will be determined principally by the power relationship existing between its parent nation and other great nations. This relationship, of course, may be exceedingly involved—indeed, no less so than the story of international wars and diplomacy. To illustrate—the Germans in Poland, Denmark, the Netherlands, Belgium, Luxemburg, France, Switzerland, Italy, Austria, Czechoslovakia, Hungary, Rumania, and so on, will present quite different problems for these states as Germany moves through its cycle of frightful power to defeat. If we could imagine the United States being defeated by, say, Japan, we could also imagine a quite different problem presented to the South American countries by various European and Asiatic subordinate nationalities.

Probably the reason why the United States does not have so serious a subordinate-nationality problem as most continental European countries is that it did not develop in a similar matrix of international conflict. To be sure, its peculiar institutions and economic base—especially the relative fluidity of its social-status system—are contributing influences. The United States, like most American countries, is a nation of immigrants. It is English-speaking without being British. The French in Louisiana have less reason to be nationalistic than the French in Canada; in Canada the British and the French tend to be subnationalities reflecting the nationalistic rivalries of their parent countries.

Just as the subordinate nationalities of a single parent nation experience different fortunes in different dominant states, so also we should expect a variety of subordinate nationalities in one state to have more or less favorable status as power groups. Among the subnationalities of European origin in the United States, the English probably have the highest status, while some one or more of the Balkan nationalities, probably the Turks, have the lowest status. The status of the Asiatic and African nationalities is complicated by racial stereotypes. However, we should probably not say that differences in language are the bases of conflict among nationalities. The bases are nationalism and the existing pattern of power relationship. Yet we should expect that, other things being equal, the greater the disparity of culture between nationalities, the greater the opportunity for the development of national antagonism.

In the United States the prestige of Americanism and the economic and political advantages available to the assimilated "foreigner" tend to lead to assimilation. In fact, in this situation of persons of different nationality we may think of them as the "foreign-born," for assimilation rather than nationalism tends to be the controlling social attitude. The different nationality groups are seldom regarded as subnations. Some of them, like the English and the French, rapidly lose themselves in the general population, and such groups as the Italians and Poles seek particularly shelter and sympathetic contact in national communities, so that the pains of assimilation may be more easily endured.

Unlike certain situations in Europe, no nationality group in the United States can reasonably hope to become independent and secede, while the disadvantages of gaining political recognition as a subordinate nation are apparently so great that no national group seems to desire it. In the United States, then, aggressive nationalism among minor nationalities is rather unknown. Consequently the group life of the various nationalities may be thought of as tribal rather than nationalistic, and the problem becomes more nearly one of assimilation than of nationalistic conflict. As we have seen, however, in the case of such groups as the Chinese, Japanese, and Mexicans, nationality problems are complicated by racial antagonisms.

Nationalism and Intolerance

Professor Salo Baron submits a "law of anti-Semitism," which may be stated briefly as follows: the larger the number of nationalities within one state, the less the likelihood of the development of anti-Semitism within that state. He defines three types of state-nationality situations: (a) those in which the purview of political power of the State coincides with the nationality, *the national State,* such as France and Italy, "because the slight minorities within their territories do not change effectively their national complexion"; (b) those in which the State includes many nationalities, *the State of nationalities,* such as Poland, Czechoslovakia, and Russia; and (c) those in which the State includes only part of a nationality, the whole being divided among two or more states, *the part-of-a-nationality-state,* such as "the German nationality, which is divided between two independent and separate States, Germany and Austria, with important sections in" other countries. "These . . . are the three types of States under which the Jewish people have lived in the Diaspora. If we . . . consider the treatment of Jewry under these various types of States, we shall . . . be able to formulate our law as follows: *The status of the Jew is most favorable in pure states of nationalities, most unfavorable in national states, and somewhat between the two extremes in states which include part of a nationality only.*[27] And in support of this hypothesis Baron continues:

> The reason is self-evident. The national state, feeling strongly the strangeness of the Jew in its otherwise homogeneous body national, has always tried to eliminate it by full assimilation, which often took the shape of enforced conversion, or of full exclusion, which generally meant expulsion. The state of nationalities, being composed of many different groups, [is] less concerned about the existence of another distinct element, and could see more clearly the meritorious qualities of a group different from all the others. . . . In the [part-of-a-nationality state] the psychological situation [is] somewhat similar to that of the national state, but the lack of complete unity often precludes a uniform policy and expulsions from one section are nullified by admissions into other regions.[28]

In other words, the greater the national solidarity within any given state, the greater the likelihood of anti-Semitism. Putting it still otherwise, anti-Semitism is an inverse function of national solidarity within independent states. But this hypothesis is hardly a complete explanation of anti-Semitism; moreover, Baron's presentation of historical support is not always convincing. There may be a high correlation between the incidence of multinationality states and tolerance; the correlation of itself, however, may not explain anti-Semitism. If the multinationality State happens to be an empire, the subjects may be a congeries of mutually alien peoples.

It does not seem to be the mere objective existence of a larger number of nationalities within the State which produces favorable treatment of the Jews but rather the extent to which the State finds a policy of "nationality" *laissez faire* most suitable to the continuance of its rule. When the State becomes militant in its attempt to achieve solidarity among its nationalities on some basis of common culture, such as a common religion or a common destiny, anti-Semitism may arise.

To be sure, it should be easier for a state that has already achieved a high degree of national solidarity to become anti-Semitic. But a state with a

[27]Op. cit., p. 506. (Italics are Baron's.)
[28]Ibid., p. 506.

nationally homogeneous population is likely to recognize foreign groups of any kind more easily and become antagonistic to them also. Apparently a social group becomes intolerant not merely because it recognizes an alien group in its midst but rather because it is able successfully to blame that alien group for some frustration to social aspiration or for instrumenting social dysphoria. Anti-Semitism, it seems, could be explained only in consideration of the peculiar unassimilability of the Jews and the social situation developing about them in relation to other peoples.

Race Prejudice, Class Conflict, and Nationalism

The United States has set the pattern of Oriental exclusion for such countries as Canada and Australia. On the Pacific Coast, and in California especially, a distinct and rather involved racial situation has developed; perhaps it may be thought of as the completion of a "race-relations cycle." Here, because of the rapid cultural advancement of these colored people, the natural history of race relations has been greatly expedited. Like all racial situations, we approach this one also from the point of view of the white man's initiative—he is the actor in chief; the Asiatics react to their best advantage.

The Asiatics came into California because there was a great demand there for their labor; they came because the relatively high wages in California enticed them. But the "pull" was far more significant than the "push." No matter how great the lure of higher wages, they could by no means have "invaded" the Coast if the encouragement and inducement of certain hard-pressed white employers did not facilitate it. The great wave of Asiatic common labor began to move upon the Western Hemisphere after the decline of the Negro slave trade—after 1845 especially. The West Indies, the Pacific Coast of America, and even South and East Africa received their quotas. The Asiatics came not as slaves but mainly as coolies; and gradually, among others, California and other Pacific states had their Chinese and Japanese problem; Trinidad and South Africa, their East Indian problem; and Cuba, its Chinese problem.

These "coolies" came mostly as contract laborers, some form of indentured-servant relationship; and "Wherever they were imported, they were used as substitutes for slave labor in plantation areas."[28a] The Japanese,

---

[28a]Carey McWilliams, *Brothers under the Skin,* p. 85.

however, came later and probably with somewhat more personal initiative. Carey McWilliams summarizes the process of their coming:

> With the conclusion of the Reciprocity Treaty of 1876 between Hawaii and the United States—which opened the islands for American capital—the sugar interests of Hawaii began to clamor for Japanese labor. As early as 1868 these interests had "practically stolen" 147 Japanese for plantation labor in the islands. Most of these initial immigrants, however, were returned to Japan in response to a sharp note of protest. The execution of the Reciprocity Treaty was followed, in 1886, by the adoption of the Hawaiian-Japanese Labor Convention. It was this agreement that, for the first time, "officially opened the doors for the immigration of Japanese laborers to the outside world." Under the terms of the agreement approximately 180,000 Japanese were sent to Hawaii—the largest single body of workers that Japan sent to any land.[29]

Following the Chinese Exclusion Act of 1882, Chinese workers on the Pacific Coast became less available and employers began to look to the Japanese for the supply of their labor deficiency. As H. A. Millis observes with respect to the agricultural interest: "Many farmers faced the practical problem of finding substitutes for the disappearing Chinese, who had shaped their investments and methods."[30] A large fraction of the immigrants came by way of Hawaii. Thus in 1910 the United States Immigration Commission reported:

> With the strong demand for common labor prevailing in the west, the Japanese contractors on the Coast, and especially those doing business in San Francisco and Seattle, induced many to come to the United States. Some of these contractors were for a time regularly represented by the agents sent to Honolulu; recourse was made to advertising in the Japanese papers published there, cheap rates were secured, and in some instances assistance was given in other ways to those desiring to reach the mainland.[31]

The Chinese, the Japanese, and a much smaller number of East Indians, then, came to the Coast as workers—mainly as common laborers.[32] And

[29]*Prejudice*, p. 304.

[30]*The Japanese Problem in the United States*, p. 109.

[31]*Reports of the U.S. Immigration Commission: Immigrants in Industries*, Vol. 23, p. 14.

[32]Concerning the Japanese, Dr. Millis concludes: "Most of those who immigrated directly or indirectly to the Pacific Coast previous to 1908 came to begin as wage earners on the lowest rung of the industrial ladder. They came to Japanese boarding houses and from there most of them secured their first employment as section hands on the railway, as agricultural laborers in the field and orchard, or as domestic servants and house cleaners in the large cities." Op. cit., p. 31.

this is probably the principal source of antagonism in this racial situation—a conflict between workers of different races. Before discussing this, however, it may be well to observe the numerical relationship among the races involved. The Asiatics were always a smaller minority in California than Negroes have been in the South. In 1920, at the height of the anti-Japanese agitation in California, the Japanese constituted about two per cent of the population, and in 1940 about one and one-half per cent. The Chinese population fell from about nine per cent in 1860 to six-tenths of one per cent in 1940.

A remarkable fact about the California anti-Oriental movements is that they have been mainly initiated by white workers instead of exploiters of labor, the class which we have attempted to show is responsible for all modern racial antagonism. In this respect the California situation appears to be the very opposite of the Negro-white relationship in the South. But first let us review briefly the role of labor in the anti-Orientalism on the Coast.

According to Lucile Eaves, ". . . from the early fifties to the present time, there have been organizations in which all classes of wage-workers joined to promote the exclusion of Asiatic labor. It is the one subject upon which there has never been the slightest difference of opinion, the one measure on which it has always been possible to obtain concerted action."[33] And further: "By the persistent efforts of the working people of California first the state and then the nation have been converted to the policy of Oriental exclusion."[34] Ever since the middle of the nineteenth century, then, when California was indeed a very young state, white workers reached consensus against the Asiatic worker.

The history of white-worker-Asiatic antagonism in California is one of considerable agitation and periodic violence against Chinese and Japanese. The influence of organized labor in politics has been stronger in California than in any other state of the United States, and apparently no small part of this influence is due to the solidarity which labor has been able to develop about a continuing menace to its welfare—the threat of competition from Asiatic labor.

[33]*A History of California Labor Legislation,* p. 6.
[34]Ibid., p. 105.

This reaction of labor, however, is not peculiarly a racial phenomenon; the conflict is essentially between employer and worker. Indeed, workers will react to inanimate objects, to machinery, in a characteristic way if the latter is introduced suddenly as a significant substitute for labor. Workers have been known to riot and attack machines in a way not unlike their attacks upon other workers who, because of lower standards, are favored by employers. In 1844 the leader of a British trade union wrote:

> Machinery has done the work. Machinery has left them in rags and without any wages at all. Machinery has crowded them in cellars, has immured them in prisons worse than Parisian bastilles, has forced them from their country to seek in other lands the bread denied to them here. I look upon all improvements which tend to lessen the demand for human labor as the deadliest curse that could possibly fall on the heads of our working classes, and I hold it to be the duty of every working potter—the highest duty—to obstruct by all legal means the introduction of the scourge into any branch of his trade.[35]

Although today trade unionists do not express themselves in this way, the attitude is not lost; workers merely approach the problem differently. They insist upon sharing the profits which accrue to the employer because of the increased productivity of the machine. But competition with substandard workers puts standard workers in an even more disadvantageous position in their struggle with capitalists. As one anti-Oriental puts it:

> Our grievance is against the humble, tireless, mean-living, unalterably alien, field and factory hand, who cuts wages, works for a pittance and lives on less, dwells in tenements which would nauseate the American pig, and presents the American workman the alternative of committing suicide or coming down to John Chinaman's standard of wages and living. Self-protection is sufficient ground on which to base exclusion.[36]

[35]Edmund Potter, head of the Potters' Trade Union, quoted by Sidney and Beatrice Webb, *Industrial Democracy,* 1920 ed., pp. 392–93; see also W. Cunningham, *The Growth of English Industry and Commerce,* 5th ed., Vol. I, pp. 444–45.

[36]San Francisco *Bulletin,* November 18, 1901, quoted by Elmer Clarence Sandmeyer, *The Anti-Chinese Movement in California,* p. 106. That this attitude is not essentially racial may be indicated by a similar expression of feeling against white immigrants on the East Coast of the United States: "This unlimited and unrestricted admission of foreign emigrants is a serious injury to the native laboring population, socially, morally, religiously, and politically; socially, by overstocking the labor market and thus keeping wages down; morally and religiously, by unavoidable contact and intercourse; and politically, by consequence of want of employment and low wages, making them needy and dependent, whereby they become the easy prey or willing tools of designing and unprincipled politicians. And in this way the native population is deteriorated and made poor, needy and subservient: and these realities

It should be noted that this attitude is not an exploitative attitude; it is a conflict between two exploited groups generated by the desire of one group of workers to keep up the value of its labor power by maintaining its scarcity. In Trinidad, British West Indies, Negro workers, in almost identical terms, fought against the continued introduction of indentured East Indian laborers;[37] and between 1930 and 1932 Negroes on the South Side of Chicago demonstrated against the employment of white "foreigners" by certain public utilities.[38] However, there is no racial antagonism between Negroes and East Indians in Trinidad, and it would be somewhat of an inversion of reason to expect Negro Chicagoans to have race prejudice toward white "foreigners." We may cite, of course, many illustrations of this attitude among whites in the United States—beginning, perhaps, with the early anti-Irish attitude in the East. Every conflict between strikers and "scabs" produces similar attitudes among the strikers. In 1910 the platform of the Socialist party of California contained this plank:

> We favor all legislative measures tending to prevent the immigration of strike breakers and contract laborers and the mass immigration and importation of Mongolian or East Indian labor, caused or stimulated by the employing classes for the purpose of weakening the organization of American labor and of lowering the standard of life of the American workers.[39]

Professor H. A. Millis presents a case of labor displacements in Florin, a small town southeast of Sacramento, which has been called "the best locality in the United States for the study of Japanese agricultural life":

> The basket factory [in Florin] was established ten years ago. At first most of the employees were white women and girls of the community. They were found to be unsatisfactory in certain respects and were rapidly displaced by Japanese. . . . It is said that the white women were difficult to manage, could not be depended upon to report for work regularly and, though paid by the piece, did

produce want of self-respect, hopelessness, laxity in morals, recklessness, delinquencies, and crimes." From *Emigration, Emigrants, and Know-Nothings,* by a Foreigner, quoted by Lawrence Guy Brown, *Immigration,* p. 94.

[37]See *Report of the Committee on Emigration from India to the Crown Colonies and Protectorates,* London, 1910.

[38]For newspaper stories of this movement, see the Chicago *Whip* from September 30, 1930, onward.

[39]Quoted in *Reports of the U. S. Immigration Commission,* Vol. 23, p. 173.

not wish to work more than ten hours per day, or work overtime, or on Sundays, as it was thought the interest of the business required. In all these matters the Japanese were more acceptable to their employers, who are white men prominently connected with shipping firms in Sacramento. Paid by the piece, they formerly worked twelve to fourteen hours per day, and on Sunday, when the demand was such as to make long hours profitable. At present all the employees, except a representative of the non-resident manager, are Japanese.[40]

This apparently racial conflict, then, is in fact an extension of the modern political-class conflict. The employer needs labor, cheap labor; he finds this in Asiatic workers and displaces white, more expensive labor with them. White workers then react violently against the Asiatics, indeed, not unlike the way in which early handicraft workers reacted against the machine. On this point Eliot Grinnell Mears observes: "The organized-labor attitude . . . while strenuously opposed in its public utterances to Oriental immigration, is actually interested in racial questions only in so far as they affect competitive conditions in industry. . . . The issue is capital and labor, not race and labor."[41]

On the Coast the Oriental may be thought of as one significant aspect of the subject matter in the conflict between capital and labor. "The Chinaman," says the Sacramento *Record Union* (January 10, 1879), "is here because his presence pays, and he will remain and continue to increase so long as there is money in him. When the time comes that he is no longer

[40]Op. cit., p. 155. And Millis continues: "Laborers reacted most strongly . . . because they thought their standards were imperiled. The Chinese acquired a firm position in the manufacture of cigars, shoes, and garments in San Francisco. They were used to defeat the ends of organized labor, and labor unionists reacted strongly against them as they do against other 'scabs' and cheap workmen. In other parts of the country, for example in the manufacture of shoes in Massachusetts, there was talk of hiring the Chinese to take the places of striking union men and to control the labor situation. They were a menace—as workingmen saw them. Were not the Japanese also? Did they not begin very much as the Chinese? . . . Were they not employed as strike breakers in the manufacture of shoes in San Francisco? White laborers reacted against the Japanese because they competed on a different level. It does not matter so much that their competition never extended far when their immigration was not greatly restricted. It was potential in any case. . . . The labor unions stand for the setting of progressive standards and offer strong resistance when any group of men or set of circumstances threaten or seem to threaten these standards. Without organization, workingmen react in very much the same way in the face of new competition." Ibid., pp. 242–43.

[41]*Resident Orientals on the American Pacific Coast,* pp. 93–94.

profitable that generation will take care of him and will send him back."[42]
And Sandmeyer observes:

> The Chinese were charged with contributing to monopoly in connection with the great landlords and the railroads. . . . Since these landed interests were among the most ardent advocates of continued Chinese immigration the charge was frequently voiced that California was in danger of having a "caste system of lords and serfs" foisted upon it. . . . The anti-Chinese element in California looked upon these "monopolists" as among the chief mainstays of the Chinese. . . . These great landowners were regarded as worse than the plantation owners of slave days.[43]

The famous California Workingmen's Party organized in 1877 was a radical, outspokenly anti-capitalist assemblage. The leaders "called upon the workmen and their friends in every county, town, city, and hamlet to organize branches of the Party at once, and prepare for a campaign that would enable them to draft a constitution which should place the government in the hands of the working people."[44] In fact, the Workingmen's Party in 1878 practically succeeded in controlling the California Constitutional Convention and got into the new constitution a considerable part of its "radical" platform.[45]

The workers were able in large measure to defeat the exploitative purpose of the ruling class in California partly by the help of that class itself. Capitalist exploiters of labor have some necessity to keep their labor freely exploitable, and one means of accomplishing this end is to keep it degraded. In California both Chinese and Japanese proved to be exceedingly intractable as a permanent labor force, and this tended to bring the primary elements of racial antagonism into play. Concerning the situation after the Chinese had been fairly well subdued, Carey McWilliams (quoting the San Francisco *Chronicle*) says: "By 1905 the fight had been narrowed down to the Japanese. 'The Chinese,' the *Chronicle* observed, 'are faithful laborers

---

[42]Quoted by Elmer Clarence Sandmeyer, op. cit., pp. 31–32. The author continues: ". . . employers and those seeking employment differed widely concerning the effect of the Chinese in the State. With few exceptions employers considered them beneficial as a flexible supply of labor, cheap, submissive, and efficient; but those whose only capital was their ability to work were almost unanimous in the opinion that the Chinese were highly detrimental to the best interests of the state." Ibid., p. 33.

[43]Ibid., pp. 32–33. See also p. 85, and Eliot Grinnell Mears, op. cit., p. 56.

[44]Lucile Eaves, op. cit., p. 31.

[45]Ibid., p. 36.

and do not buy lands. The Japanese are unfaithful laborers and do buy lands.' "[46] In this connection the United States Immigration Commission also observes:

> The representatives of several . . . boards of trade, even while opposed to the immigration of Japanese, stated that their communities would gladly make use of more Chinese if they were available. The reasons advanced for the favorable opinion of the Chinese as against the Japanese were their superiority as workmen, their faithfulness to employer, a less general desire to acquire possessions of land or to engage in business, and the absence of a desire on their part to associate with others on equal terms.[47]

On the farm these extraordinarily temporary laborers economized their earnings in wages and aspired forthwith to become independent farmers. To be sure, the Asiatics were not brought to California to become farmers; they were brought or encouraged to come as wage workers. Therefore, when a government survey reported: "There are probably more white laborers working for Oriental farmers than there are Oriental laborers working for American farmers,"[48] the anti-Oriental antagonism of the farmer became aggravated. In California a number of laws were enacted which more or less effectively excluded the Oriental from the privilege of farming.

As businessmen, also, Chinese and Japanese are out of their place. They are looked upon by other businessmen as foreign competitors, with the characteristic relationship of a struggle for markets. As H. A. Millis points out with reference to both the businessman and farmer:

> Laundrymen in San Francisco and elsewhere, barbers, proprietors of small tailor shops, and others have protested when the Japanese have entered the circle of competition and cut prices or brought about a loss of patronage. The cry of "race problem" has been employed to accomplish economic ends. The growers

[46]Op. cit., p. 19.

[47]*Reports of the U.S. Immigration Commission,* Vol. 23, p. 174.

[48]*California and the Oriental: Report of State Board of Control of California, to Gov. Wm. D. Stephens,* rev. ed., January 1, 1922, p. 115. This report continues: "The Japanese farmers and every member in the family, physically able to do so, including the wife and little children, work in the field for long hours, practically from daylight to dark, on Sundays and holidays, and in the majority of cases, live in shacks or under conditions far below the standards required and desired by Americans. . . . American farmers cannot successfully compete with the Japanese farmers if the Americans adhere to the American principles so universally approved in America." Pp. 116–17.

of vegetables about Tacoma and Seattle, and the growers of berries about Los Angeles have protested ineffectively when the acreage has been increased by Japanese growers and prices have fallen. The newcomers "ruined the market," it was said.[49]

As business competitors the Asiatics meet their most powerful white antagonists. Confronted with the negative sanctions of the latter group, they are indeed friendless. But, as we have seen, employers have been on the whole more in favor of than against them. Yet the masterly attitude of the employer group may be indicated by a suggestion to Governor William D. Stephens by a California businessman: ". . . The Mexicans are employed to do practically all the common labor in the Imperial Irrigation District. . . . If this Mexican labor could be extended up through the entire state, the white farmers could do the managing and superintending of the farms, as the Japanese and Hindus do now, and we could get along very well without our Japanese . . . in the agricultural pursuits of the state."[50]

Although the sporadic aggression of the employers gave considerable encouragement and stimulation to the anti-Asiatic movement among white workers, the latter may not have achieved the purpose of Asiatic exclusion so completely had it not been for their favorable alliance with Southern politics. It may seem strange that the politicians of the South, who advocate the interest of a ruling class that has fairly well subdued white labor through the widespread exploitation of black workers, should deem it advisable to take the side of the workingmen of California in their struggle against their employers' desire to exploit cheap Oriental labor. And yet it was probably the weight of the Southern vote in Congress which made it possible for California to put over its national policy of anti-Orientalism.

In the South organized labor is weaker than in any other section of the country; on the Pacific Coast it is stronger. The South has been powerfully dominated by a white exploiting class, so much so, indeed, that white labor has never been able effectively to organize against it. White

[49]Op. cit., p. 243. On this point Raymond Leslie Buell makes the following comment: ". . . if the anti-Japanese laws [prohibiting the purchasing or leasing of land] are religiously enforced, they will not solve America's Japanese problem. They merely transfer the Japanese from the farms to the cities. . . . Japanese competition in industry is likely to prove more harmful to American labor than if Japanese remain on farms where white labor is scarce." "Again the Yellow Peril," in Julia E. Johnsen, ed., *Japanese Exclusion*, p. 43.

[50]*California and the Oriental*, etc., p. 136.

labor had no voice at all against the immigration of black workers into the South; as a consequence white labor was considerably degraded.[51] In fact, the white common people of the South were so thoroughly propagandized that they actually helped the master class to fight the Civil War in the interest of the continued exploitation of black labor on an extremely low level.[52] In the South there is a biracial system; and since the Negroes are degraded, the work which Negroes ordinarily do also tends to be degraded. The prospects on the Coast after 1850 were very favorable for the development of a biracial system, with Asiatic coolies taking a place similar to that of Negroes in the South and part of the white common people assuming the status of poor whites.

But certain historical events, one of them the discovery of gold in California, brought a great wave of highly independent white workers into violent competition with the Asiatics, thus frustrating the tendency toward a bipartite racial system. All the whites could not take the position of a small ruling class because they always outnumbered the Asiatics. The alternative was to organize and stop the tendency toward the situation which developed in the South.

Immigration, of course, is a problem of the Federal Government; and the influencing of national policies may not be easy, especially when it is in the interest of workingmen mainly in one state.[53] However, the South came to the rescue of California not because of an interest in the white

[51]For a discussion of faint antagonism of white workers against the competition of free Negro workers and slaves, see Richard B. Morris, *Government and Labor in Early America,* pp. 182–88.

[52]In this connection Carey McWilliams observes: "With the narrow construction placed on the Fourteenth Amendment in the famous Slaughter House decision in 1873 and the decision in 1875 which held the Civil Rights Statute unconstitutional, the Supreme Court had, so to speak, let the bars down so far as the Negro problem was concerned. Prior to this time the South had shown a lively interest in the possibility of substituting Chinese coolie labor for Negro slave labor. It had been suggested in Memphis in 1869 that such a substitution might be in order; and on several occasions about this time Southern planters had visited California with this purpose in mind. Once they realized, however, that they had again regained control of the Negro, their interest in Chinese labor swiftly abated." *Brothers under the Skin,* p. 83.

[53]As we have seen, organized labor had considerable influence in the politics of California. "The labor vote had attained such proportions in numbers and solidarity as to make elections to public office almost impossible without its support, and it was generally understood that in order to secure the labor vote a candidate must declare himself against the Chinese." Elmer Clarence Sandmeyer, op. cit., p. 57; see also Lucile Eaves, op. cit., p. 23.

workers or dislike for the exploiters of Oriental labor but because it wanted to develop a national tradition to the effect that when the interests of a colored people come into conflict with those of white people the former must always give way. The problem was defined as a conflict between the whites and the Asiatics in California. If this were admitted, then white people in the South should be conceded the right to control "their" Negroes without interference from the national government. This logic was possible in spite of the fact that the articulate white people in the South were masters, while those on the Coast were organized workers. Carey McWilliams puts it in this way:

> This correlation between the Negro problem and the Chinese question is clearly indicated in the vote in Congress on the important measures introduced after 1876 affecting the Chinese. Without exception, these measures were passed by the vote of representatives from the Pacific Coast and the Deep South. Again and again, Southern Senators and Congressmen lined up with representatives of the Pacific Coast to railroad through Congress measures aimed at driving out the Chinese.[54]

But did the white workers of California have no other alternative? Suppose a very significant number of Asiatic workers had actually established residence on the Coast, could they not have been organized also? They probably could and would have been organized—even though with considerably more difficulty than if they had been white workers. The cultural bar between the European and the Asiatic makes it difficult and at certain stages practically impossible for the two groups to reach that common understanding necessary for concerted action against the employer. Moreover, the first generation of Asiatic workers is ordinarily very much under the control of labor contractors and employers, hence it is easier for the employer to frustrate any plans for their organization. Clearly this cultural bar helped to antagonize white workers against the Asiatics. The latter were conceived of as being in alliance with the employer. It would probably have taken two or three generations before, say, the East Indian low-caste worker on the Coast became sufficiently Americanized to adjust easily to the policies and aims of organized labor. Eventually, however, they would have been organized just as Negroes are being gradually organized.

[54]Op. cit., p. 83; see also Lucile Eaves, op. cit., p. 176.

But since the Asiatic was not yet a very considerable element in the population, the white workers decided not to listen to arguments from other interest groups concerning the possibility of assimilating him. Although it must be quite obvious that Orientals have been, are being, and can be assimilated to Western culture, there has been very much argument on this very question. Ordinarily their assimilation is to the advantage of white workers, for the assimilated Asiatic either ceases to be a laborer or becomes more easily organizable. Nevertheless, workers may become frantic when it is argued that since the Asiatics are assimilable they should be allowed to immigrate in unlimited numbers. They will naturally use every means, including those developed by the employer class, to demonstrate the "impossibility" of assimilating the Asiatic.

On the other hand, the assimilation of colored workers is ordinarily against the primary interest of labor exploiters. The assimilated colored worker is either lost for exploitation or becomes intractable; therefore, it is in the interest of employers to convince a certain public that the Asiatics are unassimilable. Success in this conviction will tend seriously to retard assimilation. Here again a basic conflict of interest seems to converge in an identical argument, and in this situation it is sometimes difficult to discover the interest behind the rationalization. In fact, an employer having an immediate need for more labor may even contend that the Asiatic is readily assimilated. The following illustrates the nature of the arguments against assimilation:

> Granting equality, the standards of the races are almost as opposite as the poles, and there is no possibility of a common trend ever being evolved. Assimilation is impossible. True, there are a few marriages here and there, but they are the exceptions that prove the rule. . . . The two peoples run along different lines physically. As they differ in color so do they in tradition, habits and aspirations.[55]

We should recognize, however, that many arguments in favor of the impossibility of Oriental assimilation are in reality arguments in favor of the prohibition of Oriental assimilation. By legal enactment the anti-assimilationists prohibit intermarriage between whites and "Mongolians," provide for separate schools and for residential segregation. In illustration, K. K. Kawakami tells us: "A number of Japanese farmers and business men

[55]John S. Chambers, "The Japanese Invasion," *The Annals,* Vol. XCIII, January 1921, pp. 24–25.

asked the leading Americans of the city [i.e., Lodi, a farming town] to be
their guests at a dinner. . . . Upon the heels of this meeting came a
resolution of the Lodi post of the American Legion, condemning the
American participation in the banquet and declaring: '. . . that we look with
disfavor and disapproval on any gathering intended to promote good fellowship and social affiliation between the Japanese and our own people.' "[56]
And without apparently recognizing the intent of the anti-assimilationists,
Kiichi Kanzaki declares:

> Instead of agitation, America should meet the problem with an attitude
> predicated on the policy of how to Americanize and assimilate the Japanese
> that are here, so that they may not be left as a foreign and isolated group in
> America.[57]

Notwithstanding this, however, we cannot assume that the Chinese and
Japanese culture fell off like water on a duck's back. Consider, for instance,
the simple pigtail, the queue, of the Chinese. To cut it off the Chinaman
may have to go through a terrific personality disturbance, and to keep it
may forever limit the possibility of Americans being at ease in his company.
As Millis observes: "With a different language, with queue and different
dress, with no family life, with different customs and steeled against change
as they were, the reaction against them was strong and immediate when
they ceased to be objects of curiosity."[58]

In the end the Chinese on the Coast have been practically gypsyfied.[59]
"The Chinaman was a good loser." He has withdrawn from the struggle;
he is no longer a significant threat to the standards of white labor. He may
now be treated with a high degree of indifference or even amiability.
"Except for a few large agricultural corporations, the Chinese are generally
engaged in small commercial enterprises supplying the needs of their

---

[56]"The Japanese Question," *The Annals,* Vol. XCIII, January 1921, p. 82.

[57]"Is the Japanese Menace in America a Reality?", *The Annals,* Vol. XCIII, January 1921,
p. 97.

[58]Op. cit., pp. 240–41. To be sure, a master race need not suffer in this way. According
to Jesse F. Steiner: "The American in Japan never intends to become a Japanese—he is not
laughed at because of his customs. He feels that his customs have prestige. But the Japanese
must conform in America." Op. cit., pp. 93–94.

[59]On this point see R. D. McKenzie, "The Oriental Invasion," *Journal of Applied
Sociology,* Vol. 10, 1925, pp. 125–26.

countrymen. Owing to the effectiveness of the Chinese Exclusion Act, the Chinese can not be considered a menace for the future."[60]

But the Japanese have never given up; their youthful nationalism prevents them from becoming an inconsequential people on the Coast. As one observer puts it: "The Chinese and the Hindoo may have intelligence; may have industry, but they are not aggressive, they do not seek to dominate, nor are they backed by powerful nations intent upon the domination of the Pacific Ocean, if not the world."[61]

In some respects, race relations on the Coast are internationality relations; therefore, the relationship of whites to Hindus, Chinese, or Japanese have depended to some extent upon the power relationship of the parent nations of these peoples. The local attitude toward the Asiatics has been constantly involved with international treaties and diplomacy, and Japan has been the most determined nation with which the United States has had to deal. It is not, of course, that Japanese are more nationalistic than Americans, but rather that the Japanese have had to be aggressive in their struggle for position among the actually superior white nations. Discrimination against Japanese on the Coast naturally has been taken as insults to Japan. Moreover, as H. A. Millis observes: "[Japanese] emigrants have been treated . . . almost as colonists."[62]

The more nationalistic a people, the less will be its tendency to assimilate, the more it will tend to value its culture, especially its non-material culture, its religion. Moreover, when two highly nationalistic groups come

[60]*California and the Oriental*, etc., p. 115. And according to the *Tentative Findings of the Survey of Race Relations*, 1925, ". . . there has been a clear tendency on the part of the Chinese to withdraw from competitive forms of labor and business and to enter less productive urban callings. In some cities, notably in border and sea-coast communities, there is a pronounced tendency for an increasing number of Chinese to engage in lotteries and other disorganizing callings." Quoted by Eliot Grinnell Mears, op. cit., p. 197.

[61]John S. Chambers, op. cit., p. 25. And Carey McWilliams explains: "All first-generation immigrant groups in America are inclined to be nationalistic. Until 1924, the Issei [or first-generation Japanese] were probably no more inclined in this direction than any other immigrant group; but afterwards they did develop, in some cases, what has been termed a 'suppressed nationality psychosis.' Nationalistic tendencies increased. They fought to retain the language schools despite the fact that the schools themselves were an admitted failure. They thought that the schools would be one means of instilling in their children a sense of pride in their background. They thought they might assist in bridging the chasm that had begun to separate the two generations. Their children, they said, were in danger of developing an inferiority complex and of sinking 'to the level of Indians.' " *Prejudice*, pp. 95–96.

[62]Op. cit., p. 249.

into contact, there will be mutual fear, distrust, and intolerance. On the Coast intolerance for the Japanese has been partly due to nationalistic conflicts. As one anti-Japanese saw it: "The irrigated part of Placer County is practically a little Japan. . . . Controlling the land, they can perpetuate the ideas, habits, religion and loyalties of the mother country and do this indefinitely."[63] Difference in religion may be one basic reason for intolerance for the Chinese and Japanese. A different god implies a different system of morality. "Brotherhood," says Marshall De Motte, an anti-Asiatic, "implies one father and cannot exist between peoples holding entirely different ideas as to the Fatherhood of God and man's responsibility to man."[64]

That racial antagonism is not determined by biological, innate cultural incapacity or inferiority of the subordinate group is demonstrated by this racial situation. Sometimes it is openly admitted that the Japanese are a culturally superior people. On this very account, however, it is most difficult to exploit them and consequently they are most undesirable. "We admire their industry and cleverness, but for that very reason, being a masterful people, they are more dangerous. They are not content to work for wages as do the Chinese . . . but are always seeking control of the farm and of the crop."[65] David Warren Ryder puts it paradoxically: "Because they are orderly and not in jail, because they are thrifty and energetic, because they marry, set up homes and raise families, they are 'dangerous,' they are a 'menace,' they 'threaten white supremacy.' "[66] In fact, within limits, the

[63]Elwood Mead, "The Japanese Land Problem in California," *The Annals,* Vol. XCIII, January 1921, p. 51. Carey McWilliams also observes: ". . . witnesses before the Tolan Committee advanced the usual stock arguments against the Japanese. . . . Particular emphasis was placed on the language schools, the charge of dual citizenship, and the influence of Buddhism and Shintoism upon the resident Japanese." Op. cit., p. 121.

[64]"California—White or Yellow," *The Annals,* Vol. XCIII, January 1921, p. 23.

[65]Hon. James D. Phelan, "Why California Objects to the Japanese Invasion," *The Annals,* Vol. XCIII, January 1921, p. 17. On this point Col. John P. Irish says: "As the Chinese had been condemned for their imputed vices, so the Japanese are condemned for their imputed virtues, for their sobriety, their industry, their intelligence and skill, for their respect for law and for their honesty. Dr. Benjamin Ide Wheeler, President emeritus of the State University of California, in a speech against them said: 'Their good taste, persistent industry, their excellent qualities and their virtues render their presence amongst us a pitiful danger.' " "The Japanese Issue in California," *The Annals,* Vol. XCIII, January 1921, p. 75.

[66]"The Japanese Bugaboo," *The Annals,* Vol. XCIII, January 1921, p. 51. See also H. A. Millis, op. cit., p. 139.

greater the tendency of an exploited people to overthrow the harness of exploitation, the greater the opposition from their exploiters.

We may conclude, then, that the Asiatics came to the Pacific Coast as an exploitable labor force. There they encountered the violent opposition of white workers. The white workingman's antagonism against the Asiatics was essentially a class conflict between labor and capital. The ruling class never had the opportunity to develop and maintain strong racial antagonism against the Chinese; therefore, when the latter ceased to be a threat to labor they were treated with a high degree of indifference. However, the aggressive nationalism and imperialism of the Japanese excited counternationalism, intolerance, and counterimperialism among American capitalists especially. Since both race prejudice and nationalism are based upon a potential power relationship between groups, we should expect Japanese in the long run to be most respected by the white ruling races because of their remarkable facility in modern warfare. Race relations in the Pacific— in the world, for that matter—have been revolutionized mainly because of the physical might of Japan.

4.
Race and Caste[1]

Race Relations Physical, Caste Cultural

"Just as a sudra begets on a brahman female a being excluded from the Aryan community, even so a person himself excluded procreates, with females of the four castes, sons more worthy of being excluded than himself."[2] This postulate from Manu reveals graphically a pattern of caste stratification that is the opposite of every known system of race relations. Thus, if we consider only the two castes mentioned, Brahman and Sudra,[3] it is obvious that the lawgiver maintains that successive crosses between lower-caste men and pureblood Brahman women result in offspring of increasing inferiority. In other words, the mixed progeny of a Sudra and a Brahman woman is very much superior to the man whose father is, say, one sixty-fourth Sudra along the male line, while his mother is pure Brahman. Yet so far as physical difference is concerned, it is clear that the latter must be considered virtually pure Brahman. We are not, of course, assuming here that there was originally a recognized physical difference between the two castes; the point is that the meaning of "blood" in caste relationships is not the same as in racial situations.

The crucial symbol of race relations is physical identifiability. When we speak of Chinese, Indians, Europeans, Negroes, or Filipinos, we expect responses indicating consciousness of ocular evidence of physical differentiation. But when we refer to such groups as Chamars, Banyas,

[1]In this chapter we shall refer to conditions of race relations in the United States almost exclusively. In the succeeding chapter, the problems of race relations will be discussed analytically.

[2]Manu, X, 30.

[3]We have discussed above some factors concerning the probability that Sudras constituted a single caste. [See Cox, *Caste, Class, and Race* (New York: Monthly Review Press, 1959), 16–17.] Unless confusion results, we shall continue to use the term to represent the lower castes.

Telis, Doms, Brahmans, Kayasthas, or Jolahas, no sense of physical distinction need be aroused. We see rather only East Indians. If we are familiar with these castes, one name might suggest filth and human degradation, while another might call to mind scrupulous cleanliness and superciliousness, or very likely a certain occupation, or any one of a composite of cultural traits.

To come upon a new caste in the caste system is a matter of no particular moment, but the appearance of a new race is always startling. No Hindu in Brahmanic India is ever expected to know all the castes any more than an American family is expected to know individually all other families in the United States. It is sufficient, for caste characterization, to apply certain established norms to the stranger. A new caste may be consciously organized, yet it is beyond the power of human beings to establish a new race. The caste has almost no capacity for assimilating outsiders; its membership is theoretically closed. On the other hand, there is a natural attraction between races in contact, and sooner or later they amalgamate. The concept of amalgamation is not applicable to castes, for physical *rapprochement* does not affect the distinction or stability of castes. Indeed, historically, caste rigidity in India has proceeded hand in hand with physical amalgamation. It cannot be assumed, however, that the one caused the other. Obviously, when two or more races have amalgamated, all possible "race questions" will have been answered.

It is impossible for a person to become a member of any given race other than by birth; but, although the membership of castes ordinarily is limited by birth, it is quite possible for two or more castes to merge if they so will it—consequences notwithstanding.[4] As we have mentioned above, an individual may be initiated into a caste. In the caste system the heritage which gives him distinction is cultural, hence he might be dispossessed of it; the

---

[4]"There is . . . apparently a tendency toward the consolidation of groups at present separated by caste rules. The best instance of such a tendency to consolidate a number of castes into one group is to be found in the grazier castes which aim at combining under the term 'Yadava' Ahirs, Goalas, Gopis, Idaiyans, and perhaps some other castes of milkmen, a movement already effective in 1921. . . . There is little evidence as yet that marriage is being practiced within these consolidating groups, but it is a development the possibility of which may not be overlooked. The Census Superintendent of the Central Provinces quotes 'specific instances' . . . of marriage between members of different sub-castes of Brahmans, and between members of different sub-castes of Kalars, where the union would formerly have been condemned." *Census of India, 1931*, Vol. I, Pt. 1, p. 431.

individual born of a given race, however, inherits physical marks which are not only inalienable but also beyond the discretion of the race itself. It is manifest, then, that to be born within a given race, there is no alternative but to die within it;[5] in the case of caste no such obdurate rule obtains. In fact, the individual might abandon his caste at will, while he cannot possibly give up his race.

Race problems, then, are social problems which have reference to groups physically identifiable. Therefore, we should expect two races in contact and having some basic racial antagonism to develop different problems for persons with different degrees of admixture. And such is, in fact, the case. For instance, in the United States a white person with very little Negro blood is confronted with different problems from those which either the pure white or black person must meet. Ordinarily the disinterested public treats this white Negro like a white man and insists that he behave like one. Thus he may be forcibly prevented from sitting among Negroes in public conveyances, while a dark-complexioned Negro may be assaulted on the highway because his Negro wife looks white.

These are but crude indices of the mental conflicts of these people. And so, too, for the various grades of physical distinguishability, the racial problems tend to vary. In the caste system we should not expect to find any such group of marginal persons because the criteria of belonging are not physical marks. A man either belongs to a caste or he does not. There are no half-caste persons in the sense that there are half-race men. The problem which a caste has of knowing its members is of the same order as that of a family's knowing its constituents.

A caste, should it desire to affiliate outsiders, must admit them as new members. On the other hand, if a person has the physical marks of another race, he may without any formality whatever assume that race. A white Negro, for example, may decide to "pass," and he will if his appearance does not betray him. But a person may not "pass" into a caste; he can get into it only by formal admission.[6]

[5]We are not unmindful here of the phenomenon of passing. However, only physically marginal men pass; hence, they may be said to have been born with the necessary physical characteristics.

[6]We should mention that reference is here made to the primary endogamous circle and not to the wider class group, such as Brahmans, Chamars, and so on.

After a certain pattern of race relations has been developed, official or even scientific classification of the races has little, if any, effect upon their social relationship. In the caste system, however, an official scale of caste precedence is of considerable importance to the castes concerned. Whether we call all Hindus Caucasians or not, for instance, a light- and a black-complexioned Hindu in the United States must not expect to receive similar social treatment. But in the caste system it is of tremendous difference whether the census labels a caste clean or unclean Sudra. A man in the caste system is known for what he is; in a race system he is known primarily by how he looks.

When a Hindu girl marries into a higher caste her success is not reckoned in terms of physical criteria, for, according to Western ideas of race superiority, her caste may be physically superior. She marries, so to speak, into a higher culture; into a caste, say, of merchants, priests, or landowners. Interracial marriage, however, always involves problems of amalgamation; and the more pronounced the physical distinction, the more insistent the problems. Race prejudice rests upon physical identifiability; caste prejudice is preoccupied with cultural distinction.

A recognition of this fact may be of significance as a basis of social prediction. For instance, if we assume that both types of prejudice are inimical to social well-being, then we may ask what the factors involved in their dissolution are. We have no basis for believing that time alone will dissolve the caste society, but time has probably settled most race problems. The caste system in India will yield only to the impact of a culture more powerful than itself, while amalgamation of races will be postponed only so long as the dominant race is able to retard it.

Thus in America, Negroes are not allowed freedom of opportunity to participate in the culture principally because of an apprehension of amalgamation and its meaning in Western society. Negroes and whites are constantly approaching the race problem from different points of view, yet the end must be the same. Assuming the standpoint of fundamental rights of citizens, Negroes ask only that they be permitted to participate freely in the public life of the community. On the other hand, the articulate conservative whites hold that freedom of participation in public life must inevitably lead to "social equality" and thence to unrestrained amalgamation. Thus the outstanding freedom of democracy must be denied Negroes in the interest of racial purity and dominance. There is an inherent dilemma in American race adjustment which must remain unstable until democracy has been fully achieved. In Brahmanic India, however, amalgamation is far advanced, democracy is unknown, and the society is highly integrated and at peace with its system.

In its milieu, Brahmanism is the dominant culture, and thus far only Western culture has been able to challenge its stability. Caste disorganization will proceed with the advance of Western culture; indeed, we should expect that with the incursion of Western culture caste will disintegrate, while ideas of racial distinction and social seriation will be augmented.

Structure of Caste and Race Relations

It is sometimes said that the British form a ruling caste in India. This view, however, seems to be inaccurate. The British are, in fact, a ruling race. A caste is an assimilated dependent segment of a system; consequently, it cannot be set off against the system. If the British were, indeed, a caste, they would not be known as a people, but rather as some such group as Rajanya, or Baniya, or Brahman. One of the sources of conflict in India is that the white rulers refuse to be so recognized. The British distinguish themselves by their color and they dominate the Indians. The probability that their rule has been far more humanitarian than the crude pressure of upper castes is irrelevant.

Racial antagonism tends to divide the society vertically. Although all colored people in the racial situation may be considered subordinate to whites, with the latter horizontally superposed, from the point of view of a power relationship the races tend to be diametrically opposed. The caste system, on the other hand, tends to stratify it in a status hierarchy.[7] In the latter sense there is no status-hierarchical relationship between the white ruling class in India and the dark-skinned natives. It is not a common social-status relationship at all; one group dominates while the other is dominated, and a we-feeling is virtually absent among them. The British are not the highest caste; they stand face to face with the whole caste system.

[7]It would be inaccurate, however, to say that a caste forms a "definite stratum" of the caste hierarchy.

In other words, they have no position in the caste system; their sympathies follow a color line.

Both racial and caste separation tend to inhibit social mobility, but this common factor should not be conceived of as identifying them. The mobility which racial antagonism abhors is movement across a color fence which surrounds each race regardless of social position of the individuals. The mobility which the caste system limits is movement from one corporate group to another within an "assimilated" society.

The situation may be further illustrated by considering the relationship between Mohammedans and Hindus. For centuries before British rule the Mohammedans had been a ruling power in India. Since they were not race-conscious, however, they amalgamated with the Hindus. But the Mohammedans stand in religion opposed to the Hindus, a situation which tends to divide these two groups sharply. In time the Mohammedans yielded to the social structure of the Hindus, so that today there are castes on both sides of the line. Thus there are three systems of social restriction. The castes on either side do not intermarry among themselves, while Hindus and Mohammedans stand aloof. There is a power relationship between the latter and a status relationship among their castes. The two social phenomena are distinct, for while we may speak of two sets of caste hierarchies, the relationship between Hindus and Mohammedans does not suggest a *hierarchy* at all. Neither is there any hierarchy between the East Indians as a whole and the British.[8]

The structure of race and of caste relationship is incommensurable. Caste has reference to the internal social order of a society; race suggests a whole people, wherever found about the globe, and a people in actual world dispersion will not conceive of themselves as members of a caste. While there may be rivalry for position among castes, between races in opposition there will be struggle for power. A caste—that is to say the endogamous group—is an organization; a race is not ordinarily an organization.

[8]We use the term "hierarchy" here to mean a social gradient of persons in a social-status system. Thus we do not think of conquered and conqueror as forming a hierarchy. The Germans, for instance, subdued the French, but, for that period, we do not think of the Germans and French as forming a "power hierarchy." In short, we prefer not to think of power groups as forming hierarchies.

Race and Caste Consciousness

Race sentiment and interest tend to be universal, while caste sentiment and interest tend to be circumscribed and localized. If a part of the membership of a caste were to migrate to some area beyond easy reach of the other, the likelihood is that it will become a new caste. Not so, however, with a race. The Indian people are very much concerned about the relationship of Hindus and other races over the whole world. Thus the East Indians in Africa and in the West Indies may be outcastes because of their migration from India, but they are by no means given up by the race. Caste pride is based upon internal group invidiousness, while race pride cuts across caste lines and reaches out to a whole people, commanding their loyalty in a body.

Whether caste discrimination is crueler than race discrimination is beside the point. Thus it is a common practice to throw into the laps of Indian nationalists the fact that white people are not nearly so inhuman to East Indians as the upper-caste Indians are to the outcastes, the conclusion being that the nationalists are but "sounding brass" when they oppose the British on the grounds of race prejudice. Consider, for example, the following challenge of Sir Michael O'Dwyer to the Hindus:

> What a volume of protest would be raised throughout the Empire if the Indian settlers in South Africa or Kenya were debarred the use of the public water supply or the right to use a public highway or entry to a public building or admission to state schools on grounds of social inferiority. And yet these injustices are perpetrated today everywhere in India under the sacred name of caste on some fifty millions of Indians.[9]

That the lot of the outcastes is an unhappy one is undeniable, yet we may be sure that the Indians will never see eye to eye with O'Dwyer. Indeed, it is possible for Hindu leaders to be outspokenly self-critical and still maintain a consummate hate for the dominant race. Thus Mahatma Gandhi says of his people:

[9]Quoted from O'Dwyer's article in *The Royal Colonial Institute Journal* by Albert James Saunders, "Nationalism in India," Ph.D. thesis, University of Chicago, 1925, p. 126. It should be mentioned that the attempt of the Indian Constituent Assembly to legislate against untouchability (April 1947), which indicates further weakening of the caste system, does not invalidate this discussion of basic traits of the system.

The laws of Cochin State are in a way much worse than those of South Africa. The common law of South Africa refuses to admit equality between white and coloured races. The common law of Cochin bases inequality on birth in a particular group. But the incidence of inequality in Cochin is infinitely more inhuman than in South Africa; for an untouchable in Cochin is deprived of more human rights than the coloured man in South Africa. There is no such thing as unapproachability or invisibility in South Africa. I have no desire to single out Cochin for its disgraceful treatment of untouchables; for it is still unfortunately common to Hindus all over India, more or less.[10]

This statement of Gandhi was not, of course, calculated to rouse the Hindus against anyone; it is a sort of self-criticism looking to the support of some reform movement. But those laws against people of color in South Africa have the effect of bringing every Hindu together in mortal opposition to practically every white man. Confusion of this distinction has been a source of most egregious errors in recent sociological writings, which have assumed that "whenever rights, privileges, and duties" are unequally divided between two in-marrying groups there is established a "caste system." In the caste system there is a gradient of increments of superiority and inferiority from the depths of human degradation to the exalted guru; and unless we can conceive of a society's committing suicide, we should not expect Hindus as a whole to revolt against the system.

It is so, too, for instance, with Negroes. In their relationship with whites, Negroes in America are solicitous about the fate of Negroes all over the world. The feeling arises from a consciousness of identity of interest in opposing white mastery of their race. Stories of Nazi Germans stripping France of its monuments to Negro heroes or of Jim Crow laws in South Africa concern American Negroes as a whole probably as vitally as stories of attempts to delete the Constitution from the textbooks of Negro children in Mississippi. This is race consciousness, not caste consciousness. With race the feeling of fellowship is universal; with caste it is localized within some society. The same acute sense of gratification which the defeat of Jim Jeffries by Jack Johnson brought to the hearts of American Negroes spread forthwith even among the Negroes of Central Africa. The purview of caste feeling, however, does not extend beyond the sea. Should he migrate, the

[10]*Young India, 1924–1926*, p. 726.

caste-man is readily abandoned by his caste. Slight cultural variations in religion, custom, or occupation tend to estrange or split castes. Yet these are of practically no effect when one race is opposed to the other. It may be well to discuss briefly at this point one rather covert aspect of race and caste loyalty, the phenomenon known as "passing."

Passing

Given a common culture, passing may be thought of as a procedure by which a mixed-blood person—having the physical characteristics of the dominant race—assumes full membership in that race so that he may participate in the social advantages which it has reserved to itself. One form of passing may be called *shuttling*. Here the mixed-blood moves back and forth between the two races, leading a primary, familial life in the one, and a secondary, industrial life in the other. Almost always the familial group is of the subordinate race. Of course the shuttler is open to greater risk of detection than the passer who has decided once and for all to make a complete break with one race.

A caste-man does not pass; neither is he preoccupied with passing into another caste. However, the foolhardy may shuttle in pursuit of some transient gain, such as sitting in at the feasts and celebrations of other castes. On the other hand, we should expect most, if not all, subjugated peoples to desire to pass. Obviously it is possible only for marginal men to pass, yet the general attitude is socially significant. If, for instance, the following question were put to American Negroes: "Would you wish that you were white?" the answer would be obvious.[11] It would not be so obvious, however, if the same question were put to Negroes who had not yet felt the full pressure of white exploitation.[12] But if one were to ask all East Indians

[11]A few sympathetic critics of the writer inform him that this apparently obvious expectation is really one of major social complications. Negroes, they maintain, will be horrified by the idea of becoming white. And, indeed, this is probably true. It is a remarkable psychological fact that individuals tend to like themselves, and few would voluntarily prefer to live in other bodies. But the question is: Given the existing social advantages and disadvantages of color differences in the United States, would one prefer to be born white or colored? The writer is not unmindful of the rationalization that it is fortunate to be a Negro because the Negro race has a "cause." This, it has been said, makes life dramatic, and even tragedy is better than no drama at all. Cf. E. Franklin Frazier, *Negro Youth at the Crossways*, pp. 51–53.

[12]The Bantu "feels himself an integral part of a great people, up to whose standard he is bound to live, and in whose eyes, as in his own, he is one of the goodliest and completest creatures of God's earth." Olive Schreiner, *Thoughts on South Africa*, quoted by Everett V. Stonequist, *The Marginal Man*, p. 22.

whether they would like to become Brahmans, the question would elicit the same sort of response as if Americans were asked whether they would all like to become priests, or judges, or congressmen.

We should expect that the greater the cultural advantages reserved by the dominant race, the greater will be the desire to pass. That passing is particularly a device for widening the individual's economic and social opportunities might be substantiated by the fact that it occurs most frequently during early adulthood. So far as personal initiation is concerned, it may not occur in childhood or in old age. Indeed, those unsuccessful and unencumbered colored persons who have passed often return with advancing age to their colored family tree.

Race Conflict Addressed to the System Itself

Race conflict is directed either against or toward the maintenance of the entire order of the races. On the other hand, caste rivalry never brings the caste system into question; its purview of opposition is circumscribed by identified castes. As a matter of fact, races are not status-bearing entities in the sense that castes are. For instance, Negroes and whites in the United States stand toward each other in the relationship of subordination and superordination, a relationship implying suspended conflict. Conversely, castes stand toward each other in the relationship of superiority and inferiority, a relationship implying *natural,* socially accepted, peaceful status ordering of the society. In the first case we have a power relationship in which definite aims and ends of each group are opposed; the second is a situation of mutual emulousness among little status-bearing groups.

Intercaste jealousy and invidiousness tend to strengthen the fabric of the caste system; interracial conflict, on the other hand, is usually a challenge to the pattern of interracial adjustments.[13] Thus we might say that the greater the rivalry between caste and caste, the more stable the caste system; while

[13]The following conclusion by P. S. Joshi may illustrate the point: "The South African white . . . has been and will ever be striving to perpetuate the colour bar. The South African non-white too will . . . struggle to have it effaced. If no way of a satisfactory compromise is found at this juncture, the conflict will . . . create such a havoc in South Africa that the entire white civilization will be dislocated, and an unparalleled internecine war will flare up." Op. cit., p. 7.

To the same effect Joshi quotes Professor Edgar Brookes: "To keep the [colour bar] would mean in a century's time such a state of tension as to bring the whole civilization of the sub-continent to a state of chaos and civil war." Ibid., p. 302.

the greater the conflict between race and race in one society, the greater the opportunity for settling interracial differences. It is only when the subordinate race has obtained a relatively advanced conception of itself that it will make a bid for increased "social equality." Of course failure or a definite achievement of further suppression by the superordinate race will obviously widen the breach between them.

Such Indian outbreaks as the Mutiny of 1857 and the Amritsar Affair were conflicts which cut across caste barriers on the side of the Hindus, and across class strata on the side of the British whites. They pitted each group vertically against the other, and latent race attitudes came vividly into view.

The world position of a race tends, moreover, to determine the attitude of its members in their relationships with other races. Thus Englishmen in India derive all their dominant attitude not only from the might of the nation which they represent but also from the position which white people occupy over the whole world. Mohammedans in India are humiliated by a military reverse of the Turks, and East Indians attained a new gratifying conception of themselves in the 1904–05 defeat of Russia by Japan (a colored people), while Marcus Garvey saw the hope of black men in great ships of war manned by Negroes. This principle of power and force which seems to underlie race adjustments gives it a peculiarly eruptive and unstable character.

Race Attitudes Dynamic

"What, then, is this dark world thinking? It is thinking that as wild and awful as this shameful war [World War I] was, it is nothing to compare with that fight for freedom which black and brown and yellow men must and will make unless their oppression and humiliation and insult at the hands of the White World cease. The Dark World is going to submit to its present treatment just as long as it must and not one moment longer."[14] This "rising tide of color" which is the expressed hope of some colored leaders and the fear of some whites may be rather farfetched; at any rate, it illustrates an attitude which ever strives toward realization.

While the caste system may be thought of as a social order in stable equilibrium, the domination of one race by another is always an unstable situation. In a situation characterized by race prejudice, individuals in the

[14]W. E. B. Du Bois, *Darkwater*, p. 49.

subordinate group are always seeking to destroy the social barrier; and at points of sympathetic contact between the races, members of the superordinate group are constantly devaluating racial pretensions. As an illustration, consider the following, a fairly common reaction in the Deep South:

> Stop this "lily-white" nonsense. Quit being sidetracked by this Bourbon wail of Negro. Recognize this vital force of the immovable truth that an injustice to one American citizen will react upon all. You can't have one law for the white man and another for the Negro in our form of government. You know that those who have most talked of suppressing blacks have really suppressed you . . . and most of all Southern whites.[15]

These attitudes tend to be summatory, and a day of reckoning usually becomes the goal of the dominated race. The instability of the situation produces what are known as race problems, phenomena unknown to the caste system.

Race Relations Pathological

We may call any system of group adjustment pathological which harbors latent conflict attitudes directed toward its destruction. No form of seeming oppression of one group by another is of itself conclusive. In some cultures slavery is normal, in others extreme class subordination, and in still others outcasting. A stable social adjustment may be thought of as one in which the beliefs of a people are in harmony with their practices and in which the social system itself never comes up for critical public discussion. The occasion for a defense of the social order does not arise, and this notwithstanding the possible adverse judgment of persons residing in other societies. Ordinarily the beginning of social disorganization is heralded by critical discussion and cynical appraisal of the social system by members of the society. We may illustrate the pathological nature of modern race relations with a consideration of Negro–white opposition in the United States.

Struggle of the "social conscience" with itself has characterized the mental state of whites throughout its history of dominance over Negroes. The following rationalization by the Reverend J. C. Postell of South

---

[15]Joseph C. Manning in the newspaper *Southern American,* quoted by Ray Stannard Baker, *Following the Colour Line,* p. 264.

Carolina in 1836 is not only typical of the period but also illustrates a necessary striving to synchronize beliefs and practices.

> It [slavery] is not a moral evil. The fact that slavery is of Divine appointment, would be proof enough with the Christians that it could not be a moral evil. . . . If slavery was either the invention of man or a moral evil, it is logical to conclude that the power to create has the power to destroy. Why then has it existed? And why does it now exist amidst all the power of legislation in State and Church, and the clamor of the abolitionists? It is the Lord's doings and marvelous in our eyes; and had it not been for the best, God alone, who is able, long since would have overruled it.[16]

The basic ideological problem of whites in their relationship with Negroes, then, is that of reconciling two standards of morality. The powerful democratic Christian beliefs developed in Western society are on the side of the Negro; the racially articulate whites must shoulder the task of demonstrating that these beliefs do not include colored people.[17] Thus they strive to see democracy as implying equal opportunity among whites in their exploitation of Negroes. But such an interpretation must be constantly reinforced, for it rests insecurely on a broader world view. Not infrequently it is attacked from within the ranks of whites themselves, while practically all Negroes have been opposed to it. There are probably more words spent upon the race problem in the South than on all other social problems combined.

We may think of the racial adjustment in the South as being in a state of great instability. The cultural pattern is unsatisfactory to both races, a serious problem to each, and it is antipathetic to the fundamental social norms of the country. Respect for law in a representative form of government must be relied upon for the preservation of social institutions. But in America respect for the white race takes precedence, a condition which has resulted, especially in the South, in endemic social dysphoria. Thus we may conceive of the interracial accommodation as a persistent, malignant system which remains ominous of violent interracial strife. Anxiety, fear, mutual mistrust, and social stricture are typical mental states.

---

[16]Parker Pillsbury, *The Church as It Is,* quoted by Trevor Bowen, *Divine White Right,* p. 107.

[17]To be sure, these beliefs are not in themselves social determinants; they merely evince the basic ideological conflict between two social systems—those of the democratic proletariat and the oligarchic capitalists.

In the South the most powerful means of control and of maintaining the status quo are surreptitious and indeed criminal in the light of constituted law. The established institutions of the country do not function in support of the system; they must be suspended when white dominance is threatened. The mob, night riders, gangs, and ruling-class organizations such as the Ku Klux Klan; slugging, kidnaping, incendiarism, bombing, lynching, and blackmailing are the principal reliance of the racially articulate whites for securing their position. The instability of this accommodation may be indicated by the fact that many whites are ashamed of it. The following passage by William H. Skaggs speaks for a minority of whites:

> In the romances of mythology, ancient and medieval history, the knights-errant who were the champions of women fought in the open. Neither in the Iliad, nor the Aeneid, nor in the narratives of Plutarch, or the Chronicles of Froissart, do we find the record of a gallant knight prowling around after dark and unmercifully beating some poor, unfortunate serf.[18]

It should be emphasized that although in Western society these acts of racial aggression are defined as pathological, in Brahmanic India intercaste violence may be consistent with the fundamental beliefs of the society. A Brahman need not resort to clandestine terrorization of lower-caste men in order to establish his superiority, for undisputed public opinion gives him the right overtly to subdue disrespectful inferiors. Therefore, as a constituted form of punishment, a Brahman may direct the flogging of a low-caste man. The position of high-caste Hindus is guaranteed to them in Hindu society, but in America there is no such fundamental guarantee for whites. Its establishment must be maintained from day to day.[19]

There is here, then, an irreconcilable antithesis which must inevitably remain a constant source of social unrest. The "lawlessness of judges" in deciding the law and the "unlawful enforcement of the law" by policemen are common perversions of American institutions, but they are pivotal in the racial system. The social anomaly is inherent.

There is, of course, no unlimited freedom of participation in the culture for Negroes, and freedom of speech for both races is limited by the interest of the white ruling class. Whole systems of pseudo-scientific teachings are fostered, while sympathetic knowledge of the social life of colored people

---

[18]*The Southern Oligarchy*, p. 332.

[19]This does not mean to say that the South considers its treatment of Negroes criminal.

is practically kept out of reach of white persons. In a democracy these obstacles to communication must necessarily result in pathological social strictures.

We have attempted to show in this section that racial antagonism necessitates constant vigilance and social preoccupation, and that while attitudes of white dominance are generally recognized by Negroes, they are seldom, if ever, accepted. In the caste system, on the other hand, there is social tranquillity. In attempting to explain their social systems, most peoples will seek some sort of justification in religious terms; it is a way of achieving divine sanction for the social fact. The Hindus, more than any other people of comparable magnitude, have been able to couch their social behavior in a religious frame of reference. The following is a brief view of the success which racially articulate whites have had in bending Christianity to this task.

The Church, a Factor

It was during the days of slavery that the most insistent attempts were made to develop a religious rationale for white, ruling-class policy. The Church in the South exploited every vestige of class differentiation in the Bible. God—seldom Jesus—gave his approval.[20] With the close of the Civil War, however, the arguments became more subtle. Discriminatory practices against the colored people were either condoned by some of the churches or justified on the grounds that they contributed to the welfare of Negroes.

The struggle for consistency in the basic social beliefs continues. Segregation in or exclusion from the churches and church schools is inimical to the dominant theme of Christianity. Indeed, it has been said that the Church must choose between race prejudice and Christianity, for it cannot have both.[21] While it is in the process of making this choice, the white Church, in the South especially, like the courthouses, will continue to be ominous symbols of white dominance. The dominant group must compromise with Christianity. We need hardly mention again that the Church as an instrument of the dominant interest has never been able to achieve anything approaching the consensus of Hinduism in the caste system.

[20]See Harper and Others, *The Pro-Slavery Argument,* and John H. Hopkins, "Bible View of Slavery," *Papers from the Society for the Diffusion of Political Knowledge,* No. 6.

[21]See Trevor Bowen, op. cit., p. 148; and Buell G. Gallagher, *Color and Conscience.*

Education, a Factor

We have alluded above to the fact that one of the principal sources of prestige controlled by Brahmans is learning. What the Brahmans realized so clearly some three thousand years ago has been also repeatedly adopted by other groups interested in maintaining social ascendancy. Obviously the fact of educational discrimination is not per se an index of caste relationship. There is a good deal of truth in Ray Stannard Baker's point that "every aristocracy that has survived has had to monopolize education more or less completely—else it went to the wall."[22] In the South before the Civil War the poor whites were effectively excluded from educational opportunities, and ordinarily it was criminal to teach a Negro to read. Equal educational opportunity means opportunity for inferior classes to acquire the sophistication of dominant groups, the instrument of attack upon the philosophy and pretensions of the latter. "What the North is sending the South is not money," said James K. Vardaman, a post–Civil War Southern governor, "but dynamite; this education is ruining our Negroes. They're demanding equality."[23]

Education enhances the power of communication of the subordinate group and puts it in possession of the technique of social organization. It tends, therefore, to develop a degree of social unrest among the subordinate group, a condition which cannot fail to disturb the status quo. Thus, in characteristic fashion, a leading Southern politician, Senator B. R. Tillman of South Carolina, predicted ominously:

> Every man . . . who can look before his nose can see that with Negroes constantly going to school, the increasing number who can read and write among the colored race . . . will in time encroach upon our white men.[24]

The white ruling class has not been able to keep the printed page entirely away from the Negro; it has, however, severely limited his access to it and has succeeded somewhat in channeling his thinking.

One means of limiting the effectiveness of education is the strategy of making education itself seem useless to Negroes. They are barred, by force if necessary, from opportunities which call for initiative in thinking, so that relatively their education tends to become a costly luxury deteriorating

---

[22]Op. cit., p. 247. Indeed, every ruling class is interested in education which preserves, not in that which disturbs, the status quo.

[23]Quoted, ibid.

[24]Ibid., p. 246.

rapidly from non-use. A truncated educational career becomes the disillusioning lot of many. In the caste system, an individual is naturally limited by his caste dharma, and the idea of education serving as a means of broadening the functional scope of the individual is anomalous. The British, in their limited attempts to put in practice Western principles of popular education, have sometimes felt the compelling resistance of the caste society.[25] In the caste system there is no universal right to an education, and even members of one's own caste would not appreciate his claim to a right of freedom to use his attainments. In race situations, however, whites are on the defensive in setting up barriers to free exploitation of one's ability.

Occupation

Factors influencing the choice of occupation for both races in the United States are fundamentally different from those which operate in the caste system. The questions asked by caste members in viewing the field of labor

[25]J. C. Nesfield, inspector of schools in the North-Western Provinces, relates his experiences: "In one school there was a boy of the Kurmi caste, which is one of the most industrious agricultural castes in Upper India. He had passed a very good examination in the highest standard of the village schools; after telling him that he had now completed all that a village school could give him, I inquired what occupation he intended to follow. His answer at once was—'Service; what else?' I advised him to revert to agriculture, as there was scarcely any chance of his getting literary employment; but at this piece of advice he seemed surprised and even angry.

"At another school I met a Pasi, a semi-hunting caste, much lower in every respect than that of the Kurmi. He was a boy of quick understanding and had completed the village school course in Nagari as well as Urdu, and could read and write both characters with equal facility. He asked me what he was to do next. I could hardly tell him to go back to pig-raising, trapping birds, and digging vermin out of the earth for food; and yet I scarcely saw what other opening was in store for him. At another school there was the son of a Chuhar, or village sweeper, a caste the lowest of all the castes properly so called. He was asked with others to write an original composition on the comparative advantages of trade and service as a career. He expressed a decided preference for trade. Yet, who would enter into mercantile transactions with a sweeper even if a man of that caste could be started in such a calling? Everything that he touches would be considered as polluted; and no one would buy grain or cloth from his shop, if he could buy them from any other. There seems to be no opening in store for this very intelligent youth but that of scavengering, mat-making, trapping, etc., all of which are far below the more cultivated tastes he has acquired by attending school. And in such pursuits he is not likely to evince the same degree of skill or enjoy the same contentment as one who has grown up wholly illiterate.

"In these and such like ways, the attempts made by the government to raise the condition of the masses and place new facilities of self-advancement within their reach, are thwarted by the absence of opportunities and by the caste prejudices of the country." Quoted in *Cambridge History of India,* Vol. VI, p. 343.

are different from those which confront whites and blacks. In estimating the possibilities of an occupation, the caste-man wants to know primarily the attitude of his caste and the degree of "purity" of the occupation. When the system is functioning normally, however, individual choice of occupation is ruled out; the individual inherits his vocation. To both whites and Negroes, on the other hand, income and personal adaptability to the occupation are primary considerations; the nature of competition, fair or unfair, in the field is another important factor.

At the basis of these situations lies the difference between the economic order of the two societies. The theory of production which obtains in the caste system is founded upon hereditary group specialization and co-operation. It maintains that the most satisfactory economic system is one in which each group has a specified occupation rendering service on a sort of intergroup barter basis. It holds further that, since each group must consequently be dependent upon others for more or less of its goods and services, the general welfare demands that castes do their work properly and without failure or suffer the consequences of social displeasure. No group has a right to change its work; yet in the event that some occupation becomes plethoric or unproductive, the caste may assume another *less respectable* occupation. The latter provision is necessary to make it as distasteful as possible for castes to change their occupations. Thus a man's work becomes a social duty, and to wish for change is to shirk a grave responsibility.

Here the determinism of price and equilibrium economics operate only feebly, for the system is conceived in static terms; furthermore, the state of the market is an extremely sluggish determinant of occupational structure. There is, in fact, no "labor market" in the caste system. So far as production is concerned, the caste system is not unlike, in functional conceptualization, a colony of ants or bees, with each class of insects doing its work naturally and harmoniously. Human beings may put varying estimates on the work of each class of insects; yet, for the continuance of the insect society, the work of each may be indispensable. And so, too, it is a postulate of the caste system that the occupation of the lowest caste, though relatively inferior, is none the less important to the system. We may take our analogy a little farther in observing that castes are supposed to work with the same sort of symbiotic harmony as the insects, neither envying nor usurping each other's functions.

Production in the caste economy, then, is carried out by hereditarily specialized producers' associations which have not only a social right to peaceful enjoyment of their specialty but also a sacred duty to execute it faithfully and contentedly.[26] Profits or differential income are not controlling, for the producers of goods do not measure the value of their services by what they might earn in the production of other goods. In other words, castes do not have the alternative opportunity of working in those industries which yield the largest returns. Hence, accommodation rather than opportunism is the social basis of production. Moreover, the productive activities of castes are not mere jobs or positions; they are ways of living. The individual in the caste system never thinks of occupation as a means of advancing his social status, which is so closely bound up with that of his caste.[27] We may recall also that the system is not forced, as in slavery, where the master may use his slave in a variety of occupations; but rather it is a type of social order calling for voluntary group production and exchange.

On the other hand, economic competition in America precludes dependence of one race upon the other for its material existence. In the South, Negroes are practically excluded from such occupations as the practice of law, military service in peacetime, and the holding of political office. It is necessary that the white ruling class monopolize these occupations, for they are indispensable to the strategy of white dominance. Competition of different varieties and even open exploitation tend to keep Negroes out of many employments; so far as constitutional and religious right to any given occupation is concerned, however, both Negroes and whites are on equal footing. Even though the probability of its materialization now seems little indeed, there is nothing in our social system which condemns a Negro for aspiring, say, to the presidency of the nation. In fact, he, like all others, is theoretically encouraged to "hitch his wagon to a star." Thus, not only are

[26]Caste specialization, as distinguished from modern industrial specialization, is specialization according to product. That is to say, each caste claims the production of a certain commodity or service. Castes do not come together for the purpose of producing in concert a single commodity. In fact, the assembly-line idea is not conducive to caste stability.

[27]With the incursion of Western culture, there is in urban India today some modification of the limitations of occupational choice.

the races not identified with any particular occupation, but there is also no accepted plan for the sharing of occupations.

The most that we can say is that Negroes, because of their subordination, will be found mainly on the lower rungs of the occupational ladder; as workers they are ordinarily exploited, but striving to enhance their economic participation is characteristic. In an unpublished study of the buying power movement among Negroes in Chicago the present writer discovered from an investigation of the files of the *Chicago Whip* that Negroes had applied in large numbers for a variety of jobs that were seldom if ever open to them. Many had been trained for occupations from which they were ordinarily barred.[28] We may conclude, then, that although on the surface it might appear that the occupational limitations of the caste system are comparable to those developed under a system of racial exploitation they are, in fact, two definitely distinguishable social phenomena.

Aspiration, a Factor

In practically every instance of white–colored race contacts there has been a remarkable stimulation of ambition among the colored group.[29] In most instances the white dominant group has observed this attitude with apprehension. It is, however, exceedingly pertinacious, for it goes hand in hand with acculturation.

Unlike castes in India, Negroes in America have been seeking to increase their participation and integration in the dominant culture. Cessation of such striving is an inseparable feature of the caste system. Indeed, culturally speaking, the castes in India have arrived. If, for instance, the Negro–white relationship were a caste relationship, Negroes would not be aspiring toward the upper social position occupied by whites; their concern, rather, would be almost entirely with the development of a socially sufficient internal organization. It is this centrifugal cultural drive among Negroes which produces fear and antagonism among the white ruling class. Thus the scheme of race relationship in America centers about attempts of Negroes to reach new levels of participation and opposition to these attempts by whites.

[28]See also Charles S. Johnson, *Growing Up in the Black Belt,* Table 9, p. 195, for a study of the deviations of choice of occupation of Negro children from the occupations of parents.

[29]In rare instances, as in Australia, where the black and white cultures differ very greatly, there has been only feeble effort among the colored to emulate the whites.

Even as far back as the days of slavery Negro aspiration was everywhere evident. We could not conceive of an institution of hope, such as the Negro spirituals, developing among the lower castes of India; nor of the latter's producing such masters of compromise and appeasement as the early Negro preacher personality type. The slaves sang:

Bye and bye
Ah'm gonna lay down dis heavy load
and

Walk together chillen,
Don'tcha get weary!

Probably no one who has seen the Negro preacher in his cabin church of the Deep South, marching triumphantly over the King's English amid great surges of "Amen! Amen!!" and "Yes, Lord!" lifting his congregation in repeated affirmations of faith and hope, could fail to realize that these people are far from being resigned in spirit. Their spontaneous songs of freedom and courage in the face of great trial, their incessant call at the "gates of heaven," these are not unlike in emotion the spirit of liberty which has everywhere in Christendom moved men to action. Hinduism provides no such powerful escape from the claims to superiority of dominant castes. Ray Stannard Baker tells a story of hope among post–Civil War Negroes:

> Just at the close of the war [President R. R. Wright of the Georgia State Industrial College] was a boy in a freedman's school at Atlanta. One Sunday, General O. O. Howard came to address the pupils. When he was finished, he expressed a desire to take a message back to the people of the North. "What shall I tell them for you?" he asked. A little black boy in front stood up quickly and said: "Tell 'em, Massa, we is rising."[30]

In the South, Negroes have been effectively excluded from politics, but they are by no means apathetic to the fact that they have heavy stakes in this field. In his farewell address, one of the last remaining Civil War Negro congressmen, George H. White, said:

> This, Mr. Chairman, is perhaps the Negroes' temporary farewell to the American Congress; but let me say, Phoenix-like he will rise up some day and come again. These parting words are in behalf of an outraged, heartbroken, bruised, and bleeding, but God-fearing people, faithful, industrious, loyal people-rising

[30]Op. cit., p. 92.

people, full of potential force. . . . The only apology that I have to make for the earnestness with which I have spoken is that I am pleading for the life, the liberty, the future happiness, and manhood suffrage of one-eighth of the entire population of the United States.[31]

Langston Hughes has given a sympathetic interpretation of the encouragement and sacrifices of the many colored mothers who welcome drudgery that their children may have wider social opportunities. Thus a mother counsels in the last lines of the poem, *Mother to Son:*

So boy, don't you turn back.
Don't you sit down on the steps
'Cause you finds it's kinder hard.
Don't you fall now—
For I'se still goin', honey,
I'se still climbin'
And life for me ain't been no crystal stair.

Sometimes, of course, the going is very difficult, and even strong men rail against the unyielding barriers. Again Hughes seems to symbolize this attitude:

My hands!
My dark hands!
Break through the wall!
Find my dream!
Help me to shatter this darkness,
To smash this night,
To break this shadow
Into a thousand lights of sun,
Into a thousand whirling dreams
    Of sun![32]

Among the most revealing aspects of the relationship, however, is the open criticism of whites by a minority of whites. This phenomenon seems to be present in virtually all types of race relations, but it is practically unknown in the caste system. Furthermore, its absence is not a mere chance occurrence; it is rather the peculiar social view of castes which precludes it. The following is a typical expression of the former kind of sentiment:

[31]Congressional Record, 56th Congress, 2d Sess., January 29, 1901, p. 1638.
[32]Excerpt from *As I Grew Older.* See James Weldon Johnson, *The Book of American Negro Poetry,* 1931.

> We southern whites are more the victims of slavery than the Negroes
> because, possessing a little economic advantage, we have nourished the constant
> inclination toward unfairness. The Negro, with notable patience, has neverthe-
> less not failed through the long years to be aspiring; above all in the present
> juncture, he demands justice, and here he is our master.[33]

In a previous section we have attempted to examine the function of
marriage in the caste system. We shall now look into the role of marriage
in race relations and its meaning as an identifying criterion of caste.

Race, Caste, and Intermarriage

It is common knowledge that in the United States the crucial problem
of race relations is that of Negro–white intermarriage. This is apparently
the crowning fear of white men. Very few, indeed, even of those who would
criticize their white brothers for discrimination against Negroes, have had
the courage to face the fierce opposition to any principle of free marital
preference between the races. The articulate whites have held generally
that, the larger the number of light-complexioned Negroes, the greater the
difficulty of segregating them; hence neither intermarriage nor miscegenation can be permitted. Moreover, it is not of the essence of importance
whether the father of the mixed-blood is white or black.

We think that some authors put too much emphasis upon the "sexual
gains" of whites in the South. It is true that Negro men do not have the white
man's opportunity to select women from either race, but there is reason to
believe that sometimes Negroes conceive of this disparity of opportunity
as an investment. That the ruling-class whites so understand it is manifest
from the equal application of the marriage restriction laws. On this score
Baker cites a typical attitude. "Our people," says a district attorney in
Mississippi, "Our white men with their black concubines, are destroying
the integrity of the Negro race, raising up a menace to the white race,
lowering the standard of both races, and preparing the way for riot, mob,
criminal assaults, and finally, a death struggle for racial supremacy."[34]

[33]Broadus Mitchell, *Black Justice,* American Civil Liberties Union pamphlet, May 1931,
pp. 6–7. See also Ren Maunier, *Sociologie coloniale,* pp. 77–83, for a discussion of
progressive and regressive cultural tendencies among different races in contact with Western
culture. In his speech of March 15, 1941, at the dinner of the White House correspondents'
association, President Roosevelt said: "There never has been, and there isn't now, and there
never will be any race of people fit to serve as masters over their fellow men."

[34]Ray Stannard Baker, op. cit., p. 167.

Had the Southern situation been a caste system, the sexual "loss" to Negroes might have been absolute. In America, however, regardless of which race takes the initiative in bringing it about, amalgamation is one sure way of solving race problems. The white guardians of race purity are never so bitter, never so condemnatory, as when they deal with white men's consorting with Negro women. To these guardians of the status quo it is treason against one's own race. Even though such laws were not unconstitutional, we could hardly conceive of a rule which bars the marriage of Negro men and white women and at the same time sanctions sexual relationships between white men and Negro women. It is apparent that either situation will bring about the same end.

Although in the caste system there is no particular social impulsion, other than possible physical desire, for low-caste men to covet women of higher castes, there is a definite social advantage to colored men in their marrying white women. In a racial system which puts a cultural premium upon lightness of color, a Negro man can give his children considerable advantage by such a marriage. And as a matter of fact, in those states in which intermarriage is not prohibited, it appears that some four out of every five mixed marriages are of Negro men and white women.[35] Because of the racial antagonism on this question, the couple may be embarrassed in either group. Other things being equal, however, their children should fare better than the father because of their lighter complexion. Assuming that the sex ratios are similar for the races, we should expect that, should the cultural advantage of whites decrease relatively, the number of intermarriages will increase and the ratios of men intermarrying will tend to approximate each other. It has been reported that intermarriage has increased in Soviet Russia with the extension of economic and political equality to all racial groups.[36]

Marriage Restriction Laws

Since only somewhat more than half of the states prohibit intermarriage between different races, the question arises as to the meaning of

---

[35]See Robert E. T. Roberts, "Negro-White Intermarriage," unpublished master's thesis, University of Chicago, 1940, p. 10.

[36]Bernhard J. Stern, "Intermarriage," *Encyclopedia of the Social Sciences.*

these laws[37] with respect to the race-caste hypothesis. All the states which prohibit intermarriage between whites and some other race also prohibit it between whites and Negroes. Some states which once had miscegenation laws have repealed them, while the laws which now exist have been individually enacted over a period of years. Furthermore, the laws apply only from the date of enactment, so that all prior interracial marriages are legal.

Now if we are to examine the question whether marriage prohibition is a criterion of caste in America, we should like to ask whether it is statutory or customary prohibition which is determining. It would be contrary to reason to hold that a caste system in a given state is instituted or abolished with the enactment or abrogation of an intermarriage law. Clearly, then, the statute does not establish the caste. But American Indians and Negroes are forbidden to intermarry in Louisiana and Oklahoma, while in Maryland, Negroes may not marry Malays. Could it be that these different groups are castes? In Idaho a white person may marry a Mongolian but not a Negro; shall we assume that Chinese and whites form a caste in opposition to Negroes? "Persons of different races" are prohibited from intermarrying in South Dakota; is this state most truly representative of a racial caste system in America? The mere posing of these questions seems to make it evident that the operation of the statutes provides no support to the race-caste hypothesis.

The alternative is that custom and not law provides the negative sanctions, from which fact we must conclude that custom may operate with different degrees of rigidity in contiguous states, those with and those

[37]Twenty-seven states forbid marriage between whites and Negroes: Oregon, California, Nevada, Idaho, Utah, Arizona, Colorado, North Dakota, Nebraska, Missouri, Indiana, Kentucky, Tennessee, West Virginia, Virginia, Maryland, Delaware, Oklahoma, Texas, Arkansas, Louisiana, Mississippi, Alabama, Florida, Georgia, South Carolina, and North Carolina.

Some fifteen states expressly or implicitly forbid marriage between whites and Mongolians: Arizona, California, Georgia, Idaho, Mississippi, Missouri, Montana, Nebraska, Nevada, South Carolina, Oregon, Utah, South Dakota, Wyoming, and Virginia.

Ten states implicitly or expressly forbid Malay-and-white marriage: Arizona, California, Georgia, Maryland, Nevada, Oregon, South Carolina, South Dakota, Virginia, and Wyoming.

Five bar unions with Indians: Arizona, Georgia, North Carolina, Oregon, and South Carolina. Two bar unions with Asiatic Indians: Arizona (Hindus), and Virginia (Asiatic Indians).

See Charles S. Mangum, Jr., *The Legal Status of the Negro,* p. 253.

without an intermarriage law. In the United States there is undoubtedly a definite opposition to intermarriage between whites and peoples of color, yet this attitude tends to become very much confused when we attempt to explain it in terms of caste. The possibility of hypergamous marriage among castes in India is a factor contributing to a further elucidation of these social situations.

Hypergamy

Although Herbert Risley wrote extensively on hypergamous marriage in India, he never saw hypergamy as a social phenomenon distinguishing caste and race relations. In India superior-caste males may marry inferior-caste women, and this does not result in consolidation of castes. It is declared in the laws of Manu that:

> For the first marriage of twice-born men, wives of equal caste are recommended; but for those who through desire proceed to marry again the following females, chosen according to the direct order of the castes, are most approved. . . . A Sudra woman alone can be the wife of a Sudra, she and one of his own caste, the wives of a Vaisya, those two and one of his own caste, the wives of a Kshatriya, those three and one of his own caste, the wives of a Brahmana.[38]

Thus the higher the caste, the greater the opportunity for "mixture of blood." Yet hypergamy has not resulted in a lessening of caste consciousness. "If caste was based on distinction of race," says R. V. Russell, "then apparently the practice of hypergamy would be objectionable, because it would destroy the different racial classes."[39] In the Punjab outcaste women, Chamars, are sold to Jats, Gujars, and Rajputs as wives.[40]

The taking of colored women by white men, at least in their early contact with a people of color, is also considered a form of hypergamy; in fact, some writers have found it possible to identify caste and race relations on this very point. But the significant difference between these two forms of hypergamy is that in the case of castes the identity of the groups is not affected by it; while in the case of race relations, the more frequent the intermarriages, the less clear the racial distinctions. Women taken from lower castes may be a total loss to the latter—unless it be that the lower

---

[38]Manu, III, 12–13. See also Vishnu, XXIV, 1–4.

[39]*The Tribes and Castes of the Central Provinces of India,* Vol. II, pp. 363–64.

[40]George W. Briggs, *The Chamars,* p. 42.

caste gains some spiritual gratification from a sense of one of its members participating in a higher dharma—but the gain to the people of color varies all the way from complete amalgamation to the establishment of a restless mixed-blood people, who tend to become a challenge to the pretensions of their fathers' race. Hypergamy can never become a law in a biracial system, for the system will be doomed from the moment of its enactment. Here again, then, we have a social fact which seems common to two different situations, yet whose social meanings are distinct.

Endogamy

Endogamy is self-imposed restriction upon outmarriage by a social group. Any group which explicitly limits marriage of its members to persons within the group may be called endogamous. In Western society there are negative sanctions against upper-class persons marrying lower-class persons, yet we do not ordinarily think of the upper class as being endogamous. In fact, a social class cannot be endogamous because it has no consciousness of its limits.

With the exception of hypergamy, endogamy among castes in India is a basic trait. A group cannot function within the Brahmanic system if its social area of choice of partners in marriage is undefined. The caste is a truly endogamous social entity. The prohibitions against outmarriage are not a reaction to similar actions of some other castes; they are the most reliable means available to the caste for protecting its heritage. Furthermore, the social heritage of low castes is to them as important as that of high castes is to the latter.

Some students of the caste system have concluded that endogamy among castes is similar to endogamy as they observe it between race and race in Western society. But if we return to our situation in the United States we shall see that neither Negroes nor whites belong to groups that are endogamous in the caste sense. Their choice of partners in marriage is limited only by matters of cultural compatibility or localized racial antagonisms. A caste is organized as a caste not particularly with respect to some specified group but rather with reference to every conceivable group or individual. White people in the United States, on the contrary, may marry whites from any other part of the world. Generally they are opposed to intermarriage with peoples of color, but unless racial antagonism becomes directed, a marriage

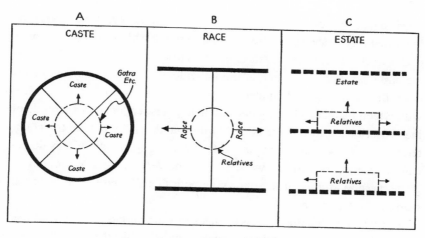

Caste, Race, and Estate Endogamy

here and there is not particularly objectionable. When the social situation is favorable, as in Hawaii, whites may intermarry more readily than some other races.

Being themselves a colored people, Negroes have only a cultural inhibition. They will intermarry comparatively freely with every other race in the United States. Indeed, as we have mentioned above, in some states whites have found it contrary to their interest to permit marriage between Negroes and other peoples of color within the state. The opposition of Negroes to intermarriage with whites is a rather complex reaction. It varies in response to the attitude of whites in different parts of the country. It may be possible to illustrate three significant types of endogamy: caste, race, and estate endogamy.

In Figure A the marriage system of castes is represented by an outer circle enclosing castes, with an inner circle marking off the exogamous parts of the castes. An individual born within a section of the small circle— sapinda, gotra, clan, sept, pravara—must look outside of it for a mate, though not beyond the limits of his caste.[41] Thus, within the system, each caste is closed to the other. Even marriage among castes of collateral status is avoided.

Figure B illustrates the pattern of race endogamy obtaining in the United States between whites and Negroes or Chinese or Indians or Japanese. The inner circle represents the familial or exogamous group, and the middle bar indicates a negative intermarriage sanction among whites against some

[41]For a discussion of this, see S. V. Karandikar, *Hindu Exogamy*.

specific race or races. Thus, with the exception of near relatives and some identified race, each race is free to marry among any of the other peoples of the world. Therefore, the race is not a closed endogamous unit. While the caste sanction declares that the individual may not marry out of his caste, the racial sanction stipulates Negroes, or Chinese, or Indians as races with which its members may not intermarry. The endogamous attitude of the proscribed colored race is ordinarily founded in resentment, a counterattitude. Some such feeling as the following is apparent: "If they do not care to intermarry with us, we shall hate the very thought of seeming to crave the opportunity of intermarrying with them." And so the color bar gains a negative support.[42]

Figure C illustrates the process of endogamy in an estate system. The inner rectangle represents the familial exogamous group, while the horizontal lines indicate more or less distinct estate barriers or strata. Within a given estate which may extend beyond national boundaries, marriage is freely sanctioned—differences in culture, of course, are limiting factors. Although lateral unions are normal, persons within the estate may seek to "marry up," a tendency which is resisted. Thus the social estate tends to be endogamous with respect to lower estates, but exogamous with respect to upper ones. Furthermore, the wider the disparity in social-estate position, the more rigid the sanctions against estate intermarriage. Practically all that we have said about estate endogamy may also be said about social classes, with the exception that it is the individual or family or clique which defends or strives after status.

We may conclude, then, that endogamy is of different significance in caste and race relations. The caste is locked within its immediate marital circle; the race, on the other hand, is opportunistic and will intermarry or refuse to do so as its interest or cultural strategy demands.

Race and Caste Stability

Rigid social sanctions are developed in both the caste system and among races in opposition. But contrary to the belief of some writers, rigidity in itself is not the distinguishing social fact. We have no definite measure of rigidity of social distance; therefore, to speak of "the *rigidity* which the

[42]According to Ray Stannard Baker, "The prejudice of white people has forced all colored people, light or dark, together, and has awakened in many ostracised men and women who are nearly white, a spirit which expresses itself in a passionate defense of everything that is Negro." Op. cit., p. 156.

caste system has attained in the South" may be misleading. Here, too, the meaning of the social phenomenon as it functions in given social situations involves the significant problem.

In the caste system each caste knows or assumes that it knows its place. The very nature of racial opposition, however, precludes attainment of such a degree of adjustment. The poet pictures some of this indecision thus:

> *My old man's a white old man,*
> *And my old mother's black;*
>
> *My old man died in a fine big house,*
> *My ma died in a shack.*
> *I wonder where I'm gonna die,*
> *Being neither white nor black?*[43]

The desire for interracial peace is certainly a desideratum among the white ruling class of the South, but in this respect Negroes are on the defensive. Observe, for example, the purpose of Hoke Smith, a typical Southern politician:

> Those Negroes who are contented to occupy the natural status of their race, the position of inferiority, all competition being eliminated between the whites and the blacks, will be treated with greater kindness.[44]

It is, notwithstanding, the Negroes' unalterable attitude against acceptance of a place of natural inferiority—that is to say, a condition of certain exploitability—which keeps race problems very much alive. There is no peace; evidently there shall never be social complacency while whites continue to maintain such a position.

> When I first went to the South [says Baker] I expected to find people talking about the Negro, but I was not at all prepared to find the subject occupying such an overshadowing place in southern affairs. In the North we have nothing at all like it; no question which so touches every act of life, in which everyone, white or black, is so profoundly interested.[45]

One factor which contributes to the flux of race relations in America is the irregularity of interracial practices and discrimination. It provides an

---

[43]Langston Hughes, *Cross.*

[44]Quoted by Ray Stannard Baker, op. cit., p. 249.

[45]Ibid., p. 26.

opportunity not only for countless attacks upon the color line, but also for a minority of whites to disregard rules favored by the articulate ruling class. Segregation and "Jim Crow" are tangible symbols of white dominance, yet these practices are sufficiently inconsistent to make their application frequently unexpected. In some cities in the Deep South white taxicabs compete for Negro passengers; in others they refuse Negro trade. In some cities Negroes must enter and leave the streetcar from the rear; in others they may enter at the center. The effect of "Jim Crow" laws as a stereotyping factor in race discrimination is graphically illustrated by Stephenson:

> Suppose, for instance, a colored passenger were to board a train at Philadelphia for Evansville, Indiana, and go through Maryland, West Virginia, and Kentucky. Pennsylvania and West Virginia have no "Jim Crow" laws, Maryland and Kentucky have. When the colored passenger reaches the Maryland line, must he enter a car set apart for colored people? When he reaches the West Virginia line, may he go back into the coach with white passengers? When, again, he reaches the Kentucky line, will he be forced to return to the car set apart for his race? And, finally, when he comes to Indiana, may he once more return to the car for white passengers?[46]

These apparently minor variations in the laws, customs, and etiquette contribute vitally to the instability of the whole system.[47] Moreover, the very dynamic character of our capitalist society precludes the attainment of that final racial adjustment so much desired by the exploiting class.

We may conclude, therefore, that race adjustment is not a static accommodation. Years ago Booker T. Washington recognized this very clearly. There have always been backward-circling currents, but the direction of the stream has been unmistakable. "The story of the American Negro has been one of progress from the first."[48] The race problems assume different aspects from decade to decade, and the issues tend to become more and more challenging.

---

[46]Gilbert T. Stephenson, *Race Distinction in American Law,* p. 217.

[47]For a discussion of legal variations in Jim Crow laws, see Charles S. Mangum, Jr., op. cit., Chap. VIII; and C. S. Johnson, *Growing Up in the Black Belt,* pp. 276–80, for variations in race etiquette in the rural South.

[48]Booker T. Washington, *The Story of the Negro,* Vol. 2, pp. 397–98; see also James Weldon Johnson, "The Negro and Racial Conflict," *Our Racial and National Minorities,* ed. by Francis J. Brown and Joseph S. Roucek, p. 350.

Dynamics of Race Relations

The fundamental social force operating among Negroes is social assimilation and amalgamation. In America there has been a strain toward assimilation among most unassimilated groups. This is particularly powerful among Negroes because their parent culture was not only designedly extirpated, but it also lost virtually all prestige on the American scene. Colored people, then, are oriented toward the broader culture of the country; only through social rebuffs are they turned back upon themselves. In this the attitude of whites and Negroes is not similar but opposed. The racially articulate whites feel that they must guard their exploitative advantage (not specifically their occupation) for exclusive enjoyment, while Negroes are seeking increasing cultural participation. The difference between the racial attitude of whites and caste attitude is that whites *wrongfully* take the position of excluding groups from participating freely in the common culture, while castes *rightfully* exclude others from participating in their dharma.

The world view of the caste is turned inward, and its force is centripetal; that of Negroes is turned outward, and its force is centrifugal. Negroes, in America at least, are working toward the end that Negroes as a social symbol would become non-existent. However, the caste of Brahmanic India of either low or high status is devoted toward the perpetuation of itself.[49] The solidarity of Negroes is admittedly temporary; it is a defense-offense technique. The ideal of Negroes is that they should not be identified; they evidently want to be workers, ministers, doctors, or teachers without the distinction "Negro workers," "Negro ministers," and so on. In short, they want to be known unqualifiedly as American citizens, which desire, in our capitalist society, means assimilation and amalgamation.

[49]According to James Weldon Johnson, "We should by all means make our schools and institutions as excellent as we can possibly make them; and by that very act we reduce the certainty that they will forever remain schools and institutions for 'Negroes only'. . . . We should gather all the strength and experience we can from imposed segregation. But any good we are able to derive from the system we should consider as a means, not an end. The strength and experience we gain from it should be applied to the objective of *entering into,* not *staying out of,* the body politic." *Negro Americans, What Now?,* p. 17. To the same effect Frederick D. Patterson writes: "If the most is made of segregated opportunities now, those who develop thereby will do much . . . to break down segregation and other barriers to normal participation." *What the Negro Wants,* Rayford W. Logan, ed., p. 274.

It may not be out of place to say in conclusion that this question about whether race relations are caste relations is not simply an argument about words. In this essay we have attempted to show that they are political-class relations. To accept one view or the other is virtually to redefine one's approach to the study of the subject. One great disappointment about the procedure of those students who have conceived of race relations as caste relations is that they have not employed the caste concept as a hypothesis or a theory, but rather they have used it mainly as a substitute title or name for "race." It is likely that if they had attempted to use caste as an instrument of analysis, they should have discovered that, thus applied, it is decidedly worthless.

5.
The Meaning of Heredity and Outcasting in Caste and Race Relations

The Problem

There are few characteristics of the caste system which are so generally recognized as heredity, and yet the function of heredity in the system has been commonly misunderstood. Almost without exception those authorities who have identified caste and race relations have been prone to mistake the meaning of heredity among castes. Consider, in illustration, the following typical conclusion:

> In essence the caste idea seems to be a barrier to legitimate descent. A union of members of the two castes may not have a legitimate child. All such children are members of the lower caste and cannot be legitimated into the upper caste by the fact that they have an upper caste father or mother.[1]

The orientation here, as usual, is biological and evidently deduced from an observation of the obdurate dichotomized type of interracial adjustment in the South. Thus an insidious truism concerning American race relations has served to skew fundamentally thinking about caste. It runs somewhat as follows: "No colored child can become white; in some colored-white societies whites have decided to ostracize all peoples of color; hence no intermarriage can result in offspring of equal status with whites. Since heredity is the 'essence' of caste, it must follow that socially bipartite race systems are caste systems." To those who think that castes are anti-color devices, this reasoning seems irrefragable. It may be shown, however, that this very idea of heredity helps us further to distinguish between caste and race relations.

[1] John Dollard, *Caste and Class in a Southern Town,* p. 63.

In the first place, it may be well to emphasize that two or more castes may have the same general status in the caste system. Therefore, when we speak of the offspring of an intercaste marriage, higher and lower status need not be necessarily implied. One might ask, then: What is the problem of legitimizing children born to members of different castes with equal status? Further: What do castes really inherit? How does this differ from the inheritance of races? Before attempting to examine the latter question, we shall discuss broadly the nature of heredity among castes.

Nature of Heredity among Castes

Of all things which children of mixed-caste marriages might inherit, the physical possibilities are of the least significance. Of primary importance seems to be an imputed character. Manu declares that from "blamable marriages spring sons who are cruel and speakers of untruth, who hate the Veda and the sacred law."[2] As a rule, the lower the caste of the man and the higher that of the woman, the more vicious the children.[3] The early Hindu law books are not always consistent on the question of the status of children of hypergamous marriages. According to John D. Mayne, "They give no conclusive evidence that the sons of all inter-caste marriages were ostracized from the upper caste."[4] One of the early law books declares: "On women of lower caste than their husbands sons are begotten who follow the caste of their mothers."[5] While Manu assures us that "he who was begotten by an Aryan on a non-Aryan female may become like to an Aryan by his virtues. . . ."[6] The estate of the father of sons born to wives of decreasing caste status goes to these sons in proportions decreasing directly with the status of their mothers.[7]

[2]Manu, III, 41.

[3]Vishnu, XVI, 3, 6, 14.

[4]John D. Mayne, *A Treatise on Hindu Law and Usage,* 8th ed., Sec. 88.

[5]Vishnu, XVI, 2.

[6]Manu, X, 67.

[7]"If there are four sons of a Brahmana springing from four different wives of the four castes, they shall divide the whole estate of their father into ten parts. Of these, let the son of the Brahmana wife take four parts; the son of a Kshatriya wife, three parts; the son of a Vaisya wife, two parts; the son of a Sudra wife, a single part." Vishnu, XVIII, 1–5. See also Manu, IX, 149, 151, and VIII, 416.

"This relationship subsisting between husband and wife of two different, not to say widely separated castes, was not held to be disgraceful or worthy of denunciation. On the contrary,

But variations in the possibilities of inheritance in the system seem to be even more widespread. The principal reason for this seems to be the absence of a physical basis of inheritance. The child of an intercaste marriage may become a legitimate member of the upper caste; it may descend to the lower caste; it may go into a caste of intermediate status, or it may fall to a position beneath that of either caste. The Chandala, a Sudra-man-Brahman-woman cross, occupies a status beneath that of either parent, while the children of Brahman men and Sudra women ordinarily have a status above Sudras, "for through the power of the seed sons are born . . . who are honored and praised."[8] Of especial interest to us is the rather frequent identification of the children of hypergamous marriages with the caste members of the father. On this point Sherring observes:

> The infanticide practiced by Rajpoots has been a fruitful cause of the intermingling of low caste blood with their own. Failing to secure wives for their sons, on account of the great paucity of girls in their own tribes, they have, for many generations, contracted alliances with girls of low castes, especially the Raj Bhars, who having been purchased or carried off from their families, have been transformed into Rajputanis, or wives of Rajpoots.[9]

One device for maintaining exclusiveness among castes is that of taking the women of a given caste but refusing to return the favor by giving daughters in marriage. "Thus, Kurils will take Dohar girls in marriage, but will not give their daughters to Dohars."[10] And the offspring of such marriages follow the caste of their fathers. "In the Kangra Hills the son of a Brahman father and a Rajput mother is reckoned a Brahman."[11]

while it was less dignified for a Brahman to marry a woman of a lower caste than a woman of his own, yet marriage in the one caste was just as legal as marriage in the other." M. A. Sherring, *Hindu Tribes and Castes,* Vol. I, p. xvi.

[8]Manu, X, 72.

[9]Op. cit.

[10]George W. Briggs, op. cit., p. 35.

[11]*Census of India, 1911,* Vol. I, Pt. 1, p. 378. "Throughout the Panjab the Jats and Gujars and certain classes of Rajputs who have not enough women of their own, sometimes buy as wives Chamar and other low caste women, accepting without inquiry the allegation that they belong to their own caste. So long as they themselves are satisfied, no one else seems to mind." Ibid. See also R. V. Russell, *The Tribes and Castes of the Central Provinces of India,* Vol. I, p. 365.

Racial Differences

In race relations it is almost always sufficient merely to look at a man to identify him; in caste relations his status must be inquired into. A man's child by a woman of lower caste, according to the pleasure of his caste, may be initiated and accepted into his caste. In the case of a racially dichotomized society it is not possible to legitimize the children of mixed marriages by their unreserved inclusion into the dominant race. This is so because nothing short of making the colored child of an interracial marriage white will be sufficient. The 1901 *Census of India* explains further certain possibilities of inheritance based upon deficiences of the sex ratio. Thus:

> Where females are in marked defect, a relaxation of the restrictions on marriage inevitably follows. Sometimes it takes the form of expressly permitting males of a higher caste to marry females of a lower one. Thus in the Panjab, Khatris will marry Arora women and the Aroras in their turn take as their wives women of lower castes. But, more often it leads to laxity in inquiring into the status and antecedents of the proposed bride, and to a willingness to accept the statements that may be made regarding her by her guardians or vendors. In this way there is in some parts a regular traffic in young females. Girls are often enticed from their homes in the Panjab and sold either in some other part of that province or in Sind. The purchasers of women in the Panjab are mainly Jats, Aroras, and Kirars, but the practice is also known among the Kombohs and Khatris.[12]

A race inherits, then, physical marks, real or imputed; the caste inherits intangible cultural or personality attributes. It is true that a person's caste ordinarily comes to him as a cultural heritage, but we may emphasize that descent within the meaning of the Brahmanical system does not have the same application as can be given it in discussions of race relationships in, say, the Southern states of the United States. To use the term at all in describing race relationships in the South, we must mean racial identity, for a person of Negro blood born in England or France or the West Indies, who happens to be in the South, must expect to assume the racial status of all other Negroes. It should be gross, indeed, to hold that all Negroes in the world belong to the same caste by descent.

If we look beyond the misguiding truth that a colored child cannot become white, then we may examine the meaning of legitimacy in racially

---

[12]Vol. I, Pt. 1, Sec. 227. See also J. J. Meyer, *Sexual Life of Ancient India,* Vol. I, p. 57; N. K. Dutt, *Origin and Growth of Caste in India,* Vol. I, p. 587.

dichotomized societies. In the first place, it appears that the mixed-blood offspring may be legitimate according to statutory law. Consequently, although mixed-blood children may not be accepted as white in any part of the United States, in all states where mixed marriages are not declared illegal the child may inherit property as though his parents were of one race.[13] In one state, Indiana, the child is legitimate, even though there is an intermarriage prohibition law.[14] In the eyes of the law, then, the mixed-blood child may be legitimate. We know of no case in Hindu law where a child who is able to inherit without discrimination the estate of his father remains debarred from inheriting his father's caste.

In the second place, the child may be unreservedly accepted by both mother and father as a natural member of their family. In Haiti, before the revolution, white planters married colored women, and their children ordinarily inherited normal parental affections. These children, however, were not regarded by the white public as its equal. The criterion of acceptance depended not upon superiority of caste but upon superiority of race; in other words, their color alone determined their acceptability. If the colored woman happened to be light enough in complexion, the children were likely to be considered white as a matter of course. And finally the child may be legally defined as a member of its colored-parent group, as in the United States; or it may enter a new group, such as the Cape Coloreds of South Africa or the Eurasians of India. However, by the very definition and purpose of a dichotomized racial situation, the children of mixed marriages can never be given social opportunities identical with the dominant whites. To be legitimized in the white group, of course, can mean only that the mixed-blood child has equal economic, juridical, and social opportunities with the whites.

All Hindus inherit not only a caste status with respect to other caste-men, but also the physical marks of Hindus. Because of the latter heritage they may be considered social subordinates of white men. But the latter assumption develops a power relationship of white dominance and not a caste position of inferiority. The Hindu's racial heritage identifies him with all other Hindus, while his caste heritage differentiates him from all other-caste

[13]Kennington vs. Catoe, 68 S. C. 470, 47 S. E. 791 (1904).
[14]Indiana Statutes Annotated (Burns, 1933), Sec. 44-107.

Hindus. All caste members must of necessity inherit some racial affiliation, but obviously racial affiliation does not presuppose caste membership.

When reference is being made to relationships between races, it becomes rather cumbersome to think of the legitimizing of children as a determining factor. If the colored parent is accepted among the whites, then the child will also be accepted; but if the parents are not accepted, the children may be. In America both parties to a mixed Negro-white marriage can belong legitimately to neither group; yet, according to the lightness of color of the colored partner, their children may become a part of either the white or the Negro group.

Outcasting

The term "outcasting" employed as a factor in discussions of race relations ordinarily refers to racial ostracism socially imposed as a penalty for intermarriage. However, the phenomenon of outcasting is far more involved than this. Restricted to the meaning presented here, the term may be suggestive in popular use. But in the hands of the student seeking an understanding of race relations, it is likely to be misleading. As a substantive, the term "outcaste" may be used in two ways to indicate: (1) a person belonging to one of the menial, depressed tribes or castes who are generally considered impure, such as the Chamar, Dom, or Bhangi; or (2) that person who has been expelled from a caste as a punishment for breach of caste rules. It is with the latter meaning that we shall now be concerned.

Outcasting, in the latter sense, is a well-recognized, dependable form of punishment in a caste system. It has the effect of not merely lowering an individual in the estimation of his fellows, but also of putting him beyond the bounds of his caste. An outcasted person does not continue to be a member of his caste. Barring the death penalty, a caste can inflict no greater punishment upon one of its members. Thus, the Abbé Dubois tells us:

> The expulsion from caste, which follows either an infringement of caste usage or some public offense calculated, if left unpunished, to bring dishonor to the whole community, is a kind of social excommunication, which deprives that unhappy person who suffers it, of all intercourse with his fellow creatures. It renders him, as it were, dead to the world, and leaves him nothing in common with the rest of society. In losing his caste he loses not only his relatives and friends, but often his wife and children, who would rather leave him to his fate

than share his disgrace with him. Nobody dares eat with him or even give him a drop of water. If he has marriageable daughters, nobody asks them in marriage, and in like manner his sons are refused wives. He has to take it for granted that wherever he goes he will be avoided, pointed at with scorn, and regarded as an outcaste.

If after losing caste a Hindu could obtain admission to an inferior caste, his punishment would in some degree be tolerable; but even this humiliating compensation is denied him. A simple Sudra with any notion of honour and propriety would never associate or even speak with a Brahmin degraded in that manner. It is necessary, therefore, for an out-caste to seek asylum in the lowest caste of Pariahs if he fails to obtain restoration in his own; or else, he is obliged to associate with persons of doubtful caste.[15]

A person once outcasted can seldom regain admission to his caste. For some offenses, however, principally those against one's relatives, the offender may be pardoned by his caste. He usually prostrates himself before the assembled caste-men, "listens without complaint to the rebukes which are showered upon him, receives the blows to which he is oftentimes condemned, and pays a fine. . . ."[16] There are many wrongs which may merit the penalty of outcasting. Among some castes the eating of beef stands as an unpardonable enormity; "people have been outcasted because they had *smelt* beef."[17] Whole families may be outcasted for becoming involved in the marriage of a widow; while refusal to attend the funeral of a relative or failure to invite certain caste-men to one's feast is to court the judgment. Prohibited intercaste marriages hold a secure place among capital offenses, but these are rare, for in India marriage is a major business of castes. Relatives and leaders of the caste assume too pivotal a role in weddings to make unsanctioned marriages a frequent occurrence. It should be remembered, of course, that the significance of caste rules ordinarily varies with the caste.

Now let us consider the possibilities of outcasting among races. It has been frequently said, in support of the race-caste hypothesis, that in the United States white persons are outcasted for marrying colored persons and vice versa. We propose to examine the accuracy of this conclusion. When we speak of a white or Negro person's losing caste for breach of caste rules,

[15]*Hindu Manners, Customs, and Ceremonies,* 3d ed., p. 38.
[16]Ibid., p. 41.
[17]J. N. Farquhar, *Modern Religious Movements in India,* p. 419.

what really do we mean has been lost? In this society only the state can punish, and outcasting is no constituted form of punishment. It is not even recognized by the state. Outcasting must mean, then, that the white or Negro race shuns one or a group of its members, though the latter may stand unblemished before the law. It seems too indefinite, however, to hold that a race can shun a person, for a race is ordinarily too socially heterogeneous. Only some persons of certain social-class levels may laugh at or ridicule the individual for breach of social-class convention. In fact, the likelihood is that social-class demotion may be mistaken for outcasting.

For the breach of many types of social sanctions, or even misfortunes, such as loss of employment, going to prison, intermarriage with Indians, Jews, or Negroes, white persons may suffer more or less serious loss of class status, yet they can never "lose caste" in the sense of becoming anything other than white persons. Far less is it possible to conceive of the "white caste" as a whole, or any significant part of it, as falling or rising into some other caste. This seems to be a vital distinction between caste and race relations.[18]

Moreover, neither a Negro nor a white person can be outcasted in the sense that a Hindu caste-man can be, for the simple reason that neither belongs to a caste as the Hindu does. Death alone can remove an individual from his race.[19] Although the latter fact seems clearly evident, much confusion has resulted from letting it out of view. A man could be expelled from his caste and forgotten; he cannot be expelled from his race. A white man in the United States who has committed the cardinal sin against his race, let us say by intermarrying, will continue to represent his race. In spite of sentiment against him, he remains a major concern of interracial policy makers.

[18]In India it seems quite possible for entire castes to change their status and identity. "The Sahnsars of Hushyarpur were admittedly Rajputs till only a few generations ago, when they took to growing vegetables, and now rank with Arains. Some of the Tarkhars, Lohars, and Nais of Siras are known to have been Jats or Rajputs who within quite recent times have taken to the hereditary occupation of these castes; and some of the Chubans of Karnal, whose fathers were born Rajputs, have taken to weaving and become Shekhs." Danzil Ibbetson, *Panjab Castes,* p. 8.

[19]The caste system presumes life membership in the caste, but the biological fact of race ensures inevitable affiliation.

Therefore, the racially articulate whites are interested, as all the interracial laws indicate, in disrupting his mixed marriage and not in outcasting him. In fact, the instrumentality of outcasting is not available in the American social order. In the caste system the outcaste is dead so far as his former caste is concerned, but a race cannot thus easily give up its members. Should the white woman or man find sanctuary among colored persons, he will remain even as threatening to white dominance as if there were no white sentiment against him.

The crux of the matter lies in the fact that no race by vote or sporadic agreement can determine who shall be included within its ranks. Sociologically speaking, races are defined by intergroup conflict and not by internal selection. A caste, however, is the sole arbiter of questions concerning its membership. It may exclude or include persons at will, and birth presents no bar to this prerogative. The destiny of a caste is consciously in the hands of its members.

6.
The New Orthodoxy
in Theories of Race Relations

In this chapter we shall discuss the racial theory of two reputable scholars, Robert E. Park and Ruth Benedict, and elaborate somewhat our own point of view.[1] We shall not, of course, give any consideration to the views of the political biologists who continue to be interested in developing somatic theories of race relations. Trying to deal scientifically with these theories is exceedingly depressing, for almost invariably their apparent objectivity is only a mask for an ulterior purpose.

We cannot defeat race prejudice by proving that it is wrong. The reason for this is that race prejudice is only a symptom of a materialistic social fact. If, for instance, we should discover by "scientific" method that Negroes and Chinese are "superior" to tall, long-skulled blonds—and this is not farfetched, since libraries have been written to prove the opposite— then, to the powers that be, so much the worse for Negroes and Chinese. Our proof accomplishes nothing. The articulate white man's ideas about his racial superiority are rooted deeply in the social system, and it can be corrected only by changing the system itself.

Race prejudice is supported by a peculiar socioeconomic need which guarantees force in its protection; and, as a consequence, it is likely that at its centers of initiation force alone will defeat it. By stepping clear of the whole unnumbered productions of intellectual apologists for Nordic racial pretensions, Adolf Hitler has come into the open and has shown quite

---

[1]In our selection of a noted sociologist and an anthropologist who have shown considerable interest in race relations, we are not primarily interested in equating theories. We shall hope only that a critical review of their position may throw light upon significant currents of thought in the field. Moreover, it does not seem necessary to refer to certain statements by these writers merely because they appear correct but have no bearing upon the thesis developed in this study. Social theories gain in meaning and significance if their authors are known; and this fact, we shall hope, is the justification for our personal approach.

clearly the real process by which "Aryans" are made and unmade. Those people are "Aryans" who have the physical might to support their claim.

The study of race relations, then, is fundamentally a sociological study. In the past, however, the sociologists have not been sufficiently convincing in their analysis to command general recognition. We turn now to a consideration of the character of their thinking.

Robert E. Park

Professor Robert E. Park needs no introduction to American social scientists. His position as a major sociologist and outstanding teacher is well known; his continued interest in the study of race relations is equally well known. He was one of the most consistent opponents of that host of pseudo scientists who take it upon themselves to explain why peoples of color are inferior to white people and how they became that way.

Dr. Park wrote no book on race relations, but he was very much concerned with the theory of race relations in his *Introduction to the Science of Sociology* done in collaboration with E. W. Burgess. His theory will be found mainly in his numerous articles, and evidently the most significant of these is that contributed to the volume *Race Relations and the Race Problem,* edited by Edgar T. Thompson.

A critical examination of Park's ideas on race relations is valuable not only because it may throw some light upon the state of conservative thinking in this field, but also because it may bring into small focus theories that have gained considerable currency in the social sciences.

The Meaning of Race Relations

In attempting to gain insight into modem race relations Professor Park goes into the life of Ancient Greece and Rome and then concludes: "It is obvious that race relations and all that they imply are . . . the products of migration and conquest. This was true in the ancient world and it is equally true of the modern."[2] This apparently truistic conclusion can have meaning only when we know that "all . . . relations of cultural or racial minorities with a dominant people may be described . . . as types of race relationship,

[2]"The Nature of Race Relations," in *Race Relations and the Race Problem,* Edgar T. Thompson, ed., p. 7.

even though no evidences exist either of race conflict, on the one hand, or of obvious racial diversity on the other."[3]

To Park, then, the mere cultural difference of a dominant and a subordinate people is sufficient to produce the phenomenon which we have come to know as "race relationship." Is it necessary to specify "dominant people"? What if the "cultural relations" take place between peoples of collateral cultural status within the same geographical area? With such a definition it becomes quite easy for Dr. Park to find race problems among the ancient Greeks. He does not differentiate significantly between the types of social systems which may or may not produce the variation in human nature necessary for an expression of racial antagonism. On this score Ruth Benedict observes interestingly:

> The principal objective of early imperialism was to secure tribute and to bind the subjugated areas to the capital, not, as in later forms, to exploit a new labor market in working mines or plantations. Therefore, it was economical to honor the most able of the conquered peoples and to depute authority to them. In regard to the folkways and cultural life of the provinces, Roman policy was one of *laissez faire.*[4]

Professor Park asserts further: "The struggles of minor nationalities for self-determination is a phase of race conflict; a phase . . . in which language rather than color is the basis of division and conflict."[5] The question here is whether either color or language has ever been *the basis* of race conflict. We shall revert to this in a later section.

It seems quite obvious that this definition is entirely too broad to be of service in analyzing race relations as they are commonly understood; and, as we shall see, Park uses it mainly as a stumbling block. It may be suggested that Dr. Park intends to refer here to something quite vital, that such contacts as take place between a dominant culture group and a "minority people" present all the characteristic relations and mechanisms that we are familiar with in the case of racial conflict. But this is the very question under consideration. Park states neither the characteristics of racial conflicts nor those of culture-group conflicts; hence, if it is necessary, we shall have to accept this identity upon his arbitrary opinion.

[3]Ibid.

[4]Ruth Benedict, *Race: Science and Politics,* pp. 160–61.

[5]Robert E. Park and Ernest W. Burgess, *Introduction to the Science of Sociology,* p. 646.

Race Prejudice

Race prejudice, Dr. Park admits, has been a very difficult social attitude to define; "no one has yet succeeded in making it wholly intelligible."[6] But our author proceeds to identify the phenomenon:

> Race prejudice is like class and caste prejudice—merely one variety of a species . . . as far as race relations are concerned, racial minorities are merely social classes . . . race prejudice in the southern states is caste prejudice.[7]

The omnibus scope of the concept of race relations is here continued until it becomes clear that there is confusion. If, so far as race relations are concerned, racial minorities are social classes, is class conflict race conflict? Is there antagonism between social classes? What, at any rate, is a social class? If race prejudice is like caste prejudice, what is caste prejudice? These queries remain unanswered.

The following definition also goes beyond mental grasp: "Race prejudice may be regarded as a spontaneous, more or less instinctive, defense-reaction, the practical effect of which is to restrict free competition between the races."[8] Could one say, for instance, that the race that is prejudiced is merely suffering from an inferiority complex? This definition seems to follow such a deduction.

Park does not even settle upon a working definition of a race, "since ethnologists themselves are not agreed upon any classification of the human family along racial lines."[9] But he says, "The closest approach we shall ever make to a satisfactory classification of races as a basis of antipathy will be that of grouping men according to color. . . . This would give us substantially the white . . . the yellow . . . and the dark . . . races. The antipathies between these general groups . . . will be found to be essentially fundamental."[10] What now becomes of our all-inclusive definitions of race relations and race prejudice? If this is in fact the author's[10a]

[6]Ibid., p. 578.

[7]"The Basis of Race Prejudice," *The Annals,* Vol. CXXXX, November 1928, pp. 11ff.

[8]Park and Burgess, op. cit., p. 623; see also Park's repetition of this definition in J. F. Steiner, *The Japanese Invasion,* p. xiii.

[9]Park and Burgess, op. cit., p. 634.

[10]Ibid., p. 636.

[10a]For simplification of reference we shall assume that the citations from Park and Burgess, *Introduction to the Science of Sociology,* are by Park.

classification of races, then race prejudice must exist only between peoples of different color. If not, he should have included in it the social phenomena of classes, castes, minority groups, and nationalities.

Moreover, Dr. Park has here made a significant assumption, the clarification of which is vital for an understanding of race relations. He assumes that there are fundamental color antipathies between whites, yellows, and blacks. Of course Park does not demonstrate this, and we might ask the question: What historical evidence is there to show that before the white man made his contact with the peoples of color there existed race prejudice among these peoples?

Caste and Race

The major part of Professor Park's racial theory is involved with his ideas of caste, and this very fact constitutes his major failing. On the origin of caste in India, he writes:

> A permanent caste system in India seems to have had its origin in the obvious diversity of racial types in the Indian population. It is a well-recognized fact that visibility is an important factor in maintaining social distance and incidentally making class distinction hereditary.[11]

This statement covers considerable ground, but it is typical of all the racial theories of "the origin" of caste. As we have attempted to show in a previous chapter, there is available no historical evidence that caste in India had a racial origin. To repeat, the deductive procedure behind this belief is that of imputing the writer's own racial conditioning to an age which could not possibly have known it. Why should "visibility" produce thousands of castes in India? The naked Indian eye has never been so delicate a color detector. But what really is Park's meaning of caste? Although he presents no clear description of it, he declares:

> The sect is a spontaneous association; the caste is, in many ways, a *forced* association. After having chosen a profession—let it be priest, soldier, magistrate—man belongs necessarily to a caste. . . . In India the caste is determined by birth, and it is distinguished by a characteristic trait: the persons of one caste can live with, eat with, and marry only individuals of the same caste.
>
> In Europe it is not only birth, but circumstances and education which determine the entrance of an individual into a caste; to marry, to frequent, to invite to the

[11]In Edgar T. Thompson, ed., op. cit., p. 16.

same table only people of the same caste, exist practically in Europe as in India. . . . We all live in a confined circle, where we find our friends, our guests, our sons- and daughters-in-law.[12]

Therefore, we might say in conclusion to this passage, everyone in the world belongs to a caste. Clearly the author has reached an almost unlimited expansion of the concept of caste. Indeed, he says: "Every religious society tends to assume the character of a caste . . . in so far at least as it prohibits or discourages marriage outside the church or the sect."[13] And "the prostitute, in America, until recently constituted a caste."[14]

We may also observe the contradiction that in India, after a man has chosen his profession, he belongs to a caste, yet his caste is determined by birth. Moreover, it should be interesting to know in what ways the caste is a forced association.

With this frame of reference Park proceeds to interpret race relations in the United States. First, however, there are some traits of caste which are particularly important in this analysis. "Etiquette," he writes, "is the very essence of caste, since the prestige of a superior always involves the respect of an inferior."[15] But why should etiquette be the essence of caste and not that of class or the family or any other little-dog–big-dog relationship?

At any rate, in an earlier statement, Park seemed to have favored a different "essence." Thus he observes:

Sighele points out that the prohibition of intermarriage observed in the most rigid and absolute form is a fundamental distinction of the caste. If this be regarded as the fundamental criterion, the Negro in the United States occupies the position of a caste.[16]

Therefore we arrive at the conclusion that race relations in the United States are in fact caste relations. "The 'color line' is . . . a local variety of what students of society and human nature call caste."[17] This was not always so, but we are not at all certain when it came about.

[12]Park and Burgess, op. cit., pp. 205–6.
[13]In Edgar T. Thompson, ed., op. cit., p. 44.
[14]Park and Burgess, op. cit., p. 722.
[15]In Bertram W. Doyle, *The Etiquette of Race Relations*, p. xx.
[16]Park and Burgess, op. cit., p. 722.
[17]Park, in Bertram W. Doyle, op. cit., p. xvii.

The social order which emerged with the abolition of slavery was a system of caste—caste based on-race and color. . . . So firmly was the system of caste fixed in the habits and customs . . . of both races in the South that all the social disorganization incident to the Civil War and Reconstruction were not sufficient wholly to . . . destroy it.[18]

The question here is: Was slavery the caste system or did the caste system arise after slavery? Dr. Park does not answer this clearly. In the passage above he seems to say that slavery was caste. And to the same effect he asserts: "It was when, after the abolition of slavery, the caste system broke down that the discords and racial animosities that we ordinarily identify with the race problem began."[19]

With this confusion we pass to another stage in the evolution of race relations: "The Negro group has gradually ceased to exhibit the characteristic of a caste and has assumed rather the character of a racial or national minority."[20] However, this appears to be contradicted forthwith. In referring to the Jim Crow experience of Congressman Mitchell on a train, the author declares: "This is an *instance of caste* a little less innocent and amiable than the casual mistake of addressing a bishop as 'boy.' "[21]

At this point we may consider Park's explanation of endogamy among Negroes. He reaches this position: ". . . restrictions on intermarriage . . . make the Negro an endogamous social group, in much the same sense that Jews, the Mennonites, and any of the more primitive religious sects are endogamous."[22] Here the author seems to be very much in error.

Negroes are definitely not endogamous as the Jews or the tribe; in fact, Negroes are not endogamous at all. Such religious cultures as Judaism and Mohammedanism tend to oppose assimilation. Intermarriage is abhorrent to orthodox Jews; and sanctions against it come from within the group itself. This is also true of certain sects. Because white people are

[18]Ibid., p. xvi.

[19]Ibid., p. xxi. Again: "The caste system as it had existed was maintained not by law but by a body of customs that was more or less self-enforcing. One evidence of the change in race relations, as a result of emancipation, was the efforts of the southern communities to enforce by statute racial distinctions and discriminations which were difficult or impossible to maintain by custom and tradition." Ibid., p. xx.

[20]Ibid., p. xxiii.

[21]Ibid., p. xxiv. (Italics added.) See also "Racial Ideologies," *American Society in Wartime,* William F. Ogburn, ed., p. 178.

[22]In Bertram W. Doyle, op. cit., p. xxii.

endogamous with respect to Negroes, it does not follow that Negroes are also endogamous. There are no primary sanctions among Negroes prohibiting outmarriage; there is too much color in the group for that. Negroes are probably the freest people in the United States, so far as attitudes against outmarriage are concerned, and this notwithstanding certain reactions against white endogamy. A recognition of this distinction should obviate many spurious comparisons between race relations and "culture-minority" problems.

The Mores and Race Relations

There is a definite ring of fatality and mysticism in Park's discussion of the stability of race relations in the South. This is evidently due to the false outlook derived from the caste belief and to an over-reliance upon the apparent extent to which race relations in the South are "in the mores," a static *laissez-faire* concept. The following illustrates his position:

> The failure of reconstruction legislation to effect any fundamental change in the South's caste system is less an illustration of the recalcitrance of the Anglo-Saxon than of Sumner's dictum that it is not possible to reform the mores by law.
>
> People not reared in the southern tradition have sometimes assumed that southern people's insistence on racial segregation is evidence that they cherish some deep, instinctive antipathy for the Negro race. Anyone who accepts that conception of the matter is likely to be somewhat mystified when he learns that the Negro is quite all right in his place. And that place, like the place of everyone else, is the one which tradition and custom have assigned him.[23]

Here is an extraordinary mixture of ideas that is indeed "mystifying." What constructive thinking about race relations might one do when one is told that "custom" assigned the Negro to his place? If not custom, then one is left to choose between "Anglo-Saxon recalcitrance" and the "mores." At any rate, let us consider the mores. To what extent are race relations in the South in the mores? Here Park follows William G. Sumner's fatalistic ideology quite closely.

According to Sumner, "Each individual is born into [the mores] as he is born into the atmosphere, and he does not reflect on them, or criticise them any more than a baby analyzes the atmosphere before he begins to breathe

[23]Ibid., p. xvi.

it." When this concept is applied to race relations in the South, the prospects of change appear dismal indeed. Thus he asserts:

> The whites have never been converted from the old mores. . . . Vain attempts have been made to control the new order by legislation. The only result is the proof that legislation cannot make mores. We see also that mores do not form under social convulsions and disorder. . . . Some are anxious to interfere and try to control. They take their stand on ethical views of what is going on. It is evidently impossible for any one to interfere. We are like spectators in a great natural convulsion. The results will be such as the facts and forces call for. We cannot foresee them. They do not depend on ethical views any more than the volcanic eruption on Martinique contained an ethical element.[24]

This is the passage from which Park took inspiration; it has also been the inspiration of the white ruling class of the South. Gunnar Myrdal is right when he asserts:

> The theory of folkways and mores has diffused from the scientists and has in the educated classes of the South become a sort of regional political *credo*. The characterization of something as "folkways" or "mores" or the stereotype that "stateways cannot change folkways"—which under no circumstances can be more than a relative truth—is used in the literature on the South and on the Negro as a general formula of mystical significance. It is expressed whenever one wants to state one's opinion that "what is, must be," without caring to give full factual reasons.[25]

At any rate, the question arises: What really is supposed to be "in the mores" and in whose mores? Clearly it could not be the whole social system of the South that is in the mores, and it would be difficult to accept the rationalization that it is the fear of intermarriage.

The "old mores," the slavery attitudes, were not the static phenomena which Sumner and Park have defined for us. They were never assimilated in the American society. Indeed, they might be compared with large stones in the stomach that were not only indigestible but also productive of increasing irritation, until at last they had to be disgorged. So, too, modern race relations keep the social system in a state of continual unrest. These race relations in the South have developed out of the immediate need of the

[24]*Folkways*, pp. 77–78. In the same vein he continues: ". . . nothing sudden or big is possible. The enterprise is possible only if the mores are ready for it. The conditions of success lie in the mores. That is why the agitator, reformer, prophet, reorganizer of society who has found out 'the truth' and wants to 'get a law passed' to realize it right away is only a mischief-maker." Ibid., p. 113.

[25]*An American Dilemma*, p. 1049; see also pp. 1045–57 for a good discussion of this subject.

white exploiting class to restore as far as possible the complete control over its labor supply, which it enjoyed during slavery. A high degree of restoration has been achieved, not through the force of "the mores," but through a continued and vigorous campaign of anti-Negro education and the creation of innumerable situations for the exercise of extralegal violence against Negroes or against whites who seek to intervene in their protection.[26]

The attitudes of the white ruling class in the South, called mores, are in fact conflict attitudes. The statement often heard in the South that "nothing, nothing will ever change the South" is like the statement, "They shall not pass." Both presume powerful antagonists; both are war cries. But whereas the general who takes the latter position may be fairly certain that he will stand his ground, the former is made by a class which recognizes that it is constantly losing ground. This class may be compared with a man rowing hard upstream, while his boat moves slowly down with a powerful current. It gives him considerable encouragement to shout that he will never go down.

Then, too, the anti-Negro attitudes which the ruling class propagates among the white masses cannot be "in the mores" of the people of the South

[26]See Carey McWilliams, "Race Discrimination and the Law," *Science and Society,* Vol. IX, Winter, 1945, pp. 1–22, where the political and economic interests behind the laws which establish anti-racial "mores" are convincingly reviewed; also Frank E. Hartung, "The Social Function of Positivism," *Philosophy of Science,* Vol. 12, April 1945, pp. 120–33; and E. B. Reuter, "Southern Scholars and Race Relations," *Phylon,* Third Quarter, Vol. VII, 1946, pp. 232–33.

In fact, it may be an advantage to clear thinking, where social controls in modern society are being analyzed, to abandon altogether the concepts "folkways" and "mores" with their magical implications. Other terms may be devised to designate customary behavior that is more or less culturally mandatory in our highly dynamic social system.

[27]This point seems so significant that we shall illustrate it by quoting at length from a feature article published in a leading white newspaper of the Deep South. Probably no right is more desired by Negroes in the South than the right of free and equal access to the ballot; and none is more effectively denied them. Let us observe the state of the mores on this score:

"Next Tuesday is . . . July 4, the day we mark radiant on our calendar as the birthday of our nation, when our forefathers signed the great charter of American democracy. Fundamental to that charter, and on which every other claim rests, is the premise: 'All men are born equal, and are endowed by their Creator with certain inalienable rights.' Next Tuesday we celebrate this birthday of democracy by substituting 'white men' for 'all men,' as we eliminate Negroes from the right of self-government. We will do this with the slogan upon our lips, 'white supremacy.' In its final analysis it may be truly said that this war which we are fighting all over the world today is in protest against the claim of one race to be supreme over another race. Thus the Japanese began their rape of China, and the Germans their slaughter of the Jews. What do we mean by race supremacy? Racial pride may be a wholesome emotion, or it may become a menace to the rights and welfare of mankind.

because at least half of them, all the Negroes and a considerable minority of whites,[27] reject them entirely. In reality race relations in the South are rather more in the trigger finger of the people than in their mores. Dr. Park might just as well argue that it is in the mores of the Germans, the "Aryan

"Here in the South we are proud of our Anglo-Saxon blood, and basing our claims on the achievements of the race in the past, proclaim the dogma that our race must be supreme. This is a fatal fallacy. Any people, or individual who claims superiority on the achievements of the fathers, denies the fundamental principle of democracy by attempting to substitute the heresy of inheritance for the test of righteousness of achievement. We can only hope to claim any vestige of superiority for the Anglo-Saxon race by maintaining today the spirit and ideals by which our fathers won their place in the world of yesterday. What was that spirit, and what were their ideals?

"The foundation of Anglo-Saxon civilization was laid at Runnymede, when the English people won from the crown the right of trial by jury. It was the birthday of the English spirit of fair play. Out of that great charter was born years after our own great charter, which without discrimination of race, color or creed declares 'all men are endowed by their Creator with certain inalienable rights.' My Anglo-Saxon pride is in their record of fair play, their fine sense of chivalry, their disciplined obedience to their own laws, and their long history of protection of the weak against the strong.

"By that record the civilization of the South must be tested today. We have in our midst—by no choice of their own—a minority race absolutely dependent upon us for 'life, liberty and the pursuit of happiness.' The traditions of our past, and the very genius of our race, demand that we grant to them the 'inalienable rights' proclaimed in the Declaration of Independence, which we glorify next Tuesday.

"Of course, the slogan 'white supremacy' was born in the South during the terrible days of 'reconstruction,' when conscienceless 'carpetbaggers' and 'scallawags' mobilized an ignorant race, just freed from slavery, and voted them en masse against the welfare of both races. The fear of Negro supremacy produced the defense of white supremacy. But it is folly not to recognize the revolutionary change which has taken place among the Negroes in 65 years. Their progress educationally and commercially is really unmatched in the story of races. There has come an intelligent racial pride, and sense of responsibility, to their own leaders, which makes it impossible for conscienceless politicians to repeat the horrors of the reconstruction political nightmare.

"Of course, we must not shut our eyes to the truth that there is still a great mass of ignorant irresponsibility among the Negroes, just as there is such a dead weight of ignorant and irresponsible mass of whites. But just here is our faith in democracy. It is not a form of government, but an educational process. It is in the exercise of freedom of choice, with its responsibility, that men develop in intelligence and character. To lose faith in this process is to lose faith in democracy.

"The story which Celestine Sibley told the other day of the schools of democracy established for Negro children was profoundly significant. It reveals the Negroes' faith in democracy, and also their faith that, despite their present attitude, eventually the white people will grant them the privileges of democracy. That is my faith also. Whatever may be the final legal interpretation of our present plan for a 'white primary,' it is so obviously an annulment of the purpose and spirit of our constitution, that it cannot stand against the growing sentiment of an enlightened democratic conscience. We cannot much longer continue to subject Negroes to 'taxation without representation' or draft them to jeopardize their lives in defense of a democracy which denies them the right of franchise." M. Ashby Jones, feature writer, in the Atlanta *Constitution,* July 2, 1944.

race," to rule over the peoples of central Europe. Even all the "convulsions and disorder" of World War I and all the attempts of the League of Nations to legislate did not disturb this attitude. Furthermore, anyone who had an opportunity in the early forties to observe the relations between the "German race" and the French people—how the crestfallen Frenchman grinned and reached for his cap as the proud German conquerors went by on the streets of Paris—cannot help concluding that it is in the mores of these people to be ruled by the master German race. Of course the utter nonsense of this hardly bears recitation, and yet it is not different from the antagonistic racial adjustment in the South. Park and Sumner see only the accommodation aspect of the interracial situation. The "convulsions and disorder" of which they speak are themselves the product of maladjustment. Convulsions and disorder do not develop out of social situations that are in the mores; moreover, the racial situation in the South remains pregnant with further possibilities for social eruptions.

Nothing is more discussed, nothing more provocative of heat, indeed, nothing more unstable than race relations in the South. The dominant attitudes supporting race relations are inconsistent with the fundamental democratic mores of the nation, and they are becoming increasingly so. The white ruling class is, to be sure, determined to keep the Negro exploitable, but it dares not rely upon "the mores" to do this. It must exercise "eternal vigilance" in maintaining an ever-present threat of interracial violence if it is to continue its exploitative social order. The Southern racial system "lives, moves, and has its being" in a thick matrix of organized and unorganized violence. As Myrdal observes, "There exists a pattern of violence against Negroes in the South upheld by the relative absence of fear of legal reprisal. Any white man can strike or beat a Negro, steal or destroy his property, cheat him in a transaction and even take his life, without much fear of legal reprisal."[28] It may not be too strong an assertion to state that such a condition in America could never become stabilized.

Poor Whites

With respect to the role of poor whites, Park seems to have accepted the popular illusion that there is a fundamental antagonism between them and the colored people. For instance, he says:

[28]Op. cit., p. 559.

> It has been the violent . . . efforts of the New South, *in which the poor white man has become the dominant figure,* to enforce upon Negroes the ritual of a racial etiquette . . . that has been responsible for a good deal, including lynchings. . . . Negroes acquired in slavery the conviction that a poor white man was an inferior white man, and the course of events since emancipation has not increased the black man's respect for the white man as such.[29]

Might we not ask what "course of events" Park has in mind which might have resulted in an increase of the Negroes' "respect for the white man as such"? In what sense is the poor white man a dominant figure in the South? Indeed, even at a lynching we do not conceive of the poor white as being the dominant figure—unless, of course, we mean that in most of the lynch mobs lower- and middle-class whites are more numerous. But this could not be Park's meaning, because white mobs have always been thus constituted. As a matter of fact, both the Negroes and the poor whites are exploited by the white ruling class, and this has been done most effectively by the maintenance of antagonistic attitudes between the white and the colored masses. Could anything be more feared, is any aspect of race relations more opposed by this ruling class than a *rapprochement* between the white and the colored masses?

This, too, is consistent with Park's belief in the stability of race relations. Those who rely upon the mores for their interpretation of racial antagonism always seek to define their problem as an irrational up-thrust of primitive folk attitudes; as having its roots in some instinctual drive toward repugnance between all biologically distinguishable peoples, a repugnance beyond the reach of cultural variations.

An Estimate

Shorn of its censual and descriptive support, Park's theory of race relations is weak, vacillating, and misleading; and, to the extent that it lends "scientific"[30] confirmation to the Southern rationalizations of racial exploi-

[29]In Bertram W. Doyle, op. cit., p. xxi. Italics added.

[30]Consider, for instance, the manner in which David L. Cohn, one of the most rabid and effective apologists for racial discrimination in the South, brings Park into his service. Says Cohn: "Let those who would attempt to solve [the race] question by law heed the words of the distinguished sociologist, Dr. Robert E. Park: 'We do not know what we ought to do until we know what we can do; and we certainly should consider what men can do before we pass laws prescribing what they should do.' " See "How the South Feels," *Atlantic Monthly,* January 1944, p. 51.

tation, it is insidious.[30] His teleological approach has diverted him from an examination of specific causal events in the development of modern race antagonism; it has led him inevitably into a hopeless position about "man's inhumanity to man," a state of mind that must eventually drive the student into the open arms of the mystic.

It may seem puerile and even unfair to criticize Professor Park's ideas and views in this fashion. Puerile because one, knowing of Park's kaleido-scopic intellectual style, has no difficulty in finding inconsistencies and occasional contradictions in his writings; and unfair because the citations have been abstracted from their animated setting. But we have been especially careful not to distort these ideas and to consider only that part of Park's theory upon which he seems to put some continued reliance. In fact, this is apparently the whole substance of Dr. Park's contributions to the theory of race relations.[31] Moreover, it is easy to discover inconsistencies but not so easy to show that these inconsistencies are inevitable.

If we know that one believes that the cultural conflicts which existed in ancient times are in fact race conflicts, that race prejudice is caste prejudice, that "the mores" of the white man determine or even maintain the pattern of race relations, then we approach his work with assurance that there will be inconsistencies. Such theories do not explain the facts, and in order to achieve some semblance of logical exposition one must inevitably become inconsistent and contradictory.

Probably the crucial fallacy in Park's thinking is his belief that the beginnings of modern race prejudice may be traced back to the imme-morial periods of human associations. As a matter of fact, however, if it is not recognized that color prejudice developed only recently among Europeans, very little, if any, progress could be made in the study of race relations. We must also recognize the peculiar socioeconomic necessity for race prejudice. Indeed, Park himself almost put his finger upon this. Thus he writes:

> There was no such thing as a race problem before the Civil War, and there was at that time very little of what we ordinarily call race prejudice, except in the case of the free Negro. The free Negro was the source and origin of whatever

[31]For a comprehensive bibliography of Park's writings, see Edna Cooper, "Bibliography of Robert E. Park," *Phylon,* Vol. VI, Winter, 1943, pp. 372–83.

[32]Ibid., p. xxi.

race problems there were. Because he was free, he was at once an anomaly and a source of constant anxiety to the slaveholding population.[32]

Although we do not agree entirely with this statement, it might yet have been observed that in the United States the race problem developed out of the need of the planter class, the ruling class, to keep the freed Negro exploitable. To do this, the ruling class had to do what every ruling class must do; that is, develop mass support for its policy. Race prejudice was and is the convenient vehicle. Apparently it now becomes possible to give meaning to the phenomenon of race prejudice.

Race prejudice in the United States is the socio-attitudinal matrix supporting a calculated and determined effort of a white ruling class to keep some people or peoples of color and their resources exploitable. In a quite literal sense the white ruling class is the Negro's burden; the saying that the white man will do anything for the Negro except get off his back puts the same idea graphically.[33] It is the economic content of race prejudice which makes it a powerful and fearfully subduing force. The "peonization" of Negroes in the South is an extreme form of exploitation and oppression, but this is not caused by race prejudice. The race prejudice is involved with the economic interest. Indeed, "one does not feel prejudice against a beast of burden; one simply keeps him between the shafts." However, it is the human tendency, under capitalism, to break out of such a place, together with the determined counterpressure of exploiters, which produces essentially the lurid psychological complex called race prejudice. Thus race prejudice may be thought of as having its genesis in the propagandistic and legal contrivances of the white ruling class for securing mass support of its interest. It is an attitude of distance and estrangement mingled with repugnance, which seeks to conceptualize as brutes the human objects of exploitation.[34] The integrity of race prejudice must be protected and maintained by the exploiters, for it is constantly strained even at the very few points where sympathetic contact is permitted between the people.

[33]In his second inaugural address President Lincoln arrived at a similar conclusion when he declared: "It may seem strange that any men should dare to ask a just God's assistance in wringing their bread from the sweat of other men's faces. . . ."

[34]It is some such idea Alexis de Tocqueville had when he wrote: "The European is to the other races of mankind, what man is to the lower animals; he makes them subservient to his use; and when he cannot subdue, he destroys them." *Democracy in America,* Vol. II, p. 182.

Race prejudice, then, constitutes an attitudinal justification necessary for an easy exploitation of some race. To put it in still another way, race prejudice is the social-attitudinal concomitant of the racial-exploitative practice of a ruling class in a capitalistic society. The substance of race prejudice is the exploitation of the militarily weaker race. The slogan that the colored man shall never have social equality merely means that the colored man must be forever kept exploitable.

We should not be distracted by the illusion of personal repugnance for a race. Whether, as individuals, we feel like or dislike for the colored person is not the crucial fact. What the ruling class requires of race prejudice is that it should uniformly produce racial antagonism; and its laws and propaganda are fashioned for this purpose. The attitude abhors a personal or sympathetic relationship.[35] The following statement by Kelly Miller seems to be relevant:

> Henry W. Grady, not only the mouthpiece, but also the oracle of the South, declared in one of his deliverances that he believed that natural instinct would hold the races asunder, but, if such instinct did not exist, he would strengthen race prejudice so as to make it hold the stubbornness and strength of instinct.[36]

This point may be illustrated further. As an American one might have a great hatred for the English; one might feel the Englishman decidedly repulsive. But normally such an attitude will be personal; it may even have to be private. There are no social sanctions for it. But if the United States should go to war with England, for what real reason the masses of people may not know, then Americans will be propagandized and made to feel dislike for every Englishman. The attitude thus becomes social, and public expressions of hatred for the English will merit the applause of the group. In this situation, to show friendship for the English is to be defined as a traitor, so that to live easily with one's fellows one should both hate and consequently fear the English. Above all, one should never seem to "fraternize" with them; and this even though one's personal experience contra-

---

[35]Under feudalism there was no opportunity for the development of race prejudice, for the community of interest among vassals, subvassals, and serfs was based upon personal ties; in modern plantation slavery, race prejudice tends to be at a minimum when personal and sympathetic relationships between master and slave achieve a degree of stability in the process of accommodation.

[36]*An Appeal to Conscience,* p. 23.

dicts the propaganda. Ordinarily, however, individual experience will tend to be consistent with social definitions and pressures.

Perhaps we can now begin to think constructively about race prejudice. The mystification is probably gone. Evidently race prejudice can never be wholly removed under capitalism, because exploitation of militarily weaker peoples is inherent in capitalism. However, within this system the form of race exploitation may be changed.

Ruth Benedict

Professor Ruth Benedict, the distinguished American anthropologist, is more careful in her study of race relations;[37] yet there remain some significant inconsistencies. She sees, as Dr. Park does not, that racial antagonism is a recent European development; moreover, she has examined with greater insight the intercultural relationships among the Grecian, Roman, and medieval peoples.[38] So far as we know, Mrs. Benedict has developed no theory which seeks to explain Negro-white relations in the United States as a relationship between two castes.

Both Benedict and Park, however, approach their problem with a concept which tends to weaken their whole discussion. "Ethnocentrism" is supposed to have some relationship to racial antagonism, but neither writer

[37]*Race: Science and Politics.*

[38]Ibid., pp. 157–66.

[39]In an article by an eminent student of Dr. Park which develops not only the letter but also the sermonizing spirit of Park's approach, "the genesis of race prejudice" is described fundamentally and in terms of universal, psychological human traits as follows: "Racial prejudice is *associated* with the disposition on the part of virtually every human group to think of itself as superior to outsiders. The notion of chosen people is quite widespread. We know of primitive communities the members of which call themselves 'men' or 'human beings' to distinguish themselves from all outsiders who are regarded as not quite human. We generally glorify the people whom we speak of as 'we,' whereas the 'others' or outsiders are depreciated and suspected. Although strangers do sometimes have a romantic fascination for us, more often than not we fear them and remain at a respectful distance from them, ready to believe almost anything about them to which we would not for a moment give credence if it concerned a member of our own group." Louis Wirth, "Race and Public Policy," *The Scientific Monthly,* April 1944, pp. 303–40. (Italics added.) This type of discussion of the behavior of "human beings" not only adds practically nothing to an understanding of race prejudice but also definitely distorts the subject. Is it really true that there is a "disposition on the part of virtually every human group to think of itself as superior to outsiders"? Do Negroes and Chinese and Indians feel superior to whites in the sense that whites feel superior to them? If they do not, it would seem that the significant problem lies in an explanation of the difference. As Emile Durkheim points out: "Social facts must be interpreted by social facts."

has been able to state clearly what this relationship is.[39] They seem to imply, at least, that ethnocentrism is incipient race prejudice. "Ethnocentrism," says W. G. Sumner, "is the technical name for this view of things in which one's own group is the center of everything, and all others are scaled and rated with reference to it."[40] Other sociologists have expressed this idea as a "we feeling" or a "consciousness of kind."

"Racism," asserts Dr. Benedict, "is essentially a pretentious way of saying that 'I' belong to the Best People. . . . The formula 'I belong to the Elect' has a far longer history than has modern racism. These are fighting words among the simplest naked savages."[41] Now it is very difficult to know what Professor Benedict means. She seems to say that modern race prejudice is merely "pretentious" ethnocentrism. But since ethnocentrism is a very ancient and rudimentary social attitude, must we conclude that race prejudice is as old as mankind? The latter conclusion is opposed to one of her basic hypotheses.

The fact is that one will be inevitably confused if he begins his study of the history of race relations by assuming that ethnocentrism precedes the phenomena. Ethnocentrism is a social constant in group association, hence it cannot explain variations in collective behavior. The "we feeling" may be present in the family, in the football team, as well as in the race or in the nation. Ethnocentrism exists today as ever, and it may continue indefinitely without evolving into race prejudice. In other words, ethnocentrism does not become anything else. When a group becomes race-conscious it will have achieved some degree of solidarity; therefore, we may expect it to show signs of ethnocentrism. But the ethnocentrism is immediately a function of its solidarity rather than of its racial antagonism. Indeed, the essential fact of ethnocentrism is not so much antagonism as it is a propensity in members of a cultural group to judge and estimate, in terms of their own culture, the cultural traits of persons in other cultures. John Linschoten, a sixteenth century white stranger among the Africans at Mozambique, described this reaction among the natives:

> . . . they take great pride, thinking there are no fairer people than they in all the

[40]Op. cit., p. 13.

[41]Op. cit., pp. 154–55. See also Robert E. Park in *Race Relations and the Race Problem*, E. T. Thompson, ed., pp. 10ff.

world, so that when they see any white people, that wear apparell on their bodies, they laugh and mocke at them, thinking us to be monsters and ugly people: and when they will make any develish forme or picture, then they invent one after the forme of a white man in his apparell, so that . . . they think and verily persuade themselves, that they are the right colour of men, and that we have a false and counterfeit colour.[42]

Ethnocentrism is always limited—both in intensity and in direction. A people's favorable conception of themselves may be affirmed by expressions of affection as well as by expressions of dislike for certain groups.[43] Therefore, to repeat, ethnocentrism may be thought of as indirectly derived from social attitudes which need not always be aggressive and antagonistic.[44] These may be (a) a friendly attitude: *We* like them; *they* are like us. We will give even our lives to help these friends when they are in serious difficulties—such as the attitude of the United States toward England in the two world wars. (b) A hostile attitude: They are barbarians, uncivilized people. We will not rest until they are subdued—such as the usual attitude of the Greek colonists toward the un-Hellenized peoples among whom they settled. (c) A conditional attitude of amiability: We like them; we are their best friends, if only they will stay in their place—such as the attitude of most white Southerners toward the colored people. (d) A defensive attitude: We have nothing against them; they are powerful, but we will fight back when they ill-treat us—such as the attitude of American

[42]Arthur Coke Burnell, ed., *The Voyage of John Huyghen von Linschoten to the East Indies,* from English trans., 1598. Vol. I, p. 271.

[43]On June 28, 1943, at the meeting of the British Empire Parliamentary Association in Ottawa, Canada, attended by members of the American Congress, the Hon. Thomas Vien, Speaker of the Canadian Senate, referred to the assembly as "the two branches of the great Anglo-Saxon family."

[44]It is likely, however, that a common hostility toward an out-group may be more productive of in-group solidarity than a common friendship. Aristotle put it strongly when he said: "A common fear will make the greatest of enemies unite."

[45]The following is Aristotle's version of the Grecian variation of this attitude: "Those who live in cold countries, as the north of Europe, are full of courage, but wanting in understanding and the arts: therefore they are very tenacious of their liberty; but not being politicians, they cannot reduce their neighbors under their power: but the Asiatics, whose understandings are quick, and who are conversant in the arts, are deficient in courage; and therefore are always conquered and the slaves of others: but the Grecians, placed as it were between these two boundaries, so partake of them both as to be at the same time both courageous and sensible; for which reason Greece continues free, and governed in the best manner possible, and capable of commanding the whole world." *Politics,* p. 213.

Negroes toward whites. (e) An egocentric attitude: the common chosen-people conception of many groups.[45] There are other possibilities. For instance, in a single social situation, the "we" feeling of one group may be graded both in intensity and in quality toward other groups. In South Africa the social solidarity of the white English and Afrikander people assumes a different aspect as it is addressed to the Jews, or the "colored," or the Asiatics, or the natives. We should expect this because the solidarity itself is a function of the peculiar social interaction between one group and another in the total ethnic situation. Extremely isolated peoples may even express ethnocentrism with reference to the animals about them.[46]

The following seem to be characteristic of the cycle of racial antagonism which includes ethnocentrism: first, a capitalist need to exploit some people and their resources; then the more or less purposeful development among the masses, the public, of derogatory social attitudes toward that particular group or groups whose exploitation is desired—here the strategy of the capitalists will depend upon the nature of the ethnic situation; a consequent public estrangement of sympathetic feeling for and loss of social identification with the exploited group—that is to say, a development of race prejudice; the crystallization of a "we feeling" and of social solidarity on the part of the propagandized group against the exploited group and a reaction of the latter; and, finally, the continual appeal to this "we feeling," consciousness of solidarity, or ethnocentrism as a means of intensifying race prejudice so that the exploitative purpose might be increasingly facilitated.[47]

Another shortcoming of Mrs. Benedict's study lies in its abstractness. It conceives of race prejudice as essentially a belief and gives almost no attention to the materialistic source of the rationalization. "Racism," she writes, "is the dogma that one ethnic group is condemned by nature to

[46]It is likely that not every primitive people would be so confident as were the early Hebrews that God gave man dominion over all the animals of the earth.

[47]This, of course, is an ideal statement. Race prejudice is a continuing, becoming, changing phenomenon. It is directly responsive to changes in the whole capitalist system. Moreover, people of all races are born into and ordinarily accept the system as they find it. In modern times capitalists never have to begin from scratch and create the social situation in which race prejudice is developed.

[48]Op. cit., p. 153. The following illustrates further the author's tendency in this respect: "To understand race conflict we need fundamentally to understand *conflict* and not *race.* . . ." Ibid., p. 237. (Italics Benedict's.)

hereditary inferiority and another group is destined to hereditary superiority. . . . [Racism] is, like religion, a belief which can be studied only historically."[48]

This is the kind of approach which unwittingly deflects the view from the real impersonal causes of race prejudice. Indeed, from this position the author proceeds to identify race conflict with religious persecution. She recognizes no significant difference whatever between "persecution" and racial aggression. The fact that the Inquisition was a religious conflict "is a reflection of the times; from every other point of view religious persecutions and racial persecutions duplicate one another." Again: "In order to understand race persecution, we do not need to investigate race; we need to investigate persecution. Persecution was an old, old story. . . ."[49] This, obviously, is misleading.

As we have attempted to show in a previous chapter, in interracial antagonism it is not exactly intolerance which actuates the conflict. The struggle is not one directed toward the achievement of enforced conversion; neither is there a secondary interest in the welfare of the group as in persecution situations. As a price of peace, the "inferior" group is not asked to recant or to renounce anything. The exploited race is all right so long as it remains contentedly exploitable;[50] the persecuted group is all right if it agrees to give up its beliefs.[51] Intolerance tends to cease with conversion or

[49]Ibid., pp. 230–31.

[50]The unvarnished purpose of all "racism" may be expressed as some variant of the following discourse delivered in 1859 by a New York advocate of the Southern system: "Now, Gentlemen, nature itself has assigned his condition of servitude to the Negro. He has the strength and is fit to work; but nature, which gave him this strength, denied him both the intelligence to rule and the will to work. Both are denied him. And the same nature which denied him the will to work, gave him a master, who should enforce this will, and make a useful servant of him. . . . I assert that it is no injustice to leave the Negro in the position into which nature placed him; to put a master over him; and he is not robbed of any right, if he is compelled to labor in return for this, and to supply a just compensation for his master in return for the labor and the talents devoted to ruling him and to making him useful to himself and to society." Quoted by W. E. B. Du Bois, *Black Reconstruction*, p. 52.

[51]Recently Hayim Greenberg introduced an article reporting persecution as follows: "Very alarming reports have reached us recently concerning the Jews in Yemen. A representative of the Yemenite Jews informed a press conference in Tel-Aviv that . . . the Jews of Yemen faced imminent prospects of extinction: they have been given the alternative of 'voluntary' conversion to Mohammedanism or of having to face such conditions as would lead to their natural death." See "In 'Arabia Felix,' " *Jewish Frontier*, July 1944, pp. 8ff.; see also, for a good discussion of medieval persecution, Joshua Trachtenberg, *The Devil and the Jews*, 1943.

recantation, while race prejudice abhors the very idea of conversion. Therefore, religious persecution and racial domination are categorically different social facts. Indeed, during the first period of European transoceanic colonization, the interest of the Roman Catholic Church and that of the capitalist adventurers constantly came into conflict; and the predominance of the one or the other materially affected the form of interracial adjustment. This does not mean to say, however, that a capitalistically exploitative purpose may not be couched in a religious context.

Probably the most tentative thesis of Dr. Benedict is her conclusion that "racism was first formulated in conflict between classes. It was directed by the aristocrats against the populace."[52] In support of this, she relies principally upon the posthumous publications of Henry Boulainvilliers and Joseph Arthur de Gobineau's *Essay on the Inequality of Human Races,* written in the middle of the nineteenth century. Although Dr. Benedict elaborates this point considerably, further discussion of it could have only some remote academic significance if it did not give us an opportunity to observe the confluence of race, class, and nationality problems.

First, however, the meaning of the term "racism" calls for a word. Most people who use the term conceive of it as a racial ideology or philosophy of racial superiority; but, in addition, they usually make the implied or expressed assumption that racism is the substance of modern race antagonism. This almost always leads to confusion because it ordinarily resolves itself into a study of the origin and development of an idea rather than the study of social facts and situations. The study of racism is a study of opinions and philosophies. However, since students of racism are seldom, if ever, concerned with the peculiar type of social organization in which race antagonism develops, they are likely to produce an apparently consistent selection of verbalizations from promiscuous intergroup conflicts as the story of the development of racial antagonism. Such is the difficulty which confronts Dr. Benedict when she declares: "Fanatical racism . . . occurred in Israel long before the days of modern racism." She reaches this conclusion on the ground that the prophet Ezra advocated tribal endogamy and that the tribes themselves practiced group exclusiveness.[53] This pro-

[52]Op. cit., pp. 174–73.

[53]Ibid., p. 163. Compare Num. 36:12 and Deut. 7:3–8.

traction of "racism" into the distant past was made even though it is a thesis of Dr. Benedict's essay that racism has a recent beginning.

Although Boulainvilliers and Gobineau seem to have been expressing a similar racial philosophy, they were in fact reacting to two fairly distinct stages in the development of modern society. It is not by mere chance that Boulainvilliers (1658–1722) was a contemporary of Louis XIV (1638–1715) and that Gobineau (1816–1882) was a contemporary of Metternich (1773–1859) and François Guizot (1787–1874). Nor should it be surprising that both Boulainvilliers and Gobineau are Frenchmen. It was Louis XIV, then the most divine and powerful monarch in Europe, who finally brought the French nobles to their knees and who derived very much of his power from the fluid wealth of the third estate. It was he who "domesticated" and pulled the teeth of the French feudal lords. It was Metternich of Austria who, after the Bourbon restoration in France, led the reactionary forces in Europe against the liberal and equalitarian philosophies which mothered the French Revolution. It was at that time also that liberal writers with Enlightenment ideologies were driven underground. Boulainvilliers and Gobineau, therefore, were reactionaries in highly reactionary social situations.

Boulainvilliers was the champion of the frustrated and weakened nobles; Gobineau was an antagonist of the Jacobins. Boulainvilliers stood between the monarch and the bourgeoisie, in which position he could develop no significant racial theory. Racism and nationalism are not ideologies of a nobility; superior right by conquest is the basis of feudal claims, and it is upon this ground that Boulainvilliers sought to rest his case for French feudalism.[54] But Gobineau's fire was directed squarely at the proletariat, especially at the exploited colored peoples of the world; he was a mature philosopher of racial antagonism. In grand style he declared, "The human race in all its branches has a secret repulsion to the crossing of blood, a repulsion which in many of its branches is invincible, and in others is only conquered to a slight extent." From the point of view of color prejudice, the *Essay* might have been written by William McDougall or Lothrop Stoddard.

There certainly is some justification for concluding that the *Essay* is

---

[54]For a brief discussion of Boulainvilliers and his contemporary, Fénelon, see Jacques Barzun, *The French Race,* Chap. VII.

anti-proletarian and, consequently, anti-democratic. But, if so, which class does it favor? Dr. Benedict thinks it is the "aristocrats." "Aristocrats" as such, however, are not a political class. Certainly Gobineau was not arguing for a return of feudalism. What he wanted was capitalism ruled by a superior bourgeoisie, probably a vestigial nobility as in England. This, together with his cult of ancestor worship as a basis of national power and aggression, his nationalism, which Dr. Benedict denies, rounds him out as the St. John of fascism. The following excerpt might have been taken from *Mein Kampf:*

> ... a people will never die, if it remains eternally composed of the same national elements. If the empire of Darius had, at the battle of Arbela, been able to fill its ranks with Persians, that is to say with real Aryans; if the Romans of the later Empire had had a senate and an army of the same stock as that which existed at the time of the Fabii, their dominion would never have come to an end. So long as they kept the same purity of blood, the Persians and Romans would have lived and reigned.[55]

To understand Gobineau and his successors properly we shall have to inquire briefly into the relationship of modern class conflict, race relations, and nationality relations. Class conflict and capitalism are inseparable; modern race relations developed out of the imperialistic practices of capitalism, while offensive and defensive nationalism provides the *esprit de corps* necessary for solidarity in exploitative group action under capitalism. Leaders of nationalism must inevitably be opposed to modern political-class conflict; that is to say, they must be against the proletariat.

These three social phenomena, all functions of capitalism, are progressive and, in given situations, they may combine with different degrees of intensity to produce different social effects. Ordinarily, the greater the imperialistic practice, the greater will be the nationalism and the less the class conflict. Therefore, the ruling capitalist class may seek to stimulate nationalism either for the purpose of suppressing class conflict or for the purpose of dividing a proletariat on racial lines so that both groups may be the more easily exploited. In recent times that imperialism which Europeans practiced so freely among the colored peoples of the world has been systematically attempted at home. In his characterization of fascism Maurice Dobb declares that we must see Hitlerism "as a monstrous system

[55]Arthur de Gobineau, op. cit., p. 33.

of exploitation of surrounding territories, treated as colonial regions for the exclusive benefit of privileged groups in the metropolis: a system of exploitation more ruthless than preceding ones, utilising more perfect and diabolic methods of repression, and essentially predatory in its economic effects."[56]

The modern nation itself is a product of capitalism; medieval peoples became nations as they developed a bourgeoisie. Moreover, the nationalism of the modern state is dynamic. The smaller nation that has become nationalistic[57] and rid itself of the immediate control of a great power tends to move from defensive to offensive nationalism.

Historically, racial ideologies were developed with reference to the relationship of Europeans with non-European peoples and subsequently refined to meet the needs of imperialism within Europe itself. Race problems and nationality problems, then, belong to the same species of social problem. However, we should not conclude, as Dr. Park does, that "language rather than color is the basis of . . . conflict" between nationalities; and it would be misleading to speak of nationality problems as a "phase of race conflict." Apparently the basis of international conflict must be sought either in the type of exploitative situation or in the competitive status of the international bourgeoisie.

A Restatement

We may restate in simple *outline* form the nexus between capitalism and race relations, with special reference to the American scene.

Capitalist, bourgeois society is modern Western society, which, as a social system, is categorically different from any other contemporary or previously existing society.

Capitalism developed in Europe exclusively; in the East it is a cultural adoption.

In order that capitalism might exist it must proletarianize the masses of workers; that is to say, it must "commoditize" their capacity to work.

[56]"Aspects of Nazi Economic Policy," *Science and Society,* Spring 1944, p. 97.

[57]In his famous book on the *National Question,* Joseph Stalin observes: "The bourgeoisie of the oppressed nation, repressed on every hand, is naturally stirred into movement. It appeals to its native folk and begins to cry out about the fatherland, claiming that its own cause is the cause of the nation as a whole." Pp. 20–21. To the same effect, see Leon Trotsky, *The History of the Russian Revolution,* trans. by Max Eastman, Vol. III, pp. 55–56.

To "commoditize" the capacity of persons to work is to conceptualize, consciously or unconsciously, as inanimate or subhuman, these human vehicles of labor power and to behave toward them according to the laws of the market; that is to say, according to the fundamental rules of capitalist society. The capitalist is constrained to regard his labor power "as an abstract quantity, a purchasable, *impersonal* commodity, an item in the cost of production rather than a great mass of human beings."

Labor thus becomes a factor of production to be bought and sold in a non-sentimental market and to be exploited like capital and land, according to the economic interest of producers, for a profit. In production a cheap labor supply is an immediate and *practical* end.

To the extent to which labor can be manipulated as a commodity void of human sensibilities, to that extent also the entrepreneur is free from hindrance to his sole purpose of maximizing his profits. Therefore, capitalism cannot be primarily concerned with human welfare. Slavery, in a capitalist society, presents an ideal situation for easy manipulation of labor power; but it is against free competition, a powerful desideratum of capitalism. Labor, under slavery, is of the nature of capital. It should be observed, however, that long-continued contact between slave and master may develop personal sympathies which tend to limit good business practice in the exploitation of slave labor.

It becomes, then, the immediate pecuniary interest of the capitalists, the bourgeoisie, not only to develop an ideology and world view which facilitate proletarianization, but also, when necessary, to use force in accomplishing this end.

So far as ideology is concerned, the capitalists proceed in a normal way; that is to say, they develop and exploit ethnocentrism and show by any irrational or logical means available that the working class of their own race or whole peoples of other races, whose labor they are bent upon exploiting, are something apart: (a) not human at all, (b) only part human, (c) inferior humans, and so on. The bourgeoisie in Europe were faced both with the problem of wresting the power from the agricultural landlords and at the same time keeping the workers from snatching any part of that power. Among the peoples of color, however, the Europeans had only the problem of converting virtually the whole group to worker status.

So far as force is concerned, we might illustrate. In the unrestrained process of "commoditizing" the labor of the American Indians the early European capitalist adventurers accomplished their complete extermination in the West Indies and decimated them on the continent.

The rationalizations for their doing this were that the Indians were not human; they were heathens; they could not be converted to Christianity; therefore, they were exploited, like the beasts of burden, without compunction for infringements of natural human rights. At that time also the argument for the exploitation of the labor of white women and white children in Europe was that the long hours of labor kept them from the concern of the devil, from idleness, and that their supposed suffering was part of the price all human beings must pay for their sins either here or hereafter.

When the great resource of African black labor became available, Indians in the West were not so much relied upon. They were largely pushed back as far as possible from exploitable natural resources.

Slavery became the means by which African labor was used most profitably; hence Negroes were considered producers' capital.

As the tendency to question such overt capitalist exploitation of human beings increased, principally among some articulate persons ordinarily not immediately engaged in business, the rationalizations about the non-human character of Negroes also increased. Moreover, the priests, on the whole, pointed out that God amply sanctioned the ways of the capitalists. The greater the immediacy of the exploitative need, the more insistent were the arguments supporting the rationalizations.

At this time, the early nineteenth century, many white workers in Europe and in America were being killed, beaten, or jailed for attempting to organize themselves so that they might limit their free exploitation by the entrepreneurs. Their unions were considered conspiracies against "society," and thus against the bourgeois state.

In 1861 the Civil War was commenced partly as a reaction to certain social pressures to break the monopoly on black labor in the South and to open up the natural resources of that region for freer exploitation.

At length, however, the Southern agricultural capitalists initiated a counterrevolution and re-established a high degree of control over their labor supply. To do this they had to marshal every force, including the emotional power of the masses of poor whites, in a fanatical campaign of race hatred, with sexual passion as the emotional core.

In support of this restoration the ruling class enacted black codes in which the principal offenses were attempts to whiten the black labor force by sexual contacts and tampering with the labor supply by union organizers or labor recruiters. All sympathetic contact between the white and black masses was scrupulously ruled out by a studied system of segregation. The whole Negro race was defined as having a "place," that of the freely exploitable worker—a place which it could not possibly keep if intermarriage was permitted.

At this time, also, the last quarter of the nineteenth century, the labor movement in the North was being driven underground. Labor had to organize in secret societies—sometimes terroristic societies. Troops, sometimes Federal troops, were being called out from east to west to put down strikes, and the Knights of Labor became a proletarian movement.

Today the ruling class in the South effectively controls legislation in the national Congress favorable to the continued exploitation of the Negro masses mainly by diplomatic bargaining with the politicians of the Northern capitalist exploiters of white labor. The guardians of the racial system in the South control or spend millions of dollars to maintain segregation devices—the most powerful illusory contrivance for keeping poor whites and Negroes antagonized—and to spread anti-color propaganda all over the nation and the world. For this expenditure they expect a return more or less calculable in dollars and cents.

Today it is of vital consequence that black labor and white labor in the South be kept glaring at each other, for if they were permitted to come together in force and to identify their interests as workers, the difficulty of exploiting them would be increased beyond calculation. Indeed, the persistence of the whole system of worker exploitation in the United States depends pivotally upon the maintenance of an active race hatred between white and black workers in the South.

The rationalizations of the exploitative purpose which we know as race prejudice are always couched in terms of the ideology of the age. At first it was mainly religious, then historico-anthropological, then Darwinian-anthropometrical, and today it is sexual, *laissez faire,* and mystical. The intent of these rationalizations, of course, must always be to elicit a collective feeling of more or less ruthless antagonism against and contempt for the exploited race or class. They could never have the meaning that, since the race or class is supposed to be inferior, superior persons ought to be humane toward it—ought to help it along the rugged road whereby full superior stature might be achieved. On the contrary, they must always have the intent and meaning that, since the race is inferior, superior people have a natural right to suppress and to exploit it. The more "inferior" the race is, the more securely the yoke should be clamped around its neck and the saddle fixed upon its back. The rationalizations are thus a defense; race prejudice is a defensive attitude. The obtrusiveness of certain social ideals developed under capitalism as concessions to the masses makes the rationalizations of racial exploitation necessary.

7.
The Modern Caste School of Race Relations

During the last decade a prolific school of writers on race relations in the United States, led mainly by social anthropologists, has relied religiously upon an ingenious, if not original, caste hypothesis. Professor W. Lloyd Warner is the admitted leader of the movement, and his followers include scholars of considerable distinction.[1] We propose here to examine critically the position of this school.

If we think of a hypothesis as a tentative statement of a theory which some researcher sets out to demonstrate or to prove, then the school has no hypothesis. But we shall quote liberally so that the authors might have an opportunity to speak for themselves about the things which they believe. These we shall call loosely the hypothesis. The school is particularly interested in race relations in the Southern states of the United States, and its members believe that they have struck upon an unusually revealing explanation of the situation. In the South, they maintain, Negroes form one caste and whites another, with an imaginary rotating caste line between them. "The white caste is in a superordinate position and the Negro caste in a subordinate social position." The following definition of caste has been most widely accepted.

---

[1] See the leading hypothesis by W. Lloyd Warner, "American Caste and Class," *American Journal of Sociology*, Vol. XLII, September 1936, pp. 234–37. See also, by the same author, "Social Anthropology and the Modern Community," ibid., Vol. XLVI, May 1941, pp. 785–96; W. Lloyd Warner and W. Allison Davis, "A Comparative Study of American Caste," in *Race Relations and the Race Problem*, pp. 219–40; W. Allison Davis and John Dollard, *Children of Bondage;* W. Lloyd Warner, Buford H. Junker, and Walter A. Adams, *Color and Human Nature;* W. Allison Davis, Burliegh B. Gardner, Mary R. Gardner, and W. Lloyd Warner, *Deep South;* John Dollard, *Caste and Class in a Southern Town;* Buell G. Gallagher, *American Caste and the Negro College;* Robert Austin Warren, *New Haven Negroes;* Kingsley Davis, "Intermarriage in Caste Societies," *American Anthropologist*, Vol. 43, September 1941, pp. 376–95; Robert L. Sutherland, *Color, Class and Personality;* Edward A. Ross, *New-Age Sociology;* William F. Ogburn and Meyer F. Nimkoff, *Sociology;*

Caste . . . describes a theoretical arrangement of the people of a given group in an order in which the privileges, duties, obligations, opportunities, etc., are unequally distributed between the groups which are considered to be higher and lower. . . . Such a definition also describes class. A caste or organization . . . can be further defined as one where marriage between two or more groups is not sanctioned and where there is no opportunity for members of the lower groups to rise into the upper groups or of members of the upper to fall into the lower ones.[2]

A class system and a caste system "are antithetical to each other. . . . Nevertheless they have accommodated themselves in the southern community. . . ." The caste line is represented as running asymmetrically diagonally between the two class systems of Negroes and whites as in the following diagram.[3]

It is assumed that during slavery the caste line, AB in diagram, was practically horizontal but that since then, with the cultural progress of Negroes, it has rotated upward. It may become perpendicular so as to coincide with the line DE; indeed, though unlikely, it may swing over toward the whites. The point here is that it would be possible for the line to take a vertical position while the caste system remains intact.

It is thought further that the social disparity between Negro classes and

Kimball Young, *Sociology;* Robert L. Sutherland and Julian L. Woodward, *Introductory Sociology;* Stuart A. Queen and Jeanette R. Gruener, *Social Pathology;* Alain Locke and Bernhard J. Stern, *When Peoples Meet;* Wilbert E. Moore and Robin M. Williams, "Stratification in the Ante-Bellum South," *American Sociological Review,* Vol. 7, June 1942, pp. 343–51; Allison Davis, "Caste, Economy, and Violence," *American Journal of Sociology,* Vol. LI, July 1945, pp. 7–15; James Melvin Reinhardt, *Social Psychology;* Guy B. Johnson, "Negro Racial Movements and Leadership in the United States," *American Journal Of Sociology,* Vol. 43, July 1937, pp. 57–71 ; M. F. Ashley Montagu, *Man's Most Dangerous Myth;* "The Nature of Race Relations," *Social Forces,* Vol. 25, March 1947, pp. 336–42; Paul H. Landis, *Social Control;* Ina Corinne Brown, *National Survey of the Higher Education of Negroes,* U.S. Office of Education, Misc. No. 6, Vol. 1; Verne Wright and Manuel C. Elmer, *General Sociology;* W. Lloyd Warner, Robert J. Havighurst, and Martin B. Loech, *Who Shall Be Educated;* St. Clair Drake and Horace R. Cayton, *Black Metropolis;* Mozell C. Hill, "A Comparative Analysis of the Social Organization of the All-Negro Society in Oklahoma," *Social Forces,* Vol. 26, 1946, pp. 70–77; and others.

The counterpart of this group of thinkers is another school which has with equal enthusiasm attempted to explain caste relationship in terms of racial antagonism.

[2]W. Lloyd Warner, "American Caste and Class," *American Journal of Sociology,* Vol. XLII, p. 234.

[3]Ibid., p. 235.

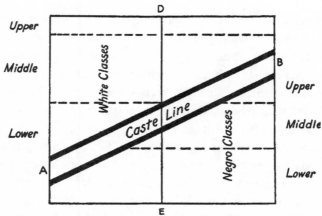

Position of "Caste Line" between Whites and Negroes in the United States.

white classes is particularly disconcerting to upper-class Negroes. The "emotional instability of many of the individuals in this group" may be readily explained since:

> In his own personality he feels the conflict of the two opposing structures, and in the thinking and feeling of the members of both groups there is to be found this same conflict about his position. . . . Although he is at the top of the Negro class hierarchy, he is constantly butting his head against the caste line.[4]

It is believed that in many countries of the world besides India there are developed caste systems, but the school has never found it convenient to demonstrate this proposition. "Caste," Warner and Davis assert without proof, "is found in most of the major areas of the world; this is particularly true of Africa, Asia, and America. The Indians of the southeastern United States and those of British Columbia have well-developed, if not castes, then caste-like structures. We cannot take time to examine those American systems, but we shall briefly summarize the material on East Indian caste. . . ."[5] Thus the caste system in India has been taken as the criterion; nowhere has the school relied upon any other system.

On the crucial question of marriage among castes Warner and Davis give Emile Senart credit for the belief that castes "isolate themselves to prevent intermarriage"; while they regard hypergamy as an example of "variations

---

[4]Ibid., p. 236. See also *Deep South* by Davis, Gardner, Gardner, and Warner, p. 13.

[5]"A Comparative Study of American Caste," in *Race Relations and the Race Problem,* Edgar T. Thompson, ed. Observe, incidentally, this editor's own involvement with the ideas of the school: ibid., p. xiii.

from the caste ideal."[6] Kingsley Davis, however, thinks that hypergamy distinguishes two major types of caste systems. In India hypergamy is possible because the Indian caste system is a "non-racial caste system"; in the United States and South Africa, on the other hand, hypergamy is impossible because there are in these situations "racial caste systems."[7] Warner and Davis depend further upon Senart and Bouglé for their significant conclusion that *"no one occupation has but one caste assigned to it."*[8]

Considerable emphasis is put upon the fact that a Negro or a white person, who is born Negro or white, could never hope to become anything other than Negro or white. "Children and grandchildren of Negroes will continue to be born into, live in, and only die out of the Negro 'caste.' "[9] Further, this biological fact of inheriting racial marks strikes Kingsley Davis as providing an ideal foundation for a caste system:

> The reason that race serves as an excellent basis of caste is that one gets one's racial traits by birth from parents having those traits, and one cannot change these traits during the rest of one's life.[10]

These, then, are some of the leading postulates of the caste school of race relations. Without continuing to introduce fragmentary statements at this point, we shall attempt an evaluation.[11]

Estimate of Basic Principles

Although the school has relied completely upon references to the caste system in India for its authority, it has nowhere made anything approaching a careful study of the caste system. Yet, even so, it has been difficult to determine which of their selected "essences" of the caste system will be controlling in given situations; and one is seldom certain about the degree of concentration of these extracts. For example, after their most elaborate discussion of caste in India, the following conclusion is reached:

[6]Ibid., pp. 229, 230.

[7]"Intermarriage in Caste Societies," *American Anthropologist,* Vol. 43, July–September 1941, pp. 376–95.

[8]In *Race Relations and the Race Problem,* p. 231.

[9]W. Lloyd Warner, Buford H. Junker, Walter A. Adams, *Color and Human Nature,* pp. 11–12.

[10]Op. cit., note, p. 387. See also *Deep South,* p. 15.

[11]We should add that sometimes members of the school speak of "the American system of color-caste" with probable implication that the Indian system is not based upon color.

There has been no attempt in these last few paragraphs to demonstrate that our caste structure and Indian caste structure are exactly the same, but rather we have attempted to show that they are the same kind of social phenomena.[12]

At this point the question may easily devolve upon the meaning of the expression "same kind." At least the reader might have expected that the authors would now attempt to show that the phenomena are indeed commensurable. But they do not. From this point on they proceed to discuss race relations in the United States, totally oblivious of a theory of caste or of whether caste ever existed in India. Apparently their thin discussion of Indian caste is merely intended to provide subject atmosphere.

We have had considerable difficulty also in finding clear-cut statements of principle. Usually some such phrase as "for our purpose," "as here used," "in so far as," or "generally" limits conclusions that are forthwith given universal applicability. To be sure, one could hardly question such a contrivance, yet it may be likened to the researcher who says: "This animal before us is not a horse, but for our purpose it is convenient to call it a horse. If you examine it closely, you will discover that it is a water buffalo. That does not matter, however, for we are not going to use it in the water-buffalo sense. Obviously, you cannot say the animal is not a horse; it is, in so far as it has four legs; and four legs are generally understood to be the essence of all horses and water buffaloes."

At points where clarity is most needed the school invariably becomes obscure, impressionistic, or circuitous. It has been accepted that the form of social organization in Brahmanic India constitutes a caste system. This system has certain distinguishing characteristics; hence we shall consider these the norm.

Definitions of a society are difficult to formulate; they are usually insufficient. For example, A. L. Kroeber wrote an article on caste[13] and came to the conclusion that a caste system is not possible in Western society; notwithstanding this, Warner, without even so much as a reference to Kroeber's negative conclusion, adopted his definition of "a caste" and reached the opposite position: "The social system of Old City [in the South] fits this definition of Kroeber's and of most of the ethnologists and social anthropologists."[14]

[12]Warner and Davis, in *Race Relations and the Race Problem*, p. 232.

[13]"Caste," *Encyclopedia of the Social Sciences*.

[14]*Deep South*, p. 9.

A play with definitions usually results in debate rather than constructive interest in the social problem. At any rate, Warner's own definition of caste considers two factors as determining: (a) that intermarriage between groups is not sanctioned, and (b) that there is no opportunity for members of lower groups to rise into upper groups, nor for those of the upper groups to fall into the lower groups.

It should be emphasized that a definition of a *caste* does not describe the *caste system*. We have shown elsewhere that upper-caste men in India have always been able to marry women of lower castes without disturbing the caste system, a procedure which could not be sanctioned in the South. Then, too, endogamy may be an isolator of social classes, castes, tribes, sects, millets, or any other social groups which think they have something to protect; hence, the final test of caste is not endogamy but the social values which endogamy secures. Indeed, A. C. Mace sees marrying out of one's class as an offense second only to the commission of crime, while Bouglé speaks of the horror of misalliances and the belief in impurity of contact between upper and lower classes in Europe.[15] Endogamy is not the essence of caste; if there is an essence of caste, endogamy merely bottles it up.

Probably the most insidious analogy between race and caste relations resides in the idea of life membership in each group. The identity of these phenomena, however, is only apparent. It must be obvious that a man born in a certain race cannot have the choice of leaving it and going into another race. But it is not at all obvious that a person born in one caste could not become a member of another caste. The biological affiliation of persons belonging to a given race has not been the position of one caste-man with respect to another in India. In fact, this very distinction should raise the suspicion that different social forces are operating in the caste system from those in situations of racial adjustment.

But what really do we mean by saying that a white man cannot fall into the Negro group? To the extent that he can have sex relations with Negro women he can "fall" biologically. The mixed-blood children that are born are, in the long run, the most potent equilibrator of the races; and the

---

[15]C. A. Mace, "Beliefs and Attitudes in Class Relations," in *Class Conflict and Social Stratification,* T. H. Marshall, ed., p. 159; C. Bouglé, *Essais sur le régime des castes,* 3d ed., p. 6.

lawmakers of the South are by no means unmindful of this fact. The Negro may "rise" biologically if he is able to pass.

From too much preoccupation with the unchangeableness of physical inheritance, the conclusion is reached that the social status of Negroes and whites in the South may become identical, yet they will continue to constitute two castes. In explaining his diagram, Warner holds that there is a theoretical possibility of Negroes advancing to the point where they may become the dominant caste. And this makes his theory particularly illogical and sterile.

So far as its logic is concerned, it asserts that Negroes may become equal to whites, evidently in wealth, in learning, in opportunity to control the government of the state; in short, culturally equal. Yet Negroes and whites will still be unequal; unequal, obviously, in color. For a person born white could never have the privilege of becoming black. Clearly, it must be on the grounds of the latter disability that his caste system will still be maintained. And since, so far as we know, time will not alter the possibility of a man's changing his racial marks, we must expect the white caste and the black caste to remain indefinitely intact—an ideal leopard-and-spots theory of race relations.

The race-caste assumption is sterile because it has no way of confronting the real dynamics of race relations. It goes happily past the meaning of the racial dichotomy in the South. Engrossed with ideas of "social structure," the school remains oblivious of the physiology of the society. It presumes that the white man is protecting his color and that the Negro is equally interested in protecting his, so that with the ballot in the hands of Negroes and with the opportunity for cultural participation open to them as normal citizens, the black code which keeps the races segregated will still be the law of the South. Elsewhere we have attempted to show, however, that the greater the relative cultural advancement of Negroes, the less will be the need of the white man's protecting his color. The theory sees a caste system set up in the South in the interest of the white man's color and, for that matter, the Negro's also.[16] Nonetheless, it may be shown that the white man

---

[16]Guided by the idea of Warner's caste line, Guy B. Johnson goes into the following monstrosity: "The great question in the coming era of race relations in the South will be, how far and how fast can the horizontal line of caste shift toward the vertical line of a biracial society? That is, how much equality can Negroes secure in the separate order? In

has no such obsession about his color. He will protect it only so long as it helps him to reserve a calculable cultural advantage.

The caste interpretation of race relations in the South cannot see that the intermarriage restriction laws are a social affront to Negroes; it cannot perceive that Negroes are smarting under the Jim Crow laws; it may not recognize the overwhelming aspiration among Negroes for equality of social opportunity; it could never realize that the superiority of the white race is due principally to the fact that it has developed the necessary devices for maintaining incontestable control over the shooting iron; and it will not know that "race hatred" may be reckoned in terms of the interests of the white ruling class. Hence, it is possible for the school to imagine the anomaly of Negroes fully assimilated culturally and yet living symbiotically apart from whites on the basis of some unexplained understanding that their colors should never be mixed. In other words, the races will, as Warner and Davis believe "isolate themselves to prevent intermarriage"! When this static approach is given up, the caste belief must also be given up.

In order that the authors might come to terms with the disturbing question of the relationship of occupation and caste, it is concluded that even in India there is no identification of every occupation with a caste. It is argued, in other words, that since many castes have the same occupation, occupation is no significant factor in the system.[17] The point to remember here, however, is that every caste has a traditional occupation or a limited number of cognate occupations, and not that every occupation has a caste.

Considerable importance is ascribed to interracial etiquette in the South as a social device supporting the supposed caste system there. Thus, according to Davis, Gardner, and Gardner:

> The most striking form of what may be called caste behavior is deference, the respectful yielding exhibited by the Negroes in their contacts with whites. . . .
> The behavior of both Negroes and white people must be such that the two are

so far as the gradual revision of racial attitudes makes caste distinctions obsolete, there will be change with a minimum of conflict." In *Race Relations and the Race Problem,* p. 150. In other words, this writer reasons that changing social attitudes are making caste distinctions obsolete, and that when all caste distinctions become obsolete, the caste line will be vertical!

[17]See Warner and Davis in *Race Relations and the Race Problem,* p. 231.

socially distinct and that the Negro is subordinate. Thus the Negro when addressing a white person, is expected to use a title such as "Sah," "Mistah," or "Boss," etc., while the white must never use such titles of respect to the Negro, but should address him by his first name or as "Boy."[18]

However, in the South there is also an etiquette intended to keep poor whites at a proper distance from the upper-class whites, and it is probably more severely non-reciprotating there than in other parts of the country. To upper-class Negroes, also, lower-class Negroes are very respectful. The titles "Boss," and so on, of themselves, may indicate only a recognition of superior rank. Indeed, a system of social etiquette which distinguishes superior persons or classes is no exclusive trait of the caste system. It is found in schools, in churches, among social classes, as well as among peoples and races who live in relationships of subordination and superordination.

The method of selecting and identifying isolatedly certain aspects of intercaste relationship, such as endogamy, non-commensality, or other marks of social distinction with their apparent counterparts in race relations, may at first seem convincing. In almost every case, however, the comparison is not between caste and race but merely a recognition of apparently common characteristics of all situations of superior-inferior or superordination-subordination relationships.[19] In conversation with the writer, one advocate of the caste school said: "No better illustration of the existence of caste in the South can be found than the practice of the races refusing to eat at the same table." But ordinarily only social equals eat, sleep, or play together. Army officers may not eat with privates, and medical doctors may resent sharing the same table with orderlies of the hospital; and so, too, a race bent upon maintaining a position of dominance can seldom engage in so socially leveling an act as that of eating together with members of the subordinate race.

The social-essence method of making comparisons between the caste system and other forms of social relationship makes it possible for different

---

[18]Op. cit., p. 22. Incidentally, we may observe that the authors present this passage concerning interracial etiquette with the implicit freshness of a discovery. No one reading it would ever suspect that *The Etiquette of Race Relations in the South,* by Bertram W. Doyle, had been on the bookshelves some years before.

[19]It is this same kind of eclecticism which leads Gunnar Myrdal to conclude that the "status" and "problems in society" of women and children reveal "striking similarities to those of Negroes." *An American Dilemma,* pp. 1073ff.

members of the caste school to choose different essences as their criterion of caste and yet not disturb the equanimity of the school. For example, according to John Dollard, the essence of caste is "a barrier to legitimate descent"; to W. Lloyd Warner, it is endogamy; to Guy B. Johnson, it is the achievement of "accommodation"; to Robert E. Park, "etiquette is the very essence of caste"; and to some, like Buell G. Gallagher, the criterion of analogy is not mentioned at all, the assumption evidently being that the identity of the phenomena should be taken for granted. Thus, it is possible for these writers to take hold of any one of a number of apparent analogues and proceed with it to identify caste and race relations.[20] If we study the caste system as the proverbial blind men studied the elephant, who will trust our conclusions?

Personality of Upper Class Negroes

It is a common belief, not peculiar to the caste school, that upper-class Negroes are especially maladjusted. The biracial system in the United States, it must be admitted, is a pathological situation; and to the extent that this is so, it affects adversely the personalities of both whites and blacks.[21] But sensitivity to social wrongs need not imply derangement or

[20]As an illustration of this possibility consider the following remarks by Jawaharlal Nehru concerning the Indian-European relations. "It was a notorious fact," he says, "that whenever an Englishman killed an Indian, he was acquitted by a jury of his own countrymen. In railway trains, compartments were reserved for Europeans; and, however crowded the train might be—and they used to be terribly crowded—no Indian was allowed to travel in them even though they were empty. . . . Benches and chairs were also reserved for Europeans in the public parks and other places. I was filled with resentment against the alien rulers of my country who misbehaved in this manner; and, whenever an Indian hit back, I was glad." *Toward Freedom,* pp. 20–21.

It would seem possible, by some ingenious eclecticism, to use even this limited information to identify Indian-European relations with caste relations, but we should expect the dullest of Hindus to remain unimpressed with the suggestion that in India there are two castes: the one East Indian and the other European. And this even though another statement by the same writer is cited in apparent support of this caste theory: "What a great gulf divides the two races, and how they distrusted and disliked each other! . . . each side was a little afraid of the other and was constantly on its guard in the other's presence. To each the other appeared as a sour-looking, unamiable creature, and neither realized that there was decency and kindliness behind the mask." Ibid., p. 3.

[21]On this point Gunnar Myrdal observes: "The conservative Southerner is not so certain as he sometimes sounds. He is a split personality. . . . The Southern conservative white man's faith in American democracy, which he is certainly not living up to, and the Constitution, which he is circumventing, are living forces of decisive dynamic significance." Op. cit., pp. 461–62.

an "off-balance" personality. We may mention at this point, however, that although this assertion calls for explanation, the caste theorists evidently do not realize that it is most damaging to their hypothesis. A person belonging to a lower caste is not "constantly butting his head against the caste line." In fact, the absence of such a phenomenon is so vital to the persistence of a caste order that it would hardly be inaccurate to maintain that it is definitely incompatible with a caste system. Caste barriers in the caste system are never challenged; they are sacred to caste and caste alike.[22] The personalities developed in the caste system are normal for that society.

Negroes are moving away from a condition of extreme white domination and subjection to one of normal citizenship. The determinant of unrest or social dysphoria among a people is not so much their state of subjugation or seeming oppression; rather it is either the process of their changing from some accommodated stage of well-being to one of subservience, or some political-class movement itself determined by some fundamental economic change. At any rate, since the Civil War the situation among Negroes in the South has been culturally progressive. Hortense Powdermaker makes the significant observation that it is not difference in class so much as difference in age which determines the attitude of Negroes toward whites. "Among the younger [Negro] generation, those in their teens, twenties, and thirties, resentment is keen and outspoken."[23] Older Negroes were reared in an earlier school of racial beliefs; and, indeed, the younger are not infrequently very impatient with their elders' compromising attitudes toward whites. Among Negroes in the South the "Uncle Toms" are distributed all through the social classes.

Of course militance in the interest of racial progress should not be mistaken for personality imbalance. In fact, dissatisfaction with the status

---

Another member of the school sees the inner strife as a personality difficulty of the whites. "With peculiar poignancy," says Buell G. Gallagher, "the individual white man feels within himself the warfare between profession and practice which he shares with his institutions. Two general streams of experience interweave in this shifting pattern of uneasiness." *Color and Conscience*, p. 24.

[22]Under the impact of Western culture the caste structure in India is being shaken, but it should be remembered that Western civilization is not attacking another civilization in the South, for this is itself Western civilization.

[23]*After Freedom*, pp. 325, 331.

quo must necessarily be the common preoccupation of all Negro leaders. There is, furthermore, some compensation to upper-class Negroes. Frequently they meet whites in flattering situations, mostly in business relations. They have considerable prestige among their own people, sometimes even more than that which whites of similar attainments can hope for within their own group. This windfall may not only compensate for loss of respect from low-class whites, but it may even result in a sort of grandiose importance inconsistent with reality. The "big Negro," a recognized personality type, is usually indelicate and grossly lacking in humility; yet he is not pathological.[24]

Upper-class Negroes do not envy poor whites in the South because the latter are beyond the purview of the black code. One might as well argue that some human beings suffer severe personality traumas because they recognize that the dogs and cats of the rich have certain advantages that they cannot have. The resentment of upper-class Negroes is rather against the ruling class, the guardians of the status quo. Enlightened Negroes recognize clearly the cultural inferiority of the poor whites. As a youth, W. E. B. Du Bois says of himself: "I cordially despised the poor Irish and South Germans, who slaved in the mills, and annexed the rich and well-to-do as my natural companions."[25] The power of sublimation and conceit to rescue persons from isolation and frustration must be reckoned with. Bitter as it is, therefore, the real conflict is usually between Negroes and their cultural equals or superiors. Sometimes it may seem to end in despair, as when Countee Cullen exclaimed:

Yet do I marvel at this curious thing:
To make a poet black, and bid him sing![25a]

Ordinarily, however, it is a persistent challenge to Negroes, an integrating force in a cause which must be served. Claude McKay, in his *America,* symbolizes this situation.

Although she feeds me bread of bitterness,
And sinks into my throat her tiger's tooth

[24]Perhaps there should be no objection to a transient assertion of personality disorganization such as the following by Gunnar Myrdal. It makes no point as a basis for significant conclusions. "This national *ethos* [the American Creed] undoubtedly has a greater force in the North than in the South. . . . But . . . even the [white] Northerner has a split personality." Op. cit., p. 439.

[25]*Darkwater,* p. 10.

[25a]From "Yet Do I Marvel" in *Caroling Dusk,* an anthology by Countee Cullen, p. 182.

Stealing my breath of life, I will confess
I love this cultured hell that tests my youth
Her vigor flows like tides into my blood,
Giving me strength erect against her hate.
Her bigness sweeps my being like a flood.
Yet as a rebel fronts a king in state,
I stand within her walls with not a shred
Of terror, malice, not a word of jeer.[25b]

At this point we should mention another crucial misconception of Warner's. He believes that Dr. Du Bois has achieved leadership of a movement for "parallelism" among American Negroes.[26] However, the fact that Du Bois as an assimilationist had a secure following, yet on his advocating a compromise with segregation was speedily wound up in his position and left to the thankless and interminable business of explaining his policy,[27] should have led Warner to give a different significance to the place of "parallelism" in the social aspirations of Negroes. He might have been on safer ground had he referred to the open plan of white South Africans ostensibly to develop a nation of whites and one of blacks within the same economically competitive area.

At any rate, segregation is a white man's principal anti-color weapon of oppression; therefore, Negroes can have but one quite obvious attitude toward it. Du Bois's leadership was doomed—and is still so—when, as he says of himself, he "proposed that in economic lines, just as in lines of literature and religion, segregation should be planned and organized and carefully thought through."[28] We may assert, as a sort of social axiom, that, with population ratios approximately as they are, the Southern aristocracy could never yield to the Negro political equality—the right to vote and to campaign for votes without intimidation—and still maintain public segregation barriers. Therefore, it is nonsense to speak of political and economic equality of opportunity with segregation.

[25b]From Claude McKay, *Harlem Shadows*, 1922.

[26]"American Caste and Class," *American Journal of Sociology*, Vol. XLII, No. 2, September 1936, pp. 235–36.

[27]See W. E. B. Du Bois, *Dusk of Dawn*, pp. 301ff., for a recent defense.

[28]Ibid., p. 305. Many years ago, when Alexis de Tocqueville said, "The Negroes and the whites must either wholly part or wholly mingle," he saw clearly the only possibilities of a stable racial adjustment; and it is doubtful whether today anyone will seriously question the inevitability of the latter alternative. See *Democracy in America*, Vol. II, p. 238.

The Social Organization of Negroes

Symptomatic of the potentialities of the caste hypothesis of race relations is the classification of societies of the world by Warner and Davis.[29]
From simple "theoretical" classless societies to "our own society [which]
possesses ranked internal structures, class and caste orders, groups with
diverse cultural [ethnic] traditions, as well as sex and age evaluations," all
the types of societies in the world are included. Thus the dichotomized
racial system in the South becomes a natural type of social ranking. "The
ranking changes from a status situation in which there is little or no ranking
to one in which almost all behavior is given an evaluation of rank."[30]

Unless clearly limited, the term "society" is very ambiguous. It is
properly used with reference to Western society or to a consumers' coop-
erative society; however, the authors did not limit the concept. It becomes
necessary, then, to settle upon some meaning of the term before discussing
it. According to John Dewey:

> Persons do not become a society by living in physical proximity any more than
> a man ceases to be socially influenced by being so many feet or miles removed
> from others. . . . Individuals do not even compose a social group because they
> all work for a common end. . . . What they must have in common in order to
> form a community or society are aims, beliefs, aspirations, knowledge—a
> common understanding.[31]

Assimilation and consensus seem to be necessary. John S. Mackenzie
emphasizes this:

> When a people is conquered and subject to another, it ceases to be a society,
> except in so far as it retains a spiritual life of its own apart from that of its
> conquerors. . . . So long as the citizens of the conquered state are merely in the
> condition of atoms externally fitted into a system to which they do not naturally
> belong, they cannot be regarded as parts of the society at all.[32]

[29]In *Race Relations and the Race Problem*, pp. 225–27.

[30]Ibid., p. 227. See also Emile Durkheim, *The Rules of Sociological Method*, trans. by
Sarah A. Solovay and John H. Mueller, pp. 81–83, for a discussion of the misleading
possibilities of such a typology of societies.

[31]*Democracy and Education*, p. 5.

[32]Quoted by F. A. McKenzie, "The Assimilation of the American Indian," *Proceedings
of the American Sociological Society*, Vol. III, p. 45; see also Emile Durkheim, op. cit., pp.
85–86. "By a society," says Robert Redfield, "is meant a recognizable system of human
relations characterizing a group, the members of which are aware of their unity and of their
difference from others." *The Folk Culture of Yucatan*, p. 80.

Another way of looking at a society is in terms of its capacity to perpetuate itself. Hinduism, or the caste society of India, is a powerful form of social organization which may go on self-satisfiedly, so to speak, forever. It carries within itself no basic antagonisms. But the social aims and purposes of whites and Negroes in the South are irreconcilably opposed. If such a situation could be termed a society at all, it must be a society divided against itself. Sapir has used this idea in his analysis of culture. Thus he writes:

> The genuine culture is not of necessity either *high* or *low;* it is merely inherently harmonious, balanced, self-satisfactory. . . . If the culture necessitates slavery, it frankly admits it; if it abhors slavery, it feels its way to an economic adjustment that obviates the necessity of its employment.[33]

In like manner we may think of the larger American society as fundamentally antipathetic to the non-Christian, non-democratic, biracial system in the South; hence it is continuously "feeling its way" to something else. To put such a situation easily into a typology of societies which includes the caste system in India, indeed to identify it with the caste system, must be misleading to say the least. The caste system of India is a minutely segmented, assimilated social structure; it is highly stable and capable of perpetuating itself indefinitely. Castes in India constitute a natural status system in one society, while Negroes and whites in the South tend to constitute two status systems, i.e., two social-class systems in two societies that are in opposition.

When two racial or nationality groups become more or less isolated from each other because of some continuing conflict situation or basic repugnance, we do not refer to them as forming a social-status hierarchy even though their relationship is one of superordination and subordination or of conqueror and conquered. As an illustration, Adolf Hitler says in his *My Battle:* "It must be held in greater honour to be a citizen of this Reich, even if only a crossing-sweeper, than to be a king in a foreign state."[34] Suppose now that this philosophy be made a reality in future German-Polish relationships; all Poles will then be considered inferior to the least of Germans, and an etiquette will be developed to implement the attitude. But there will

[33]"Culture, Genuine and Spurious," *American Journal of Sociology,* Vol. XXIX, January 1924, p. 410. See also Albert Bushnell Hart, *Slavery and Abolition, 1831–1841*, p. 32.

[34]E. T. S. Dugdale, trans., p. 182.

be here no social-status hierarchy; neither would Hitler there and then have enacted a caste system. The Poles will seek a *modus vivendi* in some sort of society of their own; and the intergroup relationship will most likely be one of antagonism, a latent power-group relationship.[35]

So, too, Negroes and whites in the Deep South do not constitute an assimilated society. There are rather two societies. Thus, we may conceive of Negroes as constituting a quasi or tentative society developed to meet certain needs resulting from their retarded assimilation. Unlike the permanence of a caste, it is a temporary society intended to continue only so long as whites are able to maintain the barriers against their assimilation.[36] It provides the matrix for a universe of discourse in which members of the group give expression to their common sympathies, opinions, and sentiments, and in which their primary social institutions function. The political and economic structure is controlled by another and larger society to which the whites are assimilated and toward which all Negroes are oriented.

The "public" of the white society includes Negroes only in the broadest sense; and when Negroes in their institutional functions declare that "everybody is invited," white people who turn up must assume the role of strangers. The "we feeling" of the white and of the Negro society tends to be mutually exclusive. Says Robert E. Park: "Gradually, imperceptibly, within the larger world of the white man, a smaller world, the world of the

[35]Consider the following circular reasoning by Guy B. Johnson, a member of the caste school: "Caste may be thought of as an accommodation, since its very existence is evidence that two or more unlike groups have worked out some sort of *modus vivendi.*" In *Race Relations and the Race Problem,* p. 126.

[36]Professor Robert Redfield described the evolution of a racial dichotomy into a social class system. It is significant to note that no such process could be suggested as a means of liquidating the caste system. "It requires little special knowledge to assert that the contact of the Spanish with the Maya, as is generally the case with long-continuing interaction between diverse ethnic groups, began with the existence of two separate societies, each with its own racial and cultural characteristics, and moved toward the formation of a single society in which the original racial and cultural differences disappear. At the time of the Conquest there were two groups that looked across at each other, both aware of the marked ethnic differences that attended their sense of distinctness one from the other. As the two groups came to participate in a common life and to interbreed, the ethnic differences became blurred, so that other criteria of difference, such as occupation, costume, or place of residence, came to be relatively more significant signs of social distinctness than was race or general culture. . . . At first there were two societies, ethnically distinct. At last there is a single society with classes ethnically indistinct." Op. cit., p. 58.

black man, is silently taking form and shape."[37] Ray Stannard Baker reports an interview with a Negro store owner in Atlanta:

"What do you mean by protection?" I asked.

"Well, justice between the races. That doesn't mean social equality. We have a society of our own."[38]

One device for retarding Negro assimilation, which does not have to be resorted to in the caste system, is the policy of guarding against any development of an overt expression of indispensability of Negroes within the social organization. Whatever their de facto importance, they must never appear as an integral part of the society. Instead, they pay little taxes; hence little or none of certain public expenditures should be diverted to their benefit. The theory of taxation according to ability to pay and expenditure according to need does not include them. Crime, sickness, high mortality rates, and poverty almost characterize Negroes, hence they are a drag on "society" and may be ostensibly sloughed off to advantage. Whites are generally protected from contact with cultured Negroes. The successful practice of this contrivance tends to give the Negro a sense of worthlessness and unwantedness, which contributes finally to the retardation of his assimilation. In Brahmanic India, however, where the population is assimilated to the caste culture, it is openly admitted that low-caste men are indispensable to the system, and this admission does not conduce to any advancement in the latter's social status.

By using the caste hypothesis, then, the school seeks to explain a "normal society" in the South. In short, it has made peace for the hybrid society that has not secured harmony for itself; and in so far as this is true, its work is fictitious.

Contribution of the School

An astonishing characteristic of this caste school of race relations is its tendency to conceive of itself as being original. It believes not only that it

---

[37]"Racial Assimilation of Secondary Groups," *Proceedings of the American Sociological Society,* Vol. VIII, p. 77.

[38]*Following the Color Line,* p. 40. Cf. Carl C. Zimmerman, "The Evolution of the American Community," *American Journal of Sociology,* Vol. XLVI, May 1941, p. 812; Hortense Powdermaker, op. cit., p. 71.

has made a discovery, but also that it has "created" something.[39] It is difficult, however, to determine wherein rests its originality. We do not know who first made the analogy between race relations and the caste system of India, but it is certain that the idea was quite popular during the middle of the last century. One of the most detailed and extended discussions of this hypothesis is that of the Hon. Charles Sumner published in 1869; and in 1904 William I. Thomas brought his full genius into play upon the subject.[40] Since then many textbooks have accepted the idea.[41] Some students, like Sir Herbert Risley, have used the hypothesis as the basis of extensive research.[42] Many writers, such as E. B. Reuter and Charles S. Johnson, have applied the term casually to the racial situation in the United States.[43] Donald Young has discussed the concept rather elaborately.[44] Among these we take somewhat at random from the writings of a journalist who in 1908 published in book form the findings of his study of race relations in the South.

In explaining the "class strata" among Negroes Ray Stannard Baker says:

> I have now described two of the three great classes of Negroes: First, the worthless and idle Negro, often a criminal, comparatively small in numbers but perniciously evident. Second, the great middle class of Negroes who do the

[39]"The view that the relationships of whites and Negroes in the South are systematically ordered and maintained by a caste structure, and that the status of individuals within each of these groups is further determined by a system of social classes existing within each color-caste, was the creation of Warner." Davis and Dollard, *Children of Bondage,* p. xvi. "The presence of caste and class structures in the society of the deep South was reported upon first by a member of our research group. . . ." Davis, Gardner, Gardner, and Warner, *Deep South,* p. 5. "An original interpretation of class and caste distinctions in the United States, providing a useful frame of reference for an appreciation of caste phenomena in this country." Ogburn and Nimkoff, *Sociology,* p. 343.

[40]Charles Sumner, *The Question of Caste.* William I. Thomas, "The Psychology of Race Prejudice," *American Journal of Sociology,* Vol. XI, March 1904, pp. 593–611. As early as 1828 Governor William B. Giles of Virginia referred repeatedly to the free Negroes as a "caste of colored population." See John H. Russell, *The Free Negro in Virginia,* p. 165.

[41]Among the best of them are C. H. Cooley, *Social Process,* p. 279, and *Social Organization,* pp. 209–28; Park and Burgess, *Introduction to the Science of Sociology,* pp. 203–6, 722.

[42]See, for example, *The Peoples of India,* p. 263, and *Census of India, 1901.*

[43]Reuter, *The Mulatto in the United States,* p. 360; Johnson, "Caste and Class in an American Industry," *American Journal of Sociology,* Vol. XLII, July 1936, pp. 55–65.

[44]*American Minority Peoples,* pp. 580–85. See also R. E. Park, "Racial Assimilation in Secondary Groups." Op. cit., p. 73.

manual work of the South. Above these, a third class, few in number, but most influential in their race, are the progressive, property owning Negroes, who have wholly severed their old intimate ties with the white people—and who have been getting further and further away from them.[45]

With respect to the color line, called a caste line by the modern school, Baker states:

> When the line began to be drawn, it was drawn not alone against the unworthy Negro, but against the Negro. It was not so much drawn by the highly-intelligent white man as by the white man. And the white man alone has not drawn it, but the Negroes themselves are drawing it—and more and more every day. So we draw the line in this country against the Chinese, the Japanese, and in some measure against the Jews; and they help to draw it.[46]

Baker then proceeds to clinch the full idea of the caste hypothesis:

> More and more they [Negroes] are becoming a people wholly apart—separate in their churches, separate in their schools, separate in cars, conveyances, hotels, restaurants, with separate professional men. In short, we discover tendencies in this country toward the development of a caste system.[47]

It is difficult to see what the modern caste school has added to this, unless it is perhaps publicity and "scientific" prestige.[48] Certainly anyone who has a taste for art might use the information given above to draw a caste line between the white and the black class structures. But Baker, like most other former advocates of the caste hypothesis of race relations in the United States, thinks almost fancifully of the idea and does not stipulate that his work should stand or fall with the belief. He realizes that the consideration of primary significance is not the "caste line" but the way in which that line holds. Thus he concludes:

> This very absence of a clear demarcation is significant of many relationships in the South. The color line is drawn, but neither race knows just where it is. Indeed,

[45]*Following the Color Line*, p. 65.

[46]Ibid., p. 218.

[47]Ibid., p. 300.

[48]It is true that sometimes members of the modern caste school have referred to race relations as "*color*-caste." But, so far as we know, they have never shown in what way "*color*-caste" is different from caste. In fact, some of the early theories on the origin of caste have sought to identify caste with racial antagonism. Therefore, the substitution of the term "color-caste" for caste does not seem to have relieved the fundamental confusion.

it can hardly be definitely drawn in many relationships, because it is constantly changing. This uncertainty is a fertile source of friction and bitterness.[49]

With respect to the scientific precision of the word "caste" the school insists: "By all the physical tests the anthropologists might apply, some social Negroes are *biologically* white," hence the term "race" cannot have meaning when applied to Negroes.[50] We should remember here, however, that the racial situation in the South never depended upon "physical tests of anthropologists." It developed long before anthropometry became of age. Furthermore, the sociologist is interested not in what the anthropometrists set up as their criteria of race, but in what peoples in interaction come to accept as a race. It is the latter belief which controls their behavior and not what the anthropometrist thinks.

But in reality the term "caste" does not economize thinking on this subject; it is a neology totally unjustified. Before we can know what the Negro caste means it is always necessary first to say what kind of people belong to the Negro caste. Therefore, in the course of defining "Negro caste" we have defined "Negro race," and the final achievement is a substitution of words only. One may test this fact by substituting in the writings of this school the words "Negroes" or "white people" whereever the words "Negro caste" or "white caste" appear and observe that the sense of the statement does not change.

For this reason the burden of the productions of this school is merely old wine in new bottles, and not infrequently the old ideas have suffered from rehandling. In other words, much that has come to us by earlier studies has taken on the glamour of caste, while the school seldom refers to the contributions of out-group students.[51]

One could hardly help recalling as an analogous situation the popularity which William McDougall gave to the instinct hypothesis. Without making

[49]Ibid., p. 31.

[50]Davis, Gardner, Gardner, and Warner, op. cit., pp. 7–8.

[51]As a typical example of this, see Davis and others, op. cit., pp. 15–136 and 228–539. Consider, in illustration, the weighty significance and originality with which the following commonplace is introduced: "The critical fact is that a much larger proportion of all *Negroes* are lower class than is the case with *whites. This is where caste comes to bear. It* puts the overwhelming majority of Negroes in the lowest class group, and keeps them there." (Italics added.) Davis and Dollard, op. cit., p. 65. This quotation also illustrates the mystical way in which real problems have been explained away.

any reference to William James, Lloyd Morgan, and others, who had handled the concept with great care, McDougall set out with pioneering zeal to bend all social behavior into his instinct theory. It was not long, however, before reaction came. And so, too, until quite recently, the race-caste idea had a desultory career. This idea has now been made fashionable, yet already students who had once used the term "caste" are beginning to shrink from it.[52] However, we should hasten to add that this school has none of the anti-color complexes of the instinct school; its leadership merely relies a little too much upon sophistry and lacks a sociological tradition.

In the following chapter we shall consider the major contribution of the Carnegie Studies, which also relies upon a "caste hypothesis" but which seems important enough to justify separate discussion.

[52]See R. E. Park in the introduction to Bertram W. Doyle, *The Etiquette of Race Relations,* and Charles S. Johnson, *Growing Up in the Black Belt.* But observe Johnson's relapse. In speaking of Negro-white relationship in the United States he says: "A racial or caste division of labor is one type of adjustment growing out of economic conflict between racial groups." In *Sociological Foundations of Education,* Joseph S. Roucek, ed., p. 423; also in *Patterns of Negro Segregation,* pp. xvi *passim.* Professor Park has been toying with the idea. For instance, Dr. Donald Pierson gives him credit approvingly for the following simple and somewhat inadequate scheme. "In a caste system," Pierson writes, "the racial lines may run thus:

	White
Race Lines	Mixed-blood
	Black

Negroes in Brazil, p. 337. For a similar diagram by Park, see "The Basis of Race Prejudice," *The Annals,* Vol. CXXXX, November 1928, p. 20. See also the preceding chapter.

8.
An American Dilemma:[1]
A Mystical Approach
to the Study of Race Relations

If the theoretical structure of our most elaborate study of race relations in America, *An American Dilemma* by Gunnar Myrdal, is correct, then the hypotheses developed in the preceeding three chapters cannot be valid, for the two views are antithetical. It thus becomes incumbent upon us to examine carefully Myrdal's approach. In this examination some repetition is unavoidable, and it seems advisable to quote rather than to paraphrase the author. This critical examination, to be sure, is not intended to be a review of *An American Dilemma.* As a source of information and brilliant interpretation of information on race relations in the United States, it is probably unsurpassed.[2] We are interested here only in the validity of the meanings which Dr. Myrdal derives from the broad movements of his data. The data are continually changing and becoming obsolescent; but if we understand their social determinants we can not only predict change but also influence it. In fact, Myrdal himself directs attention to his social logic in saying: "This book is an analysis, not a description. It presents facts only for the sake of their meaning in the interpretation."[3]

In his attempt to explain race relations in the United States the author seems to have been confronted with two principal problems: (a) the

[1]Gunnar Myrdal, *An American Dilemma.* Although this is a work of considerable scholarly collaboration, we shall, in this discussion of it, assume that it is entirely by Dr. Myrdal.

[2]Herbert Aptheker would disagree heartily with this, for he has published a small book devoted entirely to a criticism of Myrdal's factual data and of their interpretation. See *The Negro People in America.*

[3]Op. cit., p. li.

problem of avoiding a political-class interpretation, and (b) the problem of finding an acceptable moral or ethical interpretation.[4] In the first part of this discussion we shall attempt to show how his "value premise" and the caste theory are employed and, in the second part, how a shying away from the obvious implications of his data is contrived as solution for these problems. We shall not discuss the concept from which the book derives its title, for it seems quite obvious that none of the great imperialist democracies either can or intends to practice its democratic ideals among its subject peoples.[5] Myrdal does not bring to light the social determinants of this well-known dilemma; he merely recognizes it and rails against its existence. It is a long time indeed since Negro newspapers have observed: "The treatment of the Negro is America's greatest and most conspicuous scandal."[6] The dilemma is not peculiarly American; it is world-wide, confronting even the white masses of every capitalist nation.[7] At any rate, what seems to be of immediate significance is Myrdal's explanation of the basis of race relations.

"The Value Premise"

At the beginning of his study, in a chapter on "American ideals," Dr. Myrdal lays the atmosphere for his conclusions on race relations. The way in which the author handles this subject, as he himself recognizes with some contradiction, has been long in dispute among American historians. He

[4]Myrdal conceives of his problem—that is to say of race relations in the United States—as "primarily a moral issue of conflicting valuations" and of his "investigation" as "an analysis of morals." Ibid., p. xlvi. Cf. Leo P. Crispi, "Is Gunnar Myrdal on the Right Track?" *The Public Opinion Quarterly,* Summer, 1945.

[5]In a debate at an imperial conference in 1923 on the status of South African Indians, General Smuts faced the dilemma in this way: "I do not think our Indian fellow-subjects in South Africa can complain of injustice. . . . They have prospered exceedingly in South Africa. People who have come there as coolies, people who have come there as members of the depressed classes in India, have prospered. . . . They have been educated, and their children and grandchildren today are many of them men of great wealth. They have all the rights, barring the rights of voting for parliament and the provincial councils, that any white citizen in South Africa has. . . . It is only political rights that are in question. There we are up against a stone wall and we cannot get over it." Quoted in P. S. Joshi, op. cit., p. 107.

[6]Myrdal, op. cit., p. 1020. Dr. Myrdal understands clearly that expressions such as this have now achieved respectability; in fact, they are desirable, since "it is becoming difficult for even popular writers to express other views than the ones of racial equalitarianism and still retain intellectual respect." Op. cit., p. 96.

[7]Years ago Nathaniel Peffer entitled his book *The White Man's Dilemma* and sought to make it clear that "at bottom" the problem is economic—the problem of world-wide economic exploitation by "white capital," of which the American race problem is but one variation.

considers certain national ideals as if they were phenomena *sui generis,* having an existence apart from and indeed determinative of the economic life of the people. Although he concedes that "the economic determinants and the force of the ideals can be shown to be interrelated,"[8] he is mainly concerned not with showing this interrelationship but rather with elaborating an implicit hypothesis that the "American Creed" is *the* vital force in American life.

> The unanimity around, and the explicitness of, this Creed is the great wonder of America. . . . The reflecting observer comes to feel that this *spiritual convergence,* more than America's strategic position behind the oceans and its immense material resources, is what makes the nation great and what promises it a still greater future.[9]

We need not be detained here with the question as to whether either of the foregoing alternatives is the sufficient explanation of the "nation's greatness"; our immediate purpose is to observe the author's abstract orientation. He seems never to recognize the determining role of class interest but rather sets his study against a backdrop of an apparently common American ideology which he says "is older than America itself." Thus:

> Americans of all national origins, classes, regions, creeds, and colors, have something in common: a social *ethos,* a political creed. . . . When the American Creed is once detected, the cacophony becomes a melody . : . as principles which ought to rule, the Creed has been made conscious to everyone in Ameritan society. . . . America is continuously struggling for its soul.[10]
>
> The cultural unity of the nation is this common sharing of both the consciousness of sin and the devotion to high ideals.[11]

Contrary to Myrdal's rhapsodic description of class and group unity,

[8]Op. cit., p. 6.

[9]Ibid., p. 13. (Italics added.) Myrdal describes "the American Creed" as follows: "These principles of social ethics have been hammered into easily remembered formulas. In the clarity and intellectual boldness of the Enlightenment period these tenets were written into the Declaration of Independence, the Preamble of the Constitution, the Bill of Rights, and the constitutions of the several states. . . . But this Creed is . . . no American monopoly. With minor variations . . . the American Creed is the common democratic creed. 'American ideals' are just humane ideals as they have matured in our comnion Western civilization upon the foundation of Christianity and pre-Christian legalism and under the influence of the economic, scientific, and political development over a number of centuries. The American Creed is older and wider than America itself." Ibid., pp. 4, 25.

[10]Ibid., pp. 3–4.

[11]Ibid., p. 22.

James Madison, one of the Founding Fathers of the United States, had this to say about the "sentiments" and beliefs of some of the interest groups:

> The most common and durable source of factions has been the various and unequal distribution of property. Those who have and those who are without property have ever formed distinct interests in society. Those who are creditors and those who are debtors fall under a like discrimination. A landed interest, a manufacturing interest, a mercantile interest, a moneyed interest, with many lesser interests, grow up of necessity in civilized nations and divide them into different classes, actuated by different sentiments and views. The regulation of these various and interfering interests forms the principal task of modern legislation, and involves the spirit of party and faction in the necessary and ordinary operations of government.[12]

The views of Myrdal and Madison are significantly different. Myrdal is seeking to detect the harmony and "melody" in American life, which he assumes are produced by unquestioned acceptance of certain generalized national symbols by all the people. Madison, on the other hand, is trying to see what fundamentally sets group against group within the nation—what it is that produces the "spirit of party faction." We think that Myrdal is abstract and unreal because he implicitly homogeneates the material interests of the American people and then declares animistically, "America is continually struggling for its soul." Madison recognizes the importance of group sentiments, but he does not say they are determined essentially by a creed. Probably if Myrdal had approached his problem from the point of view of group interests he might have recognized the irreconcilable inconsistency even in "these ideals . . . of the fundamental equality of all men, and of certain inalienable rights to freedom." It should be recalled here that the author's assignment was that of discovering the pertinent social factors entering into a situation of continuing social conflict and antagonism.

The following is an intimation of the significance of Myrdal's creedal analysis for his main problem: "From the point of view of the American Creed the status accorded the Negro in America presents *nothing more and nothing less* than a century-long *lag of public morals*. In principle the Negro problem was settled long ago. . . ."[13] Had this statement been a mere figure of speech, it should, of course, be of no consequence. It is, however, in this

---

[12]*The Federalist,* No. 10. See, for a similar observation, Woodrow Wilson, *Constitutional Government of the United States,* pp. 217–18.

[13]Op. cit., p. 24. (Italics added.)

area of elated abstraction that our author intends to keep the subject. Probably it may be said rather conclusively that the Negro problem cannot be solved "in principle" because it is not basically an ideological problem. Indeed, speaking abstractly, we may conclude similarly that all the major social problems of the Christian world were solved "in principle" by the opening words of the Lord's Prayer—to say nothing of the whole Sermon on the Mount.

Many years ago Professor Charles A. Beard effectively criticized this romantic approach to the study of American society. He said: "In the great transformations in society, such as was brought about by the formation and adoption of the Constitution, economic 'forces' are primordial or fundamental and come nearer 'explaining' events than any other 'forces.' " And further: "Whoever leaves economic pressures out of history or out of the discussion of public questions is in mortal peril of substituting mythology for reality and confusing issues instead of clarifying them."[14] To be sure, social ideologies are always significant, but they are, on the whole, dependent social phenomena.

It is just such a relationship with which Abraham Lincoln was confronted when he declared: ". . . our fathers brought forth on this continent a new nation, conceived in liberty, and dedicated to the proposition that all men are created equal. Now we are engaged in a great civil war, testing whether that nation, or any nation so conceived and so dedicated, can long endure." Neither side in this civil war questioned the ideals, yet they were—and to this very day are—not fully agreed on the interpretation of the ideals.[15] The

[14]*An Economic Interpretation of the Constitution of the United States,* 1st ed., pp. xii, xvii.

[15]In the Federal Constitutional Convention of 1787 General Pinckney of South Carolina intimated realistically the interests behind the contemporary Negro problem. Said he: "An attempt to take away the right [to import slaves] as proposed would produce serious objections to the Constitution." And he "declared it to be his firm opinion that if he himself and all his colleagues were to sign the Constitution and use their personal influence, it would be of no avail towards obtaining the assent of their constituents. South Carolina and Georgia cannot do without slaves. As to Virginia she will gain by stopping the importation. Her slaves will rise in value, and she has more than she wants. It would be unequal to require South Carolina and Georgia to confederate on such unequal terms. . . . He contended that the importation of slaves would be for the interest of the whole Union. The more slaves, the more produce to employ the carrying trade; the more consumption also, and the more of this, the more of revenues for the common treasury." See Max Farrand, ed., *The Records of the Federal Convention of 1787,* Vol. II, p. 371.

crucial circumstances, then, are not the presumed universal acceptance of the "Creed," but rather the interests which make its peculiar and divergent interpretations inevitable. In other words, each side had different material interests and, as is ordinarily the case, the ideals of each were made subservient to the material interests. To put it otherwise, the Creed, in its formative stage, was seriously debated and contested, but since it had become stereotyped, neither side questioned it. Each side, however, insisted upon a self-interested interpretation of it.

The Declaration of Independence and the Constitution have become national symbols, like the flag. It is quite another thing, however, to say that the content of these documents is accepted even as a creed by the whole people. As E. E. Schattschneider points out: "The truth of the matter is that the American public has never understood the Constitution, nor has it ever really believed in it, in spite of the verbal tradition of Constitutionalism."[15a] One pertinent illustration is the nonacceptance of the Thirteenth, Fourteenth, and Fifteenth amendments either in spirit or in practice by the ruling class of the South. Again we cite a statement on this point by James Madison: "Neither moral nor religious motives can be relied on as an adequate control"; and, in another context: "Wherever there is an interest and power to do wrong, wrong will be done."[16]

The Constitution did not settle or remove the vitally conflicting interests of the infant capitalist system; it simply compromised or ignored them. In other words, it postponed for a later date the real solution of latent antagonisms—postponed it until such time as one side or the other developed sufficient power to force a solution in its favor. And yet the Constitution is so ample in its scope that with certain amendments and abrogations it may become the fundamental law of a consummate democracy.[17]

[15a]*Party Government*, p. 53.

[16]*Documentary History of the Constitution*, Vol. V, p. 88.

[17]"The federal Constitution was a reactionary document from the point of view of the doctrines of the Revolution. Its bill of rights was a series of amendments added by dissatisfied elements after the instrument had been drawn up and submitted to the people. The rule of the few . . . soon began, and government lent its hand to the few who could invest in its financial paper and who gave their efforts to the building of cities and commerce and industry. . . . A new order of bourgeois acquisitiveness . . . was in the saddle. Democracy, like the rest of the hindmost, was left for the devil." Avery Craven, *Democracy in American Life*, p. 13. See also Woodrow Wilson, op. cit., p. 192.

Moreover, Myrdal's "value premise" appears to be demonstrably weakened in consequence of its being built principally upon certain fictitious attributes of ideal types, such as "the citizen," "American popular thought," "the American soul," "the common good American." For instance, the foregoing concept is employed in this way: "Today it is necessary in everyday living for the common good American citizen to decide for himself which laws should be observed and which not."[18]

The Caste Hypothesis

The whole theoretical frame of reference of *An American Dilemma* is supposedly couched in a caste hypothesis. As Myrdal himself puts it: "Practically the entire factual content of . . . this book may be considered to define caste in the case of the American Negro."[19] However, it is evident that Myrdal—in spite of the lamentable use of such phrases as "in our view," "as we have defined it," and so on—does not intend to coin a new concept. In criticizing Charles S. Johnson's idea of caste he declares, "We do not believe that such a caste system as he has defined ever existed."[20] Therefore, in his explanation of race relations in the United States, our author means to accept the known concept as a norm. Of some significance is the way in which the term is selected. This is the reasoning:

> The term "race" is . . . inappropriate in a scientific inquiry since it has biological and genetic connotations which . . . run parallel to widely spread false racial beliefs. The . . . term, "class," is impractical and confusing . . . since it is generally used to refer to a non-rigid status group from which an individual member can rise or fall. . . . We need a term to distinguish the large and systematic type of social differentiation from the small and spotty type and have . . . used the term "caste."[21]

Obviously, in arriving at this decision to use the term "caste" in explaining race relations in the United States, Dr. Myrdal employs the method of successive elimination. Without attempting to be facetious, it may be compared with that of the scientist who comes upon a strange animal and, having the necessity to classify it, says to himself: "This is not a cat, I am

---

[18]Myrdal, op. cit., p. 17.
[19]Ibid., p. 669.
[20]Ibid., p. 1375.
[21]Ibid., p. 667.

sure; neither is it a dog, I am positive of that; therefore, since I do not think of anything else, I am going to call it a duck."

There is no new theory of race relations in this study, but it develops the most elaborate defense of the caste belief. Dr. Myrdal has adopted not only the whole theory of the caste school of race relations in the United States but also its procedure. Like the leadership of this school, he appears to have taken some pride in regarding as worthless a study of Hindu society as a basis for making comparisons with Western society. Yet, as we should expect, he depends entirely upon the Hindu system for his orientation.

Thus the reader is asked to accept generalizations about the caste system in America when no other reference is made to the cultural norm than the following:

> It should be pointed out . . . that those societies to which the term "caste" is applied without controversy—notably the ante-bellum slavery society of the South and the Hindu society of India—do not have the "stable equilibrium" which American sociologists from their distance are often inclined to attribute to them. . . . A Hindu acquaintance once told me that the situation in the United States is as much or more describable by the term "caste" as is the situation in India.[22]

From this, one thing is clear: Myrdal is very much in error in believing that it is recognized without controversy that slavery in the South constituted a caste system.[23] Moreover, it is difficult to see how one could avoid the conclusion that the author has descended to some vulgar means in referring to the hearsay of "a Hindu acquaintance" as authority for the sociology of caste.

The Biological Problem

Probably the crucial circumstance in attempts to use some term other than race in describing race relations is a desire to get around the biological implications in the term. Yet it has never been shown that there is a real necessity for this. In fact, those who verbally eschew the biological connotation of the term proceed, nonetheless, to make physical differences the

---

[22]Ibid., p. 668. See also note c.

[23]We cannot be certain, however, that Myrdal has a settled view on this point, for he says elsewhere: "After the [Civil] War and Emancipation, the race dogma was retained in the South as necessary to justify the caste system which succeeded slavery. . . ." Ibid., p. 88. See also pp. 221–24.

crux of their discussion. This is particularly true of Myrdal. Says he, "Negro features are so distinct that only in the Negro problem does [belief in the desirability of a light skin and 'good' features] become of great social importance."[24] And he proceeds, evidently without realizing it, to point out the relationship of skin color to caste:

> . . . the average Negro cannot effectively change his color and other physical features. If the dark Negro accepts the white man's valuation of skin color, he must stamp himself an inferior. If the light Negro accepts this valuation, he places himself above the darker Negroes but below the whites, and he reduces his loyalty to his caste.[25]

Myrdal continues his biological interpretation of race relations with great clarity. "When we say that Negroes form a lower caste in America," he asserts, "we mean that they are subject to certain disabilities solely because they are 'Negroes,' "[26] manifestly; that is to say, solely because they are colored or black. Moreover, although the writer did not elaborate this point, he refers to Asiatics, Indians, and Negroes as "the several subordinate castes."[27] It should be interesting to see how he fits these peoples into an American caste hierarchy. At any rate, with this conception of race relations, the author inevitably comes to the end of the blind alley: that the caste system remains intact so long as the Negro remains colored.

> The change and variations which occur in the American caste system relate only to caste relations, not to the dividing line between castes. The latter stays rigid and unblurred. It will remain fixed until it becomes possible for a person to pass legitimately from the lower caste to the higher without misrepresentation of his origin. The American definition of "Negro" as a person who has the slightest amount of Negro ancestry has the significance in making the caste line absolutely rigid.[28]

Myrdal is so thoroughly preoccupied with the great significance of skin color that, although he realizes that in America Negroes of lighter complexion have greater social opportunities, he believes that they may as well be

[24]Ibid., p. 669.
[25]Ibid., p. 669.
[26]Ibid., p. 669.
[27]Ibid., p. 670.
[28]Ibid., pp. 668–69.

unmixed blacks so far as the "caste line" is concerned. Accordingly he asserts: "Without any doubt a Negro with light skin and other European features has in the North an advantage with white people when competing for jobs available for Negroes. . . . Perhaps of even greater importance is the fact that the Negro community itself has accepted this color preference."[29] This, however, has nothing to do with the rigidity of the caste line.

When Dr. Myrdal strays from his physical emphasis he becomes confused. For instance, he concludes that "being a Negro means being subject to considerable disabilities in practically all spheres of life."[30] Evidently it must follow logically from this that to the extent to which these "disabilities" are removed, to that extent also a person ceases to remain a Negro. The confusion is further deepened by the combination of a cultural and biological view of caste.

> Caste . . . consists of such drastic restrictions to free competition in various spheres of life that the individual in a lower caste cannot, by any means, change his status except by a secret and illegitimate "passing" which is possible only to the few who have the physical appearance of members of the upper caste.[31]

In other words, caste consists in restrictions to free competition, but restrictions to free competition are entirely limited by a man's physical appearance. Now, we may ask, what is the nexus between physical appearance and caste?

Rigidity of the Caste System

We may reiterate that the caste school of race relations is laboring under the illusion of a simple but vicious truism. One man is white, another is black; the cultural opportunities of these two men may be the same, but since the black man cannot become white, there will always be a white caste and a black caste: "The actual import of caste is gradually changing as the Negro class structure develops—except in the fundamental restrictions that no Negro is allowed to ascend into the white caste."[32] Yet, if this is so, what possible meaning could the following observation have? "We have been

---

[29]Ibid., p. 697.
[30]Ibid., p. 668.
[31]Ibid., p. 675.
[32]Ibid., p. 693.

brought to view the caste order as fundamentally a system of disabilities forced by the whites upon the Negroes."[33]

Closely related to this amorphous concept of the rigidity of caste is the meaning given to interracial endogamy. Myrdal uses it to identify the races in the United States as castes.

> The scientifically important difference between the terms "caste" and "class" is . . . a relatively large difference in freedom of movement between groups. This difference is foremost in marriage relations. . . . The ban on intermarriage is one expression of the still broader principle . . . that a man born a Negro or a white is not allowed to pass from the one status to the other as he can pass from one class to another.[34]

Now it could hardly be too much emphasized that endogamy of itself is no final criterion of caste. Endogamy is an isolator of social values deemed sacrosanct by social groups, and there are many kinds of social groups besides castes that are endogamous. The final test of caste is an identification of the social values and organization isolated by endogamy. To say that intercaste endogamy in India means the same thing as interracial endogamy in the United States is like saying that a lemon and a potato are the same things because they both have skins.

An illustration of Myrdal's complete disregard of the nature of caste organization is his discussion of "caste struggle." This concept of "caste struggle," to be sure, is totally foreign to our norm, the Indian caste system. Moreover, this must be so because castes in Brahmanic India do not want to be anything other than castes. There is no effort or logical need to homogeneate themselves. A caste is a status entity in an assimilated, self-satisfied society. Regardless of his position in the society, a man's caste is sacred to him; and one caste does not dominate the other. The following description of caste has absolutely no application to caste in India.

> The caste distinctions are actually gulfs which divide the population into antagonistic camps. The caste line . . . is not only an expression of caste differences and caste conflicts, but it has come itself to be a catalyst to widen differences and engender conflicts.[35]

[33]Ibid., p. 669.
[34]Ibid., p. 668.
[35]Ibid., pp. 676–77.

Mysticism

If the scientist has no clear conception of the norm which he is using to interpret social phenomena, the norm itself is likely to become lost in the data. When this happens he will ordinarily have recourse to mystical flights. In our case Myrdal seems to attribute magical powers to caste. Speaking of the cause of the economic position of Negroes in the United States he says: "Their caste position keeps them poor and ill-educated."[36] And, "Caste consigns the overwhelming majority of Negroes to the lower class."[37] Indeed, the whole meaning of racial exploitation in the United States is laid at the altar of caste. Thus it is observed: "The measures to keep the Negroes disfranchised and deprived of full civil rights and the whole structure of social and economic discrimination are to be viewed as attempts to enforce *the caste principle.*"[38]

More immediately, this mysticism is due primarily to a misapprehension of the whole basis of race relations. Caste is vaguely conceived of as something, the preservation of which is valuable per se. "The caste system is upheld by its own inertia and by the superior caste's interests in upholding it."[39] It is no wonder, then, that Myrdal falls into the egregious error of thinking that the subordination of Negroes in the South is particularly the business of poor whites. In this light he reasons: "That 'all Negroes are alike' and should be treated in the same way is still insisted upon by many whites, especially in the lower classes, who actually feel, or fear, competition from the Negroes and who are inclined to sense a challenge to their status in the fact that some Negroes rise from the bottom."[40] This, obviously, is a conception of race relations in terms of personal invidiousness. Surely, to say that "Southern whites, *especially in the lower brackets . . .* have succeeded in retaining [the] legal and political system" is to miss the point entirely. We shall return to this question in the following section.

One primary objection to the use of the caste belief in the study of race relations rests not so much upon its scientific untenability as upon its insidious potentialities. It lumps all white people and all Negroes into two

[36] Ibid., p. 669.
[37] Ibid., p. 71.
[38] Ibid., p. 660. (Italics added.)
[39] Ibid., p. 669.
[40] Ibid., p. 689.

antagonistic groups struggling in the interest of a mysterious god called caste. This is very much to the liking of the exploiters of labor, since it tends to confuse them in an emotional matrix with all the people. Observe in illustration how Myrdal directs our view: "All of these thousand and one precepts, etiquettes, taboos, and disabilities inflicted upon the Negro have a common purpose: to express the subordinate status of the Negro people and the exalted position of the whites. They have their meaning and chief function as symbols."[41]

It thus appears that if *white people* were not so wicked, if they would only cease wanting to "exalt" themselves and accept the "American Creed," race prejudice would vanish from America. "Why," asks Myrdal, "is race prejudice . . . not increasing but decreasing?" And he answers sanctimoniously: "This question is . . . only a special variant of the enigma of philosophers for several thousands of years: the problem of Good and Evil in the world."[42] Clearly, this is an escape from the realities of the social system, inexcusable in the modern social scientist.[43] At any rate, the

[41]Ibid., p. 66.

[42]Ibid., p. 79. See W. Cunningham, *The Growth of English Industry and Commerce,* Vol. I, pp. 556–57, for a review of this tendency among sixteenth-century English moralists to explain social problems by attributing them to human sinfulness.

[43]Probably we should mention here another deplorable achievement of Myrdal's—his developed capacity for obscuring the basis of racial antagonism. Consider in illustration the following paragraph:

"Though the popular theory of color caste turns out to be a rationalization, this does not destroy it. For among the forces in the minds of the white people are certainly not only economic interests (if these were the only ones, the popular theory would be utterly demolished), but also sexual urges, inhibitions, and jealousies, and social fears and cravings for prestige and security. When they come under the scrutiny of scientific research, both the sexual and the social complexes take on unexpected designs. We shall then also get a clue to understanding the remarkable tendency of this presumably biological doctrine, that it refers only to legal marriage and to relations between Negro men and white women, but not to extra-marital sex relations between white men and Negro women." Ibid., p. 59.

This excerpt is not exceptional; it characterizes the writing. Its meaning is probably this: "The theory of color caste is a rationalization. Besides the economic interests upon which this rationalization is based, we should take into account certain appetites and instinctual drives common to all human beings." The conclusion in the last sentence is incorrect. It is contrary to both the logic of race relations and the data as recorded in the literature including some of the earliest court records on white-man, Negro-woman sex relations. The deplorable fact about this writing is not so much that it is obscure as that it seeks to maneuver the reader into accepting the rationalization as the real reason for racial antagonism. We could hardly emphasize too much that "sexual urges, inhibitions," and so on, traits common to Negroes as well as whites, cannot explain why certain whites dominate Negroes. Moreover, the author does not show that anyone has ever argued that the mere fact that a rationalization is recognized for what it is destroys it. This, obviously, is a straw man set up to cover the author's obsession with abstractions.

philosophers' enigma apparently leads him directly into a mystical play with imponderables. As he sees it, "white prejudice" is a primary determinant in race relations. "White prejudice and discrimination keep the Negro low in standards of living. . . . This, in turn, gives support to prejudice. White prejudice and Negro standards thus mutually 'cause' each other."[44] Moreover, "the chief hindrance to improving the Negro is *the white man's firm belief in his inferiority.*"[45] We shall discuss this controlling idea in a later section.

Poor Whites

It should be pointed out again that Myrdal not only closes his eyes to the material interests which support and maintain race prejudice but also labors the point that there is basic antagonism between poor whites and Negroes. Says he: ". . . what a bitter, spiteful, and relentless feeling often prevails against the Negroes among lower class white people in America. . . . The Marxian solidarity between the toilers . . . will . . . have a long way to go as far as concerns solidarity of the poor white American with the toiling Negro."[46] In fact, the author goes further to intimate that the poor whites may assume a dominant role in the oppression of Negroes in the South, because the interest of the poor whites is economic, while that of the ruling class is a feeling for superiority:

> Lower class whites in the South have no Negro servants in whose humble demeanors they can reflect their own superiority. Instead, they feel actual economic competition or fear of potential competition from the Negroes. They need the caste demarcations for much more substantial reasons than do the middle and upper classes.[47]

[44]Ibid., p. 75.

[45]Ibid., p. 101. (Italics added.)

[46]Ibid., p. 69. In almost identical terms André Siegfried interprets the racial situation: "In the wealthy families some of the old-time sentimentality still survives from the slave days, but the 'poor white' sees in the Negro nothing but a brutal competitor who is trying to rob him of his job. His hatred is unrelenting, merciless, and mingled with fear. To understand the South, we must realize that the lower we descend in the social scale, the more violent the hatred of the Negro." *America Comes of Age,* p. 97. See also Edwin R. Embree, *Brown America,* p. 201.

[47]Op. cit., p. 597. This social illusion concerning the naturalness of racial antagonism between Negroes and poor whites, a mirage ordinarily perpetuated by the white ruling class, is deeply embedded in the literature. For instance, Professor Louis Wirth declares with finality: "It has been repeatedly found by students of Negro-white relations in the South that

The author hesitates to come to that obvious conclusion so much dreaded by the capitalist ruling class: that the observed overt competitive antagonism is a condition produced and carefully maintained by the exploiters of both the poor whites and the Negroes. Yet he almost says this in so many words: "Plantation owners and employers, who use Negro labor as cheaper and more docile, have at times been observed to tolerate, or co-operate in, the periodic aggression of poor whites against Negroes. It is a plausible thesis that they do so in the interest of upholding the caste system which is so effective in keeping the Negro docile."[48] And even more strikingly he shows by what means white workers are exploited through the perpetuation of racial antagonism. Says he: "If those white workers were paid low wages and held in great dependence,

the so-called white aristocracy shows less racial prejudice than do the 'poor whites' whose own position is relatively insecure and who must compete with Negroes for jobs, for property, for social position, and for power. Only those who themselves are insecure feel impelled to press their claims for superiority over others." See "Race and Public Policy," *The Scientific Monthly,* April 1944, p. 304.

Now, we may ask, why should competition be more natural than consolidation in the struggle for wealth and position? Why should insecurity lead more naturally to division than to a closing of ranks? Suppose the Negro and the white proletariat of the South decide to come together and unite for increasing power in their struggle for economic position, what are the sources of opposing power—disorganizing power—that will be immediately brought into action? Wirth might just as well argue that the antagonism and open conflicts which ordinarily develop between union strikers and scabs are caused by a feeling of insecurity among the scabs. In the end this argument must be put into that category of vacuous universals which explain nothing, for who in this world does not feel insecure? And if it is a matter of the degree of insecurity, then we should expect Negroes to take the initiative in interracial aggression since they are the most insecure. In the theoretical discussion of race relations "human nature" or the behavior of human beings as such should be taken for granted.

Sometimes thought is effectively canalized by such apparently objective statements by social scientists as the following: "A standard saying among the southern common folks is that we ought to treat the Negro as we did the Indian: kill him if he doesn't behave and, if not, isolate him and give him what we want to." Howard W. Odum, "Problem and Methodology in an American Dilemma," *Social Forces,* Vol. 23, October 1944, p. 98. Clearly the implication here is that the Southern aristocrats and their university professors are the protectors of the Negroes against the pent-up viciousness of the "southern common folks"—a complete perversion of reality.

[48]Ibid., p. 598. In another context he recognizes that "there had been plenty of racial competition before the Civil War. White artisans had often vociferously protested against the use of Negroes for skilled work in the crafts. But as long as the politically most powerful group of whites had a vested interest in Negro mechanics, the protesting was of little avail." Ibid., p. 281.

they could at least be offered a consolation of being protected from Negro competition."[49]

At any rate, Myrdal refuses to be consistent. Accordingly, he asserts, attitudes against interracial marriage "[seem] generally to be inversely related to the economic and social status of the informant and his educational level. . . . To the poor and socially insecure, but struggling, white individual, a fixed opinion on this point seems an important matter of prestige and distinction."[50] It would not do, of course, to explain the situation realistically by concluding that if the revised black codes written by the white exploiting class against intermarriage were abrogated an increasing number of marriages between the white and the black proletariat would take place, the consequence of which would be a considerably reduced opportunity for labor exploitation by this class.[51]

The Ruling Class

Myrdal does not like to talk about the ruling class in the South; the term carries for him an odious "Marxist" connotation. Yet inevitably he describes this class as well as anyone:

[49]Ibid., p. 286. In the South African situation Lord Olivier makes a similar observation: "When the capitalist employer comes on the scene, making discriminations as to the labor forces he must employ for particular work in order to make his profits, which is the law of his activity to do, then, and not till then, antagonism is introduced between the newly-created wage-working proletarian white and the native—who, in regard to the qualifications which properly determine wage contracts, are on exactly the same footing." *The Anatomy of African Misery*, p. 135.

[50]Op. cit., p. 57.

[51]Hinton R. Helper, the renegade Southerner who never bit his tongue in his criticism of the white ruling class of the South and who, however, never concealed his prejudices against the Negroes, spoke more than a grain of truth when he described the position of the poor whites. It is essentially applicable to present-day conditions. "Notwithstanding the fact that the white non-slaveholders of the South are in the majority as five to one, they have never yet had any part or lot in framing the laws under which they live. . . . The lords of the lash are not only absolute masters of the blacks . . . but they are also the oracles and arbiters of all the non-slaveholding whites, whose freedom is merely nominal and whose unparalleled illiteracy and degradation is purposely and fiendishly perpetuated. How little the 'poor white trash,' the great majority of the Southern people, know of the real conditions of the country is indeed sadly astonishing. . . . It is expected that the stupid and sequacious masses, the white victims of slavery, will believe and, as a general thing, they do believe, whatever the slaveholders tell them; and thus it is that they are cajoled into the notion that they are the freest, happiest, and most intelligent people in the world, and are taught to look with prejudice and disapprobation upon every new principle or progressive movement." *The Impending Crisis*, pp. 42–44 *passim*.

The one-party system in the South . . . and the low political participation of even the white people favor a *de facto* oligarchic regime. . . . The oligarchy consists of the big landowners, the industrialists, the bankers, and the merchants. Northern corporate business with big investments in the region has been sharing in the political control by this oligarchy.[52]

And he stresses the ineffectiveness of the exploited masses. "The Southern masses do not generally organize either for advancing their ideals or for protecting their group interests. The immediate reason most often given by Southern liberals is the resistance from the political oligarchy which wants to keep the masses inarticulate."[53] Furthermore, he indicates the desperate pressure endured by Southern workers when he says: "The poorest farmer in the Scandinavian countries or in England . . . would not take benevolent orders so meekly as Negroes and white sharecroppers do in the South."[54]

Sometimes Myrdal shakes off the whole burden of obfuscation spun about caste, creeds,[55] and poor-white control to show, perhaps without intending to do so, the real interest of the ruling class and how it sets race against race to accomplish its exploitative purpose:

> The conservative opponents of reform proposals [that is to say the ruling class in the South] can usually discredit them by pointing out that they will improve the status of the Negroes, and that they prepare for "social equality." This argument has been raised in the South against labor unions, child labor legislation and practically every other proposal for reform.
>
> It has been argued to the white workers that the Wages and Hours Law was an attempt to legislate equality between the races by raising the wage level of Negro workers to that of whites. The South has never been seriously interested in instituting tenancy legislation to protect the tenants' rights . . . and the argument has again been that the Negro sharecropper should not be helped against the white man.[56]

[52]Op. cit., p. 453.

[53]Ibid., p. 455.

[54]Ibid., p. 466.

[55]This statement is made advisedly. The following unreal conflict between status and ideals may indicate further the nebulous level at which the theoretical part of this study is sometimes pitched: "The American Creed represents the national conscience. The Negro is a 'problem' to the average American partly because of a palpable conflict between the status actually awarded him and those ideals." Ibid., p. 23.

[56]Ibid., p. 456.

It seems clear that in developing a theory of race relations in the South one must look to the economic policies of the ruling class and not to mere abstract depravity among poor whites. Opposition to social equality has no meaning unless we can see its function in the service of the exploitative purpose of this class. "When the Negro rises socially," says Myrdal, "and is no longer a servant, he becomes a stranger to the white upper class. His ambition is suspected and he is disliked."[57] Again: "The ordinary white upper class people will 'have no use' for such Negroes. They need cheap labor—faithful, obedient, unambitious labor."[58] And the author observes further: "In most Southern communities the ruling classes of whites want to keep Negroes from joining labor unions. Some are quite frank in wanting to keep Negroes from reading the Constitution or studying social subjects."[59]

In the South the ruling class stands effectively between the Negroes and the white proletariat. Every segregation barrier is a barrier put up between white and black people by their exploiters. Myrdal puts it this way: "On the local scene the accommodation motive by itself does not usually encourage Negro leaders to such adventures as trying to reach behind the white leaders to the white people."[60] Moreover, it is not the poor whites but the ruling class which uses its intelligence and its money to guard against any movement among Negroes to throw off their yoke of exploitation. "In many communities leading white citizens make no secret of the fact that they are carefully following . . . all signs of 'subversive propaganda' and unrest among the Negroes in the community, and that they interfere to stop even innocent beginnings of Negro group activity."[61]

The reasoning which we are now following, it may be well to state, is not Myrdal's; we are merely culling those conclusions which the data seem to compel the author to make but which he ordinarily surrounds with some mysterious argument about caste.

From one point of view the masters did not have so great a need for racial antagonism during slavery. Black workers could be exploited in compara-

[57]Ibid., p. 593.
[58]Ibid., p. 596.
[59]Ibid., p. 721.
[60]Ibid., p. 727.
[61]Ibid., p. 459.

tive peace; the formal law was on the side of the slave owner. As Myrdal observes: "Exploitation of Negro labor was, perhaps, a less embarrassing *moral conflict* to the ante-bellum planter than to his peer today. . . . Today the exploitation is, to a considerable degree, dependent upon the availability of extralegal devices of various kinds."[62] Obviously, among these extralegal devices are race prejudice, discrimination, and violence—especially lynching and the threat of lynching. "Discrimination against Negroes is . . . rooted in this tradition of economic exploitation."[63]

Emphasis upon Sex

In spite of this, however, Myrdal refuses to accept a realistic interpretation of race relations. Throughout these volumes he warns his readers not to put too much reliance upon a socioeconomic explanation. Thus he declares: "The eager intent to explain away race prejudice and caste in the simple terms of economic competition . . . is an attempt to *escape from caste to class*."[64] The reasoning here, of course, is unrelieved nonsense. Incidentally, it illustrates the hiatus in understanding which an inappropriate use of the concepts "caste" and "class" might entail. At any rate, our author thinks it is more revealing to take sex as our point of reference. In fact, Myrdal presents a scheme of social situations in which he ranks intermarriage and sexual intercourse involving white women as the highest in motives for discrimination, while he ranks economic conditions sixth and last.

> (I) Highest in this order [of discrimination] stands the bar against intermarriage and sexual intercourse involving white women (2) . . . several etiquettes and discriminations . . . (3) . . . segregations and discriminations in use of public facilities such as schools . . . (4) political disfranchisement . . . (5) discrimination in the law courts (6) . . . discriminations in securing land, credit, jobs . . . [65]

This rank order evidences the degree of importance which "white

[62]Ibid., p. 220. (Italics added.)

[63]Ibid., p. 208.

[64]Ibid., p. 792. (Italics added.)

[65]Ibid., p. 61. In similar vein he asserts: "It is surely significant that the white Southerner is much less willing to permit intermarriage or to grant 'social equality' than he is to allow equality in the political, judicial and economic spheres. The violence of the Southerner's reaction to equality in each of these spheres rises with the degree of its relation to the sexual and personal, which suggests that *his prejudice is based upon fundamental attitudes toward sex and personality.*" (Italics added.) Ibid., p. 61.

people" attach to certain social facts calculated to keep the Negro in his place, and it is "apparently determined by the factors of sex and social status."[66] The Negroes' estimate, however, is just the reverse of this: "The Negro's own rank order is just about parallel, but inverse, to that of the white man."[67] Here, then, is a perfect example of social illusion, an illusion that must inevitably come to all those who attempt to see race relations in the South as involving two castes.

In reality, both the Negroes and their white exploiters know that economic opportunity comes first and that the white woman comes second; indeed, she is merely a significant instrument in limiting the first. Moreover, these selected elements of social discrimination should not be thought of as discrete social phenomena; they are rather intermeshed in a definite pattern supporting a dominant purpose. If the white ruling class intends to keep the colored people in their place—that is to say, freely exploitable—this class cannot permit them to marry white women; neither can it let white men marry Negro women. If this were allowed to happen Negroes would soon become so whitened that the profit makers would be unable to direct mass hatred against them[68] and would thus lose their principal weapon in facilitating their primary business of exploiting the white and the black workers of the South.[69] If a Negro could become governor of Georgia it

[66]Ibid., p. 61. It is further emphasized: "The concern for 'race purity' is *basic* in the whole issue; the primary and essential command is to prevent amalgamation.... Rejection of 'social equality' is to be understood as a precaution to hinder miscegenation and particularly intermarriage. The danger of miscegenation is so tremendous that segregation and discrimination inherent in the refusal of 'social equality' must be extended to all spheres of life." Ibid., p. 58.

[67]Ibid., p. 61.

[68]It should be made crystal-clear that the design of the ruling white people is not primarily to keep the blood of the white race "pure," but rather to prevent race mixture; it is therefore definitely as frustrating to their fundamental purpose of economic exploitation to infuse white blood into the Negro group. Their purpose can be accomplished only if the Negroes remain identifiably colored.

[69]Decades ago George W. Cable observed: "The essence of the offence, any and everywhere the race line is insisted upon, is the apparition of the colored man or woman as his or her own master; that masterhood is all that all this tyranny is intended to preserve.... The moment the relation of master and servant is visibly established between race and race there is a hush of peace.... The surrender of this one point by the colored man or woman buys more than peace—it buys amity." *The Negro Question,* pp. 22–23.

And, as if it were in confirmation of this, C. R. Goodlatte writes, "It may be said of us that we welcome the native as a servant: as a rule we treat him individually in a fairly humane fashion; we often win his esteem and trust; but in any other capacity than that of a docile

would be of no particular social significance whether his wife is white or colored; or, at any rate, there would be no political power presuming to limit the color of his wife. But if, in a "democracy," you could insist that his wife must be black, you could not only prevent his becoming governor of Georgia, but you could also make him do most of your dirty and menial work at your wages.[70] Sexual obsession, then, functions in the fundamental interest of economic exploitation.

As a matter of fact, Myrdal is apparently so concerned with his sexual emphasis that he is here led to compare incommensurable arrays: the "white man's" system of rationalization with the real basis of race relations, as the Negroes react to it. If he had been consistent in dealing with economic reality, he would probably have been able to extricate its superstructure of rationalization with sex as its emotional fundament. Indeed, this very approach might have led him to discover the pith of the problem, for Negroes "resist" least that which is of comparatively little moment and most that which is of crucial significance. Sex is not "basic" in race relations, but it is basic in the system of rationalization which supports racial antagonism.

Again our author sees the problem in this light: "It is inherent in our type of modern Western civilization that sex and social status are for most individuals the danger points, the directions whence he fears the sinister onslaughts on his personal security."[71] This passage is intended as an explanation of the "white man's theory of color caste," determined by sexual fears. However, it seems inadequate for two reasons: (a) it is not significantly characteristic of "Western civilization" and (b) it tends to conceive of race prejudice as a personal matter. In all societies "sex and social status" are "danger points" to the individual. In apparently most of

servant we consider him intolerable." "South Africa: Glimpses and Comments," *Contemporary Review*, CXXXIII, 1928, p. 347.

[70]In order to support his specious argument Myrdal relies pivotally upon such sour-grape expressions as the following by R. R Moton: "As for amalgamation, very few expect it; still fewer want it; no one advocates it; and only a constantly diminishing minority practise it, and that surreptitiously. It is generally accepted on both sides of the color line that it is best for the two races to remain ethnologically distinct." Op. cit., p. 62. This, from a Negro, is assumed to be evidence that Negroes do not want intermarriage. On its face, Myrdal might have asked: Why should something that is not wanted be practiced "surreptitiously"? Moreover, would the white ruling class be obsessed with the prevention of intermarriage if the natural likelihood of its occurring were exceedingly remote?

[71]Ibid., p. 59.

them they are much more so than in Western society; in Brahmanic India, for instance, they are infinitely more so, but there has been no race prejudice in Brahmanic India. Then, too, we could hardly overemphasize the fact that race prejudice is not a personal attitude. The individual in the South is not allowed to exercise personal discretion in this matter. Indeed, it is obviously the very fear of sexual attraction between individual members of the races which caused the ruling class to make laws supported by propaganda for its control.

The Vicious Circle

Capitalist rationalizations of race relations have recently come face to face with a powerful theory of society and, in order to meet this, the orthodox theorists have become mystics. This evidently had to be so because it is exceedingly terrifying for these scientists to follow to its logical conclusion a realistic explanation of race relations; and yet they must either do this or stultify themselves. Here the social scientist is "on the spot"; he must avoid "the truth" because it is dangerous, regardless of how gracefully he eases up to it. In illustration, Myrdal advises Negroes not to become too radical and to think of many causes as of equal significance with the material factor: "Negro strategy would build on an illusion if it set all its hope on a blitzkrieg directed toward a basic [economic] factor. In the nature of things it must work on the broadest possible front. There is a place for both the radical and the conservative Negro leaders."[72] This, obviously, will lead to a situation in which the ideas of one group of leaders will tend to offset those of another.

Although Myrdal overlays his discussion of race relations with a particularly alien caste belief, his controlling hypothesis has nothing whatever to do with caste. His "theory of the vicious circle"[73] is his controlling idea. This theory is essentially an abstract formulation, inspired by a largely inverted observation of "a vicious circle in caste" by Edwin R. Embree,[74] and rendered "scientific" by the application of certain concepts which Myrdal seems to have used to his satisfaction in his study, *Monetary Equilibrium*.

As we have seen in a previous section, the vicious circle runs as follows:

[72]Ibid., p. 794.
[73]Ibid., pp. 75–78, 207–9, and Appendix 3.
[74]Ibid., p. 1069, note.

"White prejudice . . . keeps the Negro low in standards of living. . . . This, in turn, gives support to white prejudice. White prejudice and Negro standards thus mutually 'cause' each other." These two variables are interdependent, but neither is consistently dependent; a change in either will affect the other inversely. If we initiate a change in Negro standards, say, by "giving the Negro youth more education," white prejudice will go down; if we change white prejudice, say, by "an increased general knowledge about biology, eradicating false beliefs concerning Negro racial inferiority," then Negro standards will go up.

It is this kind of mystical dance of imponderables which is at the basis of the system of social illusions marbled into Myrdal's discussion. In the first place, Myrdal does not develop a careful definition of race prejudice. He does say, however: "For our purpose [race prejudice] is defined as discrimination by whites against Negroes."[75] But he does not use this definition, in fact we do not see how he can, for race prejudice is a social attitude, an acquired tendency to act; it is not some act or action which is the meaning of discrimination.[76] Myrdal's studied analysis would lead us rather to deduce the following definition of race prejudice: a feeling of bitterness, especially among poor whites, aroused particularly by a standing sexual threat of Negro men to white women. As he sees it, the white man's "prejudice is based upon fundamental attitudes toward sex and personality."

If, according to Myrdal's "rank order of discrimination," the whites are most concerned with sex and the Negroes with economic advancement, his fundamental equilibrium of social forces should be a direct correlation between white prejudice and Negro sexual aggression—not Negro standards, which are clearly basically economic. In this way white prejudice will tend to vanish as Negro men give up their interest in white women; Negro standards will also go up, but only incidentally. If, for instance, Negro men would relinquish their desire to marry white women, "white people" would no longer be prejudiced against Negroes; the latter would be encouraged, say, to vote and campaign for political office and to demand their share of

[75]Ibid., p. 78.

[76]In another connection Myrdal seems to give a different meaning to the concept: "If for some reason . . . white workers actually came to work with Negroes as fellow workers, it has been experienced that prejudice will often adjust to the changed amount of *discrimination.*" Ibid., p. 1067. (Italics added.) See also pp. 1141ff.

jobs and public funds in the Deep South.[77] To be sure, Myrdal does not demonstrate any such proposition. We may put it in still another way: If Negro standards go up and at the same time Negroes increase their interest in white women, then, to be consistent with Myrdal's sexual emphasis, white prejudice must increase. From this it follows that Negro standards are a non-significant variable.

The point which the author seems to have avoided is this: that both race prejudice and Negro standards are consistently dependent variables. They are both produced by the calculated economic interests of the Southern oligarchy. Both prejudice and the Negro's status are dependent functions of the latter interests. In one variation of his theory of the "vicious circle" Myrdal reasons:

> Assuming . . . that we want to reduce the bias in white people's racial beliefs concerning Negroes, our first practical conclusion is that we can effect this result to a degree by *actually improving Negro status*. . . . The impediment in the way of this strategy is . . . that white beliefs . . . are active forces in keeping the Negroes low.[78]

Here beliefs are assumed to be prime movers; they "keep the Negroes low." This is mysticism. If we can "improve Negro status" the reason for the existence of derogatory beliefs about Negroes is, to the extent of the improvement, liquidated. With a rise in the standard of living of Negroes there tends to be merely a concomitant vitiation of the rationalizations for the depressed conditions of Negroes. The belief is an empty, harmless illusion, like beliefs in werewolves or fairies, without the exploitative interest with which it is impregnated. If the economic force could be bridled, the belief would collapse from inanition. There is a vested interest in anti-racial beliefs.

The effective interest is a need for slaves, or peons, or unorganized common laborers—a need for "cheap, docile labor." The latter interest, of course, is involved in a complicated web of feeling established by both

---

[77]"Negroes are in desperate need of jobs and bread. . . . The marriage matter [to them] is of rather distant and doubtful interest." Ibid., p. 6. The Negroes, thus goes the logic, want jobs and the white men want to protect their women from Negro men. But white men are rather willing to let Negroes have jobs, while Negro men are not particularly interested in white women. If this is so, if these two admittedly antagonistic groups are vitally interested in different things, why is there antagonism at all? It would seem that men fight only when they are possessed of conflicting interests in the same object.

[78]Ibid., p. 109. (Italics added.)

immemorial and recent rationalizations. If beliefs, per se, could subjugate a people, the beliefs which Negroes hold about whites should be as effective as those which whites hold about Negroes.

This assumption of Myrdal's, that racial beliefs are primary social forces, leads him to conclude almost pathetically that the "white man's" beliefs are only a "mistake," which he would gladly correct if only he had truthful information. Accordingly our author suggests the following attack upon the beliefs themselves:

> A second line of strategy must be to rectify the ordinary white man's observations of Negro characteristics and inform him of the specific mistakes he is making in ascribing them wholesale to inborn racial traits. . . . People want to be rational, to be honest and well informed.[79]

Evidently the misapprehension in this presentation inheres in Myrdal's moral approach. He does not recognize consistently that the propagators of the ruling ideas, those whose interest it is to replace debunked beliefs with new ones, are not mistaken at all, and that they should not be thought of merely as people or white people. They are, in fact, a special class of people who fiercely oppose interference with the established set of antagonistic racial beliefs. The racial beliefs have been intentionally built up through propaganda. They are mass psychological instruments facilitating a definite purpose; therefore, they can best be opposed by realistic aggressive propaganda methods.[80] It is, to repeat, consummate naïveté to assume that the ruling class in the South will permit a free, objective discussion of race relations in its schools or public places.[81] Today such a practice can succeed only as a hazardous underground movement.

Furthermore, the author's unstable equilibrium between race prejudice and Negro standards is evidently too simple. For instance, if Negro standards go up because of interference from some outside force, say the Federal Government, the cultivated race prejudice among the poor whites may tend to diminish, but at the same time the hostility of the ruling-class whites may increase. The reason for this is that, because of the interference, the status and problems of Negroes and those of the poor whites may be made more

[79]Ibid., p. 109.

[80]This view also holds against certain popular conceptions of race prejudice as "superstition" or "myth."

[81]On this point, see Stetson Kennedy, *Southern Exposure,* p. 349.

nearly to coincide and thus enhance the possibility of an establishment of a community of interest between these two groups, a process diametrically opposed to the purpose and interests of the white ruling class. Therefore, it becomes incumbent upon the latter class to re-establish its position by bringing into play those very well-known means of reaffirming racial antipathy.

Although Myrdal never permits himself to accept a consistently realistic approach to the study of race relations, he recites as historical fact that which his theory confutes. For instance, the following historical passage says quite clearly that race prejudice is an attitude deliberately built up among the masses by an exploiting class, using acceptable rationalizations derogatory to the Negro race, so that the exploitation of the latter's labor power might be justified.

> The historical literature of this early period . . . records that the imported Negroes—and the captured Indians—originally were kept in much the same status as the white indentured servants. *When later the Negroes gradually were pushed down into chattel slavery* while the white servants were allowed to work off their board, *the need was felt* . . . for some kind of justification *above mere economic expediency and the might of the strong.* The arguments called forth by this need . . . were broadly these: that the Negro was a heathen and a barbarian, an outcast among the peoples of the earth, a descendant of Noah's son Ham, cursed by God himself and doomed to be a servant forever on account of an ancient sin.[82]

Now there is no mysticism here—nothing about "sexual drives," "fears," "inhibitions," "labile balance," and so on—the historical process is clear. The exploitative act comes first; the prejudice follows. It explains unequivocally that a powerful white exploiting class, by "the might of the strong" and for "economic expediency," pushed the Negroes down into chattel slavery and then, as a justification and facilitation of this, utilized the means of propaganda, which are ordinarily in its control, to develop racial antagonism and hate in the white public for the Negroes.[83]

Attacking beliefs by negation is obviously a negative procedure—some-

[82]Op. cit., p. 85. (Italics added.)

[83]It is interesting to observe with what anonymity Myrdal uses such key concepts as "imported," "captured," "kept," "pushed down," and so on. One would think that the subject referred to by these terms of action would be of primary concern in the investigation. It is, however, highly impersonalized, and the whole social situation tends to remain as if it were an act of Nature.

times even a futile one. In an essay of epoch-making significance, written in about the year 1800, Henri Grégoire[84] demonstrated, probably as clearly as ever, that the white man is "making a mistake in ascribing Negro characteristics to inborn racial traits"; yet this assignment is still freshly advocated. As a matter of fact, Count Arthur de Gobineau almost put men like Grégoire out of existence.[85] In like manner, Dr. W. T. Couch, formerly editor in chief of probably the most influential Southern press, proceeds to "gobinize" Myrdal.

Couch, in a caustic criticism of Myrdal, referring to him as "silly" and "ignorant," says the white man cannot make concessions to Negroes because these will ultimately lead to Negro men's marrying white men's daughters. "One concession will lead to another, and ultimately to inter-marriage."[86] Here the thinking of both authors is bogged down in the slough of sexual passion from which we may not hope for light on race relations. Moreover, in this unrealistic world of beliefs Couch has Myrdal where he wants him; he seems to triumph with such intuitive declarations as: "The assertion of equality is an assertion of values."[87] And, in a charac-teristically pre–Civil War, slaveholders' contention about the meaning of the Declaration of Independence, he becomes involved with Myrdal's

[84]*An Inquiry Concerning the Intellectual and Moral Faculties, and Literature of Negroes,* trans. by D. B. Warden, Brooklyn, 1810.

[85]After Professor Donald Young had completed his examination of the conditions of American minority peoples he made the following conclusionary statement: "Action, not cautious and laborious research, is demanded of those who would lead the populace. Thus a Chamberlain, a Gobineau, or a Stoddard attracts myriads of followers by a pseudo-scientific program based on a doctrine of God-given white supremacy . . . while the very names of Franz Boas, Eugene Pittard, Herbert A. Miller, E. B. Reuter, Friedrich Hertz, and other scholarly students of the peoples of the world are unknown outside of a small intellectual circle. 'Give us the solution and let sterile scholars while away their time with obscure facts which lead but to quibbling books!' is the cry of the masses." Yet the reason that Gobineau *et al.* have been widely accepted by the white ruling classes of the world is not that they presented a course of "action" but that they had the timely ingenuity to contrive a system of plausible logic which justified an accomplished act: the white racial mastery of the world. Explanations and justifications were desperately needed. For the most part the scholars mentioned have been able only to point out flaws in the anti-racial arguments; they had already lost their conviction when they innocently accepted the spurious grounds of discus-sion which the apologists of racial exploitation had chosen. They apparently did not recognize that both the racial antagonism and its pseudo-scientific rationalizations are products of a peculiar social system.

[86] *What the Negro Wants,* Rayford W. Logan, ed., p. xvi.

[87]Ibid., p. xvii.

moral orientation. "I believe," says Couch, *"An American Dilemma* was written under gross misapprehensions of what such ideas as equality, freedom, democracy, human rights, have meant, and what they can be made to mean."[88] Thus, without restraint and without enlightenment, the mystics, steeped in metaphysical truck, set upon each other.

A positive program, on the other hand, calls for an attack upon the source of the beliefs, so that it might be divested of its prestige and power to produce and to substitute anti-racial beliefs among the masses. In other words, the problem is that of converting the white masses to an appreciation and realization of the ruling-class function of the beliefs and their effect as instruments in the exploitation of the white as well as of the black masses. Then, not only will the old beliefs lose their efficacy, but also the new ones will die aborning.

A positive program calls for the winning of the white masses over to a different system of thinking—not merely a campaign of scholarly denials of spectacular myths about creation, stages of biological progress, cultural capacity, and so on. Indeed, such negation may even play into the hands of the "racists," for they may not only divert attention from the realities of race relations but also help to spread and implant the myths among the public. However, the effectuation of such a program, the intent of which must be to alienate public support of the aristocracy, will undoubtedly evoke terrific opposition from this class. To be sure, this fact merely demonstrates further the basis of racial antagonism in the South and the correctness of the suggested positive program. At the same time, of course, Negroes must learn that their interest is primarily bound up with that of the white common people in a struggle for power and not essentially in a climb for social status.

At any rate, it is precisely this realization which Dr. Myrdal constantly seeks to circumvent. Accordingly he argues inconsistently that the ruling class in the South is the Negroes' best friend.

> Our hypothesis is similar to the view taken by an older group of Negro writers and by most white writers who have touched this crucial question: that the Negroes' friend—or the one who is least unfriendly—is still rather the upper class of white people, the people with economic and social security who are *truly a "non-competing group."* [89]

The author, by one symptom or another, cannot help showing of what

[88]Ibid., p. xv.

he is really apprehensive: the bringing into consciousness of the masses the identity of the interests of the white and the black workers. In accordance with this attitude he takes a superficial view of the economic order and asks Negroes to go to the labor market and see who is their real enemy. Thus he asserts:

> The aim of [the theory of labor solidarity] is to unify the whole Negro people, not with the white upper class, but with the white working class. . . . The theory of labor solidarity has been taken up as a last solution of the Negro problem, and as such is escapist in nature; its escape character becomes painfully obvious to every member of the school as soon as he leaves abstract reasoning and goes down to the labor market, because there he *meets caste* and has to talk race, even racial solidarity.[90]

As a justificatory illustration of the validity of his principle of "cumulative causation," the summatory interaction of the elements of Negro standards and other social factors, Myrdal says: "The philanthropist, the Negro educator, the Negro trade unionist . . . and, indeed, the average well-meaning citizen of both colors, pragmatically applies the same hypothesis."[91] In reality, however, this is not a confirmation of a sound theory of race relations; it is rather an apology for reformism. Within the existing system of power relationships this is the most that is respectably allowed. Reformism never goes so far as to envisage the real involvement of the exploitative system with racial antagonism. Its extreme aspiration does not go beyond the attainment of freedom for certain black men to participate in the exploitation of the commonalty regardless of the color of the latter. This aspiration is the prospect which the Southern oligarchy with some degree of justification ordinarily refers to as "Negro domination."

Then, too, with reformation as an end, the logical "friend" of the Negro leader must necessarily be this same white aristocracy; for he must ultimately become, like the aristocracy, the inevitable economic adversary of the exploited masses; he must become, in other words, a "black Anglo-Saxon." Indeed, assuming bourgeois proclivities, his very appeal to the

---

[89]Op. cit., p. 69. (Italics added.) It is interesting to observe how Dr. Myrdal has finally become almost reactionary in the sense of the incorrigible segregationist, W. T. Couch, who also says: "Nothing is more needed in the South today than rebirth of [Booker Washington's] ideas, restoration of the great leadership that he was giving." Op. cit., p. xxiii.

[90]Myrdal, op. cit., p. 793. (Italics added.)

[91]Ibid., p. 1069.

masses for support in his struggle for "equality" is an unavoidable deception. The reformer seeks to eliminate only the racial aspects of the exploitative system; he compromises with the system which produces the racial antagonism. But the white ruling class cannot willingly accept even this compromise, for it knows that the whole system is doomed if Negroes are permitted to achieve unlimited status as participating exploiters. In such an event there would be no racial scapegoat or red herring to brandish before the confused white commonalty as a means of keeping them and the Negro masses from recognizing the full impact of political-class oppression.

Today "conservative" theories of race relations are not merely denied; they are confronted with a countertheory, the theory that racial antagonism is in fact *political-class* antagonism and that race prejudice is initiated and maintained by labor exploiters. It is not, it would seem clear, that the aristocracy is less antagonistic to the Negroes but that this class uses more respectable weapons against them, which are also infinitely more powerful and effective. As a matter of fact, the poor whites themselves may be thought of as the primary instrument of the ruling class in subjugating the Negroes. The statement attributed to a great financier, "I can pay one half of the working class to kill off the other half," is again in point.

As we have seen, Myrdal does not favor this explanation. He declares that all the Negro's troubles are due to the simple fact that "white people" want to be superior to colored people; or, indeed, merely to the fact that the Negro is colored. His argument follows:

> We hear it said . . . that there is no "race problem" but only a "class problem." The Negro sharecropper is alleged to be destitute not because of his color but because of his class position—and it is pointed out that there are white people who are equally poor. From a practical angle there is a point in this reasoning. But from a theoretical angle it contains escapism in a new form. It also draws too heavily on the idealistic Marxian doctrine of the "class struggle." And it tends to conceal the whole system of special deprivations visited upon the Negro *only because he is not white.*[92]

Throughout the study the author has frequently found it sufficient simply to mention the name of Karl Marx in order to counter views based upon the determining role of the "material conditions of production" and distribution.[93] After a studied argument in favor of the futility of Negroes

[92]Ibid., p. 75. (Italics added.)

adopting a Marxian view of society, he concludes: " 'Even after a revolution the country will be full of crackers' is a reflection I have often met when discussing communism in the Negro community."[94] The least we could say about this is that it is very crude. On this kind of thinking John Stuart Mill is emphatic: "Of all the vulgar modes of escaping from the consideration of the effect of social and moral influences on the human mind, the most vulgar is that of attributing the diversities of conduct and character to inherent natural differences."[95] More especially it expresses the fatalism upon which the whole orthodox school of race relations inevitably rests.

Myrdal, as a confirmed moralist, is not concerned with problems of power but rather with problems of "regenerating the individual" by idealistic preachments. If only the individual could be taught to accept the morality of the Creed, then society would lose its fever of racial pathologies and settle down to a happy existence. However, the point we are trying to make is that, in a feudal system, serfdom is natural and the serf will be treated like a serf regardless of whether the lord is a bishop or a secular noble; in the slavocracy of the South the slave was treated like a slave, whether his master was white or black; in modern capitalism black workers are exploited naturally and race hatred is a natural support of this exploita-

---

[93]And yet Myrdal has shown himself to be vitally wanting in an understanding of the difference between status rivalry and class struggle. Observe, for instance, the following typical confusion: "Our hypothesis is that in a society where there are broad social classes and, in addition, more minute distinctions and splits in the lower strata, the lower class groups will, to a great extent, take care of keeping each other subdued, thus relieving, to that extent, the higher classes of this otherwise painful task necessary to the monopolization of the power and the advantages.

"It will be observed that this hypothesis is contrary to the Marxian theory of class society. . . . The Marxian scheme assumes that there is an actual solidarity between the *several lower class groups* against the *higher classes,* or, in any case, a potential solidarity. . . . The inevitable result is a 'class struggle' where all poor and disadvantaged groups are united behind the barricades." Ibid., p. 68. (Italics added.) Myrdal thinks that Marx thinks the *upper class* and the *lower class,* mere social illusions, are in conflict. No wonder he seems to conclude that Marx is rather foolish. And he does not trouble himself at all to explain how the "higher classes" exercise the "necessary painful task" of keeping the lower classes subdued when, perchance, the latter stop fighting among themselves and turn their attention to their common enemy. This is, to use the term so frequently employed by Myrdal, "escapism."

[94]Ibid., p. 509.

[95]*Principles of Political Economy,* Vol. 1, p. 390. Long before this John Locke had said quite as much; see *Essay Concerning Human Understanding.*

tion. In other words, morality is a function of the social system, and a better system can change both morality and human nature for the better.

There will be no more "crackers" or "niggers" after a socialist revolution because the social necessity for these types will have been removed. But the vision which the capitalist theorist dreads most is this: that there will be no more capitalists and capitalist exploitation. If we attempt to see race relations realistically, the meaning of the capitalist function is inescapable. At any rate, although Myrdal criticizes Sumner and Park for their inert and fatalistic views of social change, he himself contends that any revolutionary change in the interest of democracy will be futile:

> . . . a national policy will never work by changing only one factor, least of all if attempted suddenly and with great force. In most cases that would either throw the system entirely out of gear or else prove to be a wasteful expenditure of effort which could be reached much further by being spread strategically over various factors in the system and over a period of time.[96]

This is not the place to discuss the theory of revolution, but it must be obvious that the purpose of revolution is not to "throw the system out of gear." It is to overthrow the entire system, to overthrow a ruling class; and the cost of revolution did not frighten the capitalists when it became their lot to overthrow the feudalists.

An American Dilemma, the most exhaustive survey of race relations ever undertaken in the United States, is, for the most part, a useful source of data. In detail it presents many ingenious analyses of the materials. But it develops no hypothesis or consistent theory of race relations; and, to the extent that it employs the caste belief in interpretations, it is misleading. Clearly, the use of "the American Creed" as the "value premise" for his study severely limits and narrows Dr. Myrdal's perspective. Even though we should grant some right of the author to limit the discussion of his subject to its moral aspects, he still develops it without insight. He never brings into focus the two great systems of morality currently striving in our civilization for ascendancy, but merely assumes a teleological abstraction of social justice toward which all good men will ultimately gravitate. Moreover, since we can hardly accuse him of being naïve, and since he clearly goes out of his way to avoid the obvious implications of labor exploitation in the South, we cannot help concluding that the work in many

[96]Op. cit., p. 77.

respects may have the effect of a powerful piece of propaganda in favor of the status quo. If the "race problem" in the United States is pre-eminently a moral question, it must naturally be resolved by moral means, and this conclusion is precisely the social illusion which the ruling political class has constantly sought to produce. In this connection we are conscious of the author's recognition that "social science is essentially a 'political' science." One thing is certain, at any rate: the work contributes virtually nothing to a clarification of the many existing spurious social theories of race relations—indeed, on the latter score, Myrdal's contribution is decidedly negative. And for this reason evidently he has been able to suggest no solution for the dilemma, but, like the fatalists whom he criticizes, the author relies finally upon time as the great corrector of all evil.

9.
The Area of Caste Society
and Practical Value of the Concept

The System Limited

We now come to the question: where in the world outside of Brahmanic India do caste systems exist? And the answer must be briefly: Practically nowhere. The caste system is an Indian cultural invention, and the fact that it did not diffuse may be due to the comparative isolation and sedentariness of the Hindus, besides the probable difficulty of reorganizing other societies under the peculiar aegis of godlike priests. An economic system in which occupational specialization is presumed to inhere in corporate social groups producing out of a sense of religious duty in the interest of social peace—in which leadership is atomized and loyalty passionately bestowed upon the producing unit—is to be found only in India.[1] A number of authorities, among them Bouglé, Hutton, Senart, and Risley,[2] have reached a similar conclusion.

[1] There are evidently some real vestiges of the caste system among the islands off the coast of southern India. The caste culture was carried there by early migrations. See Miguel Covarrubias, *Island of Bali,* pp. 52–57; Jane Belo, "A Study of a Balinese Family," *American Anthropologist,* New Series, Vol. 38, 1936, pp. 12–31. See also Clive Day, *The Dutch in Java,* p. 9, and Raymond Kennedy, *The Ageless Indies,* pp. 32–36.

[2] "Even in ancient times," says Bouglé, "western civilization has set its face against such a system." *Essais sur le régime des cartes,* 3rd ed., p. 11. J. H. Hutton, census commissioner of India, thinks that the caste system is a form of social organization unique in the world, for "there is no other country or nation which possesses anything approaching the elaborate caste system of India, nor is there any other country known to have possessed one of the same kind." *Census of India,* 1931, Vol. 1, Pt. 1, p. 433; see also for a similar statement by Hutton, *Caste in India,* pp. 41–42. And Senart concludes: "Caste exists only in India. It is therefore in the situation peculiar to India that we must seek its explanation. . . . We must turn to the facts themselves . . . to . . . study the characteristic elements of the system. . . ." *Caste in India,* p. 174. See also p. 32. Although Risley reached some rather astonishing conclusions in support of his race-caste theory, he writes: "Nowhere else in the world do we find the people of a

Many others, however, think that caste systems have existed at various periods and in different areas of the world. Yet none of this group has ever gone to the pains of assuring himself that the system under consideration stood up in careful comparison with Hindu society. Consider, in illustration, the treatment of this subject by the eminent anthropologist, Robert H. Lowie. In a discussion of caste among the Natchez Indians he asserts:

> The Natchez evidently had a most interesting caste system. . . . The common herd were designated by the unflattering term *Stinkards* and were sharply set off from the nobility. This latter group was subdivided into three ranks of Honored People, Nobles and Suns, the ruler standing at the head of the scale as Great Sun. . . . The Natchez were not only permitted but prescribed the marriage of Suns with commoners, the regulation affecting both sexes. When a Sun woman espoused a Stinkard, the customary patriarchal arrangements of the tribe were suspended, the husband occupying the status of a domestic not privileged to eat in his wife's company and being liable to execution for infidelity. The working of the scheme has been thus summarized by Swanton: "The Suns comprised children of Sun mothers and Stinkard fathers; the Nobles were children of Noble mothers and Stinkard fathers, or of Sun fathers and Stinkard mothers; the Honored People included children of Honored women and Stinkard fathers, and of Noble fathers and Stinkard mothers; finally, the large class of Stinkards was recruited from plebeian intermarriages or from unions of Stinkard mothers and Honored men."[3]

We have quoted at length from Dr. Lowie, for we know of no other discussion of caste systems independent of India which improves significantly upon his. Critically, however, it may be said that this whole description appears irrelevant to basic principles of caste organization. From the foregoing description, the Natchez society appears to be a type of matriarchate with some sort of estate system.[4]

of a large continent broken up into an infinite number of mutually exclusive aggregates, the members of which are forbidden by an inexorable social law to marry outside the group to which they themselves belong." *The People of India,* p. 24. To the same effect, see also Max Weber, *Gesammelte Aufsatze zurReligionssoziologie,* Vol. II, Sec. 1. Weber thinks that Jews in Europe have been a caste similar to the outcastes of India, "a Pariah folk." He distinguishes the Jewish situation, however, with the modifications that the Jews lived in a casteless milieu, that they were never spiritually resigned, and that they possessed a rational religion. Ibid., pp. 2–7. Notwithstanding these modifications, the analogy remains questionable.

[3]Robert H. Lowie, *Primitive Society,* pp. 351–52.

[4]For a discussion of the estate systems of the Aztecs and Incas, see Bailey W. Diffie, *Latin-American Civilization,* pp. 165–78. It should be observed that although the caste system of India is very ancient it involves a highly developed civilization, and in consequence we should not expect to find it in decidedly primitive cultures.

Some students have been very much troubled about the tendency to limit caste society to India. Thus it has been said to the writer: "If you require, for a society to be characterized by 'caste,' that it resemble the Indian situation in every important particular, then of course there is no instance of caste in the world except that found in India; and it further follows that 'caste' cannot be the name of a class of phenomena and is no concept."[4a] Clearly, such a view opens the way for endless debate. At any rate, we feel rather like Professor MacIver, who explains: "If we are to study a thing together we must, when we use a word or phrase, be denoting, mentally pointing out as it were, the same object."[5]

At any rate, this contention should be met directly. It is not so much an insistence that every social fact in the caste system of Brahmanic India must be identical or duplicated in detail in the social structure of race relations in the United States as it is absolutely necessary that at least every detail, which the race-caste hypothesis itself considers significant enough to mention in its own support, should be tested and compared to the social norm. We should consider the race-caste hypothesis invalid if its postulates are inconsistent with the caste system of India. If not India, then the theorist is obviously limited to two alternatives: (1) He should state explicitly which other caste system or systems he is using as a social prototype, or (2) he should indicate clearly that his assumed caste system is a fictitious construct. In either case the validity of his reasoning will depend upon the acceptability of his criteria and assumptions. Thus far, however, no race-caste theorist known to us has followed either of these two procedures.

The caste system is not a social concept in the sense that social status is one. Social status is a universal attribute of human societies. Just as, for

---

[4a]For a rather loose discussion of this point, see M. F. Ashley Montagu, "The Nature of Race Relations," *Social Forces,* Vol. 25, March 1947, p. 339.

[5]R. M. MacIver, *Society, Its Structure and Changes,* p. 5. Moreover, to conceive of a social concept as definitive of a type of social organization, which the concept of a caste system must necessarily imply, and to impute this concept to some social fact in a totally different type of social organization can hardly be a valid procedure. Raymond Bauer makes this point when he observes: "To study culture one must study it as a complete pattern of functionally related institutions. As a matter of fact, even individual institutions should not be studied apart from an explicitly stated cultural framework, since the significance of any one institution lies in its functional relationship to the entire pattern." Review of *The Social Systems of American Ethnic Groups* by W. Lloyd Warner and Leo Srole in *Science,* Vol. 103, February 1, 1946, p. 150.

instance, warm blood does not differentiate species of Mammalia, so also social status of itself does not differentiate types of societies. But the caste system is not merely an attribute of society; it is itself a type of society. It will make no sense at all to speak of a caste society as an attribute of a capitalist society. These two are distinct social systems, with entirely independent cultural histories and with mutually antagonistic social norms. It is beyond all social logic, moreover, to conceive of a caste system developing spontaneously within a capitalist system. We cannot even conceive of social status, as it manifests itself in the caste system, having an identical or similar manifestation in the capitalist system.

A concept which changes its meaning according to the convenience of the student may complicate rather than clarify thinking on the subject. The sociologist who says that the caste system of India represents a unique form of social organization is evidently on better ground than he who asserts that wherever you find a society whose social-status structure is rigid with one or more in-marrying groups, there you have a caste system. And this admission of uniqueness does not mean that Hindu society is an anomalous social phenomenon, for this pattern of culture reveals social situations which might have developed in other societies. Its very uniqueness should present a tempting field for study. The caste system, like capitalism, is a form of social organization; both of these are types of societies. Clearly, it is as logical to think of the caste system as having developed independently in India as it is for us to realize that modern capitalism is exclusively a European-culture development.

Furthermore, the indiscriminate use of a concept naturally tends to limit its effectiveness. If, according to the predilection of the writer, he might extract any one or a selection of attributes of the caste system to verify his hypothesis that castes exist in Haiti, or in England, or in the United States, or, for that matter, in the Army, or in the Church, then indeed we have a concept of wide serviceability but at the same time sociologically meaningless.

Another tendency, which should rather be deplored among sociologists and anthropologists, is that of using the term "castelike" when an accurate description of the social situation evidently seems too abstruse. The term "castelike," even more so than the term "caste," confuses the problem. Obviously a castelike society may be defined only by saying that it represents a social system which looks like or behaves like a caste system. This done, however, we are faced with the query, How does a caste system look? The ocular connotation of this type of adjective apparently detracts from its value in describing societies. When we say a thing is manlike, or doglike, or redlike, our meaning is ordinarily quite clear. There is no mistaking the gorilla for a man, or the dog for a wolf, or purple for red; acceptance of the one when the other is desired may mean all the difference in the world. But in the case of abstract phenomena, the common assumption seems to be that "likes" may be identified *for all practical purposes.*

In his study of race relations in the United States Dr. Sutherland explains that "the term 'castelike' is used in describing the relations of the Negro and white groups. This has been done because the separation of the two groups is neither complete nor uniform."[6] Before this statement, however, Sutherland prepared his readers with the following postulate: "In a class system individuals can move from one level to another by acquiring the proper symbols. In a *caste society* mobility is *not permitted* so long as the individual possesses the symbol which has been used to separate the groups."[7]

Here, then, reappears the "symbol" criterion of caste society. Evidently this standard of social mobility excludes the possibility of degrees of effective caste systems. Just how much prevention of symbol acquisition constitutes "castelike" and what determines the permitting agency are questions, unfortunately, left to the reader. Probably one might say that Negro-white relationship in the North is not so "castelike" as it is in the South. But the question arises: Who prevents whites in the United States from acquiring any of the symbols which Negroes now possess? And if perchance the answer is, "Obviously nature," then we have again returned quite smugly to the leopard-and-spots hypothesis of caste society. According to the interest of the person who derives the meaning, the term "castelike" may be interpreted as racelike, guildlike, labor-union-like, classlike, and so on. Its value to the sociologist seems to lie principally in its power to obscure social problems.

[6]Robert L. Sutherland, *Color, Class, and Personality,* p. xix.
[7]Ibid., pp. xviii–xix.

Practical Value of the Concept

In conversation some thoughtful persons have suggested to the writer that although the American application of the term "caste" may not be "scientific," it is nonetheless a very effective word in the service of the orator or the journalist. Since we have built up negative stereotypes about the caste idea, the use of the term "caste" in describing the racial system in this country may have a quite desirable result. We should remember, however, that truth is on the side of colored people and that they probably need few, if any, artificialities to support it. Ray Stannard Baker says well: "The situation in the South has made some people afraid of the truth."[8]

Furthermore, there is usually some unexpected, distasteful rebound in compromising with untruth. For instance, it is not unlikely that the propagandists will awaken to discover that they have played into the hands of the ruling class in the South. It has been an old practice of the Southern aristocracy to stifle any incipient discontent among the un-privileged whites by pointing to a two-class system—all whites above and all blacks below. By this method they have been able to strengthen their political-class position. It worked well with the slaveholders and has continued to function admirably. As Roger W. Shugg says: "To parry the thrusts of Abolitionists, Free Soilers, and Republicans, the southern planters consolidated support at home by spreading their mantle over all classes and denying the existence of any class except the white and black races."[9]

To be sure, no one need be overmeticulous about an offhand use of the term "caste" in discussions of race relations. In formal sociological writ-ings, however, its indiscriminate use may be insidiously misleading. In-deed, attempts to give the vulgar use of this term scientific precision have probably divested it of much of its former odium. In the sociology books it has been objectified and desiccated so that race relations in the Southern states, for instance, are sometimes made to appear as one of the natural forms of social organization. The idea of a "type of society" obscures the

[8]Op. cit., p. 258.
[9]*Origins of Class Struggle in Louisiana*, p. 33.

actual pathological racial antagonism, leaving some diffused impression that it is socially right, even as the caste system in India is right.[10]

The terms "race prejudice" and "racial discrimination" have already been defined in the world view of Western society as social sins per se. However, such subjects as race prejudice and discrimination call for delicate handling in the textbooks. Consequently many writers will find it more incommodious to discuss and explain these phenomena than to couch the situation in the euphonious terminology of "American caste."

If we have caste among blacks and blacks in Haiti,[11] among peoples of color in India, and among whites and whites in England,[12] then there may be all the more reason and justification for having caste between whites and blacks in the South. The implication of the "naturalness" of caste provides a comforting blanket assumption.

[10]Observe, in illustration, with what nicety of reasoning Guy B. Johnson gets around his problem: "There has lately been much agitation for the suppression of lynching by Federal law. Some people, with characteristic faith in the magic of legislation, imagine that Federal law can stop lynching. Any custom which is as deeply rooted in caste consciousness as lynching is, will not be eradicated easily." See "Patterns of Race Conflict," in *Race Relations and the Race Problem,* p. 146.

[11]John Lobb, "Caste in Haiti," *American Journal of Sociology,* Vol. XLVI, July 1940, pp. 23–34.

[12]*The University of Chicago Round Table,* December 8, 1940, p. 20.

10.
The Race Problem in the United States

The Problem

We shall limit this discussion to Negro-white relationships; these are the races ordinarily referred to when the race problem is considered. Moreover, we shall consider mainly the situation in the South because it is more obvious; that in the North differs mainly in degree. The "race problem" includes all the immediate or short-run instances of overt friction between Negroes and whites; maladjustments due to disparity in population characteristics, such as death rate, disease, unemployment, poverty, illiteracy, and so on, and innumerable conflicts of opposing attitudes and policies. The whites determine the pattern of these problems and the grounds upon which they must be thrashed out. Broadly speaking, the general policy of the nation follows the scheme developed in the South, and the ruling-class whites in this area are explicitly devoted to the ideal that Negroes shall never be assimilated. The race problem, then, is primarily the short-run manifestations of opposition between an abiding urge among Negroes to assimilate and a more or less unmodifiable decision among racially articulate, nationalistic whites that they should not.

The Problem of Assimilation

The solidarity of American Negroes is neither nationalistic nor nativistic. The group strives for neither a forty-ninth state leading to an independent nation nor a back-to-Africa movement; its social drive is toward assimilation. In this respect Negroes are like most other American immigrants; it is well known that the social tendency toward assimilation is an American cultural trait. Therefore, the solidarity of Negroes is defensive and tentative only, while their social orientation is centrifugal. For them social solidarity is not a virtue in itself. Their society is not designed for self-perpetuation; it will endure only so long as the white ruling class is successful in opposing their assimilation.

The urge toward assimilation and away from group solidarity is so compelling among Negroes that few, if any, of the organizations maintained by whites which offer reasonably unrestricted participation to Negroes can be developed by Negroes for Negroes. As a rule, only those types of white enterprises which discriminate against Negroes can be developed among Negroes. If the white society were to be impartial to Negro participation, no business, no school, no church would thrive among Negroes. Negroes are old Americans. The businesses of Negroes are mainly those of catering; their church had its birth in reaction to white discrimination, and their separate schools belong to the system of white race segregation. In short, Negro business enterprises and social institutions may be thought of as crystals of reaction to white race discrimination.

One of the most powerful techniques utilized by the white ruling class for retardation of assimilation of the races is segregation. Segregation obviously limits the opportunity for communication and interracial understanding and makes possible an easy exploitation of antagonistic stereotypes. The refined Negro is most carefully guarded against, so that in the South the principal racial contact is between the white upper class and Negro domestic servants.

If the races live in protected residential zones and are kept apart in schools, in churches, in cemeteries, on the playgrounds, in hotels and restaurants, on transportation vehicles, and so on, they will tend to believe in a disparity of every possible group interest and purpose, a social fact which is basically antipathetic to assimilation.

In the United States white foreigners are ordinarily encouraged to assimilate, but peoples of color are not. The Christian democratic world view of the nation, however, is not thus selective. In fact, this world view is a prepotent force tending to counteract and subordinate the immediate anti-assimilation attitudes of the white racially articulate class. Therefore, with respect to the basic ideals of Western civilization, the position of this class must necessarily be defensive; and this, even though its rationalizations may seem aggressive.

The Meaning of Assimilation

According to Albert Ernest Jenks: "Only when the individuals or ethnic groups are emotionally dead to all their varied past, and are all responsible solely to the conditions of the present, are they assimilated people."[1] To be assimilated is to live easily and unobtrusively in the society. One must be at home, so to speak, with the dominant social organization. So long as a group is identified or remembered as alien, it will be forced to have a divided allegiance. Naturally, the assimilation ideal of American Negroes is to be recognized as unqualified Americans.

It would seem paradoxical, however, to assume that the more assimilated Negroes become, the more socially maladjusted they are. According to Ogburn and Nimkoff :

> The Negroes today are largely assimilated, yet as a group they are now less well adjusted to the white man's world than they were in the earlier period of slavery. . . . The more thoroughly assimilated Negroes become, the more they realize the limitations and discriminations under which they must live and the more resentful they become. The more assimilated the Negro, the more nearly he approaches the white man in competitive skill; hence the greater becomes the white man's resentment against him.[2]

Apparently there are two questions raised in this conclusion: (a) What do we mean by the term "largely assimilated"? and (b) To what extent does interracial conflict represent mutual maladjustment? It is possible that Negroes are farther away from ultimate oneness and belonging in the general American social order than any white European group that might currently enter the country. If this is so, then Negroes in America are less well assimilated than any conceivable white immigrant group. According to Robert E. Park, "Assimilation may in some senses and to a certain degree be described as a function of visibility. As soon as an immigrant no longer exhibits the marks which identify him as a member of an alien group, he acquires by that fact the actual if not the legal status of a native."[3] Thus acculturation alone may not be sufficient for assimilation; in other words, the mere assumption of the dominant cultural patterns has not been suffi-cient to assure complete integration of the group.

[1]"Assimilation in the Philippines," *Proceedings of the American Sociological Society,* Vol. VIII, 1913.

[2]*Sociology,* pp. 385–86.

[3]"Assimilation," *Encyclopedia of the Social Sciences.*

In fact, the dominant attitude in the South is that cultural disparity is of exceedingly minor significance when compared with difference in skin color. So great indeed is the alleged alienating power of the latter that it is sometimes believed that difference in color forever precludes the possibility of the two groups achieving cultural parity. In his argument that the Negro is not assimilated, Park concludes: "This distinction which sets him apart from the rest of the population is real, but it is based not upon cultural traits but upon physical and racial characteristics."[4] The Negro is very much more assimilated today than in 1860 in the sense that if it now becomes possible to overthrow the Southern oligarchy with its racial ideologies by extirpating it, then Negroes would be in a much better position to assume the role of normal citizens in harmony with the rest of the population.

With respect to the point that Negroes are becoming increasingly less well adjusted, it is significant to observe that increasing interracial conflict is a problem of both races. A race riot may result in the death of both blacks and whites, while a lynching is a disturbing event as well for white people. Booker Washington's aphorism that "you can't hold a man down in the ditch without staying down there with him" is homely but eminently suggestive.

Much of the racial aggressiveness of white people runs counter to the basic ideals and social ethics of Western society. Its satisfactory operation necessitates a relegation of the laws and a reliance upon spontaneous elemental force. In this sense whites may be thought of as culturally maladjusted. The most significant of these acts of racial aggression is the well-known practice of lynching. At this point we shall attempt an analysis of this phenomenon; it is the fundamental reliance of the white ruling class in maintaining its racial superiority.

Lynching

Quite frequently lynching has been thought of as a form of social control consisting in the taking of the life of one person or more by a mob in retribution for some criminal outrage committed by the former. This method of unceremonial punishment is assumed to be common on the frontier where there is no constituted juridical machinery and where, in the interest of social order, the group finds itself constrained to act spontane-

---

[4] Ibid. However, this statement by Park should not be taken too literally; the fact is that the Negro is marked by his color for the purpose of achieving an ulterior cultural advantage.

ously. Furthermore, it is known to occur in organized society where some crime is of such a heinous and socially revolting nature that an angry crowd gathers spontaneously and passionately mangles the criminal to death. Even in this situation, however, the police may be ineffectively organized, as is ordinarily the case in rural communities.

At any rate, these two situations do not involve significant social problems in America; in fact, they hardly refer to lynching as a social institution.[5] They have no racial, nationality, or political-class significance. Justice among frontiersmen has never been a pressing problem for the nation. Furthermore, lynching must not be confused with the "hue and cry" of the general mob in medieval times. Here indeed was a recognized method of arrest, with its system of sanctuaries and sanctuary law.

Lynching may be defined as an act of homicidal aggression committed by one people against another through mob action for the purpose of suppressing either some tendency in the latter to rise from an accommodated position of subordination or for subjugating them further to some lower social status. It is a special form of mobbing—mobbing directed against a whole people or political class.[6] We may distinguish lynching from race rioting by the fact that the lynching mob is unopposed by other mobs, while it tends to be actuated by a belief that it has a constituted right to punish some more or less identified individual or individuals of the other race or nationality.

Lynching is an exemplary and symbolic act. In the United States it is an attack principally against all Negroes in some community rather than against some individual Negro.[7] Ordinarily, therefore, when a lynching is indicated, the destruction of almost any Negro will serve the purpose as well as that of some particular one. Lynchings occur mostly in those areas

[5]We may mention incidentally that a rather puerile approach to a study of the institution of lynching is to derive hypotheses from an examination of the history of *the term* "lynching."

[6]Recently there has been a tendency, especially among journalists, to call any kind of mobbing a lynching. This, however, gives us no basis for an understanding of lynching as an intergroup problem.

[7]Francis W. Coker says well that "as violent manifestations of a racial antagonism mixed with economic rivalry the pogroms of czarist Russia and the terrorist activities against Jews in Germany and the states of southern Europe are in a class with lynching. Similarly, the conflicts between labor and capital [political class action] often give rise to what are in essence lynching." "Lynching," *Encyclopedia of the Social Sciences*.

where the laws discriminate against Negroes; sometimes, in these areas, the administrative judicial machinery may even facilitate the act. However, the lynching attitude is to be found everywhere among whites in the United States.

A lynching, as the definition given above suggests, is not primarily a spontaneous act of mob violence against a criminal. Where the interracial situation is not agitated, it will not occur. There seems to be a recognizable lynching cycle, which may be described as follows:

(a) A growing belief among whites in the community that Negroes are getting out of hand—in wealth, in racial independence, in attitudes of self-assertion, especially as workers, or in reliance upon the law. An economic depression causing some whites to retrograde faster than some Negroes may seem a relative advancement of Negroes in some of the latter respects.

(b) Development, by continual critical discussion about Negroes among whites, of a summatory attitude of racial antagonism and tension.

(c) The rumored or actual occurrence of some outrage committed by a Negro upon some white person or persons. The ideal act is the rape of a white girl. But if the tension is very high, whites will purposely seek an incident with the Negroes.

(d) The incident having occurred, the white mob comes into action, lays hands upon the Negro, and lynches him. He is burned, hanged, or shot in some public place, preferably before the courthouse, and his remains dragged about the Negro section of the community. Ordinarily, in the heat of mob action, other Negroes are killed or flogged, and more or less Negro property is destroyed—houses are burned, places of business pillaged, and so on. There is usually a scramble among the mob for toes, fingers, bits of clothing, and the like, which are kept as souvenirs of the lynching occasion.

(e) During a lynching all Negroes are driven under cover. They are terrified and intimidated. Many put themselves completely at the mercy of their non-militant "white friends" by cowering in the latter's homes and pleading for protection from the enraged mob. Sometimes they leave the community altogether.

(f) Within about two or three days the mob achieves its emotional catharsis. There is a movement for judicial investigation, and some of the "best white people" speak out against lynching. On the following Sunday a few ministers of great courage declare that lynching is barbarous and un-Christian; and in time the grand jury returns its findings that "the deceased came to his death by hanging and gunshot wounds at the hands of parties unknown."

(g) There is a new interracial adjustment. Negroes become exceedingly circumspect in their dealing with whites, for they are now thoroughly frightened. Many are obligated to their "white friends" for having saved their lives, and few will dare even to disagree with white persons on any count whatever. The man who does so is not considered a hero by the majority of Negroes; rather he earns their censure.

(h) In a more or less short period of time Negroes begin to smile broadly and ingratiatingly over the merest whim of white men.[8] They are eager to show that they bear no malice for the horrible past.[9] Lynching has accomplished its purpose, social euphoria is restored, and the cycle is again on its way.

Some lynchings may appear to have a high degree of spontaneity. It should be remembered, however, that in the South the threat of lynching is continually impending, and this threat is a coercive force available to white people as such. Says Arthur F. Raper, "Lynching is resorted to only when the implied threat of it appears to be losing its efficacy."[10] Both the overt

[8]Gunnar Myrdal makes an observation in point: "Much of the humor that the Negro displays before the white man in the South is akin to that manufactured satisfaction with their miserable lot which the conquered people of Europe are now forced to display before their German conquerors. The loud, high-pitched cackle that is commonly considered as the 'Negro laugh' was evolved in slavery times as a means of appeasing the master by debasing oneself before him and making him think that one was contented." Op. cit., p. 960.

[9]"Law and order" in the South implicitly but resolutely insist that the family or, worse still, Negroes of the community upon whom this appalling atrocity has been committed do nothing to show that they harbor resentment. The lynching, to be successful, must have so cowed the Negroes that even a gratuitous offer of possible legal assistance would be rejected by them. In a recent Mississippi lynching a white Northern reporter tactfully avoided interviewing the colored family of two lynched boys "because a man in Quitman told me quietly, 'It wouldn't do them niggers any good to be seen talking to you.' " (Victor H. Bernstein, in the Pittsburgh *Courier,* October 31, 1942.) The overwhelming terror among Negroes in the lynching situation is evoked principally by the awareness that there is in effect no legal power presuming to question the free violence of the lynchers.

It is to this social attitude which Mrs. Atwood Martin, Chairman of the Association of Southern Women for the Prevention of Lynching, refers when she says: "Knowing at the start that if we went too fast . . . it would be the Negro population that would suffer, we have refrained from overzeal until sure of our support." See Jessie Daniel Ames, *The Changing Character of Lynching,* p. 68.

threat of lynching and prevented lynchings function to maintain white dominance. They provide, in fine, the socio-psychological matrix of the power relationship between the races.

Lynching in the South is not a crime, and this notwithstanding the fact that a few state statutes apparently proscribe it.[11] It is quite obvious that the constitutions of the Southern states and their supporting black codes, the system of discriminatory laws intended to keep Negroes in their place, intentionally put the Negro beyond the full protection of the law, and that the former take precedence over any contravening statute. Furthermore, it is clear that the political power of the area aims at class exclusiveness. Consider, for example, the following not uncommon public threat to Negroes of South Carolina by a United States senator—the normal attitude of the Southern politician:

> Whenever the Constitution comes between me and the virtue of the white women of South Carolina, I say, "To hell with the Constitution" . . .
>
> When I was governor of South Carolina you did not hear me calling out the militia of the State to protect Negro assaulters.
>
> In my South Carolina campaigns you heard me say, "When you catch the brute that assaults a white woman, wait until the next morning to notify me."[12]

---

[10] *Preface to Peasantry,* p. 23. In discussing a lynching situation Raper says also: "While these seventy-five thousand people were members of actual mobs but one day in the year, they were most probably mob-minded every day in the year. Millions of others were mob-disposed, and under provocation would have joined a mob, killing or standing sympathetically by while others killed." *The Tragedy of Lynching,* p. 47.

[11] Cf. James H. Chadbourn, *Lynching and the Law,* Chapter III; James E. Cutler, *Lynch Law,* pp. 1–12; and Frank Shay, *Judge Lynch,* p. 8.

[12] Cole Blease, quoted in Arthur F. Raper, *The Tragedy of Lynching,* p. 293. In November 1942, at the national poll-tax filibuster, Senator Doxey said confidently, "Mississippi and the other Southern states will uphold Anglo-Saxon supremacy until the lofty mountains crumble to dust." No one has the slightest doubt about the means which the senator and the entire legal machinery of the Southern states employ and will continue to employ in the interest of this brand of democracy. Doxey knows that he has behind him the firmly established and effective Southern institution of interracial violence; hence he speaks to the nation with conviction. Moreover, he is able to speak with this degree of finality because he is assured that the United States Senate dares not challenge his position—at least he knows that the moral level of the Senate is far below that necessary to cope with the probable cost of instrumenting such a challenge.

Nothing serves to bring the Southern congressmen so solidly in opposition as a national movement to pass legislation making lynching a crime. We should expect this because to make lynching a crime would be to strike at the pivot of white dominance in the South; to

It is certainly true that all white people in the South will not thus express themselves, and some are decidedly opposed to this view. But where a leading politician could hold himself up for election on the grounds that he is a potential lyncher, the presumption is inevitable that lynching is not a crime.

The dominant opinion of the community exalts the leaders of the mob as "men of courage and action."[13] Raper reports an incident in point:

> Women figured prominently in a number of outbreaks. After a woman at Sherman had found the men unwilling to go into the courtroom and get the accused, she got a group of boys to tear an American flag from the wall of the courthouse corridor and parade through the courthouse and grounds, to incite the men to do their "manly duty."[14]

To be a crime lynching must be an offense against the local state, but the propagandized sentiment of the community registered by votes determines what offenses shall be. "Mobs do not come out of the nowhere; they are the logical outgrowths of dominant assumptions and prevalent thinking. Lynchings are not the work of men suddenly possessed of a strange madness; they are the logical issues of prejudice and lack of respect for law and personality."[15] To be sure, the law loses respect naturally when it seems to contravene the powerful interests which lynching protects.

Moreover, the sense of penal immunity which pervades the mob, amounting frequently to elation in performance of a social service, tends to belie the theory that lynching is criminal. A story of crime does not read like the following:

> Shortly before midnight, with an acetylene torch and high explosives, a second story vault window was blown open and the Negro's body was thrown to the crowd below. It was greeted by loud applause from the thousands who jammed

make lynching a crime would be to indict the political leadership of the South; indeed, to make lynching a Federal crime would be to bring before the nation the full unfinished business of the Civil War. An effective anti-lynching law must inevitably inculpate the deepest intent of Southern constitutions. Remarkable as it may seem, the most sacred and jealously guarded right of the Southern states is undoubtedly the right to lynch Negroes; consequently, any Federal law seeking to limit this right will be promptly construed to be an infringement upon the sovereignty of states. It is in this light that the impotence of the Fourteenth Amendment in protecting the life and liberty of Negroes in the South must be estimated.

[13]Walter White, *Rope and Faggot,* p. 4.

[14]Arthur F. Raper, op. cit., p. 12; see also p. 323.

[15]Ibid., p. 27.

the courthouse square. Police directed traffic while the corpse was dragged through the streets to a cottonwood tree in the Negro business section. There it was burned.[16]

A person or group of persons committing crime might be expected to go to great pains in relieving themselves of any trace of the act. Lynchers, however, expect to be glorified in identifying themselves. In reviewing one case Ray Stannard Baker writes: "They scrambled for the chains before they were cold, and the precious links were divided among the populace. Pieces of the stump were hacked off, and finally one young man . . . gathered up a few charred remnants of bone, carried them uptown, and actually tried to give them to the judge."[17]

The mob, then, is seldom, if ever, apprehensive of punishment. The law stands in a peculiar relationship to lynching. Nowhere is lynching advocated on the statute books; yet there is a prepotent sanction in the South that whites may use force against any Negro who becomes overbearing. According to Raper, "The manhunt tradition rests on the assumption of the unlimited rights of white men and the absence of any rights on the part of the accused Negro."[18] Negroes can ordinarily be taken from police custody because there is a controlling assumption that the formal law is not available to Negroes. The mob is composed of people who have been carefully indoctrinated in the primary social institutions of the region to conceive of Negroes as extralegal, extrademocratic objects, without rights which white men are bound to respect. Therefore, most Southern official criticism of mob action against Negroes must necessarily be taken largely as pretense. The jury and courts could hardly be expected to convict, since their "hands are even as dirty."[19] Mrs. Jessie Daniel Ames puts it in this way:

Newspapers and Southern society accept lynching as justifiable homicide in defense of society. When defenders of society sometimes go too far in their

[16]Ibid., p. 7. Sometimes the scheduled lynching of a Negro is announced in the newspapers. See William H. Skaggs, *The Southern Oligarchy*, p. 300.

[17]*Following the Color Line*, p. 187.

[18]Op. cit., p. 9.

[19]The tables of convictions for lynchings and attempted lynchings presented by Chadbourn, op. cit., pp. 14–15, are not very revealing. They may include contempt cases and cases falling within the two possible meanings of lynching suggested in the introduction to this analysis. The situations may be further complicated by lynchers doing more or less serious violence to white persons who may attempt to protect the Negro.

enthusiasm, as in the Winona, Mississippi, torch lynchings of 1937, public opinion regrets their acts, deplores them, condemns, but recognizes that too much blame must not be attached to lynchers because their provocation is great and their ultimate motives are laudable.[20]

Such functionaries as the sheriff, mayor, or prosecuting attorney have not only been known to take part in lynchings, but also the court sitting formally has answered the purpose of the mob. "Mobs do not loiter around courtrooms solely out of curiosity; they stand there, armed with guns and threats, to see that the courts grant their demands—death sentences and prompt executions. Such executions are correctly termed 'legal lynchings,' or 'judicial murders.' "[21]

We should make the distinction between that which is socially pathological and that which is criminal. Although these two phenomena may converge, they are nevertheless capable of separate existence. All criminal acts indicate some form of social maladjustment, but not vice versa. In illustration, certain types of speculation on the stock and commodity exchanges may be socially pathological and yet not crimes. If the economic system and supporting laws are such that unwholesome speculation cannot be but inevitable, then clearly it will not be criminal. In like manner, although the lynching of a Negro involves some social wrong against Negroes besides some increment of degeneracy among the lynchers, statutory impotency or even implied encouragement may necessarily exclude it from the category of crime.

Lynching is socially pathological only in the sense that it is incompatible with the democratic Christian spirit of the Western world. The spirit of the age is antipathetic to both the Southern system of social values and its stabilizer, lynching; but lynching happens to be the more obtrusive. Like a society of head-hunters or cannibals where the individual hunter is never inculpated in terms of the values of his society, the Southern lyncher can be considered criminal and degenerate only in the judgment of an outgroup.

[20]Op. cit., p. 51.

[21]Arthur F. Raper, op. cit., p. 46. See also page 13, and Walter White, op. cit., p. 32. In this connection Mrs. Ames observes: "In more than one prevented lynching a bargain was entered into between officers and would-be lynchers before the trial began in which the death penalty was promised as the price of the mob's dispersal." Op. cit., p. 12.

Lynching is crucial in the continuance of the racial system of the South. From this point of view lynching may be thought of as a necessity.[22] This is not to say, however, that lynching is "in the mores"; it is rather in the whip hand of the ruling class. It is the most powerful and convincing form of racial repression operating in the interest of the status quo. Lynchings serve the indispensable social function of providing the ruling class with the means of periodically reaffirming its collective sentiment of white dominance. During a lynching the dominant whites of the community assume an explicit organization for interracial conflict. By overt acts of aggression they give emotional palpability to their perennial preoccupation with racial segregation and discrimination. Their belligerency tends to compel the conformity of possible indifferent whites in the community, and it defines opposing whites as unpatriotic and traitorous to the cause of white dominance.

Furthermore, there is an inseparable association between Negro disfranchisement and lynching. Disfranchisement makes lynching possible, and lynching speedily squelches any movement among Southern Negroes for enfranchisement. In the South these two are indispensable instruments in the service of the status quo. Indeed, as Jessie Ames concludes: "Negroes, as a voteless people in a Democracy, [are] a helpless people."

Clearly, the lynching would be of no particular concern to Negroes if custom in the South prescribed, as punishment for certain offenses, public hanging and mutilation. We should not expect Negroes to be any more occupied with problems of such a practice than they are, say, with the current question of capital punishment. Indeed, there is a sense in which Negroes may prefer public retribution for such a crime as rape. The act of penalizing is itself a factor contributing to social cohesion.[23] If Negroes were permitted to attend in concert with whites the public execution of a white or a Negro rapist, we should expect the event to engender a degree

[22]In criticizing the policy of Southern newspapers, Jessie Daniel Ames declares: "They cannot defend lynching as a necessary form of violence to insure white supremacy. All the country holds the philosophy of white supremacy . . . but nationally it is not good sales talk to advertise that white supremacy can be maintained in the South . . . only by force, coercion, and lynching." Op. cit., p. 54.

[23]For a general discussion of the nature of negative sanctions, see Emile Durkheim, *The Division of Labor in Society,* Chap. II.

of solidarity between them. Such interracial action, however, is not at all intended by a lynching. Lynching is not punishment; it is racial aggression.

"In the states where most lynchings have occurred, white people generally justified slavery. . . . They justified methods of terror employed to intimidate and disfranchise the Negroes; and they later enacted laws and perfected party procedures to restore and preserve white supremacy."[24] Through the instrumentality of these laws and political contrivances the Southern aristocracy returned to power and relegated the protection of the Negro to the benevolence of white people as individuals. Having defined Negroes basically as extralegal objects, some sort of informal means of violent coercion, ranging all the way from an occasional blow to floggings, mutilations, and lynchings, had to be relied upon.

Lynchings were excluded, *ipso facto,* from the category of criminal offenses when Negroes were disfranchised by the Southern state constitutions; the black codes support the constitutions. As we have attempted to show in our chapter on situations of race relations, the type of racial situation determines the pattern of white-colored relationship, while some sort of political-class interest is fundamental. The planter, exploitative class interest dominates the social life of the South, and lynching is bound up with the latter interest.[25] In South Africa, where the racial situation is in many respects similar to that of the South, the same need for extralegal violence against the colored people presents itself. As one writer concludes: "The history of the century [in South Africa] would hardly show an instance of a single white man awarded capital punishment for the murder of a native. But it will bring to light scores of cases in which the white murderer escaped scot-free or only with nominal punishment. . . . [The natives] get nominal wages and heaps of insults. The white farmer could . . . whip

---

[24]Arthur F. Raper, op. cit., p. 50.

[25]"The Black Belt lynching is something of a business transaction. . . . Negroes are in least danger in these plantation counties. The whites, there, chiefly of the planter class and consciously dependent upon the Negro for labor, lynch him to conserve traditional landlord-tenant relations rather than to wreak vengeance upon his race. Black Belt white men demand that the Negroes stay out of their politics and dining rooms, the better to keep them in their fields and kitchens." Ibid., pp. 57–58.

This inherent requirement of Southern economy tends to set the dominant theme of race relations, so that even poor whites may seem to exploit the advantage in their competitive contacts with Negroes.

them and make them slave for him."[26] In South Africa, however, the lynching pattern is not exactly duplicated because personal violence against the natives is, to a considerable extent, permitted in the formal law.

This is a consideration of highest importance in understanding the determining force in the pattern of race relations in the South. The insistence upon a personal right of white men to control Negroes has its roots in the Southern system of slavery. The landlords had achieved such a right over their Negro slaves, and their vision of losing it was clearly the most galling aspect of the Civil War. As Hinton R. Helper says with acrimony: "All slaveholders are under the shield of a perpetual license to murder."[27] It is this right which the counterrevolution of the aristocracy practically restored. Its brilliant self-satisfying outer covering was extended to the white commonalty as a reward for their counterrevolutionary support.[28] The aristocracy retrieved this right of personal control over the Negro at greater cost than that of any other right known to their constitutions. This class is naturally sensitive about it and cannot be expected either to accept or to make laws which will abrogate it.[29] Then, too, the rights secured by belonging to a dominant race must necessarily be personal.

Lynching, besides, is integral in the Southern system. To remove the threat of it is to overthrow the ruling class in the South and to change the basis of Southern economy. "Threats, whippings, and even more serious forms of violence have been customary caste sanctions utilized to maintain a strict discipline over Negro labor."[30] Where the system is functioning most

[26]P. S. Joshi, *The Tyranny of Colour,* pp. 18, 20.

[27]Op. cit., p. 140.

[28]Even before Emancipation the white commonalty was allowed a superior right of violence over Negroes. This had to be done, for it was upon the white masses that the slaveholders depended for protection against insurrection. The practice involved the poor whites in deep antagonism with the Negroes, while the masters held the property right to sue these whites for damages in case of "unreasonable" injury to the slave.

[29]At a recent court hearing in Mississippi, prosecuted by the Federal Government, the Southern attorney defending the lynchers of Howard Wash said: "The people of this great Southland are on trial. We may as well face the truth. This is not a trial to vindicate the lynching of Howard Wash, the Negro, nor is it a trial only to convict the three defendants. . . . It is just another effort to see how much we of the South will permit invasion of state rights." The newspaper reported that "a popular subscription, conducted by leading citizens of southeastern Mississippi, was launched for a defense fund." The jury, of course, did not convict. See Pittsburgh *Courier,* May 1, 1943.

[30]Gunnar Myrdal, op. cit., Vol. I, p. 229.

effectively, lynching tends to become natural even to Negroes. Arthur F. Raper observes a case in point: "The Negroes were not greatly disturbed by the lynching, being already inured to the undisputed domination of whites. In Bolivar County, with an average of one lynching every four years, such occurrences are part of the normal picture."[31] One is in error, then, in thinking that it is possible to eradicate mob action in the South, as it may be possible to stamp out, say, the crime of kidnaping, without also questioning the foundations of the Southern social order. Jessie Daniel Ames, Executive Director of the Association of Southern Women for the Prevention of Lynching, sees the alternatives thus: "To those who believe lynchers are criminal devils, inherently wicked and depraved, then punishment, swift, severe, and sure, appeals; to those who believe lynchers are born into a social and economic system which turns them to acts of brutal violence, then change of the system appeals."[32]

We have seen that lynching is a form of interracial conflict facilitated by the fundamental laws of the Southern states. By lynching, Negroes are kept in their place; that is to say, kept as a great, easily exploitable, common-labor reservoir.[33] It is not essential, therefore, that the victim be actually guilty of crime. When the situation of interracial tension is sufficiently developed, a scapegoat will do.[34] Negroes have been lynched for such apparent trivialities as "using offensive language," "bringing suit against white men,"[35] "trying to act like white men," "frightening women and children," "being a witness," "gambling," "making boastful remarks," and "attempting to vote."[36]

[31]Op. cit., p. 97.

[32]Op. cit., p. 59.

[33]In the period of early Reconstruction, Judge Humphrey of Alabama expressed the fundamental economic purpose of the ruling class. "I believe," he said, "in case of a return to the Union, we would receive political co-operation so as to secure the management of that labor by those who were slaves. There is really no difference, in my opinion, whether we hold them as absolute slaves or obtain their labor by some other method." Quoted by W. E. B. Du Bois, *Black Reconstruction*, p. 140.

[34]"Two of the 1930 mob victims were innocent of crime (they were not even accused), and there is grave doubt of the guilt of eleven others. In six of these eleven cases there is considerable doubt as to just what crimes, if any, were committed, and in the other five, in which there is no question as to the crimes committed, there is considerable doubt as to whether the mobs got the guilty men." Arthur F. Raper, op. cit., pp. 4–5.

[35]Ibid., p. 36.

[36]From Tuskegee Institute's unpublished records on lynching.

Yet there is a peculiar and consistent association of the crime of rape committed by Negroes upon white women and lynching. Indeed, the arguments in favor of lynching have consistently justified it on the grounds that Negroes can be deterred from venting their asserted vicious sexual passion upon white women only by the constant threat of lynching.[37] Our problem here is not to disprove this position (many Negro women have been lynched), but rather to indicate further the relationship between lynching and the social system.

There are two principal reasons why the accusation of rape is apparently the best available defense of lynching. In the first place, rape, especially when committed upon a child, is probably the most outrageous of crimes in modern society. Mob action against a rapist, then, tends to be excused in the mores. In fact, the lynchers of such a criminal, like the men of the New Testament who threw stones, expect some sort of social approbation as a reward for their chivalry. Hence supporters of lynching find it expedient to hold out the crime of rape to a censuring world and to focus all discussion upon it. On this ground they are able to develop any degree of eloquence and heat in justification of the institution.

In the second place, as we have attempted to show in a previous chapter, the white woman holds a strategic position in the interracial adjustment of the South. To the extent that the ruling interest in the South can maintain eternal watchfulness over her, to that extent also the system may be perpetuated. The belief that Negroes are surreptitiously using white women to "mongrelize" the population produces a bitter sense of frustration, calling for practically unlimited violence against Negroes. It is principally on the latter score that the white ruling class has been able to corral the white masses for expressions of mob violence. Clearly a "mongrelized" South will ultimately mean not only a non-segregated South but also a non-aristocratic South, the perennial nightmare of the Southern oligarchy.

[37]"Regardless of the cause of the particular lynching there were always those who defended it by the insistence that unless Negroes were lynched, no white woman would be safe, this despite the fact that only one-sixth of the persons lynched in the last thirty years were even accused of rape. Regardless of the accusation, an example must be made of the accused Negro for the sake of womanhood." Arthur F. Raper, op. cit., p. 20. Says Walter White, "Sex and alleged sex crimes have served as the great bulwark of the lyncher." Op. cit., p. 55.

Therefore, in order that the Negro-man, white-woman emotional set might be exploited, lynchers and their defenders always seek to manipulate the story of a lynching to include rape as a crime of the victim. Success in this would disarm almost any Southern judge, jury, or defending attorney. The latter, like the majority of the propagandized population, are naturally predisposed and receptive to arguments founded upon sexual precaution. In the final analysis, then, the shibboleth of white womanhood provides the most effective rationale of the interests of the Southern aristocracy.

Since the act of lynching is directed particularly against the Negroes of the community, wide publicity and exemplary cruelty are desirable. The purpose of the lynching is not merely the elimination of a dangerous individual from society; rather the ideal is to make the occasion as impressive as possible to the whole population.[38] To Negroes it involves a challenge and a setting at naught of all that they might have held as rights to integrity of person and property, while to whites it is a demonstration and reaffirmation of white dominance. As one Southern writer asserts: "Lynching is a symptom of weak, inefficient rule. . . . Lynching will disappear when the white race is satisfied that its supremacy will not be questioned. . . ."[39]

Sometimes outsiders wonder at the presence of women and children at lynchings. For instance, Arthur F. Raper quotes the Raleigh *News and Observer* on a 1930 lynching as follows:

> It was quite the thing to look at the bloody dead nigger hanging from the limb of a tree near the Edgecombe-Wilson County line this morning. . . . Whole families came together, mothers and fathers bringing even their youngest children. It was the show of the countryside—a very popular show. Men joked loudly at the sight of the bleeding body . . . girls giggled.[40]

However, as a means of schooling white children in the Southern principles of race relations, there could hardly be a more effective method. On the other hand, the custom of mutilating, burning, or dragging the

[38]The following is a report on one lynching: "In Baker County, Ga., a Negro killed a white bootlegger at a Negro dance. When the 'right man' could not be found, two unaccused Negroes were lynched as an object lesson." Jessie D. Ames, op. cit., p. 66.

[39]Allen Tate in *The American Review*, II, February 1934, quoted by Sterling A. Brown in *What the Negro Wants*, p. 323.

[40]Op. cit., p. 114.

victim's body in the Negro community produces the obverse side of the lesson.

Recently there have been considerable discussions among statisticians and lawmakers concerning the exact definition of a lynching. Persons who tabulate the number of lynchings per year feel a great need for accuracy and reliability, while lawmakers want to be certain that the concept is limited so as to exclude other forms of violence and homicide. Thus far, however, these problems have not been settled—and for good reason. Everyone knows what an ordinary lynching is, but there are marginal cases difficult to define. What is a mob? Two or ten times two people? In Mississippi a Negro and a white man are gambling. The white man kills the Negro in a fight and goes free. Is that a lynching?

The reason why lynching is difficult to define for purposes such as those mentioned above is that the lynching, the culminating act of continuing white aggression against Negroes, cannot be completely extricated from the social matrix which produces it. In the South the lyncher is involved in the dominant theme of the society. Indeed, lynching should be thought of as homicidal but not necessarily homicide. Any one of the unnumbered insults, slaps, cuffs, and kicks which white persons deal to Negroes daily in the South may be described as a lynching situation.[41] So far as its effect upon Negroes of the community is concerned, the flogging of a Negro boy by a few white men is not very much different from a full-blown lynching. Specifically, we may think of a lynching situation as one in which one Negro or several encounter one white or more and in which they find themselves exposed to coercion, insult, or violence, their rightful reaction to which, as normal citizens, threatens to lead either to their being beaten or killed by one white or by a mob of white persons; and, for this impending exercise of arbitrary violence, there is a consciousness on both sides that the law will not punish and that the organized ruling class in the community will show condonement.

[41]Gunnar Myrdal observes graphically the summary character of interracial violence in the South: "A Negro can seldom claim the protection of the police and the courts if a white man knocks him down, or if a mob burns his house or inflicts bodily injury on him or on members of his family. If he defends himself against a minor violence, he may expect a major violence. If he once 'gets in wrong' he may expect the loss of his job or other economic injury; and constant insult and loss of whatever legal rights he may have had." Op. cit., p. 485.

We do not mean to say that every act of violence by whites against Negroes in the South, without exception, has gone unpunished. Ordinarily such acts do go unpunished; yet there are situations unfavorable to lynchers. The following are some of them: (a) a lynching motivated by a highly personal controversy in a community where the Negroes are well behaved; that is to say, where they are working honestly and industriously for the "big white folk"; (b) where the occasion for the killing, the lynching, is clearly a "drunken prank": of "white trash" in a "peaceful" Negro community; and (c) where uninformed whites accidentally become involved with and lynch some trusted and dependable Negro leader of the community. In the border states, especially, there is some remote likelihood that such lynchers may be sentenced to prison. On the periphery of the Deep South the definition of acts of extralegal violence which contribute to the support of white dominance and exploitation tends to contract.

It is sometimes believed that all the "best white people" in the South are opposed to lynching. Nothing is farther from the truth. In fact, we should expect the leading Southern citizens to be most deeply affected by a policy so significant to the continuance of the social system as mob violence.[41a] When it is possible for a sheriff, in answer to an accusation of nonfeasance, to declare that "nearly every man, woman and child in our community wanted the Negro lynched,"[42] it is difficult to exculpate the leading citizens from the charge of mob sentiment or condonement of it. In reality lynching is an institution maintained by leading white people of the South; it serves as a powerful support of the ruling class.

The "best white people" may be classified into the following groups:

(a) Those who are convinced of the wrongness of lynching and speak directly against it. This group does not see the place of lynching in the Southern system. There are, naturally, degrees of enthusiasm among them.[43]

[41a]As Bernard Shaw puts it satirically: ". . . when a Negro is dipped in kerosene and set on fire in America at the present time, he is not a good man lynched by ruffians: he is a criminal lynched by crowds of respectable, charitable, virtuously indignant, high-minded citizens." *Man and Superman,* p. 214.

[42]Walter White, op. cit., p. 25.

[43]The following excerpts are intended to represent types of reaction for these groups:

"It was the average man," declares the Macon *Telegraph* editorially, "who took the vicious Negro, James Irwin, from the sheriff and mutilated and lynched him. For their crime there is not a shadow of excuse. . . . By their deed they wiped their bloody feet on society's rule

(b) Those who recognize that white violence and general aggression against Negroes is determined by the political-class system but who, confronted with the magnitude of the problem involved in attacking the system, remain silent.

(c) Those who understand the relation of the system to lynching and actually speak out against the system. These constitute a very small minority of white people who live precariously in the South.[44]

(d) Those who attack lynching as a means of restoring the good name of the community in the eyes of critical outsiders. This procedure is essentially a matter of good business policy.[45]

(e) Those who are convinced about the rightness of lynching and who either silently approve of or openly justify it as inevitable. Sometimes these people actually attend the lynching ceremony. Evidently this group is in the overwhelming majority.[46]

rule of law. By their deed they lynched justice in Georgia and did almost as terrible a thing to society as did the Negro." Quoted by Arthur F. Raper, op. cit., p. 154.

For a discussion of duplicity in Southern newspaper practice concerning lynching, see Jessie D. Ames, op. cit., pp. 51–58.

[44]Among these, William H. Skaggs is typical. This critic writes: "Both social and economic conditions in the South are conducive to propagation of crime. Punishment alone will not prevent crime, so long as the economic and social causes remain. . . .

"The revival of lynching after the [Civil War] was caused by economic conditions; the claim that it was for the protection of white women was an afterthought." Op. cit., pp. 309, 319.

[45]"Mob-law . . . struck . . . at the sensitive pocket of the business interests of the county. . . . It was just at the beginning of the cotton picking season, when labor of every sort was much needed, Negro labor especially. It will not do to frighten away all the Negroes. . . . Some of the officials and citizens of Statesboro got together, appointed extra marshals, and gave notice that there were to be no more whippings, and the mob-spirit disappeared." Ray Stannard Baker, op. cit., p. 188.

[46]"At Scooba, Mississippi, where a double lynching occurred, the two men reported to have organized and engineered the mob from start to finish were leading people in the community and prominently identified with the local church, school and other community activities.

"In every community where lynching occurred in 1930 there were some people who openly justified what had been done. All walks of life were represented among the apologists: judges, prosecuting attorneys, lawyers, business men, doctors, preachers, teachers." Arthur F. Raper, op. cit., pp. 11, 19. As an example of studied justification for lynching among the better class, see also David L. Cohn, *God Shakes Creation,* pp. 92ff. Here one may observe with what elfish art the case for lynching is built up, and how pointedly ranchers and those who, like this writer, provide the rationale of lynching direct their antagonism against colored people as a whole rather than against any allegedly offending Negro person.

During a lynching it would be foolhardy for Negroes of the community to seek the protection of the police station, the sheriff's office, or the courthouse; to be sure, they will never dream of seeking shelter in a white church. To enter the police station on the assumption that their persons would be defended against the mob is to infuriate the mob. In other words, such a course would symbolize to the white mob that Negroes expect to utilize the machinery of the law to protect their rights, which is the antithesis of the lynchers' objective. The custom of Negroes is rather to go to the homes of "white friends," who would be able to certify to the lynchers that they are *"hard-working,* well-behaved niggers." In discussing one case Raper writes: "Most of the Negroes had gone to the homes of white friends, or had left town. . . . At midnight when other Negroes called the police-officers and Rangers and militia men for protection, they were told that nothing could be done for them, that they had better get out of town or stay at the homes of 'white friends.' "[47]

This act of relying upon white friends for primary security has a double significance. It demonstrates to the lynchers that the Negro is willing to accept the personal authority and guardianship of white people as the final guarantee of any possible rights which he may have. It is a sort of admission that he has divested himself of any hope of reliance upon institutions intended to safeguard the rights of citizens as such. He prostrates himself, as it were, before white men in recognition that Negroes may enjoy a degree of well-being only by sufferance of their white neighbors.

In the second place, the practice is significant in that it provides an invaluable lesson to possible intractable Negroes. Negroes who have been saved by their white friends are indebted to the latter, and subsequently such Negroes tend to act as a check upon any of their fellows who might harbor ideas of revolt. Most Negroes come to know these "sympathizers" as the "good white folk" of the community. The combined effect is to make Negroes aware of their dependence upon whites and to put at rest any tendency to criticize the whites for their partiality in government,

[47]Op. cit., p. 438. In a pamphlet issued by the Southern Conference of Human Welfare, *The Truth about Columbia Tennessee Cases,* 1946, describing a lynching situation in Columbia, Tennessee, Clark H. Foreman observes: "The people of Columbia are not responsible for this outrage. . . . It was the State forces sent in from outside that organized the armed invasion and pillaging of the Negro business section. Even the killing in the jail was done by state officers."

education, economic dealings, and so on. Out of this situation is produced the finally accommodated Negroes known as "Uncle Toms."

We have considered at some length the problem of lynching because mob violence against Negroes occupies a dominant role in the interracial adjustment. We have mentioned also the fact that Negroes have great difficulty of access to the law. One secondary reason for this is that Negro legal talent is practically excluded from the South. Of all functions among Negroes, with the possible exception of the Negro politician, the Negro lawyer is most insufferable. He is an affront to the courts, and it is a decided humiliation for white advocates to debate the law with him. Most of the authorities in the Southern states hold Negroes presumptuous merely on application for admission to the bar, and by devious means they are fairly well excluded from the practice of law. An effect of this is that the ruling-class whites are able to keep the Negro under their surveillance by denying him a sympathetic access to the forum of justice.

The National Conscience

Recently social scientists have been giving considerable attention to "the national conscience." To be sure, this is an analogical concept, the use of which is subject to the dangers of its being identified with reality. In the person, conscience may be thought of as the personality disturbance produced by conflicting definitions of ethical or moral situations. There is, therefore, no conscience unless there is conflict. In modern democracies the conflict develops principally between the ideals of the two great political classes; that is to say, between the democratic and the oligarchic ideals. But these ideals are functions of distinct types of economic organization and are not in themselves primary social determinants. To believe that they are is to run the risk of becoming mystical. In the stable feudal system of Europe the serfs did not conceive of certain ideals of Christianity as ideological weapons for their liberation, for the social and economic system was such that they did not want liberation. Serfdom per se was not conceived of as oppression. To the extent that the feudal system was superseded by a new economic order, however, serfdom became oppression.

So, too, the greater the decline of the bourgeois social order, the more intense the ideological conflict in the "democracies."[48] Probably one reason for whites dealing so brutally with Negroes in interracial conflicts is the necessity for their summoning of passions sufficient to overcome possible inhibitions of conscience—sufficient to overcome the distracting proletarian world view. The frantic, orgiastic behavior at lynchings may testify to this. Unceasing racial aggression becomes a necessary opiate. Both the black and the white schoolboy have an opportunity to hold up Thomas Jefferson as an ideal. The little black boy is on reassuring ground when he reads "that justice is the fundamental law of society; that the majority, oppressing an individual, is guilty of crime, abuses its strength, and by acting on the law of the strongest breaks up the foundation of society."[49] The white boy, however, has a life question for decision; a dilemma which Gunnar Myrdal has made the theme of his discussion. Should he accept the policy of white dominance, then the weaker his rationalizations, the more ferocious he is likely to become toward Negroes. There is only one position for him to take if he dares discuss this question with the little black democrat; hence, in order to avoid it, he ordinarily defends himself by segregation, from which position he strikes mercilessly at his challengers.

But the white rulers of the South must be forever watchful, because the sands of a false position are always moving under them. According to John Stuart Mill:

> The real advantage which truth has consists in this, that when an opinion is true, it may be extinguished once, twice, or many times, but in the course of ages there will gradually be found persons to rediscover it, until some one of its appearances falls on a time when, from favorable circumstances, it escapes persecution until it has made such head as to withstand all subsequent attempts to suppress it."[50]

[48]Indeed, in all capitalist countries there is an incurably and increasingly affected "national conscience." It is, in fact, the unconscious internalization of the conflict of ideals of the two major political classes by the most sensitive, "disinterested" thinkers. The high bourgeoisie, the defenders of the status quo, do not have a troubled conscience, for they are convinced that the system is right. The exploited proletariat does not have a troubled conscience, for it is the object of the "social injustice." A troubled conscience is mainly the lot of the undecided participators in the spoils of the system, whose social position is mainly that of a public of the ruling class.

[49]Thomas Jefferson, *Democracy,* ed., Saul K. Padover, p. 29.

[50]*On Liberty and Other Essays,* pp. 34–35.

Although in practice Negroes in the South have no opportunity to claim rights, privileges, and duties on an equal footing with whites, they nevertheless possess the right to believe that they have a claim to rights equal to those of whites.

This is vouchsafed them by the democratic orientation of the dominant culture, which obviously transcends local and current practice; and which increases in force as the masses rise in social importance. Even in the darkest of the Deep South, where Negroes are most accommodated to discrimination, there is always this powerful group expectation. It articulates the race problem and prevents the vicissitudes of race relations from attaining consensus or crystallizing. It never gets into what Sumner calls the mores.

One is amazed at the strength of the simple faith of the older, unlettered, rural Negroes. Powerless in the hands of their white exploiters, they go beyond them directly to their omnipotent God, almost happy in the assurance that retribution will come. Indeed, the sense of being wronged suffuses the thinking of the entire people. Powdermaker puts it in this way:

> The Negro feels guiltless with regard to the racial situation, and deeply wronged; whereas the white feels guilty, sometimes consciously and sometimes—perhaps more injuriously—without admitting it to himself. Even though he accepts the status quo and feels the Negro essentially inferior, he still cannot quite escape the realization that his actions run counter to the professed beliefs of democracy and Christianity. . . . The Negro's bitterness is intensified by a scorn for what he considers white hypocrisy, but this makes him feel all the more in the right.[51]

Respect for law is indispensable in a democracy. But a very large part of the social thinking in the South is in terms of lawlessness. Racial domination and respect for law are incompatible. Almost any day one may read in some of the more liberal Southern newspapers such expressions of qualms as the following:

> The spectacle of more than a dozen bombings of Negro homes in Dallas in the last six months without a single arrest is a shameful commentary on our respect for civil rights. If anyone thinks that this condition would have persisted in a

[51]Hortense Powdermaker, *After Freedom*, pp. 361–62. See also Robert E. Park, "Racial Assimilation in Secondary Groups," *Publications of the American Sociological Society*, Vol. VIII, 1913, p. 82.

residential area occupied by leading citizens, he is either naïve or has a poor understanding of the American police system.

Citizens, black or white, have a right to expect protection from lawless acts. If this is withheld from Negroes, the rights of the rest of us are in jeopardy. The difference as to vigilance of protection may involve the color of skin in one case, and in another the poverty or wealth of the victim. . . . Local democratic self-government cannot live in such weed-infested soil.[52]

It may be said finally that no system which depends for its existence principally upon anti-social acts, upon inevitable violence, can hope to perpetuate itself indefinitely.

Changing Social Status

It seems quite evident that the status of Negroes in the United States has changed considerably since 1865. It is exceedingly infrequent, however, that we are able to observe the immediate incidence of change. Sometimes it is difficult to determine whether the race is advancing toward a more favorable position within the larger society, for the apparent solution of some one of the innumerable race problems usually precipitates a multiplicity of them. Symptoms of the changing social status are many and divergent. However, any socially significant act or condition is an index of relative readjustment of racial position only in so far as it limits or enhances freedom of participation of Negroes in the general culture. Hence it is toward the fretting away of such limitations as segregation, intergroup etiquette and deferences, economic restrictions, intermarriage prohibitions, and political ostracism that Negroes continually address themselves.

A people may derive a conception of itself only by invidious comparisons of its cultural and physical attainments and attributes with those of other competitively related groups. When the frame of reference is the general American culture, however, Negroes cannot revert to a cultural history and mythology of such a character as would inspire a significant in-group sentiment of nativistic pride.[53] Thus the race is not oriented toward its past but toward its present capacity and "right" to participate freely in the culture. The American Negro's past seems to be no longer a cause. The teachings of democracy, science, and Christianity evidently afford a more

[52]C. P. Brannin, letter to the Dallas *Morning News,* April 17, 1941.
[53]Cf. Melville J. Herskovits, *The Myth of the Negro Past.*

consistent basis for the group's achievement of a new conception of itself than a knowledge of the past cultural contribution of the race to world civilization. Moreover, this is largely true because American Negroes have no social urge for nationalism. René Maunier has made a similar observation in his conclusion that American Negroes are influenced by an idea of progress, while the cultural aspirations of such peoples as the Chinese, Hindus, and North African whites tend to regress toward earlier civilizations.[54]

At the basis of assimilation is the social phenomenon of persons attaining new conceptions of themselves. A people's conception of itself is a social force which constantly seeks expression, and it may be extinguished only after considerable struggle with opposing ideas. Even after this it may unexpectedly return to life, especially among those who possess a written history. "The role of the controlling ideas," says Gustave le Bon, "has always been so significant that peoples have never been able to change them without changing also the whole course of their history. And if in our day some benevolent divinity wanted to transform Europe, he would have only to modify the conceptions which orient certain peoples."[55]

Before any real increment of status advancement can be attained, therefore, the group must be able to conceive of itself as meriting it. Accommodation may be so nearly complete that even slaves may rest contented with their status. There is probably a grain of truth in Edward B. Reuter's statement: "Slavery did not rest upon force except in the early stages of the institution. . . . The forces that controlled the slaves were within the slaves themselves."[56] The white masters, of course, were, in a sense, also resigned to their own position. In fact, to this day there is a degree of naïve adjustment of superordination and subordination between the races

[54]"Among Negroes of the United States it is the idea of advancement which actuates them today. While among the Chinese and even among the whites of Africa, among the Arabs and the Berbers, it is the idea of regress and not the idea of progress that determines their behavior. It is an aspiration toward the past, a desire to go backwards, a need for restoration and reconstruction. . . . These attitudes are especially striking in the teachings of Gandhi. We should differentiate then, between the black and the yellow movement." *Sociologie coloniale,* pp. 77–78.

[55]*Premieres Consequences de la guerre,* p. 324.

[56]*The American Race Problem,* p. 105. For an elaborate discussion of continuing unrest among slaves in the United States, see Herbert Aptheker, *American Negro Slave Revolts.*

in the South. The situation, however, is extremely unstable. Both groups are constantly preoccupied with it.

An advance in social status of a subordinate group involves a concession to it, the result of which is a reciprocal redefinition of intergroup position. This concession to status may be voluntary or involuntary, but it is always an admission that the "distanced" group merits the right to be included further in the "we" feeling of the dominant group. In the United States, Negroes strive constantly to obtain these admissions.

A people without a culture peculiar to itself, but having only a truncated pattern of the general culture within which it lives, might be expected to rely upon decisions of the privileged group for estimates of its own achievements. In most parts of the South, therefore, the Negro leader is one who is "liked" by white people; and the first Negro to go beyond some barrier of the status quo almost invariably has prestige within his group. He is a symbol presaging the group's formation of a new conception of itself; he has attained recognition among those having access to the vertex of the culture; he has wrested a voluntary or involuntary concession leading to wider cultural participation for his group.

Although comparatively isolated achievements of Negroes may result in some form of redefinition of group position, the situation which produces the more radical changes is success in direct competition, rivalry, or conflict. For this reason, especially in the South, some whites have found it necessary to prohibit any situation involving a direct matching of abilities between the races. At any rate, the process of assimilation involves a psychological narrowing of intergroup estimations of themselves. Hence, of major significance to a true advance in status for Negroes is a conscious realization on their part that they have an unquestionable right to some immediate social position.

Negroes in the North

It may seem paradoxical that Negroes suffer less from race prejudice and discrimination in the North where capitalism is farther advanced. A friendly critic of the writer put the question thus: "Why does anti-Negro, anti-Semitic, anti-alien activity not attain quite the same ferocity in the highly industrialized North, with its need for an 'exploitable labor force,' as in the South?" The answer is, apparently, not far to seek. In the North the proletariat is farther advanced than it is in the South. In fact, we may think of advanced capitalism as a state in which the proletariat has attained some considerable degree of power. In other words, the farther the progress of capitalism, the greater the relative power of the proletariat.

In the North democracy, the proletarian system of government, is much more developed than in the South, where the white and the black proletariat has been consistently suppressed. The first great aim of the proletariat in all countries has been the capture of the ballot. In the North the workers now have the ballot, but in the South it is still limited among whites and virtually denied to Negroes. It must be obvious that if the common people, regardless of color, were as free to vote in Mississippi as they are, say, in Illinois, Mississippi could never be the hotbed of racial antagonism that it is.[57]

Industrialization creates the need for an exploitable labor force, but it is in this very need that the power of the proletariat finally resides. The factory organization not only provides the basis for worker organization but also facilitates the development of a consciousness of class power and indispensability. Social equality is not an aspiration unique among Negroes; it has been an explicit objective of the whole proletariat, regardless of color or country, almost from the dawn of industrial capitalism. Therefore, as the stronger white proletariat advanced toward this end in the North, Negroes have advanced also. In the South the white proletariat is weak and Negroes, almost totally proletarian,—that is to say, propertyless wage workers with a very small upper crust holding relatively insignificant productive property precariously—are weaker still. To the extent that democracy is achieved, to that extent also the power of the ruling class to exploit through race prejudice is limited.[58]

---

[57]Stetson Kennedy puts it in this way: ". . . short of another civil war, the southern Negro must be emancipated economically and politically before he can be emancipated socially. This means that he must first join democratic unions and beat a democratic path to the polls. Once these two things have been accomplished—gains in one will facilitate gains in the other—the abolition of Jim Crow will be as inevitable as was the abolition of chattel slavery after civil war broke out. Once the economic and political functions of Jim Crow have been negated, its social function will vanish as the subterfuge that it is." "Total Equality, and How to Get It," *Common Ground,* Winter, 1946, p. 66.

[58]On this point Gunnar Myrdal makes a pertinent observation: "The South, compared to the other regions of America, has least economic security, the lowest educational level, and is most conservative. The South's conservatism is manifested not only with respect to the Negro problem but also with respect to all other important problems of the last decades—

Negroes' Approach to the Problem

Because the racial system in the United States is determined largely by the interests of a powerful political class, no spectacular advance in status of Negroes could be expected. This, of course, might happen if the Southern oligarchy were liquidated in revolution. Revolution, however, cannot be initiated by Negroes. If it comes at all, it will be under the aegis of the democratic forces of the nation. Basically, therefore, Negroes as a whole are not radical. They tend to be conservative and forgiving, though not resigned. Their policy is that of whittling away at every point the social advantages of the whites. By continual advances, no matter how small, the Negro hopes to achieve his status of complete equality as an American citizen.

With the exception of the power philosophy of Marcus Garvey,[59] the racial rationale of Negroes is based upon Western ideas of right and justice. Considerable reliance is put upon simple logic in exposing the inconsistencies of race prejudice. Consider, for instance, the following few sentences by Kelly Miller:

> They sometimes tell us that America is a white man's country. The statement is understandable in the light of the fact that the white race constitutes nine-tenths of its population and exerts the controlling influence over the various forms of material and substantial wealth and power. But this land belongs to the Negro as much as to any other, not only because he has helped to redeem it from the wilderness by the energy of his arm, but also because he has bathed it in his blood, watered it with his tears, and hallowed it with the yearnings of his soul.[60]

Two principal ideas of racial policy seem to divide the allegiance of Negroes, the one that "Negroes should stick together" and the other that "Negroes should shift for themselves individually, since the individual can advance more easily than the group as a whole." In reality, however, these two plans of action are correlated. The first is a necessity, the second an aspiration. Negroes "stick together" when, in attempting to act as individuals, they are rebuffed or disadvantaged. Nevertheless, there is a continuing

woman suffrage, trade unions, labor legislation, social security reforms, civil liberties—and with respect to broad philosophical matters, such as the character of religious beliefs and practices. . . . There are relatively few liberals in the South and no radicals." Op. cit., p. 73.

[59]For a discussion of Marcus Garvey, see Ira De A. Reid, *The Negro Immigrant*, pp. 147–56.

[60]*An Appeal to Conscience*, pp. 72–73.

ideal that they should be free to act on their individual merits. As social pressure about them is relieved, they automatically become individualists. Negro leaders who do not perceive the latter aspiration and advocate solidarity as an ideal readily lose favor among Negroes.

The Problem of Negro Leadership

One of the most persistent laments among Negroes in the United States is that the race has no great leader. There is a sort of vague expectation that someday he will arise. But Negroes will not have a "great leader" because, in reality, they do not want him. The destiny of Negroes is cultural and biological integration and fusion with the larger American society. Opposition by the latter society is generally directed against this aspiration of Negroes. Therefore, a great leader, whose function must be to bring about solidarity among Negroes, will facilitate the purpose of the opposition. The old-fashioned great leader of the post-slavery period, the almost unreserved appeaser of the Southern aristocracy, is gone forever. To develop a powerful leader Negroes must retract themselves, as it were, from their immediate business of achieving assimilation, and look to him for some promised land or some telling counterblow upon their detractors. At present, however, the most that the race can hope for is many small torchbearers showing the way upon innumerable fronts.

These leaders cannot give Negroes a "fighting" cause. None can be a Moses, George Washington, or Toussaint L'Ouverture; he cannot even be a Mohandas Gandhi[61]—a Lenin will have to be a white man. The task of leaders of the race is far more delicate. They must be specialists in the art of antagonistic co-operation. Their success rests finally in their ability to

---

[61]In commenting upon the wonderful power which Gandhi wields in India, the noted Negro publicist, George S. Schuyler, inquires despairingly: "Can the American Negro use soul force to win his battle for equal rights? Have we any leader who is ready to starve himself to death that freedom may live? Or to be beaten or shot for his convictions?" The Pittsburgh *Courier*, February 27, 1943. The answer is evidently yes; there are probably hundreds who will be ready to do so, if only for the glory of it. But, alas, even glory is not available to such a martyr. Unlike the East Indians, Negroes will not achieve their liberty through these methods. Leaders are in large measure produced by their followers; therefore, the question may be put thus: "Will American Negroes arise solidly in revolt behind a Negro holy man starving to death, say, for the purpose of having the modern black codes abrogated in the South? Or will they be aroused in a body to take action against American whites because a Negro offers himself to be shot in the interest of the race?" By putting the query in this way the answer becomes obvious. Surely the Negroes might make Father Divine a universal symbol if such a prospect would not make their cause seem ridiculous.

maintain peace and friendship with whites; yet they must seem aggressive and uncompromising in their struggle for the rights of Negroes. They dare not identify all whites as the enemy, for then they will themselves be driven together into a hostile camp.

This tentative nature of Negro solidarity presents a particularly baffling problem for the Negro leader. He must be a friend of the enemy. He must be a champion of the cause of Negroes, yet not so aggressive as to incur the consummate ill will of whites. He knows that he cannot be a leader of his people if he is completely rejected by whites; hence no small part of his function is engaged in understanding the subtleties of reaction to the manipulations of the whites of his community.

No contemporary Negro leader of major significance, then, can be totally void of at least a modicum of the spirit of "Uncle Tom"; ingratiation, compromise, and appeasement must be his specialties. Hence, "a great leader," who might with one blow realize the racial dreams of Negroes, will never appear; he is destined to remain a fantasy of Negroes. Booker T. Washington symbolizes the old Southern Negro leader. He was placed between a victorious counterrevolutionary South and an apathetic North; he could not help compromising. At least the alternative of compromise must have been an unproductive, unexpressed, sullen hate.[62] Those Negro leaders who advocate Negro solidarity for purposes of nationalistic aggression will be short-lived. Indeed, in the South, the Negro who addresses his attack directly to the status quo may be feared by Negroes and marked by whites.

Probably this technique of alternate smiling and sulking will never be sufficient to reduce the obdurate racial antagonism of whites in the South. Yet it is certain that open hostility on the part of Negroes alone will not accomplish the latter end. If there is to be an overthrow of the system, it will be achieved by way of a political-class struggle, with Negroes as an ally of white democratic forces of the nation. It will not come by way of an

---

[62]Yet it should be remembered that Washington was completely void of any sense of a social mission in the common people; he stands out as the ideal Negro bourgeois, who apparently miscalculated the implacable purpose of the white ruling class in the South to keep the whole race proletarianized. He believed that Negroes, by their sweat, upon the soil especially, could unobservedly slip off their yoke of exploitation to become companion exploiters with the white oligarchy. In this, to be sure, he underestimated the intelligence of the ruling class.

open interracial matching of power. As a matter of fact, the struggle has never been between all black and all white people—it is a political-class struggle.

But just at this point Negro leadership seems to be weakest. Today very few of those who have the ear of the public appear to appreciate the significance of the modern political-class movement. Some, like W. E. B. Du Bois, are frightened by the prospects of violence.[63] Others, like George S. Schuyler, think, as the ruling class would have them, that communism and fascism are bedfellows; therefore, they declare that good Negroes should have nothing to do with either.[64] And still others, like most of the college presidents and bishops, believe that it is safer not to talk about

[63]See *Dusk of Dawn,* pp. 301–2. This citation also shows the extent to which intelligent Negroes have absorbed even the comic anti-proletarian propaganda of the ruling class. See, however, "Prospects of a World without Race Conflict," *American Journal of Sociology,* March 1944, where Du Bois takes a more serious attitude toward the potentialities of socialism; *What the Negro Wants,* Rayford W. Logan, ed., pp. 60–62; and his *Color and Democracy.*

[64]See Schuyler's column in the Pittsburgh *Courier,* where he criticizes communism interminably. The following illustrates the rash criticism which some Negro journalists reserve for the communist system of the USSR: "Here is a state in which lackeyism is carried to the nadir of nausea; in which bureaucracy is elevated to a tragic absurdity; in which integrity is a dangerous addiction. In the Kremlin sits the Russian Gremlin, a crude, ignorant, egotistic, ruthless monster who has violated every human law, killed the revolution, slaughtered millions of his loyal followers; jailed ten times as many, and whose policies brought Russia and the world to the brink of disaster. . . . Only American Lend-Lease saved Russia—that, and the tremendous distances, plus ice, snow and mud." George S. Schuyler, in a favorable book review of *One Who Survived,* by Alexander Barmine, a Russian political refugee, in the Pittsburgh *Courier,* October 20, 1945.

To this group of thinkers socialism is not a social movement, in the sense that the bourgeoisization of Western society was a social movement, but rather a problem of conflicting personalities. Their common approach to the subject centers about a criticism of "those communists whom I have met" as unscrupulous or insane; therefore, at best, the movement must be described as the rantings of a cult of charlatans. To be sure, this is not a peculiarity of Negroes; it is merely their adoption of current propaganda.

More specifically, there is a large number of journalists and popular writers, white and black, who are sincere in their beliefs that they have reached some ultimate in an understanding of the social movement. The fact seems to be, however, that they have attained only to the personality or "gossip" stage of perception. Socialism to them involves an analysis of the character and foibles of certain leaders, or of the idiosyncrasies of certain "little commies" within their acquaintance, or of immediate practices, many of which must necessarily be underground and dissimulative. These persons are obviously buried under the very transpiration of a social movement more gigantic and significant than any—in so far as human initiation is concerned—that the world has ever seen. Compare, however, a responsible reporter's account: John Scott, *Europe in Revolution.*

"isms" at all. Of course, that small group, *la petite bourgeoisie noire,* the successful Negro businessman, cannot be expected to harbor proletarian ideas. In so far as we know, none of the leading newspapers seems to realize even remotely the significance of the social movement for the future welfare of Negroes.

And yet Negroes as a whole are not anti-communist; they are indeed more decidedly potentially communists than whites. At present they seem to sense some deep meaning and value in the movement, but under the tremendous weight of anti-communist propaganda they tend to remain somewhat bewildered. Then, too, they cannot be expected to take the initiative in this movement. Probably most of them would express some such basic sympathy as the following by Congressman Adam Clayton Powell, Jr.: "Today there is no group in America including the Christian church that practices racial brotherhood one-tenth as much as the Communist Party."[65] Indeed, in New York, communism among Negroes has made some tangible headway; they have recently elected a Negro communist to the city council of Manhattan.

The Problem of White Leadership

The problem of extending democracy to Negroes in the South involves one of the most frightful prospects in American social life. The Southern oligarchy has set its jaws against any such plan, which necessarily holds for them revolutionary economic consequences. The prospects are frightful because, like a true political class, the rulers of the South are prepared to hold their position even at a high cost in blood. Confronted with this terrible decision, the minority of liberal whites in the South are easily overwhelmed. Here too, therefore, as in the case of the white common people, democracy involves a conquest of the bourgeois oligarchy.

To be sure, at a certain cost the articulate leaders in this region can be overthrown. Without them the masses will soon reach a satisfactory way of living, consistent with democratic principles. Modern democracy is something to be won; it has always been withheld by some ruling class. We should miss an understanding of the political-class interest in the racial situation of the South if we were to think as some writers that:

[65]*Marching Blacks,* p. 69.

> Underlying all is the great need of every man, however humble and stupid, to feel that there is some one or some group still lower than he is. Thus only can the craving for a sense of superiority be fed. In the case of the Negro, it is notoriously the poor whites who are bitterest, who most tenaciously hold to the doctrine that he must be kept down at any cost either to himself or to the community.[66]

This kind of reasoning is common, and it has the significant—though frequently unintended—function of exculpating the Southern ruling class. But clearly, we could never explain the social order in the South by resorting to some socio-psychological constant in human nature. That which is assumed to be common to all human behavior cannot explain behavior variations; therefore, "the craving for a sense of superiority" tells no crucial story. The attitude of the poor whites is rather more an effect than a cause. "The Poor White, in his occasional expressions of race antagonism, acts for those Whites who tacitly condone and overtly deplore such behavior."[67] We may take it as axiomatic that never in all the history of the world have poor people set and maintained the dominant social policy in a society.

The Civil War was a war between two dominant political classes; it resulted in a partial limitation of the scheme of life of the Southern aristocracy, yet it neither extirpated nor defeated the essential purpose of this class. The South is still very much aristocratic and fascist. "The present white aristocratic party in the South is defending itself exactly after the manner of all aristocracies. . . . Having control of the government it has entrenched itself with laws."[68] From her recent study

[66]Edwin R. Embree, *Brown America*, p. 201.

[67]Hortense Powdermaker, op. cit., pp. 334–35. The makers of the laws of the South ingeniously set the stage for the encouragement and perpetuation of racial antagonism. "If there were more real contact between [poor whites and Negroes] some of the fierce hatred might be drained off, or even converted into fellow-feeling based on the similarity of their positions as agricultural workers struggling against great disadvantages." Ibid., p. 29. In these dichotomized racial situations the poor whites are always a danger to the position of the ruling class. Says Brookes: "The economic pressure to which the Bantu has been increasingly subjected since 1924 arises principally from solicitude for the class known as 'Poor Whites.' This solicitude is the result . . . of a feeling on the part of nationalist thinkers that the Poor Whites represent a submerged part of the South African nation. Bantu encroachment is to be resisted, not only because the Poor White may starve, but also because he may, under pressure of living conditions, betray his colour and mix his blood with the members of the Bantu proletariat. . . . A great part of the driving force which leads parties and governments to restrict fields of employment for the Bantu in favour of the Poor Whites is nationalism." Edgar H. Brookes, *The Colour Problems of South Africa*, pp. 28–29.

of a Southern community Hortense Powdermaker refers to the aristocracy as follows:

> This class and the old South are inseparable, and both play an enormous part in sanctioning the beliefs by which the middle class today guides and justifies its course. The superiority of the white man is the counterpart of Negro inferiority. And the aristocrat is a superior white *par excellence,* for his own qualities and because he is associated with the glory of the old days when the South was not at a disadvantage.[69]

The present Southern aristocracy is not that natural aristocracy among men, "the most precious gift of nature," of which Thomas Jefferson spoke. Rather it is represented by such classic expounders of conservative, nationalistic, social philosophy in the South as Governor James K. Vardaman and Senator Theodore G. Bilbo of Mississippi, Senator Jeff Davis of Arkansas, Governors Hoke Smith and Eugene Talmadge of Georgia, and Senators B. R. Tillman and Ellison D. (Cotton Ed) Smith of South Carolina.

> This is the same ruling class that has condoned lynchings, disfranchised most Negroes, kept the Negroes confined to work as sharecroppers, laborers, and domestics, retained the racial pollution laws, and used the newspapers, radio and school books to mould the minds of the white masses against equality of Negroes.[70]

The "aristocrats" maintained their power not only by their exploitation of Negroes but also by their exploitation of poor whites, who are artfully played against colored people.

It should be emphasized that the guardians of the economic and social order in the South are not poor whites; indeed, it is sheer nonsense to think that the poor whites are the perpetuators of the social system in the South. The fierce filibustering in the national Congress against the passage of an anti-lynching bill, or against the abolition of the poll tax; the hurried conferences of governors to devise means of emasculating a Supreme Court decision for equal educational opportunities; the meeting of attorneys general for the purpose of sidetracking an anti-Jim Crow decision for railroads; the attitude of Southern judges toward Negroes in courtrooms—these are obviously the real controlling factors in the

---

[68]Ray Stannard Baker, op. cit., p. 245. See also William H. Skaggs, op. cit., pp. 20, 58.
[69]Op. cit., p. 26.
[70]George Schuyler in the Pittsburgh *Courier,* March 15, 1942.

Southern order.[71] The poor whites are not only incapable but evidently also have no immediate interest in the doing of such things.

Moreover, in the very amiability which upper-class whites sometimes seem to have for Negroes lies a most powerful attitude of social distance. It is a condescending, patronizing attitude, which is the complete expression of racial superiority and prejudice. This attitude is hardly available to poor whites. The Southern "aristocracy," as the modern capitalist ruling class of this area is sometimes called, could not endure without the hatred which it perpetuates among the white and black masses, and it is by no means unmindful of that fact. No single social problem, whether of war or of peace, is as important to the Southern aristocracy as that of keeping the Negro in his place.[72]

[71]On almost any day we may clip such declarations as the following from newspapers in the South: "If the Supreme Court of the United States rules that Negroes must be admitted [to the Democratic primaries of Texas]," says W. S. Bramlett, Dallas County Democratic Chairman, "I will contribute all my experience as a lawyer and as a Democrat to nullify the ruling; and I believe most county and state party leaders will feel the same way." Reported in the Dallas *Morning News,* December 1, 1943.

[72]It is questionable whether such off-color statements as the following by Dr. Louis Wirth contribute to our understanding of race relations: "In a period of war we realize more clearly than ever . . . that racial, religious, and other prejudices constitute a danger to our national unity and it begins to dawn upon us that, however deep-seated our own internal conflicts may have been, they are as nothing compared with the conflicts between us and our enemies." *The Scientific Monthly,* April 1944, p. 305. The textbooks put the latter idea in this way: The greater the intensity of conflict between two groups, the greater the internal solidarity of each. But Wirth seems to be very much in error when he applies this concept unrefinedly to that situation. In this war, World War II, Quislings and fifth columnists were political-class leaders and members who were natural friends of the "enemy." Moreover, it is misleading to say, "We realize that prejudices constitute a danger to our national unity." The Southern prejudice against Negroes was not given up. There was "unity" only so long as Negroes did not demand that the South give up its prejudice. If such a demand had threatened to become effective, the ruling class in the South would have done exactly what the leaders of a number of European nations did; that is to say, make a choice between the Negroes, i.e., the proletariat, and Hitler; and the likelihood of Hitler's being chosen was great indeed. Anyone, for instance, might have tested this by trying to put through an anti-lynching bill in the national Congress. In such an event it would soon have become evident that matters concerning the war were quite secondary in importance.

For a realistic approach to this problem, see Stetson Kennedy, *Southern Exposure,* pp. 107–8 and 341ff.; also Theodore H. White and Annalee Jacoby, *Thunder Out of China,* pp. 45–47. It is reported that Chiang Kai-shek declared in 1941: "You think it is important that I have kept the Japanese from expanding during these years. . . . I tell you it is more important that I have kept the Communists from spreading. The Japanese are a disease of the skin; the Communists are a disease of the heart." Ibid., p. 129.

The problem of the democratic white leadership of the nation, then, is not to think of the exploitative order in the South as a Negro problem but rather as a political-class problem of the first magnitude for the nation. The Southern "aristocrats" should be understood in the light of what they really are, and the cost of reducing them should be estimated in the light of political-class practice. The alternative is a continued divided nation, for a political class has never been known to give up its position because of logical conviction. The interest of the ruling class rests in the Negroes' and poor whites' being and feeling inferior and antagonistic. This class insists that any plan for improving Southern conditions must first satisfy the latter interest.

It is not possible to speak with any degree of comprehensiveness about the problem of white leadership without reviewing somewhat its more inclusive world context. In our chapter on race relations we attempted to develop the hypothesis that modern race prejudice is rooted in certain attitudes and economic needs of the white race and that race prejudice has been diffused throughout the world by the white race. We should reiterate, however, that we do not mean to say that race prejudice has a somatic determinant. Commercial and industrial capitalism, which involved the organized movement of Europeans to distant lands, created the cultural situation favorable for the development of white race prejudice.

In our own day this very capitalism has undoubtedly passed the noontide of its vigor and is giving place to another basic form of social organization. With the change of the dominant economic organization of the world, we should expect fundamental changes in social attitudes.

In a previous chapter we have attempted to show also that two major systems are contending for primacy in the suppression of the present hybrid social order: fascism and communism. Fascism must obviously be transitory; it is an aggravation of the worst aspects of capitalism. We may think of fascism as the deathbed attendant of a moribund system, or indeed as the last great spasm in the death throes of capitalism.[73] "The chills and fever of

---

[73]Cf. J. Kuczynski and M. Witt, *The Economics of Barbarism,* and John Strachey, *The Coming Struggle for Power.* "It is our fate to live in one of those times in history when a whole economic system is in decay. History teaches us that once that process has begun there is no way of saving the dying economic system. The only way out is to put a new one in its place. That is what we must, can, and will do." John Strachey, *Socialism Looks Forward,* p. 100.

capitalism, observed since its infancy, shake and burn its whole body more drastically as it approaches old age."[74] In degenerating into organized fascism, capitalism surrenders very much of its adopted ideals of political democracy, but it has no alternative. Fascism is the only significant device developed by the established political class for the purpose of both reinvigorating capitalism and combating the democratic forces which are naturally antipathetic to capitalism.

Fascism, then, is defensive and, to repeat, necessarily exalts the worst traits of capitalism. So far as race relations are concerned, it makes a fanatic religion of white race superiority. But this is merely a function of its imperialistic obsession, which in turn stimulates nationalism. Those persons, then, who are honestly concerned with the elimination of race prejudice and race exploitation by the white ruling class must be concerned also with the elimination of world imperialism. It will probably not be inaccurate to state that the world stronghold of imperialism and colonialism is symbolized by the British Crown supported finally by the military and economic power of the United States.

The British Crown is a device kept sacrosanct by the great capitalists of the British Empire principally to overawe and exploit the larger part of the colored peoples of the world.[75] It is a putative institution serving as cover and shock absorber for the great imperialists and is completely without purpose in a non-capitalist democracy. As Mr. Laski puts it: "British

[74]George Soule, *The Coming American Revolution*, p. 148.

[75]Probably no historical situation illustrates better than the semi-bourgeois interlude of the Russian Revolution the great value of a decadent and impotent monarchy to a rising bourgeoisie. Behind the controlled divinity of the royal family the bourgeoisie is able to put into effect schemes of mass exploitation, both at home and abroad, that would be otherwise unthinkable.

In his discussion of another situation, John Scott makes the following observation: "Russian prestige among eastern peoples is today higher than ever before, owing to an inexcusable American blunder at San Francisco. Having raised the issue of the ultimate independence of colonial peoples, the American delegation joined the British in voting for a sterile formula promising colonial peoples little, and allowing the Russians to stand before the world as champions of the hundreds of millions of dependent eastern peoples. This single action quite unnecessarily deprived America of its historic rôle as champions of liberty [?] in the eyes of millions, and turned this invaluable asset over to the Russians.

"Unfortunately the same blunder has occurred repeatedly in Europe on less spectacular issues. We have given in to pressure from the British, and from our own reactionaries and have identified ourselves with the dusty little kings and equally dusty outmoded ideas from the nineteenth century, allowing the Russians to champion progress." Op. cit., pp. 233–34.

imperialism has deliberately elevated the prestige of the Crown as a method of protecting the ends it seeks to serve."[76] About fourteen out of every hundred people in the British Empire are white. Without reviewing the imperialistic practices of other nations[77] it should be apparent that race exploitation cannot be eliminated from the world without first eliminating capitalism and attacking vigorously the imperialism of Great Britain.

It should be emphasized, however, that the capitalism and imperialism of Great Britain could not survive without the sustaining hand of the American ruling class. Mr. Winston Churchill, in his Fulton, Missouri, address, might have gone even farther to say that not only *must* the United States and Britain establish a permanent military alliance—which for all practical purposes is already in effect—but also an economic brotherhood. The burden of making a capitalism, collapsing all over the world, work rests squarely on the shoulders of the American ruling class; and since capitalism no longer has a morality, the people of the United States will have to keep it resuscitated and defended by pouring into it an endless stream of wealth. In a very real sense the United States today must finance world capitalism, for it cannot convince peoples by any logical argument of the social and economic value of capitalism to them. Churchill knows that the United States must pay for capitalism or speedily become aware that it is "encircled" by a socialist world, hence he speaks with oracular confidence. Capitalism cannot offer to the masses of people that better world for which they now hunger and thirst; it can give them only reaction supported by military might and a strategic distribution of a relatively few full bellies.

The American ruling class, in its own interest, must make "lend lease" permanent, even though it is disguised in the form of loans or outright gifts to "suffering humanity." This class will have to see that food and "supplies" are rushed all over the world to strengthen the position of the various national bourgeoisies as the common people gather about them to exact an accounting of the use of their resources. In a sense, then, the United States is already fighting its own proletarian revolution on foreign battle fields.

[76]*Parliamentary Government in England,* p. 330.

[77]For broad views on this question, see Parker Thomas Moon, *Imperialism and World Politics,* and Benjamin H. Williams, *Economic Foreign Policy of the United States.*

The new economic system which will naturally supplant the old is socialism, the system whose normal emphasis is upon human welfare. The relation of socialism to racial exploitation may be demonstrated by the fact that the greater the immediacy of the exploitative practice, the more fiercely socialism is opposed. In other words, in those areas where whites live by the immediate exploitation of colored people, in those areas also socialism is most abhorred. For instance, a white communist in the Deep South is regarded in about the same light as a Negro man with a white wife. They are both threats to the exploitative system, and the ruling class has provided for their violent dispatch.[78] Indeed, the method of "solving the race issue" is identical with the method by which capitalism is being liquidated by proletarian action.

There is an increasing number of people all over the world who are willing to accept socialism with all its implications for the abandonment of mass exploitation. Some of these people understand that there will be no possibility of giving up race prejudice while still retaining the system which produced it. They recognize consequently that the problem of white leadership is no longer that of appeasing plantation capitalists but rather that of striking decisively at the very root of the social order, and they are under no illusions about the fact that the "capitalist power will not surrender its privileges without fighting for them."[79]

In the process of bringing the Southern Negro into full manhood and citizenship, therefore, the white leader has a responsibility of considerable importance. It involves the liberation of the Southern poor whites as well. A great leader of Negroes will almost certainly be a white man, but he will also be the leader of the white masses of this nation; and of course, whether

[78]It may be observed further that the pith of the argument that race prejudice will not exist in a socialist society necessarily rests on the fact that this indispensable economic drive of capitalism—exploitation, and human exploitation especially—will also cease to exist. In a capitalist system human beings live and labor in the interest of private enterprise; and the fact that a goodly number of them are impersonally degraded and consumed in the latter interest is consistent with the ethics of the system. On the contrary, in a socialist system human welfare becomes the dominant purpose of production, and the ethics of that system abhor the idea of such human degradation. In other words, increasing productivity is made dependent upon increasing development of the human intellect, tastes, and ambition. Human beings are freed and elevated beyond the elevation of their material resources.

[79]On this Daniel Guerin remarks advisedly: "Although socialism utilizes all the legal methods supplied by the law or the constitution, it does so, without the slightest illusion; it knows that the victory in the end is a question of force." *Fascism and Big Business,* p. 109.

they are permitted to recognize him or not, he will eventually prove to be the emancipator of the poor whites of the South. For example, without any considerable attention to the "Negro problem" particularly, President Franklin D. Roosevelt undoubtedly did more to elevate the status of Negroes in the United States than all other leaders, white and black together, over a period of decades before him. Negroes are auxiliary in the American proletarian struggle for power. James Madison probably had more vision than he thought when he referred to Negroes as that "unhappy species of population abounding in some of the states who, during the calm of regular government, are sunk below the level of men; but who, in the tempestuous scenes of civil violence, may emerge into human character and give a superiority of strength to any party with which they may associate themselves."[80]

In the Deep South, ruling-class whites have taught Negroes to look to them personally for guidance; in fact, these whites have controlled Negroes through their own black leaders. The successful Negro leader has learned to be sensitive to the wishes of whites. In any political-class struggle in the South, therefore, this attitude should be capitalized by the radical white leadership.

Although Negroes have become increasingly intractable to being thus indirectly led, they have yet a certain faith in "what the white man says." It is this faith to which the white radical leader, interested in breaking up the Southern social order, has access. Many overcautious and conservative Negro leaders, who have no patience with militant Negroes, become readily animated when white functionaries speak to them of equal rights. When the time comes for the South to be purged of its present political-class leadership, it will surely be easier for most Negroes to follow convinced whites than to tread behind the uncertain feet of their familiar black leadership.

Moreover, it is also the responsibility of white leaders to conduct the struggle according to principles of political-class conflict. That is to say, the aristocratic Southern ruling class must be defeated not only in an open matching of power but also broken in spirit, a social aspiration which the military victors of the Civil War failed to achieve.[81]

[80] *The Federalist,* No. 43.

[81] The same necessity for psychological defeat which the Hon. Henry A. Wallace recommended in dealing with foreign countries should also prove effective in dealing with domestic fascists. "A special problem that will face the United Nations immediately upon the

In this we should not be mistaken as to the source of antagonism against any serious attempt to extend democracy in the South. The standard bearers of the area have repeatedly and most bluntly stated that the issue could be settled only by open violence. Thus the noted Southern writer, David L. Cohn, declares: "I have no doubt that in such an event [that is to say, an attempt to abolish the terrible segregation laws] every Southern white man would spring to arms and the country would be swept by civil war."[82] Again, when the United States Supreme Court decided eight to one that Negroes should be allowed to vote in state primaries, the South Carolina General Assembly passed a number of bills to emasculate the decision, and "the House . . . applauded a speech by Representative John Long . . . who said he was willing to 'bite the dust as did my ancestors' to prevent Negroes from participating in the white Democratic primaries."[83] In many parts of the modern world democracy is feverishly seeking to get such a hold of itself as to be able to say to this characteristic, anachronistic challenge: "You shall have your wish."

The problem of racial exploitation, then, will most probably be settled as part of the world proletarian struggle for democracy; every advance of the masses will be an actual or potential advance for the colored people. Whether the open threat of violence by the exploiting class will be shortly joined will depend upon the unpredictable play and balance of force in a world-wide struggle for power.

attainment of victory over either Germany or Japan," he said, "will be what to do with the defeated nation. . . . We must make absolutely sure that the guilty leaders are punished, that the defeated nation realizes its defeat and is not permitted to rearm. The United Nations must back up military disarmament with psychological disarmament—supervision, or at least inspection, of the school systems of Germany and Japan, to undo so far as possible the diabolical work of . . . poisoning the minds of the young." Radio address, December 28, 1942.

[82]"How the South Feels," *The Atlantic Monthly,* January 1944, p. 50.

[83]The Dallas *Morning News,* April 18, 1944.

Bibliography

This is a list of most of the works referred to in the text.

Acton, Lord. *The History of Freedom and Other Essays,* London, 1909.

Adams, Romanzo. *Interracial Marriage in Hawaii,* New York, 19937.

Ames, Jessie Daniel. *The Changing Character of Lynching,* Atlanta, 1942.

Aptheker, Herbert. *American Negro Slave Revolts,* New York, 1943.

Arendt, Hannah. "Race-Thinking before Raceism," *The Review of Politics,* Vol. 6, Jan. 1944.

Azurara, Gomes Eannes de. *The Discovery and Conquest of Guinea,* trans. by C. R. Beazley and E. Prestage, London, 1896–99.

Baker, Ray Stannard. *Following the Colour Line,* New York, 1908.

Baron, Salo Wittmayer. "Nationalism and Intolerance," *The Menorah Journal,* Vols. XVI, XVII, Jun. 1929 and Nov. 1929.

Barzun, Jacques. *Race, A Study of Modern Superstition,* New York, 1937.

Beard, Charles A. *An Economic Interpretation of the Constitution of the United States,* New York, 1943.

Beard, Charles A., and Mary R. *The Rise of American Civilization,* New York, 1930.

Benedict, Ruth. *Race: Science and Politics,* New York, 1945.

——————. *Patterns of Culture,* Boston, 1934.

Bouglé, Celestin C. A. *Essais sur le régime des castes,* 3d ed., Paris, 1935.

Bousquet, Georges Henri. *A French View of the Netherlands Indies,* trans. by Philip E. Lilienthal, Oxford, 1940.

Bowen, Trevor. *Divine White Right,* New York & London, 1934.

Briffault, Robert. *The Decline and Fall of the British Empire,* New York, 1938.

Briggs, George W. *The Chamars,* Oxford, 1920.

Brookes, Edgar H. *The Colour Problems of South Africa,* London, 1934.

Brown, Francis J., and Roucek, Joseph S. *Our Racial and National Minorities,* New York, 1937.

Bryce, James. *The Relations of the Advanced and Backward Races of Mankind,* 2d ed., Oxford, 1903.

Bucher, Carl. *Industrial Evolution,* trans. by S. M. Wickett, New York, 1907.

Buell, Raymond Leslie. *The Native Problem in Africa,* New York, 1928, Vols. I, II.

Cable, George W. *The Negro Question,* New York, 1903.

California and the Oriental: Report of the State Board of Control of California, Jan. 1, 1922.

Cambridge History of India, Vol. I, Cambridge, 1922.

Census of India, 1921, Vol. I, Pt. 1.

Chambers, John S. "The Japanese Invasion," *The Annals,* Vol. XCIII, Jan. 1921.

Cheyney, Edward Potts. *European Background of American History,* New York, 1904.

Cohn, David L. *God Shakes Creation,* New York, 1935.

Craven, Avery. *Democracy in American Life,* Chicago, 1941.

Crooke, William. *Things Indian,* London, 1906.

Cunningham, W. *The Growth of English Industry and Commerce,* 5th ed., Vol. I, Cambridge, 1915.

Danvers, Frederick Charles. *The Portuguese in India,* London, 1894.

Davis, Gardner, Gardner, and Warner. *Deep South,* Chicago, 1941.

Day, Clive. *The Dutch in Java,* New York, 1904.

De Motte, Marshall. "California—White or Yellow," *The Annals,* Vol. XCIII, Jan. 1921.

Detweiler, Frederick G. "The Rise of Modern Race Antagonisms," *The American Journal of Sociology,* Vol. 37, Mar. 1932.

Diffie, Bailey W. *Latin American Civilization,* Harrisburg, 1945.

Dollard, John. *Caste and Class in a Southern Town,* New York, 1937.

Doyle, Bertram W. *The Etiquette of Race Relations,* Chicago, 1937.

Drake, St. Clair, and Cayton, Horace R. *Black Metropolis,* New York, 1945.

Du Bois, W. E. B. *Black Reconstruction,* New York, 1935.

——————. *Darkwater,* New York, 1921.

——————. *Dusk of Dawn,* New York, 1941.

Dubois, Abbé Jean Antoine. *Hindu Manners, Customs, and Ceremonies,* 3d ed., Oxford, 1906.

Durkheim, Emile. *The Rules of Sociological Method,* trans. by Sarah A. Solovay and John H. Mueller, Chicago, 1938.

Dutt, Nripendra Kumar. *Origin and Growth of Caste in India,* London, 1931.

Eaves, Lucile. *A History of California Labor Legislation,* Berkeley, 1910.

Evans, Maurice S. *Black and White in South East Africa,* London, 1911.

Faris, Ellsworth. *The Nature of Human Nature,* New York & London, 1937.

Farquhar, J. N. *Modern Religious Movements in India,* New York, 1915.

Furniss, Edgar S. *The Position of Labor in a System of Nationalism,* Boston, 1920.

Gallagher, Buell G. *Color and Conscience,* New York & London, 1946.

Gandhi, Mahatma. *Young India, 1924–1926,* New York, 1927.

Glotz, Gustave. *Ancient Greeks at Work,* New York, 1926.

Gobineau, Arthur de. *The Inequality of Human Races,* trans. by Adrin Collins, New York, 1915.

Graeber, Isacque, and Britt, S. H., eds. *Jews in a Gentile World,* New York, 1942.

Guerin, Daniel. *Fascism and Big Business,* trans. by Frances and Mason Merrell, New York, 1939.

Hall, Josef W. (Upton Close). *The Revolt of Asia,* New York & London, 1927.

Hammond, J. L., and Hammond, Barbara. *The Town Labourer, 1760–1832,* London, 1917.

Hayes, Carlton J. H. *Essays on Nationalism,* New York, 1926.

Heckscher, Eli Filip. *Mercantilism,* trans. by Mendell Shapiro, London, 1935.

Helper, Hinton Rowan. *The Impending Crisis,* New York, 1860.

Hitler, Adolph. *Mein Kampf,* New York, 1940.

Hobson J. A. *Democracy and a Changing Civilization,* London, 1934.

Huxley, Julian. *Race in Europe,* Oxford Pamphlets on World Affairs, No. 5, Oxford, 1939.

Ibbetson, Denzil. *Punjab Castes,* Lahore, 1916.

Johnson, Julia E., ed. *Japanese Exclusion,* New York, 1925.

Johnson, Charles S. *Growing Up in the Black Belt,* Washington, D.C., 1941.

Johnson, James Weldon. *Negro Americans, What Now?,* New York, 1935.

——————. *The Book of American Negro Poetry,* New York, 1931.

Jones, Chester Lloyd. *Caribbean Backgrounds and Prospects,* New York, 1931.

Joshi, P. S. *The Tyranny of Colour,* Durban, 1942.

Kanzaki, Kuchi. "Is the Japanese Menace in America a Reality?" *The Annals,* Vol. XCIII, Jan. 1921.

Karandikar, S. V. *Hindu Exogamy,* Bombay, 1929.

Kawakami, K. K. "The Japanese Question," *The Annals,* Vol. XCIII, Jan. 1921.

Kennedy, Raymond. *The Ageless Indies,* New York, 1942.

Kennedy, Stetson. *Southern Exposure,* New York, 1946.

Kohn, Hans. *The Idea of Nationalism,* New York, 1944.

Landis, Paul H. *Social Control,* Philadelphia, 1939.

Laski, Harold F. *Parliamentary Government in England,* New York, 1940.

——————. *Reflections on the Revolution of Our Time,* New York, 1943.

——————. *The Rise of Liberalism,* New York & London, 1936.

Levinthal, Louis E. "The Case for a Jewish Commonwealth," *The Annals,* Vol. 240, Jul. 1945.

Lobb, John. "Caste in Haiti," *American Journal of Sociology,* Vol. XLVI, Jul. 1940.

Logan, Rayford W., ed. *What the Negro Wants,* Chapel Hill, 1944.

Lowie, Robert H. *Primitive Society,* New York, 1920.

Maciver, R. M. *Society, A Textbook in Sociology,* New York, 1937.

MacNutt, Francis Augustus. *Bartholomew De Las Casas,* New York & London, 1909.

Magnum, Charles S., Jr. *The Legal Status of the Negro,* Chapel Hill, 1940.

Mantoux, Paul. *The Industrial Revolution in the Eighteenth Century,* trans. by Marjorie Vernon, New York, 1928.

Masouka, Jitsuichi. "Race Preference in Hawaii," *The American Journal of Sociology,* Vol. XLI, Mar. 1936.

Maunier René. *Sociologie Coloniale,* Paris, 1932.

Mayne, John D. *A Treatise on Hindu Law and Usage,* 8th ed., Madras, 1914.

McWilliams, Carey. *Prejudice,* Boston, 1944.

————. *Brothers under the Skin,* Boston, 1943.

Mead, Elwood. "The Japanese Land Problem in California," *The Annals,* Vol. XCIII, Jan. 1921.

Mears, Eliot Grinnell. *Resident Orientals on the American Pacific Coast,* Chicago, 1928.

Mill, James. *The History of British India,* Vol. I, London, 1840.

Miller, Kelly. *An Appeal to Conscience,* New York, 1918.

Millis, Harry A. *The Japanese Problem in the United States,* New York, 1915.

Montagu, M. F. Ashley. *Man's Most Dangerous Myth: The Fallacy of Race,* New York, 1942.

Moon, Parker T. *Imperialism and World Politics,* New York, 1932.

Morel, E. D. *The Black Man's Burden,* New York, 1920.

Morris, Richard B. *Government and Labor in Early America,* New York, 1946.

Myrdal, Gunnar. *An American Dilemma,* New York, 1944.

Nehru, Jawaharlal. *Toward Freedom,* New York, 1942.

Nicolay, John G., and Hay, John. *Abraham Lincoln: Complete Works,* Vol. I , 1894.

Olivier, Lord. *The Anatomy of African Misery,* London, 1927.

O'Malley, L. S. S. *Modern India and the West,* London, 1941.

Oviedo Gonzalo Fernandez de. *Historia General y Natural de las Indias,* Madrid, 1885.

Park, Robert E., and Burgess, Ernest W. *Introduction to the Science of Sociology,* Chicago, 1924.

Peffer, Nathaniel. *The White Man's Dilemma,* New York, 1927.

Phelan, James D. "Why California Objects to the Japanese Invasion," *The Annals,* Vol. XCII, Jan. 1921.

Pierson, Donald. *Negroes in Brazil,* Chicago, 1942.

Powdermaker, Hortense. *After Freedom,* New York, 1939.

Raper, Arthur F. *Preface to Peasantry,* Chapel Hill, 1936.

————. *The Tragedy of Lynching,* Chapel Hill, 1933.

Rees, J. F. "Mercantilism and the Colonies," *Cambridge History of the British Empire,* Vols. I, II.

Reinhardt, James Melvin. *Social Psychology,* Philadelphia, 1938.

Report of the Committee on Emigration from India to the Crown Colonies and Protectorates, London, 1910.

Reuter, Edward Byron. *The Mulatto in the United States,* Boston, 1918.

Reuter, Edward Byron, ed. *Race and Culture Contacts,* New York & London, 1934.

Reynolds, Reginald. *The White Sahibs in India,* London, 1937.

Risley, Sir Herbert Hope. *The People of India,* Calcutta, 1908.

Ruggles, Thomas. *History of the Poor,* London, 1793.

Russell, R. V. *The Tribes and Castes of the Central Provinces of India,* London, 1916.

Ryder, David Warren. "The Japanese Bugaboo," *The Annals,* Vol. XCIII, Jan. 1921.

Sandmeyer, Elmer Clarence. *The Anti-Chinese Movement in California,* Urbana, 1939.

Sapir, E. "Culture, Genuine and Spurious," *American Journal of Sociology,* Vol. XXIX, Jan. 1924.

Schmoller, Gustav. *The Mercantile System,* New York, 1897.

Scott, John. *Europe in Revolution,* Boston, 1945.

Senart, Émile. *Caste in India,* trans. by Sir E. Denison Ross, London, 1930.

Shapera, I., ed. *Western Civilization and the Natives of South Africa,* London, 1934.

Shay, Frank. *Judge Lynch,* New York, 1938.

Sherring, M. A. *Hindu Tribes and Castes,* Calcutta, 1879.

Shridharani, Krishnalal. *Warning to the West,* New York, 1942.

Shugg, Roger W. *Origins of the Class Struggle in Louisiana,* Baton Rouge, 1939.

Skaggs, William H. *The Southern Oligarchy,* New York, 1924.

Smith, William C. "Minority Groups in Hawaii," *The Annals,* Vol. 223, Sept. 1942.

Sombart, Werner. *Socialism and the Social Movement in the 19th Century,* trans. by Anton P. Atterbury, New York, 1898.

Stalin, Joseph. *Leninism,* New York, 1942.

Stark, Herbert Alick. *Hostages to India,* Calcutta, 1926.

Steiner, Jesse Frederick. *The Japanese Invasion,* Chicago, 1917.

Stephenson, Gilbert. *Race Distinction in American Law,* New York, 1910.

Stonequist, Everett V. *The Marginal Man,* New York, 1937.

Strachey, John. *Socialism Looks Forward,* New York, 1945.

Sullivan, Louis R. "The Labor Crisis in Hawaii," *Asia,* Vol. XXIII, No. 7, Jul. 1923.

Sumner, William G. *Folkways,* Boston, 1906.

Sutherland, Robert L. *Color, Class, and Personality,* Washington, D.C., 1942.

Sutherland, Robert L., and Woodward, Julian L. *Introductory Sociology,* Philadelphia, 1940.

Sweezy, Paul M. *The Theory of Capitalist Development,* New York, 1942.

Tawney, R. H. *Equality,* New York, 1929.

Thompson, Warren S. *Danger Spots in World Population,* New York, 1930.

Thurston, Edgar. *Castes and Tribes of Southern India,* Vol. II, Madras, 1909.

Tocqueville, Alexis de. *Democracy in America,* 3d ed., trans. by Henry Reeve, London, 1838.

Trachtenberg, Joshua. *The Devil and the Jews,* New Haven, 1943.

Trotsky, Leon. *History of the Russian Revolution,* Vol. III, New York, 1922.

Wallace, Kenneth E. *The Eurasian Problem,* Calcutta, 1930.

Warner, Lloyd, and Srole, Leo. *The Social Systems of American Ethnic Groups,* New York, 1945.

Washington, Booker T. *Working with the Hands,* New York, 1904.

Webb, Sidney and Beatrice. *Industrial Democracy,* London, 1920.

White, Walter. *Rope and Faggot,* New York & London, 1929.

Wilson, Woodrow. *Constitutional Government in the United States,* New York, 1918.

Woolf, Leonard. *Imperialism and Civilization,* New York, 1928.

Yat-sen, Sun. *Le triple Demisme,* French trans. by Pascal M. d'Elia, Shanghai, 1930.

Young, Donald. *Research Memorandum on Minority Peoples in a Depression,* Bulletin No. 31, 1937.

Yutang, Lin. *Between Tears and Laughter,* New York, 1943.

Index

in South Africa, 3*n*
Southern, obsession with Negroes
    among, 143
"white man's burden," 30-31
women, 75-79
working-class, racism among, xiii
white supremacy, 20, 166*n*
Wiley College, xxi-xxiii, xxxix*n*
Williams, Bruce, xxvii
Wirth, Louis, xxi, 172*n*
    "minority group" defined by, 91-92*n*
    on Negro-white relations in South, 219-20*n*
    on prejudice, 21*n*, 281*n*
women
    as booty, in original-contact situation, 42
    hypergamous marriages of, 139-40
    in intermarriages in bipartite
        situation, 50-51
    in lynchings, 254

in master-slave sexual relations, 44-45
sale of, between castes, 150
white, 75-79
white, exploitation of, 182
white, lynchings in defense of, 261-62
Woolf, Leonard, 22*n*, 32*n*, 60
workers
    anti-Asian feelings among, 100-101
    Asiatics as, 101-9
    organization of, 182
Wright, R.R., 134

Yemen, 176*n*
Young, Arthur, 24
Young, Donald, 92*n*, 202, 232*n*
Yutang, Lin, 33-34*n*

Zeno, 8
Zionism, 94